SCOTS LAW FOR JOURNALISTS

AUSTRALIA
LBC Information Services—Sydney

CANADA and USA
Carswell—Toronto

NEW ZEALAND
Brooker's—Auckland

SINGAPORE and MALAYSIA
Thomson Information (S.E. Asia)
Singapore

SCOTS LAW FOR JOURNALISTS

SEVENTH EDITION

Alistair J. Bonnington
*Solicitor to BBC Scotland
and Lecturer at Glasgow University*

Rosalind McInnes
Assistant Solicitor to BBC Scotland

Bruce McKain
Law Correspondent, The Herald

W. GREEN/Sweet & Maxwell Ltd
EDINBURGH
2000

Published in 2000 by W. Green & Son Ltd
21 Alva Street
Edinburgh EH2 4PS

Typeset by LBJ Typesetting Ltd of Kingsclere
Printed and bound in Great Britain by
MPG Books Ltd, Bodmin, Cornwall

No natural forests were destroyed to make this product;
only farmed timber was used and replanted

A CIP catalogue record for this book is available from the British Library

ISBN 0 414 01372 7

© A. Bonnington, R. McInnes and B. Mckain 2000

FOREWORD

*By The Right Honourable Lord Rodger of Earlsferry, Lord President
of The Court of Session and Lord Justice General of Scotland*

In the five years since the last edition of this much-respected work
the pace of technological and other developments of which Lord
Hope of Craighead wrote in his Foreword has not diminished and
has, if anything increased. The arrival of the internet as an
everyday tool of communication has meant that the opinions of our
judges are now available instantaneously to people not only in
Britain but throughout the world. Satellite news broadcasts from
beyond the shores of the United Kingdom have also become an
accepted feature of everyday life and certain Scottish legal events,
notably the Lockerbie trial, have attracted wide media attention all
over the world. With the Scotland Act 1998 and the Human Rights
Act 1998 the legal framework within which the courts and journalists have to work has also changed significantly. As a result, over
the last few years, in particular, the courts have become
increasingly aware of the need to ensure that our law relating to
contempt of court by journalists and publishers is in tune with
these developments. This has led to a series of decisions by the
Appeal Court which affect all those who report the proceedings in
our courts, at whatever level.

These changes have meant that, inevitably, the last edition of
this work was coming to look increasingly out of date. That is
particularly unfortunate in the case of a book which is designed to
provide reliable guidance to journalists, who cannot be expected
themselves to follow every twist and turn of the developments in
our law. The authors' work in revising the text and incorporating
the changes in so many areas of our law is therefore particularly
welcome. This new edition will give journalists an up-to-date
account not merely of the law which applies to them, but, more
generally, of the law which applies to the cases that they are
reporting. As the Appeal Court has recently had occasion to
observe, accurate reports of the proceedings in our courts act as a
safeguard against what Lord Diplock described as "judicial

arbitrariness or idiosyncrasy". The role of journalists who provide the public with those accurate reports is unlikely to be less important for our public life in the future than it has been in the past.

Edinburgh
October 2000

Alan Rodger

PREFACE

When Scots Law for Journalists first saw the light of day in 1965 in its stout, red, hard-backed cover, it ran to a total of 216 pages. The fact that this, the seventh edition, has more or less doubled in size is an accurate indication that for the journalist as well as the lawyer the subject has become much more complex.

It would be fair to say that the early editions concentrated on the medium of print journalism, but time has moved on.

The aim is still to provide a guide to the law and outline the pitfalls that lie in wait for the unwary, but the increasing prominence of television and radio in the gathering and disseminating of news has demanded a significant shift in the focus of the book.

Since the last edition appeared nearly six years ago the governance of Scotland has also undergone its biggest upheaval in nearly 300 years. We now have our own Scottish Parliament with the power to make its own laws.

Hardly less earth-shattering has been the incorporation of the European Convention on Human Rights into our domestic law. It has heralded radical change in the detail of our law and led to a searching re-examination of the philosophical basis some our most venerable legal institutions whose merit had not been questioned until now.

We have tried to outline these momentous events in the new edition as well as reflect the many other important changes that have taken place since 1995.

The traditionally dour Scottish approach to contempt of court seems to have become more liberal, largely due to the freedom of expression provisions in the European Convention on Human Rights.

The 1996 Defamation Act is now in force and we have seen the first ever attempt to prosecute the media in the U.K. under the Judicial Proceedings (Regulation of Reports) Act 1926.

These are dealt with in the seventh edition as are the significant developments in the areas of privacy, freedom of information, the Internet and data protection.

Scots Law for Journalists was originally compiled by Dr Eric Clive, an outstanding legal academic who has now retired after many years of distinguished service at the Scottish Law Commission, and George Watt who set unrivalled benchmarks of accuracy and interpretation of the law as the (then) Glasgow Herald's Court of Session Correspondent.

Sadly, George Watt has passed on since the last edition of this book was published and the present authors have tried to ensure that the latest work lives up to the standards he first set with Eric Clive more than three decades ago.

CONTENTS

Foreword... *v*
Preface.. *vii*
Table of Cases .... *xi*
Table of Statutes... *xv*

1: Introduction... 1
2: The Legal Practice 12
3: Criminal Courts and Procedure 16
4: Civil Courts and Procedure......................... 42
5: Miscellaneous Special Courts 57
6: Other Bodies.. 65
7: The Court Reporter................................. 80
8: Access to Information 92
9: News Gathering 114
10: Contempt of court 121
11: Photography.. 168
12: Matrimonial Proceedings........................... 180
13: Children.. 190
14: Judicial Review..................................... 199
15: Titles and Terminology 203
16: Essentials of Defamation........................... 206
17: Defences.. 219
18: Damages and other Remedies 233
19: Letters, Articles and Advertisements................ 239
20: Actionable Non-Defamatory Statements: Verbal Injury 242
21: Differences in English Law......................... 247
22: Intellectual Property................................ 250
23: Rights of Access 260
24: Broadcasting 266
25: Human Rights Act 1998 and Privacy................ 291
26: The Rehabilitation of Offenders Act 1974 300
27: Printer and Publisher............................... 306
28: Advertisements 308
29: Race Relations 319
30: Official Secrets 323
31: Reports of English Committal Proceedings 331
32: Breach of Confidence............................... 335

33: The Internet 340

Appendices:
   Appendix 1: Contempt of Court Act 1981 346
   Appendix 2: Broadcasting Standards Commission—
      Codes of Guidance 356
   Appendix 3: Press Complaints Commission—Code of
      Practice..................................... 386
   Appendix 4: Defamation Act 1996, Sched. 1. 392

Glossary 397
Index.. 407

TABLE OF CASES

para.

A.B. v. Blackwood & Sons (1902) 5 F. 25............................ 16.19
Adamson v. Martin, 1916 S.C. 319.................................... 16.34
Advocate, Lord, v. Scotsman Publications [1990] 1 A.C. 812; [1989] 3 W.L.R.
    358..09.03, 30.25, 30.35
Advocate, H.M., v. Church, 1995 S.C.C.R. 194........................ 03.93
—— v. Danskin, 2000 S.C.C.R. 101................................... 10.157
—— v. Elliot, 1995 S.C.C.R. 280................................... 03.93
—— v. George Aitken, 1984 S.C.C.R. 81.......................... 13.05, 13.43
—— v. Stuurman, 1980 J.C. 111; 1980 S.L.T. 182... 10.10, 10.115, 10.116, 10.120,
                                                         10.181, 24.04
Aitchison v. Bernardi, 1984 S.L.T. 343; 1984 S.C.C.R. 88............... 10.75
Ampthill Peerage [1977] A.C. 547; [1976] 2 W.L.R. 777................. 12.05
Archer v. Ritchie & Co. (1891) 18 R. 719......................... 17.09, 19.01
Argyll v. Argyll [1967] Ch. 302.................................. 11.39, 12.15
Atkins v. London Weekend Television Ltd, 1978 S.L.T. 76.... 10.20, 10.28, 10.29,
                                                         11.11
Att.-Gen. v. BBC [1981] A.C. 303; [1980] 3 W.L.R. 109................. 05.03
—— v. English [1982] 3 W.L.R. 278............................... 10.21
—— v. ITN [1995] 2 All E.R. 370; (1995) 1 Cr. App. R. 204.............. 24.03
—— v. News Group Newspapers [1989] Q.B. 110..................... 10.97

Baigent v. BBC, 1999 S.C.L.R. 787............................ 16.15, 18.03
Bergens Tilende v. Norway, May 2, 2000 E.C.H.R., unreported........... 25.21
Bonnard v. Perryman [1891] 2 Ch. 269..................... 18.12, 18.13, 24.11
Boyd v. BBC, 1969 S.L.T. (Sh.Ct) 17............................... 18.12
Bradbury v. Beeton (1869) 18 W.R. 33............................. 22.13
Brims v. Reid (1885) 12 R. 1016............................ 17.25, 19.05
British Sugar v. Robertson [1997] E.T.M.R. 118; [1996] R.P.C. 281......... 22.42
Broom v. Ritchie & Co. (1904) 6 F. 942........................... 16.37
Bruce v. Ross & Co. (1901) 4 F. 171............................ 16.26
Bunn v. BBC [1998] 3 All E.R. 552; [1998] E.M.L.R. 846................ 32.12

C v. M, 1923 S.C. 1... 18.10
Campbell and Steele v. H.M. Advocate, 1998 S.C.C.R. 214............... 03.85
Capital Life v. Sunday Mail (1979) *The Scotsman,* January 6, 1979, unre-
    ported... 16.39
Cowan (Forbes) Petr (1999) 2 Jur.R. 129; High Court, March 17, 1998, High
    Court at Edinburgh, unreported............................... 10.73
Cronin (John), Media Lawyer, May/June 1997, pp. 27–8................ 10.128
Cunningham v. Duncan & Jamieson (1889) 16 R. 383........ 18.06, 18.09, 19.04
—— v. Scotsman Publications, 1987 S.L.T. 698........ 07.33, 08.15, 08.22, 08.26,
                                                         08.34, 17.18

xi

Daily Record case (*aka* Cox and Griffiths Petrs) 1998 J.C. 267...... 10.43, 10.80, 10.137, 10.196
Derbyshire C.C. v. Times Newspapers [1993] A.C. 534; [1993] 2 W.L.R. 449.. 17.04, 17.35, 17.36, 25.25
Drew v. Mackenzie (1862) 24 D. 649................................. 16.03
Duncan v. Associated Newspapers, 1929 S.C. 14....................... 17.14

Egger v. Chelmsford (Viscount) [1965] 1 Q.B. 248..................... 19.05
Evening Times case (*aka* H.M. Advocate v. Scottish Media Newspapers) 2000 S.L.T. 331... 10.152

Fairbairn v. Scottish National Party, 1979 S.C. 393; 1980 S.L.T. 149........ 16.09
Fielding v. Variety Inc. [1967] 2 Q.B. 841............................. 18.06
Fletcher v. Wilson (1885) 12 R. 683.................................. 16.11
Forbes Cowan, 1998, Juridical Review 129, March 17, 1998.............. 10.76
Fraser v. Mirza, 1993 S.L.T. 527..................................... 17.23

Garbett v. Hazel Watson & Viney Ltd [1943] 2 All E.R. 359.............. 16.34
Gaskin v. UK [1990] 1 F.L.R. 167; (1990) 12 E.H.R.R. 36............... 25.19
Gilbraith v. H.M. Advocate, 2000 G.W.D. 31–1223................... 10.61–63
Girvan v. Inverness Farmers Dairy, 1995 S.L.T. 735.................... 04.47
—— v. ——(No. 2), 1998 S.C. (H.L.) 1; 1998 S.L.T. 21.................. 04.47
Godfrey v. Demon Internet [1999] 4 All E.R. 342; [1999] E.M.L.R. 542..... 33.14
—— v. W. & D.C. Thomson (1890) 17 R. 1108........................ 16.22
Grainger v. Stirling (1898) 5 S.L.T. 272............................... 19.14
Grapelli v. Derek Block Holdings Ltd [1981] 2 All E.R. 272............. 20.05

Hall v. Associated Newspapers Ltd, 1979 J.C. 1; 1978 S.L.T. 241..... 10.28, 10.29
Harkness v. The Daily Record Ltd, 1924 S.L.T. 759..................... 16.17
Harper v. Provincial Newspapers, 1937 S.L.T. 462..................... 17.18
Hedley Byrne and Co. Limited v. Heller and Partners Limited [1964] A.C. 465.. 20.09
Hope v. Leng Ltd (1907) T.L.R. 243.................................. 17.19
Hulton v. Jones [1910] A.C. 20...................................... 17.26
Hunter v. Ferguson & Co. (1906) 8 F. 574............................ 16.33
Hyde Park Residence v. David Yelland [2000] 3 W.L.R. 215; [2000] E.C.D.R. 275.. 22.25

Jersild v. Denmark (1995) 19 E.H.R.R. 1............................. 24.42

Kemp, Petrs, 1982 S.L.T. 357.. 10.109
King (Tom) case (*aka* McCann, Cullen and Shanahan) (1991) 92 Cr.App.R. 239... 10.123

Landell v. Landell (1841) 3 D. 819................................... 04.49
Langlands v. Leng, 1916 S.C. (H.L.) 102........................ 17.09, 17.35
Leon v. Edinburgh Evening News, 1909 S.C. 1014.................. 16.18, 19.01
Lingens v. Austria (1986) 8 E.H.R.R. 407............... 04.58, 16.04, 17.35
Lonrho plc., Re [1990] 2 A.C. 154; [1989] 2 All E.R. 1100.............. 10.85

McAliskey v. BBC, 1980 Northern Irish Reports 44..................... 24.52
Mackellor v. Sutherland (Duke of) (1859) 21 D. 222................... 16.26

McKerchar v. Cameron (1892) 19 R. 383. . . . . 16.26, 19.05
McLean v. Bernstein (1900) 8 S.L.T. 42. . . . . 19.12
Macleod v. J.P.s of Lewis (1892) 20 R. 218. . . . . 17.16
—— v. Lewis Justices (1892) 20 R. 218. . . . . 07.33, 08.37, 08.42, 08.44, 08.45
Macphail v. Macleod (1896) 3 S.L.T. 91. . . . . 16.36
McRostie v. Ironside (1849) 12 D. 74. . . . . 16.26
Marshall v. BBC [1979] 3 All E.R. 80. . . . . 24.50
Milburn, 1946 S.C. 301. . . . . 10.189
Milne v. Walker (1893) 21 R. 155. . . . . 16.11
Monson v. Tussauds [1894] 1 Q.B. 671. . . . . 16.34
Morrison v. Ritchie (1902) 4 F. 645. 16.33, 17.25, 18.09
Moynihan v Moynihan (Nos 1 and 2) *sub nom* Moynihan, Re [1997] 1 F.L.R.
    59; [1997] Fam. Law 88. . . . . 12.28, 12.29, 12.37
Mutch v. Robertson, 1981 S.L.T. 217. . . . . 17.35

O'Callaghan v. Thomson & Co., 1928 S.C. 532. . . . . 16.12
Ogston & Tennant v. Daily Record, Glasgow, 1909 S.C. 1000. . . . . 19.04
Oliver v. Barnet (1895) 3 S.L.T. 163. . . . . 16.26
Osborne v. BBC, 2000 S.C. 29; 2000 S.L.T. 150. . . . . 09.03, 32.09

Pope v. Outram, 1909 S.C. 230. . . . . 17.14

R v. Brent Health Authority, ex p. Francis and Community Rights Project
    [1985] 1 All E.R. 74. . . . . 23.23
—— v. Home Secretary, ex p. Brind [1991] 1 A.C. 696; [1991] 2 W.L.R.
    588. . . . . 24.26
—— v. Tronoh Mines Ltd [1952] 1 All E.R. 697; [1952] 1 T.L.R. 461. . . . . . 28.36
Referendum Party v. Business Age [1997] All E.R. 268; [1998] 2 W.L.R.
    435. . . . . 17.04
Reynolds (Albert) v. Times Newspapers [1999] 3 W.L.R. 1010; [1999] 4 All
    E.R. 609. . . . . 16.01, 16.04, 17.08, 17.35, 17.36
Richardson v. Wilson (1879) 7 R. 237. . . . . 07.32, 07.34, 08.10, 08.19, 10.163
Royle v. Gray, 1973 S.L.T 31. . . . . 10.190
Russell v. Stubbs, 1913 S.C. (H.L.) 14. . . . . 16.33

Secretary of State for Defence v. Guardian Newspapers Ltd [1985] A.C. 339;
    [1984] 3 W.L.R. 986. . . . . 10.40
Service Corporation International plc & Associated Funeral Directors
    Limited v. Channel Four Television (1998) ENT. L.R. Vol. 9, Issue 6,
    211. . . . . 32.07
Shanks v. BBC, 1993 S.L.T. 326. . . . . 04.39, 16.20
Sindicic (Vinko) (*aka* H.M. Advocate v. News Group Newspapers, Irvine
    and Scottish Express Newspapers) 1989 S.C.C.R. 157. . . . . 10.03, 10.08
Smith v. Ritchie (1892) 20 R. 52. . . . . 10.28, 10.80
—— v. Wood, *The Times*, April 10, 1963, unreported. 19.08
Spring v. Guardian Assurance plc. [1994] 3 All E.R. 129. . . . . . 17.23, 20.01, 20.10
Spycatcher Case (*aka* Att.-Gen. v. Guardian Newspapers Ltd [No. 2] [1990]
    1 A.C. 105. . . . . 09.03, 32.02, 32.03, 32.05
Stein v. Beaverbrook Newspapers Ltd, 1968 S.L.T. 401. . . . . 16.33, 18.06
Stirling v. Associated Newspapers Ltd, 1960 S.C. (J.) 5; 1960 S.L.T. 5. . . . . . 10.29
Sullivan v. New York Times (1964) 376 U.S. 244. . . . . 17.08, 17.35, 17.36

Thomson v. Crowe, 2000 J.C. 173. .... 03.27
Thompson v. Fifeshire Advertiser, 1936 S.N. 56. .... 19.13
Thomson v. Munro and Jamieson (1900) 8 S.L.T. 327. .... 17.19
Times Newsapers v. Att.-Gen. [1992] 1 A.C. 191. .... 10.104
Trainer (Joseph) Case, see "Contempt of Court: A Practitioners Viewpoint",
    1985 S.L.T. (News) 33. .... 10.125
Tudhope v. Glass, 1981 S.C.C.R. 336. .... 10.181
Turnbull v. Frome, 1966 S.L.T. 24. .... 24.21

Waddell v. BBC, 1973 S.L.T. 246. .... 17.09, 17.23, 17.35, 18.12
Walker v. British Picker Co. [1961] R.P.C. 57. .... 22.10
Webster v. Paterson & Sons, 1910 S.C. 459. .... 19.14
Williams v. Settle [1960] 2 All E.R. 806. .... 11.40, 22.22
Winter v. News Scotland Ltd, 1991 S.L.T. 828. .... 18.05
Wright & Greig v. Outram (1890) 17 R. 596. .... 16.03, 16.05, 17.15

X Ltd v. Morgan-Grampian (Publishers) Ltd, Re Goodwin [1991] 1 A.C. 1;
    [1990] 2 W.L.R. 1000. .... 10.38, 10.43

Young v. Armour, 1921 S.L.T. 211. .... 08.30, 08.33

Zircon Case (*aka* British Broadcasting Corporation v. Jessop, February 12,
    1987, *Glasgow Herald,* unreported). 30.10

TABLE OF STATUTES

1686 Evidence Act (c. 30)..... 07.19
1693 Court of Session Act
 (c. 42)............. 07.19
1707 Act of Union (c. 7)...... 01.02,
        01.04
1815 Jury Trials (Scotland) Act
 (55 & 56 Geo. 3, c.
 42)................ 04.37
1869 Newspapers, Printers and
 Reading Rooms
 Repeal Act (32 & 33
 Vict. c. 24).... 27.02, 27.04
1889 Indecent Advertisements
 Act (52 & 53 Vict. c.
 18)................ 28.33
1911 Official Secrets Act (1 & 2
 Geo. 5, c. 28).. 24.34, 30.32
 s. 1 ...... 30.01, 30.02, 30.09
 s. 2 ...... 30.03, 30.04, 30.33
 s. 9 .... 30.10
 Copyright Act (1 & 2 Geo.
 5, c. 46)............ 27.05
1921 Tribunals of Inquiry (Evidence) Act (11 & 12
 Geo. 5, c. 7)....... 10.172
1925 Criminal Justice Act (15 &
 16 Geo. 5, c. 86).... 11.16,
        11.18
1926 Judicial Proceedings (Regulation of Reports) Act
 (16 & 17 Geo. 5, c. 61).....
 12.01, 12.02, 12.05, 12.10,
 12.12, 12.18, 12.23, 12.28,
 12.29, 12.30, 12.33, 12.37,
   12.38, 12.41, 13.32
 s. 1 .... 12.27
 (i)(a) 12.03
  (b) 12.06, 12.25, 12.33
1933 Administration of Justice
 (Scotland) Act (23 &
 24 Geo. 5, c. 41)........
 s. 10 .... 07.26, 07.27
 (3) 07.28, 07.29
 (8) 07.29

1937 Children and Young Persons (Scotland) Act
 (1 Edw. 8 & 1 Geo. 6,
 c. 37).............. 13.36
 s. 46 ..... 13.33, 13.36, 13.47
1939 Cancer Act (2 & 3 Geo. 6,
 c. 13)—
 s. 41 .... 28.02
1947 National Health Service
 (Scotland) Act (10 &
 11 Geo. 6, c. 27)..... 06.14
1952 Defamation Act (15 & 16
 Geo. 6, c. 66).. 21.02, 21.09
 s. 3 .... 20.07
 s. 4 .... 17.28
 s. 5 .... 16.12
 s. 6 .... 17.09
 s. 12 .... 16.05, 18.11
1953 Accomodation Agencies
 Act (c. 23).......... 28.38
1955 Children and Young Persons (Harmful Pub-
 lications) Act (3 & 4
 Eliz. 2, c. 28)........ 28.34
1956 Food and Drugs
 (Scotland) Act (4 & 5
 Eliz. 2, c. 30)........ 26.08
1958 Matrimonial Proceedings
 (Children) Act (6 & 7
 Eliz. 2, c. 65)........ 28.14
 Prevention of Fraud
 Investments Act (6 &
 7 Eliz. 2, c. 45)..... 28.10
1959 Obscene Publications Act
 (7 & 8 Eliz. 2, c. 66) 24.44
1960 Public Bodies (Admission
 to Meetings) Act (8
 & 9 Eliz. 2, c. 67)... 23.21,
        23.22
 Sched. 23.21
1961 Trusts (Scotland) Act (9 &
 10 Eliz. 2, c. 57).... 04.32,
        04.35

1961 Printers Import Act
(c. 31)............. 27.02
1965 Law Commissions Act
(c. 22)............. 01.06
1966 Armed Forces Act (c. 45) 05.27
1967 Marine etc. Broadcasting
(Offences) Act
(c. 41)............. 28.30
Criminal Justice Act
(c. 80)............. 31.02
1968 Trade Descriptions Act
(c. 29)............. 28.29
Social Work (Scotland)
Act (c. 49).... 03.09, 13.20,
13.25, 13.46
s. 58 .... 13.25
Civil Evidence Act
(c. 64)—
s. 13 .... 16.13
Gaming Act (c. 65)...... 28.23,
28.26
Medicines Act (c. 67).... 28.03,
28.07
s. 94 .... 28.06
Law Reform (Mis-
cellaneous Pro-
visions) (Scotland)
Act (c. 70)—
s. 12 .... 16.13
1969 Representation of the
People Act (c. 15)—
s. 9 .... 24.56
(1) 24.53
1971 Interest on Damages
(Scotland) Act
(c. 31)............. 04.41
Sheriff Courts (Scotland)
Act (c. 58)......... 06.60
Tribunals and Inquiries
Act (c. 62)......... 06.02
1972 National Health Service
(Scotland) Act
(c. 58)............. 23.22
European Communities
Act (c. 68)......... 01.11
1973 Prescription and Limitation (Scotland) Act
(c. 52)............. 17.34
Local Government
(Scotland) Act
(c. 65)............. 23.21

1974 Consumer Credit Act
(c. 39)............. 28.11
Health and Safety at Work
Act (c. 37)......... 06.35
Rehabilitation of Offend-
ers Act (c. 53)..... 16.14 ,
26.01, 26.26
1975 Criminal Procedure
(Scotland) Act
(c. 21)........ 03.34, 11.23
Sex Discrimination Act
(c. 65)............. 28.39
s. 38 .... 28.39
Employment Protection
Act (c. 71)......... 06.07
1976 Fatal Accidents and Sudden Deaths Inquiry
(Scotland) Act
(c. 14)........ 13.40, 13.48
Lotteries and Amuse-
ments Act (c. 32).... 28.16
Race Relations Act
(c. 74)........ 29.05, 29.06
Sexual Offences (Amend-
ment) Act (c. 82).... 03.36
1977 Presumption of Death
(Scotland) Act
(c. 27)—
s. 14 .... 12.25
Housing (Homeless Per-
sons) Act (c. 48)..... 04.30
1978 Adoption (Scotland) Act
(c. 28)............. 28.13
1980 Bail etc. (Scotland) Act
(c. 4).............. 03.88
Magistrates Courts Act
(c. 43)............. 31.03
Law Reform (Mis-
cellaneous Pro-
visions) (Scotland)
Act (c. 55)......... 04.37
Criminal Justice (Scot-
land) Act (c. 62).... 03.63,
03.65, 10.30

1981 Contempt of Court Act
(c. 49)...... 03.69, 03.74,
05.03, 06.05, 06.63, 08.05,
08.29, 08.33, 08.103, 10.06,
10.18, 10.19, 10.22, 10.31,
10.47, 10.68, 10.80, 10.94,
10.96, 10.97, 10.137, 10.144,
10.147, 10.154, 10.163,
10.187, 10.197, 11.03, 11.10,
11.15, 17.13, 24.02, 24.22,
33.22
   ss. 1–6......... **Appendix 1**
   s. 2................ 10.157
   (2)........ 10.87, 10.157
   s. 3................. 24.22
   s. 4.... 10.49, 10.158, 10.160
   (2)... 10.57, 10.60, 10.74,
31.13
   s. 5............ 10.32, 10.33
   ss. 8-11......... **Appendix 1**
   s. 8................. 10.91
   s. 10..... 10.37, 10.39, 10.42,
10.44, 10.45
   s. 11........... 07.31, 10.64
   s. 13........... **Appendix 1**
   s. 15.... 10.158, **Appendix 1**
   s. 19..... 05.01, **Appendix 1**
   ss. 20-21....... **Appendix 1**
   Sched. 1........ **Appendix 1**
   Sched. 2........ **Appendix 1**
  Betting and Gaming
Duties Act (c. 63)... 28.22
1982 Civic Government (Scotland) Act (c. 45).... 11.50,
24.43, 28.33
   s. 51................ 27.08
  Criminal Justice Act
(c. 48)—
   Sched......... Appendix 1
1983 Representation of the
People Act (c. 2).... 16.09,
24.48, 24.50, 28.35, 28.37
   s. 93........... 24.49, 24.56
  Divorce Jurisdiction, Court
Fees and Legal Aid
(Scotland) Act (c. 12)......
12.02
  Mental Health Act (c. 20)
   Sched. 4,
    para. 57(c)... Appendix 1
  Solvent Abuse (Scotland)
Act (c. 33).......... 03.13

1984 Data Protection Act
(c. 35).. 08.82, 08.83, 09.06
  Mental Health (Scotland)
Act (c. 36)—
   Sched. 3,
    para. 48...... Appendix 1
  Cable and Broadcasting
Act (c. 46)—
   Sched. 5,
    para. 39(1)... Appendix 1
    (2)...... Appendix 1
1985 Company Securities (Insider
Dealing) Act (c. 8)... 10.42
  Local Government (Access
to Information) Act
(c. 43).. 23.13, 23.21, 23.31
  Surrogacy Arrangements
Act (c. 49).......... 28.32
  Interception of Communi-
cations Act (c. 56).. 08.111
1986 Animals (Scientific Pro-
cedures) Act (c. 14).. 28.09
  Legal Aid (Scotland) Act
(c. 47)—
   Sched. 5........ Appendix 1
  Financial Services Act
(c. 60)............. 10.41
  Public Order Act (c. 64) 24.42,
29.19
   s. 19................ 29.01
   s. 22................ 29.03
1988 Merchant Shipping Act
(c. 12)............. 01.10
  Legal Aid Act (c. 34)—
   Sched. 6........ Appendix 1
  Copyright, Designs and
Patents Act (c. 48).. 22.02,
22.17, 22.19, 22.44, 22.46
   s. 11(2)............. 22.17
   s. 30................ 22.23
   s. 58........... 22.28, 22.30
   s. 85................ 22.20
1989 Official Secrets Act
(c. 6)... 30.04, 30.08, 30.28,
30.33
1990 Law Reform (Miscellaneous
Provisions) Act (c. 40) 02.02,
03.28, 06.49, 06.51
  Courts and Legal Services
Act (c. 41)......... 02.15
  Broadcasting Act (c. 42) 24.67,
24.71, 24.78, 24.79, 24.76,
27.10, 29.01, 30.11

1990 Broadcasting Act—*cont.*
    s. 19 .... 24.73
    s. 83 .... 24.76
    s. 87 .... 24.71
    s. 90 .... 24.77
    s. 109(3) 24.79
    s. 110 .... 24.79
    s. 145(5) 24.35
    s. 163 .... 24.43
    s. 164 .... 24.42
    s. 167 .... 24.31, 24.33
      (6)(b) 24.34
    Sched. 20,
      para. 31(1) ... Appendix 1
      (2) ... Appendix 1
    Sched. 21 .... Appendix 1
1993 Damages (Scotland) Act
    (c. 5)............. 16.38
    s. 3 .... 16.38
    Trade Union Reform and
    Employment Rights
    Act (c. 19).......... 06.09
1994 Criminal Justice and
    Public Order Act
    (c. 33)—
    Sched. 4, para. 50 Appendix 1
1995 Children (Scotland) Act
    (c. 36).. 03.09, 03.18, 13.25,
        13.46
    Criminal Procedure (Conse-
    quential Provisions)
    (Scotland) Act (c. 40)—
    Sched. 4,
      para. 36 ...... Appendix 1
    Criminal Procedure (Scot-
    land) Act (c. 46).... 03.55,
        03.56
    s. 14 .... 10.30
    s. 26 .... 03.102
    s. 47 ..... 11,46, 13.02, 13.03,
        13.09, 13.11,
        13.25, 13.44
    s. 50 .... 13.29
    s. 106 .... 03.84
    s. 175 .... 03.84
1995 Disability Discrimination
    Act (c. 50).......... 06.13
1996 Industrial Tribunals Act
    (c. 17)............. 06.09
    Criminal Procedures and
    Investigations Act
    (c. 25)............. 31.11

1996 Criminal Procedures and
    Investigations
    Act—*cont.*
    s. 56 .... 07.10
    s. 57 .... Appendix 1
    s. 58 .... 07.11
      (4) 07.10
    Defamation Act (c. 31).. 16.05,
      16.40, 17.12, 17.23, 17.29,
      21.08
    s. 1 .... 24.17
      (1) 33.14
    ss. 2–4 .... 17.28
    s. 2 .... 17.29
    s. 12 .... 16.13
    s. 14 .... 17.20, 17.21
    Sched. 1 .... 17.20, 17.38,
      Appendix 4
    Armed Forces Act (c. 46) 05.21
    Broadcasting Act (c. 55)
    s. 107 .... Appendix 2
    s. 108 .... Appendix 2
1997 Crime and Punishment
    (Scotland) Act (c. 48)......
      03.20, 03.55, 03.69
    s. 1 .... 03.69
    s. 13 .... 03.20
1998 Competition Act 1998
    (c. 11)............. 08.111
    Data Protection Act
    (c. 29).. 08.82, 08.83, 08.88,
      08.116, 09.06, 09.17, 25.34
    Crime and Disorder Act
    (c. 37)............. 31.08
    Human Rights Act (c. 42)......
      04.62, 04.63, 04.65, 08.111,
      09.16, 09.17, 16.01, 24.29,
      25.04, 25.34, 25.36, 32.10,
      32.21
    s. 12 ..... 09.15, 18.13, 18.14,
      22.25, 24.11,
      25.28, 25.29,
      32.18, 32.20,
      33.26
    Scotland Act (c. 46)..... 01.38,
      04.62, 04.63, 04.65, 06.61,
      06.63, 10.50, 10.159, 14.11,
      15.06, 25.04
    s. 41 .... 01.32
    s. 42 .... 01.32
    s. 95 .... 06.57, 06.59
2000 Regulation of Investiga-
    tory Powers Act 2000
    (c. 23)............. 08.111

2000 Bail, Judicial Appoint-
       ments etc. (Scotland)
       Act 2000 (asp 9). 03.55

2000 Regulation of Investiga-
       tory   Powers
       (Scotland) Act 2000
       (asp 11). 08.115

CHAPTER 1

INTRODUCTION

THE NEW SCOTTISH LEGAL FRAMEWORK

There shall be a Scottish Parliament. With that confident and **01.01** ringing declaration the Scotland Act 1998 heralded the most fundamental constitutional change in Scotland for nearly 300 years.

Scotland was often said to be the only country in the world with its **01.02** own distinctive legal system but without a Parliament of its own to pass laws. That was not entirely true because, strictly speaking, England was in the same position. From the time of the Act of Union in 1707 the life of both Scots and English Parliaments was extinguished and a new body, the United Kingdom Parliament, created to replace them. Given that the Parliament was based in London, however, Scots could be forgiven for thinking that it was their legal system rather than the English that was at a disadvantage. Legal commentators frequently argued that the Scottish legal system had been ill-served by the failure of the Westminster Parliament to find enough time to pass distinctive laws for Scotland.

The situation changed dramatically in 1999 with elections for **01.03** the first Scottish Parliament in 292 years, heralding momentous changes for our legal system and the people involved in it. While the finer details are beyond the scope of this book, a broad outline of the main changes are covered in this chapter.

Over the centuries Scots law has survived as a distinct system, **01.04** largely based on Roman law while English law was essentially a home-grown product. The basic differences between the two systems were preserved by the Act of Union of 1707 which provided that no alteration was to be made in Scottish private law "except for the evident utility of the subjects within Scotland".

Although Scots law retains its own terminology and many **01.05** distinct features such as the not proven verdict and the 110-day rule (the time within which an accused person in custody must be brought to trial), the laws of the two countries have become much more similar than they were in 1707. There has been a constant

1

tendency towards harmonisation, particularly in recent years. Many Acts of Parliament apply to the whole United Kingdom and great stretches of the law, particularly in the fields of taxation and commerce, are the same on both sides of the Border.

01.06 An important development in the reform of the two systems along the same lines began with the setting up in 1965 of the Scottish Law Commission and the Law Commission for England and Wales. Under the Law Commissions Act of 1965 the Scottish Law Commission has the duty of keeping under review all the law of Scotland "with a view to its systematic development and reform". It has a chairman, who is a judge, and three full-time and one part-time commissioners. In pursuit of its law reform projects it issues consultative documents exploring areas of possible reform, seeks reactions from people and organisations with specialised knowledge as well as from the general public and prepares draft Bills for submission to the Scottish Parliament.

01.07 In several important respects Scots law has led the way in recent years both in development of the common law and through legislation. This revival has been accompanied by growing support for the publication of Scottish law books, giving Scots lawyers better access to the sources they require for practice, research and teaching.

01.08 Scotland has pioneered and developed the modern shift in the approach to children in trouble, from punishment towards care and protection. The passing of legislation to combat alcohol abuse and crowd violence at sports meetings originated here—as did, much earlier, the system of independent local prosecutors under the Crown, now emulated in England and Wales. England's abandonment of its insistence upon the unanimous jury verdict goes part-way at least towards acceptance of what has been the position north of the Border for centuries.

01.09 Another major and growing influence on Scots law stems from our membership of the European Community. Jacques Delors, former President of the European Commission, stated that in the 1990s 80 per cent of economic and social law would come from Brussels and it is clear that in areas such as agriculture, fishing, immigration, commercial and tax law, Europe exercises a profound influence on legal systems in the United Kingdom.

01.10 This even extends to traditional views on the sovereignty of Parliament. In the *Factortame* case in 1991 the European Court of Justice ruled illegal and unenforceable provisions of the Merchant Shipping Act 1988, legislation which had been validly introduced at Westminster. The European Court said the Act discriminated against people from other Member States on the ground of nationality and was therefore contrary to Community law.

In his book *Scots Public Law*, author Mungo Deans stated: **01.11**

"On joining the (European) Community (in 1973) the United Kingdom accepted a new legal order imposed by community law. Parliament enacted provisions in the European Communities Act 1972 whereby Community law would become part of United Kingdom law. Over the years the courts have acknowledged that where there is a conflict between Community law and law originating in the United Kingdom, ie domestic law, Community law should prevail unless Parliament states a clear intention to the contrary. . . . In practice the Community is gradually replacing Parliament as the supreme source of law in the United Kingdom."

For journalists in particular, the European Court of Human Rights **01.12** in Strasbourg has also issued decisions of major importance in recent years, especially in areas such as freedom of speech and contempt of court. (See Chapter 10.) When the new Labour administration came to power in May 1997 it enacted its commitment to incorporate the European Convention on Human rights into our domestic law and introduced a Human Rights Bill into the House of Lords in October that year. The Bill became the Human Rights Act 1999 (brought into force in October 2000) and provided that it would be unlawful for public authorities to act in any way incompatible with Convention rights. The rights included the right to life, the right to a fair and public trial within a reasonable time and freedom of expression.

Even before that, under the Scotland Act, the Scottish Executive **01.13** and the Scottish Parliament had to comply with the rights set out in the Convention in exercising their powers. The Scotland Act provided that an Act of the Scottish Parliament should not include any measure incompatible with Convention rights. For most purposes that took effect on July 1, 1999. As far as criminal proceedings were concerned, it became possible for an accused person to challenge the actions of the prosecution on the basis of the Convention from May 20, 1999. That was when the Lord Advocate, who is responsible for the conduct of criminal proceedings in Scotland, became a member of the Scottish Executive. Lawyers began testing the water immediately on issues such as the right to a fair and public hearing within a reasonable time by an independent and impartial tribunal. Courts were asked to decide whether a 14-year-old boy with a mental age of eight or nine who was charged with murder could understand enough of what was happening in court to receive a fair trial. They were also asked to decide whether temporary sheriffs, appointed on an annual basis, had the necessary security of tenure to be regarded as a tribunal independent from the Lord Advocate who in effect could hire and fire them.

Sources of law

01.14 Apart from the recent European influences there are four main sources of legal rules—legislation, precedents, writers and custom.

01.15 Legislation or enacted law is the first and most important. This includes Acts of Parliament and subordinate legislation made under powers conferred by Parliament. We will now have legislation passed by the Westminster Parliament and also Acts of the Scottish Parliament in areas where responsibility has been devolved. Subordinate legislation may take the form of Orders in Council (made in theory by the Queen in Council; in fact by the Government), regulations made by Government Ministers, or rules of procedure made by courts.

01.16 The term "statutory instruments" is used to describe most such legislation. In Scotland the rules made by the Court of Session to regulate procedure in civil cases are known as "Acts of Sederunt", while the rules made by the High Court of Justiciary for regulating procedure in criminal cases are known as "Acts of Adjournal". Subordinate legislation also includes the bye-laws of local authorities and other bodies.

01.17 Precedent or case law is the second source of legal rules. Any body having to make decisions over a period of time tends to seek consistency. Courts of law are no exception. The decisions and opinions of judges in important cases are recorded in law reports and constitute "precedents" if a similar case arises again.

01.18 The general rule is that a court is bound to follow a previous decision of itself and any higher court in the same hierarchy. However, the House of Lords, the highest court in a Scottish civil case, does not now regard itself as absolutely bound by its own previous decisions. Within the Court of Session there is a very convenient procedure whereby a case can be referred to a larger court when it may be necessary to overrule an awkward precedent.

01.19 Not everything said in a case is equally authoritative. A judge may make incidental comments which are not necessary for the decision of the case before him. Statements made "by the way" in this manner are known as *obiter dicta* and are not binding on other judges.

01.20 Writers are the third source of legal rules. Their authority varies. Some, such as Stair (seventeenth century) and Erskine (eighteenth century), are known as "institutional writers" and enjoy a very high authority in Scotland. English law too has its great writers, such as the eighteenth century Blackstone, but they carry less weight than their Scottish counterparts.

Custom is a subsidiary source of law. The Scottish institutional **01.21** writers took customary rules and amalgamated them with Roman law to form a coherent system. Custom therefore played an important part in the development of Scots law. In comparatively rare cases custom may still be recognised as a source of law, provided it is certain, fair and not contrary to a definite legal principle. The courts, for example, have applied a custom of the Stock Exchange and a local custom of Caithness regulating the rights of tenants against their landlords.

Two meanings of "common law"

The journalist may often come across a reference to the phase **01.22** common law, which can have two meanings. First, it can refer to all law other than that introduced by legislation. Rules derived solely from custom, precedents and the institutional writers, are rules of common law. Secondly, common law is often used in the sense of "English common law". A common law system is one, as in Australia, deriving its inspiration from the English common law.

Two meanings of "civil law"

Civil law sometimes means Roman law. A civil law system is one, **01.23** like that of France or, to a lesser degree, Scotland, deriving its inspiration from Roman law. In this sense, civil law is contrasted with the second meaning of common law given above.

The term "civil law" is more often used in contrast to criminal **01.24** law. The civil law is concerned with, for example, divorce, contract, property and actions for damages. The criminal law deals with wrongful acts which are harmful to the community as a whole and which are punished by the State. The same act, for example careless driving, may give rise to both a criminal prosecution and a civil law claim for damages.

Private and public law

We have already used the term "private law" in quoting from the **01.25** Act of Union. Broadly speaking private law regulates relations between subject and subject while public law regulates relations between State and subject. The law of divorce is a branch of private law. Criminal law is part of public law.

DEVOLUTION

As we noted at the beginning of the chapter, Scotland now has its **01.26** own Parliament sitting in Edinburgh for the first time in nearly 300 years. When the Labour Party won the general election in May

1997 with an overwhelming majority of 179 seats, it quickly put into effect its pledge to publish a White Paper on a devolved Scottish Parliament. This was followed by a referendum in which the Scottish people voted decisively in favour of a Parliament which was to have wide-ranging powers, including varying the rate of income tax, although the Parliament at Westminster retained ultimate legislative supremacy. The next stage was the publication of the Scotland Bill in December 1997 and the Bill became an Act almost a year later.

01.27 The approach favoured by the Government was to list the matters reserved to Westminster such as the constitution of the United Kingdom, defence and national security, United Kingdom foreign policy and fiscal economic and monetary policy, but this left a large range of devolved powers for the 129 new Scottish Members of Parliament (MSPs) to deal with. In the legal sphere these include criminal law, criminal justice and prosecution, the civil and criminal courts, legal aid and prisons and most judicial appointments. More generally the Parliament will be dealing with such major issues such as health, education, social work, housing and land-use and the environment.

01.28 In their book *Devolution and the Scotland Bill*, Chris Himsworth and Colin Munro of Edinburgh University state: "There is a clear intention underlying the devolution package that the Scottish Parliament should have general powers to amend and perhaps codify the private law and the criminal law of Scotland. . . . The point is to provide (or restore) a law-making capacity to a legal system which has to its detriment lacked its own legislature in modern times."

01.29 The Scottish Parliament sits for a fixed term of four years (unless an extraordinary general election has been called) and MSPs are elected by an additional member system, unlike the traditional "first past the post" system used for Westminster. In effect an elector casts two votes—one for a candidate to represent the constituency, the second for a party—the idea being to increase the relationship between seats won and votes cast while at the same time preserving the constituency link. Of the 129 MSPs 73 are elected on the first past the post basis, more or less from the Westminster constituencies (with Orkney and Shetland becoming two constituencies rather than one) and the remaining 56 under a regional list system. The eight European Parliament constituencies in Scotland will each return seven regional members to the Scottish Parliament. An elector can vote once in the constituency election and a second time for a political party which has submitted a list of candidates, or for an individual standing as an independent candidate.

The Scotland Act provides the Scottish Parliament with the **01.30** power to make laws—Acts of the Scottish Parliament—subject to the proviso that they must be within the legislative competence of the Parliament. There are a number of grounds upon which an Act of the Scottish Parliament will be *ultra vires* or outwith its powers. This would be the case if the would-be legislation attempted to deal with issues reserved for Westminster, formed part of the law or a territory outside Scotland, attempted to modify the terms of the Scotland Act or was incompatible with any European Community Law or the European Convention on Human Rights. The Scotland Act contains provisions designed to avoid this happening.

A member of the Scottish Executive in charge of a particular Bill **01.31** is obliged to make a statement to the effect that in his view an Act of the Scottish Parliament containing the same provisions as those in the Bill would be within the legislative competence of the Parliament. The standing orders of the Parliament also provide that no Bill can be introduced if the Presiding Officer decides that it would be outside the Parliament's legislative competence. The Presiding Officer, elected from the MSPs, is charged with ensuring the efficient conduct of Parliamentary business. The role is roughly that of the Speaker of the House of Commons. It is also his or her job to present Bills for Royal Assent. Questions as to whether a Bill would be within the Parliament's powers can be referred to the Judicial Committee of the Privy Council by the Advocate General (see later), the Lord Advocate or the Attorney-General. At a later stage the question of whether any Act of the Scottish Parliament is within its legislative competence—a "devolution issue"—can be referred to the Court of Session or High Court with an appeal to the Privy Council. The court or tribunal before which an alleged devolution issue arises has the power to decide that the claim is frivolous or vexatious.

Reporting proceedings of the Scottish Parliament

Reports and broadcasts of what takes place in the Scottish **01.32** Parliament are protected from the law of defamation and contempt of court, but on a more restricted level than proceedings in Westminster. Section 42 of the Scotland Act provides that for the purposes of contempt the strict liability rule (see Chapter 10) shall not apply to any publication made in proceedings of the Parliament in relation to a Bill or subordinate legislation or to the extent that it consists of a fair and accurate report of such proceedings made in good faith. It will be seen that the exemption from the law of contempt applies only to some proceedings of the Scottish Parliament. To take the example of the Dunblane atrocity, if Thomas

Hamilton, the perpetrator, had survived the incident, and in a general debate following his arrest or in questions to Ministers an MSP had suggested that Hamilton should have shot himself to save wasting public money on a trial, such remarks would not be protected by section 42. The protection is limited to fair and accurate reporting of potentially prejudicial comments about active legal proceedings made during the course of debate on a Bill or subordinate legislation. The immunity provided by section 42 also does not cover contempt at common law. As far as defamation is concerned section 41 of the Scotland Act provides absolute privilege for any statement made in the proceedings of Parliament and for the publication of any statement made under the authority of Parliament.

The Scottish Administration

01.33 The Scotland Act establishes a Scottish Executive, led by the First Minister, Ministers appointed by him and the Lord Advocate and Solicitor-General. The First Minister is nominated from the members of the Parliament and appointed by the Queen on the recommendation of the Presiding Officer.

Role of the Secretary of State for Scotland

01.34 There was some debate as to whether the office of Scottish Secretary would be either necessary or desirable in a devolved Scotland. The White Paper saw the Secretary of State's role as ensuring the passage and implementation of the legislation to establish the Scottish Parliament. Once that had been established his or her role would be to promote communication between the Scottish Parliament and the Executive and Westminster and to represent Scottish interests in reserved matters. In Himsworth and Munro's view:

> "The Secretary of State will, it seems, be something of a midwife for the birth of a Scottish Parliament, and for a while afterwards will be the health visitor who passes on folk wisdom and ensures healthy bonding. ... Over a longer timescale, some commentators consider that the Scottish arm of the United Kingdom Government, being less able to claim to represent Scotland than representatives of the directly elected Parliament, will wither and die. Certainly, when different parties are in London and Edinburgh, the position of Secretary of State is likely to be distinctly less comfortable."

Minister of Justice

Another consequence of devolution was the setting up of a **01.35** Ministry of Justice headed by a Justice Minister. The first holder of the office was Mr Jim Wallace, a Liberal Democrat MSP and a Queen's Counsel. The Justice Minister's responsibilities include civil law and criminal justice, police, drugs, community safety and crime prevention, prisons, parole and miscarriages of justice, legal aid, courts administration (apart from tribunals), land reform and the Scottish Law Commission. The stated aim of the Justice Department was to bring together under one Minister all the policy responsibilities for criminal justice and civil law.

Mr Donald Dewar, who became the First Minister of the new **01.36** Scottish Administration, announced that the Justice Ministry would also be responsible for taking forward the Government's commitments on judicial appointments. He said the Government was keen to make the selection process more open and to see a broader base for appointments, although ability to do the job would remain the most important quality. The Government began carrying its intentions into effect in December 1999 when Justice Minister Jim Wallace announced the appointment of Mrs Rajni Swanney, the first Asian to be appointed as a sheriff in Scotland on a full-time basis. The present system of appointing judges and sheriffs has been described by legal commentators as being "shrouded in mystery". Appointments are made by the Queen acting on "advice" but the precise role of the various advisers, such as the Lord Advocate and Lord President has never been entirely clear. The Scotland Act provides for the appointment of High Court and Court of Session judges and, for the first time, sets out a clear procedure for removing them from office on the grounds of inability, neglect of duty or misbehaviour. (See Chapter 6.)

The Law Officers

The Office of Lord Advocate is one of the most ancient and **01.37** powerful in the Scottish legal system, dating back to at least 1483. He is head of the Crown Office and Procurator Fiscal Service which conducts prosecutions and investigates deaths in Scotland. In that capacity he acts independently of other Ministers and is not subject to the ordinary rules of collective ministerial responsibility. In practice he has traditionally been closely involved in considering the names of candidates for the High Court, Court of Session and Sheriff Court benches.

Under the ill-fated Scotland Act of 1978 the Lord Advocate **01.38** would have remained a part of the United Kingdom Government, but this idea has now been discarded. Under the 1998 Scotland Act both the Lord Advocate and his second-in-command, the Solicitor-General for Scotland, are appointed by the First Minister and become law officers of the Scottish Administration. As such they are responsible for giving legal advice to the Scottish administration, particularly over whether a proposed piece of legislation is within the legislative competence of the Edinburgh Parliament.

01.39 Such is the value placed on the independence of the Lord Advocate that the Edinburgh Parliament is specifically prevented by the Scotland Act from removing him from office. Any such attempt would be beyond the competence of the Parliament. The Scotland Act also provides that "any decision of the Lord Advocate in his capacity as head of the systems of criminal prosecution and investigation of deaths in Scotland shall continue to be take by him independently of any other person". The law officers do not have to be members of the Scottish Parliament but are entitled to take part in debates and answer questions about their responsibilities, although they cannot vote if they are not MSPs. They can decline to answer any question if the answer might prejudice a prosecution or otherwise damage the public interest.

01.40 The critical issue of the Lord Advocate's independence from political influence was raised in two instances as the Scotland Bill was making its way through Parliament. One case involved the decision to agree to a prosecution outside Scotland of two Libyans accused of murdering 270 people by blowing up a plane over Lockerbie. The other was a decision to lodge a Crown appeal against sentences of four years imposed on three youths convicted of culpable homicide. In both cases Lord Hardie, the Lord Advocate, strenuously denied suggestions in some sections of the media that he had succumbed to pressure from Government colleagues in making the decisions. He insisted that the final decisions had been his and his alone.

01.41 The Lord Advocate became a member of the cabinet of the first Scottish administration and this again led to suggestions in some quarters that his independence as a prosecutor might be compromised. Mr Donald Dewar, the First Minister, countered by saying:

> "It has been suggested that the Lord Advocate's and indeed the Lord Chancellor's position at Westminster run counter to the doctrine of separation of powers. . . . It is an odd theory because that particular doctrine has never found favour in this country. If it did the Prime Minister, Ministers and indeed their Scottish equivalents would not sit either in the Commons or the Scottish Parliament. . . . Can I stress that the Lord Advocate has indeed no inalienable right to dodge scrutiny.

The Lord Advocate can be questioned in the Parliament here in Edinburgh on presentation and policy, can be summoned before committees. . . . He can block a question only if it is likely to prejudice proceedings in any case or is contrary to the public interest. In terms of accountability we have strengthened the safeguards, brought this great office into the mainstream."

Advocate General

One of the consequences of a devolved Parliament was the creation of a new Scottish law officer whose job was to advise the United Kingdom Government on all questions of Scots law reserved or devolved, and European law. The Advocate General assumed responsibility for advising United Kingdom government departments whether a proposal of the Scottish administration or the Parliament might conflict with the terms of the Scotland Act. The need for the new post of Advocate General for Scotland was identified because both the Lord Advocate and the Solicitor-General became part of the new Scottish set-up instead of being United Kingdom law officers. The first holder of the new office was Ms Lynda Clark, Q.C., a leading member of the Scottish Bar. 01.42

KEY POINTS

Scots Law is a distinct system with the basic differences from England preserved by the Act of Union. United Kingdom-wide legislation in areas such as company law means that the two systems now share common features, but Scots law retains many distinctive characteristics such as the children's hearing system, the not proven verdict and the 110-day rule. European law is also an increasing influence and the European Convention on Human Rights has now become part of our domestic law. Following elections in May 1999, Scotland now has its own Parliament based in Edinburgh for the first time in nearly 300 years. The Parliament has wide-ranging powers to legislate on Scottish affairs. The new Scottish administration created the post of Minister of Justice. Both Scottish law officers, the Lord Advocate and Solicitor-General, are part of the devolved set-up and can be questioned in the Edinburgh Parliament. The post of Advocate General has been created to advise the United Kingdom Government on Scots law issues. 01.43

CHAPTER 2

THE LEGAL PROFESSION

02.01 The legal profession in Scotland is divided into two main branches—solicitors and advocates. Solicitors deal directly with clients and handle all kinds of legal business. Although they plead on behalf of clients in the sheriff and district courts on a daily basis, traditionally they could not, with certain limited exceptions, appear in the Court of Session or in the High Court of Justiciary.

Solicitor Advocates

02.02 The privilege of appearing in the Supreme Courts was reserved for members of the Faculty of Advocates. However, this was changed under the Law Reform (Miscellaneous Provisions) Act 1990 which granted solicitors with the required qualifications and experience rights of audience in the higher courts. Under rules drawn up by the Law Society of Scotland and approved by the Lord President, solicitors wishing to plead in the House of Lords, High Court or Court of Session have to lodge an application with the Law Society and undergo a course of "induction training" at the Court of Session to familiarise themselves with procedural rules. They may also have to "sit-in" on cases for a specified number of days. The rules also provide for examinations to test the suitability of would-be pleaders and Supreme Courts training courses, including lectures and practical sessions, for solicitors seeking extended rights of audience.

02.03 Although solicitor-advocates are a relatively recent phenomenon, they have made significant inroads into work, particularly criminal cases, which had previously been passed by solicitors to the Faculty of Advocates. By the year 2000 there were 128 solicitor advocates, although only two were qualified to appear in both the High Court and the Court of Session. They had also formed their own representative body, the Society of Solicitor Advocates.

02.04 Mr Francis Mulholland, a member of the procurator fiscal service who qualified as a solicitor advocate, became the first fiscal to prosecute in the High Court. He was appointed by the Lord

12

Advocate of the day, Lord Mackay of Drumadoon, and appeared successfully in several important trials. However, Lord Mackay's successor, Lord Hardie, decided not to make any further such appointments. Although he was satisfied as to the competence of procurators fiscal to prosecute in the High Court, Lord Hardie took the view that it was necessary for the proper operation of the prosecution system in Scotland to maintain the traditional separation between the role of fiscals and Crown counsel. He felt this was necessary to ensure independence of decision-making and prosecution in the High Court.

Solicitors

The solicitor intending to practise must have completed the three **02.05** or four year university LL.B. course or passed the professional examinations set by the Law Society of Scotland. He or she must also attend a post-graduate course for 26 weeks and pass examinations to qualify for the Diploma in Legal Practice. The diploma course supplements the degree studies with emphasis on skill training and the practical day-to-day aspects of work in a law office. It is followed by two years of practical office training during which the trainee must, from 2002 onwards, return to university and complete a three-week "professional competence course". Towards the end of the training all trainees will, from 2003 onwards, sit a compulsory "test of professional competence" (TPC). Practising certificates are issued by the Law Society, the governing body of Scottish solicitors.

There are various societies of solicitors whose names may cause **02.06** confusion. Writers to the Signet (W.S.) and Solicitors in the Supreme Courts (S.S.C.) at one time had special privileges in Court of Session work. Other local societies include the Royal Faculty of Procurators in Glasgow and, particularly confusing, the Society of Advocates in Aberdeen. In spite of the diverse names, members of these societies are simply solicitors. The advantages of membership include widows' pensions and library facilities.

Many solicitors are also notaries public (N.P.s). This privilege, **02.07** obtained by presenting a petition to the Court of Session, enables the solicitor to act as an official witness to important formal documents.

Advocates and Barristers

Advocates, also referred to as counsel, are not allowed to deal **02.08** directly with clients and must, as a rule, rely on solicitors for their cases. The solicitor takes the litigant's instructions, interviews witnesses and does all the background work in the case. The advocate will advise on points of law and frame some of the documents involved but his main function is to plead in court.

02.09 To be admitted as an advocate an intrant must have passed, or gained exemption from, certain examinations. He must also have completed a period of professional training in a solicitor's office, and a period as a "devil" or, more accurately, pupil to a practising advocate. In 1999, for the first time in Scotland the number of members of the Faculty of Advocates passed the 400 mark.

02.10 Advocates who build up a successful practice may, after some years, apply to become a Queen's Counsel (Q.C.). This is known as "taking silk". They are then senior counsel and will frequently appear only in cases where a junior appears with them. They will tend to be engaged in fewer, but more difficult and more rewarding, cases.

02.11 Advocates are called barristers in England. Their training is in some respects more colourful than that of their northern counterparts. They must join one of four Inns of Court and eat a prescribed number of dinners each term for three years—a system surviving from the days when the main part of the barrister's training consisted of discussion with his peers and superiors at table. Nowadays this, valuable as it may be, is supplemented by more formal instruction, culminating in the sitting of the Bar examinations.

02.12 It has now become fairly common for Scottish advocates to "take chambers" under the English system and to qualify by "eating dinners" to become qualified barristers in England. It is perfectly possible to be an advocate in Scotland and a barrister in England at the same time.

02.13 Barristers tend to specialise much more than advocates and several of those specialising in a particular field often share one set of chambers and one clerk. In Scotland the system is different. Counsel's chambers are generally in their own houses in Edinburgh or elsewhere. They are not, as in England, in the nature of "offices" shared by a group. In Scotland clerical and secretarial services are provided centrally at Parliament House, Edinburgh (where the Court of Session sits), by a number of advocates' clerks and by an organisation called Faculty Services Ltd.

02.14 The traditional monopoly enjoyed by barristers of audience before the English High Court of Justice was for the first time broken when, in May 1986, Mr Leo Abse, M.P., made a brief appearance before Mr Justice Caulfield in London. He read an agreed statement in settlement of a libel action which he and 24 other M.P.s brought against Mr Cyril Smith, M.P., for an alleged statement by him during the Falkland Islands conflict accusing them of treason on opposing the Government.

This was followed by the Courts and Legal Services Act 1990 **02.15** which aimed to allow solicitors much wider rights of audience in the higher courts than they had previously enjoyed. Generally, English solicitors were allowed to appear only in the magistrates courts and county courts. From 1993, however, a solicitor with at least three years' experience could apply for a higher courts qualification from the Law Society and compete with barristers in representing clients.

In 1997 two solicitors became the first in private practice to be **02.16** appointed Queen's Counsel and later that year were also authorised to sit as deputy High Court judges, one in the Chancery Division, the other in the Queen's Bench Division. Announcing the decision, Lord Irvine, the Lord Chancellor, said that he intended to recognise the talents of all parts of the legal profession, to reward the ablest practitioners and open up the ranks of the higher judiciary. Lord Irvine also announced his intention to allow salaried lawyers from the Crown Prosecution Service full rights of audience in the Crown Court. This was criticised by the distinguished legal commentator Michael Zander who disagreed with the Lord Chancellor's view that the lawyers would be sufficiently independent of their employers. Professor Zander's view was that it would lead to a "regrettable deterioration" in decision-making in serious criminal cases.

KEY POINTS

The two main branches of the legal profession are advocates and **02.17** solicitors. Senior advocates can apply to take silk and become Queen's Counsel. Generally, the solicitor deals directly with the client and instructs the advocate who appears in court. Solicitors with the required training and experience have now been granted the right to plead in the High Court and Court of Session.

CHAPTER 3

CRIMINAL COURTS AND PROCEDURE

SCOTTISH CRIMINAL COURTS

Jurisdiction

03.01 In dealing with courts the word "jurisdiction" constantly occurs. Its basic meaning is simply a power to hear and decide. A court has appellate jurisdiction if it has power to hear and decide appeals, original jurisdiction if it has power to hear and decide cases coming before it directly, at first instance, and not on appeal from another court. Territorial jurisdiction describes the area of Scotland over which a particular court has jurisdiction. District courts and sheriff courts have restricted jurisdiction over an area defined by statute. The High Court, however, has jurisdiction over the whole of Scotland.

Summary and solemn jurisdiction

03.02 Courts of summary jurisdiction deal with the less serious crimes. Proceedings begin with a complaint (sometimes called a summons) and there is no jury. The punishment which can be imposed is limited. The courts of summary jurisdiction in Scotland are the sheriff courts and district courts.

03.03 Courts of solemn jurisdiction deal with the more serious crimes. Proceedings take place on an indictment and there is always a jury of 15 (the one exception to this is the Lockerbie prosecution, which proceeds in the special circumstances of an Order in Council allowing this case to be heard in Holland before a panel of three Scottish Judges sitting without a jury). The sheriff courts and the High Court of Justiciary are the only courts of solemn jurisdiction in Scotland. The sheriff court has both summary and solemn jurisdiction, the sheriff sitting alone in summary cases and with a jury in solemn cases.

District courts

District courts sit in each local government district or islands area **03.04** unless the Secretary of State directs, in view of the likely lack of business, that no district court shall be established for a particular district. As from May 1975 they replaced the former justice of the peace courts, burgh courts and police courts. The judges are either lay justices of the peace or legally qualified stipendiary magistrates. Most justices of the peace are appointed by the Secretary of State for Scotland but, in addition, each local authority can nominate up to one quarter of its members to serve as *ex officio* justices for its area. A stipendiary magistrate is appointed by the local authority. He must have been an advocate or a solicitor for at least five years. Only a few district courts have stipendiary magistrates. The majority consist of justices of the peace. Normally the court consists of one or two justices.

The district courts have jurisdiction over a wide range of minor **03.05** offences, such as breach of the peace and many offences under local authority bye-laws. Except where particular statutes provide otherwise, their powers of punishment are limited to a fine of up to £2,500, or 60 days' imprisonment or both. A district court when constituted by a stipendiary magistrate has, in addition to the above jurisdiction and powers, the summary criminal jurisdiction and powers of a sheriff.

Prosecutions are conducted by the procurator fiscal who must **03.06** comply with directions given by the Lord Advocate regarding prosecutions in the district court and must report to the Lord Advocate, if called upon to do so, on matters concerning the discharge of his functions. The clerical work of the court is the responsibility of the clerk of the district court, who is appointed and employed by the local authority. He may be full-time or part-time, and must be an advocate or a solicitor. The clerk also acts as legal assessor in the court, advising the justices about the law and procedure. In busy district courts such as Glasgow, the clerk carries out this function through part-time depute assessors.

The procedure and rights of appeal in district courts are similar **03.07** to those in summary procedure in the sheriff courts and will be considered later.

Justices over the age of 65 are put on a supplemental list and **03.08** cannot perform judicial functions. The Scottish Ministers has power to place justices under the age of 70 on the supplemental list in certain circumstances—for example, if they decline or neglect to take a proper part in the exercise of their judicial or other functions or to attend suitable courses of instruction. In terms of the Bail, Judicial Appointments etc. (Scotland) Act 2000 "signing justices" will appear on the supplemental list. "Full justices" cannot be removed if the tribunal set up under the 2000 Act decides. The tribunal comprises the Lord President, a sheriff principle, an experienced lawyer and a lay person.

Children's hearings

03.09 Children's hearings are not really courts at all, although they do in fact deal with most offences committed by children. (See also Chapter 12.) "Children" for this purpose means anyone under the age of 16 and certain children over that age who are already subject to a supervision requirement or who have been referred to the hearing from another part of the United Kingdom. The policy behind the Social Work (Scotland) Act 1968, which introduced children's hearings, is based on therapy rather than punishment. The law on children's hearings is now to be found in the Children (Scotland) Act 1995.

03.10 In certain circumstances children may be "in need of compulsory measures of care". These circumstances include cases where the child is beyond the control of his or her parent; where through lack of parental care he or she is falling into bad associations or is exposed to moral danger; where he or she has been the victim of certain offences (such as cruelty); or where he or she has failed to attend school regularly without reasonable excuse.

03.11 The circumstances also include the commission of an offence, and in fact a large proportion of the cases brought before children's hearings are brought on the offence ground. The hearing does not, however, conduct trials. If the grounds of referral are accepted by the child and his or her parent the hearing proceeds to decide what course would be in the best interests of the child; it may, for example, decide to place him or her under the supervision of a local authority social work department, or it may decide to send him or her to a residential establishment. But if the grounds are not accepted—as would be the case if the referral was based on the belief that the child had committed an offence but the child denied committing the offence—the children's hearing does not proceed. Instead it must either discharge the referral or have the case referred to the sheriff for a finding as to whether the grounds are established.

03.12 A referral hearing before a sheriff takes the form of a proof as in a civil court. Witnesses are put on oath and their evidence is subject to cross-examination. The standard of proof which the sheriff applies is the same as in civil courts—on a balance of probabilities. It is important to note that the sheriff does not dispose of the case himself even if he is hearing a referral. If he finds the facts established he simply remits the case back to the children's hearing for disposal. To use a criminal analogy (although it is not entirely appropriate), the sheriff decides on conviction, but not sentence.

The same result follows if the hearing considers that the grounds **03.13** have not been understood by the child. This can be a case where the child is too young to understand. In some cases new-born babies have been taken into care if the social work authorities believe the parents are not capable of taking care of the child or if the child is in some form of danger. For example, an elder brother or sister may have been assaulted or abused in the past. If the sheriff finds the ground established the case goes back to a children's hearing for the appropriate measures to be taken. Hearings also have power to deal with cases referred under the Solvent Abuse (Scotland) Act 1983.

The people who sit on children's hearings are lay volunteers **03.14** drawn from carefully selected children's panels. The organisation of hearings and the referral of cases to them are the responsibility of an officer called (rather confusingly) "the reporter", who is appointed and paid by the local authority. Procedure at the hearings is quite informal. The public is not admitted, but bona fide press representatives may attend. There is a strict ban on identifying any child in any way concerned in a hearing.

It is increasingly common for the children involved in hearings **03.15** or court proceedings to be separately represented from their parents. One method of achieving this end is to appoint a "safeguarder" to the child, who will usually be a solicitor or someone with a social work background. It is necessary for a sheriff or a children's panel hearing a case involving a child to consider the necessity of appointing a safeguarder. The safeguarder must represent the child's interests in the proceedings. But a safeguarder is not a legal role. It is the safeguarder's task to ascertain the whole family circumstances of the child. The safeguarder must represent the child's interests as opposed to that of the parents or other family members, although on many occasions these interests may coincide. By using safeguarders, the Scottish system hopes to live up to the UN Convention on the Rights of the Child which requires domestic courts to afford a child involved in proceedings the right to have his or her views taken into account. In most cases, the safeguarder's task is completed by summarising the views and interests of the child in question and reporting these to the court or hearing. Safeguarders do not require to attend the hearing itself, although in practice many do so.

Another method of having a child's interests protected is for the **03.16** hearing or the sheriff to appoint a curator ad litem to the child.

Again the aim is to make sure that the views of the child are placed before the hearing or the court. The appointment of a curator ad litem is a more formal step than the appointment of a safeguarder. A curator ad litem will almost invariably be a legally qualified person, who will appear at the hearing or court and assist the court in coming to a decision. It should be noted that the curator ad litem, which is a much more well-established concept than that of safeguarder, has the task of representing the child's interests. Common sense shows that the child's interest will often diverge from the child's views. (For example, it may not necessarily be in the child's interest to live with his aunt because his aunt gives him more sweeties.)

03.17   Appeal from any decision of the children's hearing lies to the sheriff. Appeal from any decision of the sheriff in relation to the children's hearing lies to the Court of Session by way of stated case (explained later) on a point of law or in respect of any irregularity in the conduct of the case.

03.18   The role of the media in covering children's hearings was a central issue in the long-running inquiry, beginning in August 1991, into allegations of child sex abuse on Orkney. Some sections of the media were severely criticised for "taking the side" of parents whose children were said to have been abused. The conduct of the media was given as one of the reasons why place-of-safety orders could not continue in force and children had to be returned home. The case illustrated the extreme difficulties of producing balanced reports in this type of case where one side, the reporter, feels unable to comment because of confidentiality. Because of what happened in the Orkney case, submissions were made to Lord Clyde, the judge in charge of the inquiry, that the media should no longer be allowed to attend children's hearings. Lord Clyde did not accept these submissions and the media continue to be allowed to attend children's hearings under the provisions of the Children (Scotland) Act 1995.

Sheriff courts

03.19 The sheriff courts deal with most criminal cases in Scotland. The judge is either the sheriff or the sheriff principal. Both are appointed by the Crown on the recommendation of the First Minister for Scotland who in turn acts on the advice of the Lord Advocate. Both must be advocates or solicitors of at least 10 years' standing. There are six sheriffdoms in Scotland—Grampian, Highland and Islands; Tayside, Central and Fife; Lothian and Borders; Glasgow and Strathkelvin, North Strathclyde; and South Strathclyde, Dumfries and Galloway. Each is headed by a sheriff principal who, in addition to his judicial functions, has a general duty to secure the speedy and efficient disposal of business in the sheriff courts of his sheriffdom and who has correspondingly wide administrative functions. During the 1980's and 1990's the increased use of temporary sheriffs meant that it was highly likely that an accused person would be tried by a temporary sheriff rather than by a full-time sheriff. Temporary sheriffs were solicitors and advocates to similar standing of full-time sheriffs. However, they held a Commission to act as temporary sheriffs on a year-to-year basis. They could sit on any court in Scotland. They are paid a daily fee for their work. They were not prevented from appearing for accused persons or as prosecutors on the days when they were not sitting as temporary sheriffs. Temporary sheriffs could hold their commission for a period of 12 months only. There was concern that this form of tenure may not accord with the requirements of Article 6 of the European Convention on human rights which requires judges to be "independent". In the case of *Starrs* in December 1999 the High Court ruled that temporary sheriffs did not comply with the requirements of the Convention (Art. 6) as their continued tenure was within the gift of the Lord Advocate who was also prosecutor in the case. This breached the " fair and impartial tribunal" part of Article 6. It is important to note that the High Court proceeded on the basis of perception of justice being done rather than the standards of justice achieved in courts where "temps" were sitting. It was announced following the *Starrs* decision that part time sheriffs would be appointed to replace temporary sheriffs. The part time sheriff would enjoy secure tenure, and avoiding the kind of objection taken in the *Starrs* case to the "temps".

The sheriff courts have a very wide criminal jurisdiction, both **03.20** solemn and summary. There are three limitations. First, the jurisdiction is limited geographically. As a general rule a sheriff can deal only with crimes committed within his sheriffdom. Secondly, the jurisdiction does not extend to certain crimes, of which the most important are treason, murder and rape. Thirdly, the sheriff's powers of punishment are limited to three months' imprisonment in most summary cases. This goes up to six months if the accused has an analogous previous conviction for violence or dishonesty and three years' imprisonment in solemn cases. The Crime and Punishment (Scotland) Act 1997 increased the potential powers of the sheriff considerably. In terms of section 13 of that Act, the sheriff will be able impose up to five years' imprisonment when sitting with a jury. This provision has not yet been brought into force. When sitting summarily, the sheriff's powers will be to impose six months' imprisonment or 12 months' imprisonment where there is a second or subsequent conviction involving violence or dishonesty. Similarly, this provision has not yet been brought into force.

03.21 The prosecutor in the sheriff court is almost invariably the procurator fiscal or his depute. In cases of considerably seriousness, an advocate-depute, the Solicitor-General, or even the Lord Advocate, might appear. The administrative work is done by the sheriff-clerk and his deputes.

Sheriff Court: Summary and Solemn Procedure

03.22 There are two forms of procedure followed in the sheriff court when dealing with criminal cases. In summary cases the sheriff sit alone without a jury. This, procedure is used for the vast majority of criminal prosecutions. There is no need for advance notification of the witnesses who will be called, no need for shorthand notes or any formal record and no need to lodge productions prior to the trial diet. The only record kept of the proceedings are the sheriff's notes and any minutes the clerk of court may be instructed to make by the sheriff. The sheriff's powers of punishment in summary proceedings are, as already noted, restricted in most cases to three months imprisonment or six months imprisonment if there is an analogous previous conviction involving violence or dishonesty. However, in certain situations the sheriff sitting summarily is permitted by a statute to exceed the six month limit for a particular crime. An example is the Misuse of Drugs Act where in certain cases one year's imprisonment maybe imposed.

03.23 Appeals from a summary case are normally taken by way of stated case to the High Court. As with solemn cases leave to appeal to the High Court is required from a single "sifting" High Court judge.

03.24 In solemn procedure the sheriff sits with a jury of 15. In this case proceedings are formally recorded by tape recorder or a shorthand writer. The procedure followed is basically the same as that to be found in the High Court when sitting as a trial court.

03.25 Although there are no opening speeches in Scottish cases many sheriffs think it useful to give an explanatory introductory address to the jury regarding their function in the case. There are closing speeches from the Crown and then the defence. In solemn procedure unlike summary procedure if there is a conviction it is necessary for the Crown to move for sentence before sentence will be pronounced. Sentencing is automatic in summary cases. It is a very rare event in solemn procedure for the Crown not to move for sentence, but it does occasionally happen, for example if the accused has spent time in custody awaiting trial but is only found guilty of a very minor part of the indictment.

No case to answer submission

In both solemn and summary procedure it is possible for the **03.26** defence to make a motion at the end of the Crown case that there is no case to answer. This submission concerns the quantity of evidence which has been led. Quality is not an issue at this point. It should be noted that a no case to answer submission will only be successful if the evidence led by the Crown does not justify conviction on the charge/charges of the law court or any other competent charge/charges. Accordingly a no case to answer submission would fail in a house breaking case if the Crown had brought forward enough evidence to justify a conviction on a charge of reset. It would be perfectly possible for the defence to make a submission to the effect that a conviction of reset only would be competent. But that would be a different form of submission. A no case to answer submission is restricted to the circumstances where conviction on any competent charge cannot follow on from the evidence which the Crown has led in the case.

Trial within a trial

The trial within a trial procedure had fallen into disuse until the **03.27** landmark decision in the case of *Thomson v. Crowe* in 1999. That five judge decision made it clear that a trial within a trial is competent , and indeed necessary, in certain circumstances in both solemn and summary procedure. A trial within a trial is necessary when one party questions the admissibility of evidence which the other proposes to adduce before the court. In almost all cases it will be the defence who are claiming that evidence is inadmissible, *e.g.* because the police forced a confession out of the accused person by means of threats or inducements. In these circumstances the sheriff will hear the evidence from the witnesses and hear submissions at the end of this section of the evidence of the admissibility of that evidence. In the case of a jury trial the sheriff will hear the evidence outwith the presence of the jury. If the sheriff decides that evidence is admissible it would be necessary to bring the jury back into court and then recall all the relevant witnesses and have them go through their evidence once more because the jury did not hear the evidence on the first occasion. Journalists must be aware that although they may remain in court when the jury is excluded, they cannot report the evidence led during the trial within a trial procedure. That is because if the sheriff takes the view that the evidence is inadmissible then the jury should not be aware of that inadmissible evidence.

High Court of Justiciary

03.28 The judges of the High Court of Justiciary are the Lord Justice-General (who is the same person as the Lord President of the Court of Session), the Lord Justice-Clerk and Lords Commissioners of Justiciary. All are also judges of the Court of Session and Senators of the College of Justice. They are appointed by the Crown on the advice of the Lord Advocate and can be removed from office only for gross misconduct. The 1990 Law Reform Act also made provision for "temporary" High Court judges, leading to the appointment of two leading Q.C.s and two sheriffs. The number of temporary judges soon increased to eight. These temporary Court of Session and High Court Judges were not used following the *Starrs* decision (see para. 3.21). But the challenge to temporary judges failed. Temporary judges hold their commission for three years rather than the temporary sheriffs' one year. Also they are appointed by the Lord Justice General rather than the Lord Advocate. These factors were crucial in the Court's reasoning when rejecting the challenge to Temporary judges in the Scottish Supreme Courts (High Court and the Court of Session). In light of increased court workload and to take account of the absence of four judges for perhaps as long as a year at Camp Zeist for the Lockerbie trial, the number of possible judicial appointments was raised to 32 in late 1999

03.29 The seat of the High Court is at Parliament House in Edinburgh, but it also goes on circuit to other parts of Scotland. All of the judges do not, of course, sit in each case. Normally there is only one but difficult cases can be heard by two or more. In 1999 the unusual precedent for a Scottish court sitting outside the United Kingdom was seen in the Lockerbie case. However, strictly speaking, either Camp Zeist or Kamp van Zeist in Holland was legally designated to be part of Scotland.

03.30 The High Court deals with the most serious crimes and is the only court which can try treason, murder or rape. Prosecutions are conducted by the Lord Advocate, the Solicitor-General, or, more usually, an advocate-depute.

03.31 The High Court also has jurisdiction to hear appeals from and review the decisions of cases heard on summary procedure. When sitting for this purpose it consists of at least three judges and is commonly referred to as the Justiciary Appeal Court. It has the important duty of reviewing proceedings in all inferior criminal courts with a view to seeing that justice is done.

Rape cases

Judges of the High Court of Justiciary normally "close the doors" **03.32** while the evidence of an alleged victim of rape or attempted rape is being heard, the object being to protect the witness from anything which might inhibit her in giving evidence. It has also become the practice of the judges to allow reporters covering the proceedings to remain in court provided they do not identify the witness in their reports.

This practice was judicially recognised in a case in 1983 in which **03.33** Lord Avonside said: "In our courts a victim alleged to have been raped almost invariably gives evidence behind closed doors. In such a situation the public is not permitted to hear her evidence. It has been the practice, particularly in Glasgow, to allow the Press reporters to remain. They are asked to exercise a wise discretion, and, in my experience, this they do admirably. The trial judge could, of course, if he thought it desirable, exclude the Press and clear the court completely".

Besides the powers the judges have under statutes of the Scottish **03.34** Parliament—under the Criminal Procedure (Scotland) Act 1975 they may, from the opening of the evidence in a rape trial "or the like", clear the court of all persons except those actually involved in the proceedings. Judges can now also give directions to prohibit publication of "a name or other matter" where they were already able merely to prohibit disclosure of it in open court.

The law in England on rape reporting has a much more **03.35** chequered history, perhaps illustrating the wisdom of a voluntary code.

In England identification in court reports of the alleged victim of **03.36** rape or attempted rape was banned by the Sexual Offences (Amendment) Act 1976, which also made it an offence to identify the accused in such cases unless and until he was convicted. The absurd consequences emerged in a number of cases, in particular in a case in 1986 when a man charged and named by the police in connection with a series of murders became anonymous when he was charged also with rape. Apart from the difficulties this created for the media, the police were hampered in circulating details of the man wanted for the crimes. It became clear also that a man acquitted of rape and convicted of murdering his victim could be jailed for life but not identified by the media, which, however, would be free in law to name the victim.

Following the Ealing Vicarage rape case in London in which the **03.37** victim was identified in a number of reports, major changes were made in England under the Criminal Justice Act 1988. The Act did away with the anonymity of rape accused and increased restrictions on identifying the victim. The law is now contained in the Sexual Offences (Amendment) Act 1992, which protects the victims of other sexual attacks.

03.38 The position in England now is that after an allegation of a rape offence, the name, address, or picture of the woman cannot be published in her lifetime if this is likely to lead to her being identified by members of the public as an alleged victim. Also, after a person is accused of rape, or information is laid before a magistrate accusing him of rape, nothing may be published in the woman's lifetime to identify her as an alleged victim.

03.39 The restrictions apply in cases of rape, attempted rape, aiding, abetting, counselling or procuring rape or attempted rape, incitement to rape, conspiracy to rape and burglary with intent to rape. They also apply in civil cases, for example if the woman claims damages for rape.

03.40 The restrictions may be lifted in certain circumstances, for example if the woman was charged with a criminal offence arising from the rape allegation, such as wasting police time because of a false allegation.

03.41 The woman may also be named if, before trial, the accused satisfies a Crown Court judge that this is necessary to bring witnesses forward and the defence will be prejudiced if the restriction is not lifted; the court is satisfied that anonymity places an unreasonable restriction on reporting the trial; or the alleged victim gives her written consent to what is published.

Court of Criminal Appeal

03.42 Strictly speaking, there is no such court in Scotland. However, the "Scottish Court of Criminal Appeal" is a convenient term frequently used instead of the more correct but cumbersome "High Court of Justiciary sitting as a Court of Criminal Appeal". The court hears appeals against conviction or sentence in trials heard on solemn procedure. Traditionally, it is the highest Scottish criminal court. There is no appeal to the House of Lords. But under the Scotland Act a "devolution issue" can now be taken to the Judical Committee of the Privy Council which sits in Downing Street, London. The judges of the Judicial Committee are basically the judges of the Judicial Committee of the House of Lords. There is now a "sift" procedure whereby it is necessary for an appellant to obtain leave to appeal before proceeding to the full hearing. The sift takes place on the basis of the documents lodged by the appellant's solicitors. If the single "sifting" judge rejects the appeal, the appellant can apply to a quorum of the High Court for a review of the single judge's decision. Experience has shown that few appellants take this course of action. Current information suggests that about three-quarters of all appeals are dismissed by the sifting judge.

In addition to appeals at the instance of the accused person, **03.43** cases may be referred to the High Court by the Scottish Criminal Cases Review Commission. Such cases are treated by the court in the same way as a normal appeal. The Scottish Criminal Cases Review Commission will normally only consider a case once a first appeal has been taken and rejected by the High Court.

Although not strictly appeals, another form of procedure occa- **03.44** sionally found is a reference by the Lord Advocate to the High Court on a point of law. The High Court's decision in this case does not overturn a decision of a lower court. However, it may give guidance as to the conduct of future cases. Some significant matters have been considered by the High Court in this way. In 1992 the High Court decided that crime carried out as a joke still attracted criminal penalties. In 1995 the court decided that the supply of a controlled drug to someone who dies as a result of taking that drug was a good legal basis for a charge of culpable homicide. At the time of writing the High Court has before it a case in which Sheriff Margaret Gimblett appeared to accept a defence of necessity under international law principles in a prosecution of three women accused of damaging material at the Trident base at Faslane.

Of those appeals which proceed to the full court hearing, **03.45** sentencing appeals are disposed of by a bench of two judges and appeals involving conviction by three judges. Occasionally in a case of importance a larger bench of five or more judges will be convened.

SCOTTISH CRIMINAL PROCEDURE

Although the details of criminal procedure can be left to the **03.46** lawyer, the journalist should know the steps in outline so that he can tell what is happening and what is about to happen. In this field the laws of Scotland and England are very different. To take only one example, private prosecutions are common in England but very rare in Scotland. An outstanding case occurred in 1982 when, after the Crown had decided not to prosecute three youths following a particularly vicious attack upon a woman in Glasgow, the High Court granted her authority to bring a private prosecution (by the old process of issuing a bill for criminal letters). The case went to trial and resulted in convictions for rape against one youth and for indecent assault against two others. It was the first private prosecution to have been allowed under this procedure in Scotland since 1909. The three judges who authorised the private prosecution described the case as strange and unique, the Crown having earlier dropped proceedings against the youths following a psychiatric report that the risk of damage to the victim's health if she appeared in court made it inadvisable that she be called as a witness. The court's decision to allow her to proceed was reached after the judges were satisfied that she would after all be able to appear and give evidence, without which it was originally thought a prosecution could not succeed. The court ruled that there was no doubt the woman had the necessary title and interest to prosecute privately, and this course was not opposed by the Lord Advocate. This so-called "Glasgow rape case" has not been followed by other private prosecutions. In 1992 a woman who claimed she had been raped in her own home by three men applied to the court for authority to take private proceedings against them. However, her application for a bill of criminal letters to prosecute the three men privately was refused by the High Court.

03.47 The Lord Advocate, assisted by the Solicitor-General for Scotland, is responsible for the investigation and prosecution of crime in Scotland. Both are appointed by the Crown. In terms of the Scotland Act, both the Lord Advocate and the Solicitor-General for Scotland are members of the Scottish Parliament *ex officio*. The Lord Advocate and the Solicitor-General have the function of supplying legal advice to the Scottish Executive, *i.e.* the Scottish Ministers. In practice the Lord Advocate delegates most of his responsibility in criminal matters to advocates-depute who work, along with a staff of officials, at the Crown Office in Edinburgh. The procurators fiscal investigate crime at the local level under the general supervision of the Crown Office. In the case of minor offences the procurator fiscal has a discretion whether or not to prosecute, or to issue a formal written warning, with the implied sanction of a prosecution if the warning is not heeded. He reports more serious crimes to the Crown Office which decides whether to prosecute and, if so, in which court.

03.48 Two general principles should be noted at this stage. The first is that everyone is innocent until he is proved guilty beyond reasonable doubt (and in Scotland the proof must normally be by the evidence from two independent sources). The second is a principle of great importance to journalists which will be dealt with in more detail later. It is that there must be no publicity which may seriously prejudice a person's trial. (See Chapter 10.)

03.49 As already noted there are two types of criminal procedure— summary and solemn. Different rules apply but the preliminary steps are the same. The first stage is generally the police investigation under the authority of the procurator fiscal. Newspapers have sometimes played an active part in the exposure of crime but there is a grave risk of contempt of court if anything is published after arrest has been made or a warrant granted for arrest which creates a substantial risk of seriously prejudicing or impeding the course of justice. Journalists should understand that it is the creation of the *risk* of prejudice which constitutes contempt of court. It is not necessary that a journalist has created *actual* prejudice.

The police often enlist the help of the media in their inquiries **03.50** and there is probably no danger in assisting as requested. In certain cases, however, it may be wise to check that the request has been cleared by the procurator fiscal. This would be advisable, for example, if the request is to publish a photograph of a wanted man in a case where the question of identification could arise at a later stage. Even if the Crown approves the release of a photograph, or an identikit likeness, it should be remembered that the defence can independently raise the issue of contempt. However, a finding of contempt would be extremely unlikely in these circumstances.

The investigations may result in an arrest. Normally a warrant is **03.51** required but some statutes allow arrest without warrant. A policeman can arrest without warrant when he finds a person committing or attempting to commit a serious crime or when he is told by the victim or a credible eye-witness that this has just occurred. He can also arrest without warrant in cases of breach of the peace or threatened violence or in certain circumstances when he finds a person in possession of stolen goods and unable to give a satisfactory explanation.

Summary procedure

Where the accused has not been arrested, but has simply been **03.52** cited to appear, he may plead in person, through a solicitor or by letter. If he pleads guilty in his absence, he may, subject to certain safeguards, be sentenced there and then. If he pleads not guilty a date will be fixed for a trial. If the accused is refused bail, the trial must commence within 40 days of his first appearance in court (see para. 03.47).

If an accused person has pled "not guilty", the court will hold an **03.53** intermediate diet three weeks prior to the trial diet. The purpose of the intermediate diet is to ascertain the state of preparedness of the parties. The sheriff will wish to ascertain if there are areas of the evidence which can be agreed so that certain witnesses need not be called to give evidence at the trial proper. It is perfectly possible for an accused person to choose to plead "guilty" at the intermediate diet. There is no evidence led at the intermediate diet.

03.54 The procedure at the trial is straightforward. The prosecutor calls his first witness and examines him. The defence can cross-examine (leading questions are allowed at this stage), after which the prosecution has a limited right to re-examine. After all the evidence for the prosecution has been led, the defence may advance a "no case to answer submission" which argues that there is insufficient evidence to convict the accused of the crime charged or any competent alternative. Such a submission deals only with the quantity of evidence. Its quality cannot be assessed at this stage. If there is no such submission, or if it is unsuccessful, then the evidence for the defence is led. The defence is not compelled to lead evidence. Even if they do so, the accused need not go into the witness box. After the hearing of all evidence the prosecutor addresses the court, followed by the accused or his agent and the judge pronounces his finding. This may be either guilty, not guilty or not proven. A finding of not proven has the same effect as a finding of not guilty. It is used where the court is not satisfied that the man is innocent but the prosecution has failed to prove that he is guilty. (Note that the correct terminology is "the charge was found not proven". It is not "the accused was found not proven".) If the accused is found guilty he is allowed to address the court before sentence is pronounced. Normally this is done by his solicitor, who tenders a "plea in mitigation" to the court.

Criminal Procedure (Scotland) Act 1995

03.55 Criminal procedure in Scotland is consolidated in the Criminal Procedure (Scotland) Act 1995 as amended by the Crime and Punishment (Scotland) Act 1997 and the Bail, Judicial Appointments etc. (Scotland) Act 2000. In the legislation, there is to be found provision on anonymity of children involved in criminal cases as accused or victims.

03.56 The 1995 Act gives police powers to detain a suspect for up to six hours while they make investigations to enable them to decide whether there is sufficient evidence to arrest him. The strict liability rule under the contempt of court law (outlined in Chapter 10) does not come into operation until the arrest stage is reached or a warrant is granted but the journalist must still exercise great caution about what he reports at the detention stage. Publication of information which creates a serious risk of prejudice to any future trial before an arrest is made or a warrant issued may be regarded as contempt at common law.

03.57 There are safeguards for the detainee: he is not obliged to answer any questions other than those intended to find out his name and address; he has to be told the nature of the suspected offence; he is entitled to have his detention intimated to a solicitor and one other person of his choice; and if not arrested at the end of six hours' detention he must be released and cannot again be detained on the same grounds. If he is arrested he is entitled to have this fact intimated to a person named by him without unnecessary delay. There are special safeguards for children.

The Act gives an accused the right to petition the sheriff to have **03.58** an identification parade held where the prosecutor has not already made arrangements for one and the sheriff considers it reasonable.

In summary cases an accused who is refused bail by the court **03.59** and is kept in custody must not be detained for more than 40 days after his initial court appearance. The court, however, has power to grant an extension for reasons similar to those provided under solemn procedure (referred to below), and subject to a right of appeal by either side.

Solemn procedure

In solemn procedure the accused's first appearance in court is on **03.60** petition in chambers before a sheriff, and all that can be published about the proceedings at this stage, besides the identity of the accused (unless he is a child) is a general indication of the nature of the charges, supplied usually by the procurator fiscal. It is important to remember that the fiscal may later proceed on an amended charge, or charges, or even drop proceedings altogether, although this is unusual. The accused may apply for bail at this hearing. If bail is refused the accused will be detained "for further inquiries" for a period of up to eight days. When brought back to a second private hearing in the sheriff's chambers (called the full committal diet) he may apply for bail again. If bail is refused the accused is detained "until liberated in due course of law". There is legal presumption in favour of bail being granted. But a bad record of previous convictions or reasonable belief that the accused might abscond or interfere with evidence or witnesses would point towards bail being refused. Journalists must note that the reasons for a refusal of bail cannot be revealed until the trial is completed. The United Kingdom Government conceded in the European Court of Human Rights in Strasbourg in February 2000 that the provisions in United Kingdom domestic law preventing someone from applying for bail if appearing in court on a second charge having already been convicted on a previous occasion were in breach of the Convention. In practice it is unlikely that persons accused of such serious offences (culpable homicide, attempted murder, rape, attempted rape) would be granted bail if already convicted of one of these crimes. However, from February 2000 they were to make the application. The position was regularised in terms of statute in the Bail, Judicial Appointments etc. (Scotland) Act 2000.

03.61 Pleading diets occur automatically in sheriff and jury cases. In the other form of solemn procedure, namely that before the High Court and a jury, there will only be a preliminary diet if one of the parties asks for this. Usually, a preliminary diet is requested where there is a preliminary legal matter which the defence wish to argue. For example, they may claim that the terms of the indictment lack specification, *i.e.* there is insufficient detail. They might also argue that the indictment does not disclose a crime known to the law of Scotland. However, a preliminary or pleading diet can explore any legal matter if the court is willing to listen.

03.62 In recent years there has been a revival of judicial examination as à method of discovering, at a hearing in chambers before a sheriff, what explanation or comment the suspect may have on any incriminating statement he is alleged to have made. He can be questioned by the fiscal under the control of the sheriff who must ensure questioning is fair. The accused has a right to be represented by a solicitor and to consult him before answering any question, and the solicitor may ask him questions to clear up any ambiguity. A shorthand record is kept of the examination and a copy of the transcript must be made available to the accused. As an additional safeguard, a tape-recording of the proceedings is kept. The record, or any part of it, may be used in evidence. The journalist is not allowed into these proceedings and will have to rely on the procurator fiscal or the defence agent for information as to what took place. In that situation, particular care must be taken with any report.

03.63 The Act requires that a trial under solemn procedure must start within 12 months of the accused's first appearance on petition; otherwise he must be discharged and cannot be charged again with the same offence—unless delay has been caused by his failure to appear or an extension has been granted by the court. The Act also requires that an accused must not be kept in custody for more than 80 days before being served with an indictment, and the trial must commence within 110 days of his appearance in court at his full committal. Full committal usually takes place one week after the first appearance of the accused. The 110 days limit can be extended if the court is satisfied that this is justified because of illness of the accused or a judge, absence or illness of a necessary witness, or other "sufficient cause". The grant or refusal of an extension is subject to appeal.

If during the trial the court decides that, because of the accused's **03.64** misconduct, a proper hearing cannot take place unless he is removed, it may order that the trial proceed in his absence, although he must be legally represented.

In court the accused is called "the panel". The trial takes place **03.65** before a judge and a jury of 15. Neither Crown nor defence now have any challenges to the jurors called unless on cause shown. Once the jury is empanelled, the trial will begin. The clerk reads out the indictment to the jurors and puts them on oath to "well and truly try the accused according to the evidence". A juror may wish to affirm rather than take the oath. Normally, jurors are given copies of the indictment and copies of any special defence (alibi, incrimination, insanity and self-defence) lodged. There are no opening speeches in Scottish criminal procedure. The Crown calls its witnesses and the defence are entitled to cross-examine. The prosecutor may re-examine. The judge may ask questions to clarify points of confusion. After the Crown case is complete, if the defence pleads that insufficient evidence has been led to convict the accused, they can advance a submission of "no case to answer". It is important for journalists to understand that this submission is based purely on the question as to whether or not in law a sufficient quantity of evidence has been led to go to the jury. It does not deal with the question of the quality of the evidence.

The prosecution and the defence address the jury in turn and the **03.66** judge charges the jury. The general principle is that the jury are masters of the facts and the judge master of the law. His main duty in charging the jury is to set out the law applicable to the case but he may also make fair and impartial comments on the evidence. After the charge the jury retire to consider their verdict. The verdict need not be unanimous it may be by a majority, even 8–7. The verdicts available to the jury are "guilty", "not guilty" or "not proven". In the rare case where the accused is found to have been insane at the time of the alleged crime, he will be found not guilty on the ground of insanity. An accused person found not guilty on the ground of insanity can still be made subject to a Hospital Order by the court. Such a Hospital Order may require its subject to be detained in the state hospital at Carstairs. An individual subject to a Hospital Order has the right to appeal on an annual basis to the sheriff of the area in which he is detained for review of his detention. The terms of the Mental Health legislation required that the person detained had to be receiving some form of medical treatment to justify continued detention. This famously caused controversy with the release of Noel Ruddle in July 1999 when the weight of psychiatric evidence brought before Sheriff Douglas

Allan at Lanark Sheriff Court was to the effect that Mr Ruddle was not being treated within Carstairs. The Scottish Parliament rushed through amending legislation aimed at ensuring that in future sheriffs could refuse to release such persons if it was felt their release would cause a danger to the safety of the public. This legislation has survived a challenge to its competency based on the European Convention on Human Rights.

03.67 If the verdict is "guilty" then, after the prosecutor has moved for sentence and any previous convictions have been admitted or proved, the accused or his counsel or solicitor may make a plea in mitigation of sentence. The judge will then pronounce sentence, but if the trial has been in the sheriff court and the sheriff thinks the offence merits a heavier sentence than he can impose, he can remit to the High Court for sentence.

03.68 After the initial petition procedure but before service of the indictment the accused may inform the Crown that he wants to plead guilty and have his case be disposed of as quickly as possible. He gets a shortened form of indictment and appears for sentence on what is known as a section 76 hearing.

03.69 The only sentence for murder is life imprisonment except where the person convicted is under 18, in which case the sentence is detention without limit of time in a place and under conditions to be directed by the First Minister. If he is over 18 but under 21, the sentence is detention for life at first in a young offenders' institution and then in prison. Where the sentence passed is for life the judge may recommend the minimum term to be served and must give his reasons if he does so; a recommendation is appealable as part of the sentence. The Crime and Punishment (Scotland) Act 1997 makes provision for the imposition of life imprisonment for certain offenders—namely those who have been convicted of a "qualifying offence" committed after "the relevant date". "The relevant date" is the date on which section 1 of the 1997 Act is brought into force. At the time of writing, this section has not been brought into force. Qualifying offences are such things as culpable homicide; attempted murder; incitement to commit murder or conspiracy to commit murder; rape or attempted rape; sodomy or attempted sodomy; assault to severe injury of the danger of life; robbery with a weapon; various firearms offences; lewd, indecent or libidinous practices; unlawful intercourse with a girl under the age of 13 years. In light of the incorporation of the European Convention into the domestic Scots Law it seems increasingly unlikely that this provision will ever be activated.

03.70 No prison sentence may be imposed on a person over 21 who has not previously been so sentenced to detention, unless the court thinks no other course is appropriate. No one under 21 may be sent to prison, and borstal training is replaced by detention in a young offenders' institution.

As already noted at the close of the prosecution evidence in **03.71** either solemn or summary procedure the accused is entitled (in solemn procedure in the absence of the jury) to submit a plea that there is no case to answer. If the plea is sustained the accused is acquitted, if refused the trial proceeds to defence evidence. Any report of submissions made on such a plea in a solemn case can be safely published only after the proceedings have ceased to be "active" (see Chapter 10, Contempt of Court).

Offenders can be ordered to pay compensation to their victims, **03.72** either instead of or in addition to any other method the court may select for dealing with them, for personal injury, loss or damage caused by their offences. The provisions do not apply to loss resulting from death or from a road accident unless caused by the convicted person. There is no limit to compensation under solemn procedure, but in summary cases the limits are set by statute. Where the convicted person's means are insufficient to meet a fine besides compensation, priority is given to compensation. A compensation order is treated as a sentence for appeal purposes.

The main differences between summary and solemn procedure **03.73** can be summed up as follows. In summary procedure there is no petition for committal. Proceedings begin with the complaint. In solemn procedure there is usually a petition for committal and proceedings are on indictment. Cases under summary procedure are heard in the sheriff courts or district courts. There is no jury. Cases on solemn procedure are heard in the sheriff or High Court and there is a jury. Appeal in summary procedure is by stated case or bill of suspension to three judges sitting as the Justiciary Appeal Court. Appeal in solemn procedure is to at least three judges of the High Court sitting as a Court of Criminal Appeal.

Summary appeals

Summary appeals against conviction normally proceed by a method **03.74** called "a stated case". Occasionally where the appeal is based on the argument that the court has done something which is incompetent, the method will be bill of suspension. The initial step is an application for a stated case, note of appeal (against sentence only) or bill of suspension, which must take place within one week of the decision under appeal (the stage at which the proceedings again become active under the Contempt of Court Act 1981—see Chapter 10 for the extent to which a journalist is restricted from writing about a case when it is under appeal).

03.75   The draft stated case prepared by the sheriff or justice is subject
to adjustments proposed by either side if they are agreed at a
hearing arranged for this purpose. The judge stating a case for
appeal must give his reasons if he refuses any adjustments, and
these may be taken into account by the appeal court, which also
has power to hear additional evidence or order that this be heard
by a person it appoints for the purpose. The appeal court may also
appoint an assessor with expert knowledge to assist in deciding an
appeal.

03.76   There is also a right of appeal against conviction by way of bill of
suspension where the stated case procedure would not be appropriate or competent. The prosecutor may appeal against acquittal or
sentence on grounds, in either case, of alleged miscarriage of
justice. The court may remit a case back with directions to affirm
the verdict, quash the verdict and authorise a new prosecution (to
be begun within two months) on the same or similar charges as
before. Where an appeal against acquittal is sustained the court
may convict and sentence the respondent, remit the case back to
the court below with instructions to do so, or remit back to the
lower court with the appeal court's opinion and direction.

03.77   As stated above, all criminal appeals by the accused now require
leave of a single "sifting" judge of the High Court before they can
proceed to a full appeal hearing. Summary appeals have a particularly high rejection rate at the "sift" stage.

Solemn appeals

03.78 Where the appeal court in solemn procedure has allowed an
appeal against conviction on the ground that there has been a
miscarriage of justice, a new prosecution may be brought within
two months charging the accused with the same or any similar
offence arising out of the same facts. However, no sentence may be
passed which could not have been passed in the original
proceedings.

03.79   In the first case to be brought under this provision, a man who
had been charged in 1982 with the murder of his wife's lover was
convicted of culpable homicide in the High Court at Inverness. He
appealed successfully, on the ground that a misdirection by the trial
judge had led to a miscarriage of justice. Under the old law he
would have been freed, but under the provisions introduced by the
1980 Criminal Justice (Scotland) Act the Lord Advocate was
granted authority by the appeal court to bring a fresh prosecution.
This time, the man was charged with culpable homicide and the
second trial took place at Edinburgh to avoid the risk of prejudice
from local knowledge, in Inverness, of the original hearing and

conviction. The charge was found not proven and the accused was released. Evidence at the two trials was for the most part identical. A somewhat surprising use of this power came in the case of Alexander Hall. An ex-police officer, Mr Hall had served 12 years' imprisonment for the crime of murder when his second appeal, heard in 1998, was successful. The Crown asked for and were granted authority to bring a fresh prosecution, which they did in May 1999. The fresh prosecution was unsuccessful.

While in theory there is no limit to the number of retrials in any **03.80** case, in practice more than one is unlikely. The High Court will take various factors into account in deciding whether or not to grant authority to bring a fresh prosecution. Experience has shown that it is the exception rather than the rule for the High Court to allow a second prosecution. Even in cases where the error in the lower court has not been the Crown's but that of the judge (in misdirecting the jury), the court will not necessarily grant authority.

The procedure is exceptional, compared to practice in England **03.81** where retrials are relatively common, but the 1980 Act brought to an end the fundamental rule in Scotland that an accused could not be tried more than once on the same charge. In such a case the proceedings remain active under the Contempt of Court Act from the time authority for a new prosecution is granted by the court, until a new trial is concluded or a decision is taken to drop further proceedings. There are however a few instances of retrials in Scottish procedure. These present particular difficulties for the journalist in making sure that nothing printed or broadcast prejudices the forthcoming retrial proceedings. A great deal of the information is already in the public domain. However, journalists would do well to remember that courts accept the point that the public mind is "notoriously short". Journalists cannot proceed on the basis that, because something has already been printed in a newspaper, it can be reprinted prior to the second trial. Journalists must exercise considerable discretion in dealing with these difficult situations. It must be remembered that contempt of court can be committed by raising a risk that the evidence of witnesses will be affected by what is read in newspapers, heard on radio or seen on TV. Contempt is not restricted to prejudicing the minds of jurors. No doubt this was the main reason why, in 1999, journalists were extremely careful not to re-visit the facts which came out at the original trial in 1985 of former policeman Alexander Hall, when the High Court overturned his conviction but allowed the Crown authority to bring a fresh prosecution (see para. 03.63 and also fuller discussion on contempt in Chapter 10).

An accused may appeal against conviction, sentence, or both, on **03.82** grounds of alleged miscarriage of justice, and formal notice has to be lodged at the Justiciary Office in Edinburgh within two weeks. This has special significance when the question of publicity arises after the end of a trial. The appeal court may uphold the verdict, quash the conviction, substitute an amended verdict of guilty (and pass a different sentence from that already passed), or, as we have seen, set aside the verdict and grant authority for a new prosecution. Where the appeal is against sentence the court has power not only to reduce but also to increase the original sentence.

03.83　Since October 1993 the Crown has had a right of appeal against (what it feels) are unduly lenient sentences in solemn cases. An appeal can be taken by the Crown against a sentence imposed by either a sheriff or a High Court judge. The appeal court has made it clear that it will only increase a sentence if "the sentence must be seen to be unduly lenient. That means that it must fall outside the range of sentences which the Judge at first instance, applying his mind to all the relevant factors, could reasonably have considered appropriate". Sentencing appeals are now heard by two judges.

03.84　In both solemn and summary appeals there is provision for the hearing of additional evidence not available at the trial, and in either situation the Crown may appeal by bill of advocation. The High Court also has power under sections 106 (solemn cases) and 175 (summary cases) of the Criminal Procedure (Scotland) Act 1995 to allow the hearing of new evidence of any witnesses whether or not they were called at the trial. The applicant must provide an explanation as to why this evidence was not brought to the attention of the trial court. However, the legal test for admitting fresh evidence was lowered in 1997 and it already appears that the Appeal Court is willing to look at new evidence more readily than under the old legislation. The 1997 legislation followed a somewhat embarrassing public disagreement between the then Lord Justice-General, Lord Hope, and the then Lord Justice-Clerk, Lord Ross, over the interpretation of the old test for admitting fresh evidence. In *H.M. Advocate v. Church* (1995) Lord Hope put a very liberal interpretation on the old legislation, while Lord Justice-Clerk Ross, presiding over a court of five Judges a few weeks later in *H.M. Advocate v. Elliot* (1995) followed the traditional, more strict approach. That controversy has, however, been superseded by the new test, which came into force in 1997. The law is now found in section 106 (solemn) and section 175 (summary) of the Criminal Procedure (Scotland) Act 1995.

03.85　The High Court considered the new legislation in the high-profile case of *Campbell and Steele v. H.M. Advocate*, 1998—the so-called "ice-cream wars case". In that case the appeal was based in part on the change of evidence of a material witness. The majority of the judges took the view that, under the new legislation, the applicant was still required to provide a reasonable explanation to the court as to why the fresh evidence was not heard at the trial. The Lord Justice-Clerk and Lord Sutherland went on to say that only if they were satisfied by the applicant's reasonable explanation on that point would they go on to consider a second explanation from the witness as to why the fresh evidence now being proffered to the court had not been given at the original trial. That explanation, like the first, would have to be "reasonable". The third judge, Lord McCluskey, did not feel that this two-stage approach was necessary. It appears therefore that the law in this difficult area remains a little unclear.

Scottish Criminal Cases Review Commission

Since April 1, 1999 an accused person who has exhausted all rights **03.86** of appeal may apply to the Scottish Criminal Cases Review Commission. The purpose of applying is to request the Commission to refer the case back to the High Court sitting as the Court of Appeal. The Commission itself has no powers to overturn a conviction. In effect, the Commission replaced the referral function formerly undertaken by the Secretary of State for Scotland. There was a feeling that the system, although it may have worked well in practice, did not fulfil the requisite test of independence. One Government Minister (the Secretary of State for Scotland) was being asked to review the work of another (the Lord Advocate). If the English experience is mirrored in Scotland, the new Commission may expect to be inundated with applications from persons who have been convicted before both solemn and summary courts and have had their initial appeals refused.

Bail

An accused person is presumed innocent until proved guilty and **03.87** should not, without good reason, be deprived of his or her liberty before conviction. It is reasonable, however, that if he goes free he should be required to give some security that he will appear at later stages in the proceedings. Bail is a means to this end.

Until the passing of the Bail etc. (Scotland) Act 1980, the normal **03.88** security took the form of a payment of money under a bail bond, but the Act effectively abolished money bail except in special circumstances. Bail is now granted subject to conditions, laid down by the court or the Lord Advocate, to which the bail applicant must subscribe.

These will, for example, be that he will appear at a court diet **03.89** when required, does not commit an offence while on bail or interfere with witnesses or obstruct the course of justice in any other way. He may also be required to make himself available to enable inquiries to be made or a report prepared to assist the court, or be required to report regularly at a police station, or stay away from his wife or family or other person(s) specified in the conditions attached to his bail. In special circumstances either the accused or someone on his behalf may be required to lodge money in court to ensure his attendance at a future hearing. The money may be forfeited if he fails to attend.

03.90 Liberation on bail may also be granted by the police after arrest on a summary charge, and if the accused is refused bail at this stage he may apply to the court for bail. Because the conditions of bail are contained in a document, a copy of which the accused must receive, and which must show also his normal place of residence, access to the addresses of accused persons is more readily available to the media under the terms of the Bail Act than before it, when the accused was frequently cited at the sheriff clerk's office.

03.91 In deciding whether or not to grant bail the court may take into account the type of crime charged—whether, for example, it involves alleged interference with witnesses—or whether the applicant has a criminal record, and if so what bearing that may have upon the possibility of his being in breach of conditions attached to bail. In each case the court has to balance the right of the untried person to the presumption of innocence against the risk of justice being frustrated by his failure to keep his part of the bargain.

03.92 For breach of his undertaking, the person granted bail may be fined and jailed for a maximum of three months in a summary case in the sheriff court, or a similar sum and 60 days in the district court. If he is charged on indictment, he is liable to a fine (with no maximum laid down) and imprisonment up to two years. Any penalty imposed may be in addition to the sentence passed by the court in respect of the original offence.

03.93 Traditionally in Scots law, murder and treason were not bailable crimes. Exceptionally, a person accused of one of these crimes could be released by authority of the Lord Advocate or the High Court. However, the list of non-bailable crimes was considerably extended by the Criminal Procedure (Scotland) Act 1995 (s. 26). In terms of that statute, a person accused for a second time of the following charges was to be automatically be refused bail: attempted murder; culpable homicide; rape; attempted rape. But these rules of Scots law breached the rights of accused persons under the European Convention on Human Rights. The Scottish Parliament dealt with the matter in the Bail, Judicial Appointments etc. (Scotland) Act 2000.

Now all accused persons have the right to apply for bail even if they are accused of the most serious crimes such as murder, rape and treason. Previous convictions of serious crimes are no longer an automatic bar to bail being granted. However, the seriousness of the charge and the existence of previous convictions make a grant of bail much less likely.

In addition to the provisions for pre-trial bail, anyone convicted **03.94** and sentenced to jail or detention may be granted bail pending disposal of an appeal. However, it should be noted that a convicted person who lodges an appeal does not automatically return themselves to the position of a person accused of a crime at the outset of proceedings. Once a person has been convicted and sentenced to imprisonment, they have a difficult task in persuading the court that they should be released pending the appeal hearing.

There is a right of appeal against refusal or against the condi- **03.95** tions attached to the granting of bail. The Crown may appeal against the granting of bail. In either case the appeal is normally heard by a High Court judge in chambers. The proceedings are kept private to protect the accused from possible prejudice arising from publicity given to statements made as a necessary part of information required by the judge. These may relate to the accused's record or other matters likely to influence the minds of potential jurors or witnesses at a subsequent trial. This kind of information must not appear in any report at this stage. Reporters, however, have a right of access to the decision, and this information is usually supplied by the Justiciary Office.

KEY POINTS

There are three criminal courts—High Court, sheriff and district. **03.96** The Lord Advocate is responsible for the investigation and prosecution of crime. Private prosecutions are extremely rare. Solemn procedure (dealing with the most serious cases) begins by way of a petition and cases are heard by a judge or sheriff and a jury of 15. Maximum sheriff court sentence is three years. Certain cases such as murder and rape must be taken in the High Court. There is no opening speech and the verdict can be by a simple majority. Summary cases start with a complaint and are heard by justice or sheriff sitting alone. Appeal against conviction in initially a "sifting" single judge and then if leave is granted to three High Court judges—or two judges in sentence only appeals. In certain cases the Appeal Court can grant authority for a retrial.

CHAPTER 4

CIVIL COURTS AND PROCEDURE

SCOTTISH CIVIL COURTS

Sheriff court

04.01 Scotland is divided into six regional sheriffdoms containing a total of 49 sheriff courts. Each sheriffdom has a sheriff principal who, as well as hearing appeals in civil cases, is responsible for the way business is conducted in the courts.

04.02 The sheriff court has a very wide civil jurisdiction extending to almost all types of action—such as adoption of children, liquidation of companies, club and gaming licence applications, bankruptcies and fatal accident inquiries. Exceptions are actions of reduction of deeds and actions to prove the tenor of lost documents. Legislation introduced in 1982 gave sheriffs jurisdiction to deal with divorce actions (see Chapter 12). They already had power to handle actions for judicial separation, separation and aliment, or affiliation and aliment. Actions involving amounts under £1,500 must be brought in the sheriff court. They cannot be heard by the Court of Session. There is no upper limit to the value of cases which can be dealt with in the sheriff court. Civil jury trial in the sheriff court was abolished in 1980.

04.03 An important part of the sheriff court's work is its commissary jurisdiction involving the appointment and confirmation of executors to administer the estates of people who have died. Only when he has obtained confirmation is an executor entitled to ingather and administer the estate.

04.04 Procedure in civil cases in the sheriff court was modified by the introduction of the summary cause in 1971 and again by the introduction of the small claims procedure in 1988. Certain cases, including all actions for payment of sums of money between £750 and £1,500 (excluding interest and expenses) are known as summary causes. They are begun by filling in a printed form of summons. Evidence is not recorded. Appeal lies from a final judgment of the sheriff to the sheriff principal on any point of law, and then from the sheriff principal to the Inner House of the Court of Session if the sheriff principal certifies the case as suitable for such an appeal.

The small claims procedure applies to actions where the money **04.05** value does not exceed £750. It was introduced after criticism of court procedures by the consumer lobby, which claimed that even the summary cause procedure was too difficult for lay people to understand. In small claims cases both pursuers and defenders are encouraged to "do it yourself". There is a preliminary hearing at which the sheriff tries to determine the issue between the parties. This takes the form of an informal discussion involving the sheriff, pursuer and defender or their representatives. If matters cannot be resolved at this stage the case is adjourned for a proof hearing at which, again, the emphasis is on informality. There is a right of appeal on a point of law to the sheriff principal, although appeals in small claims cases are extremely rare. The system seems to have been based on the arbitration procedure used for low value cases in the English county courts. The impression among sheriffs, solicitors and the consumer lobby appeared to be that the system was not working satisfactorily.

The procedure in ordinary causes, including actions for amounts **04.06** over £1,500, is more formal and follows the lines of Court of Session procedure, with some modifications which are noted later. Appeal is either to the sheriff principal and from him to the Inner House of the Court of Session, or else direct to the Inner House of the Court of Session. The monetary limits for small claims and summary causes are currently under review following the Scottish Executive's "Access to Justice" consultation paper.

The Court of Session

The Court of Session sits in Edinburgh and consists of the Lord **04.07** President, Lord Justice-Clerk and 30 other judges. The total number of judges was increased to 32 in 1999 to cope with the absence of four members of the Bench to try the Lockerbie case in the Netherlands and the demands placed on the Lord Justice-Clerk who headed the inquiry into the Paddington railway disaster. As we have seen, the personnel is the same as that of the High Court of Justiciary. Because of pressure of business, the 1990 Law Reform Act provided for temporary judges to sit in the High Court and Court of Session. The first four appointments were two leading Queen's Counsel and two sheriffs. They sit on the Bench dressed as Q.C.s, and do not wear the traditional judges' robes.

The court is divided into an Inner House which is largely an **04.08** appeal court, and an Outer House which deals with cases at first instance. The Court of Session remains one court, however. The division between Inner and Outer House is not a strict one. Judges from the Inner House may sit as single judges in the Outer House to help with pressure of work, and judges from the Outer House may be brought in to make up an additional appellate bench, known as the Extra Division. In theory, the court could still sit as a whole court to hear cases of particular difficulty but the raising of the number of judges and limitations of space have made this impracticable.

04.09　The Inner House is in turn divided into two divisions of equal status, the First Division and the Second Division. The First Division consists of the Lord President and three judges. The Second Division consists of the Lord Justice-Clerk and three judges. The Outer House consists of judges who sit singly and are known as Lords Ordinary. The reason for this peculiar name is that at one time there were two types of judges in the Court of Session, Ordinary Lords and Extraordinary Lords, the latter being nominees of the King and needing no legal qualifications. The power of appointing Extraordinary Lords was lost in 1723.

04.10　The Inner House is mainly an appeal court, hearing appeals from the sheriff courts and from the Outer House as well as from various other special courts and tribunals. It also has an original jurisdiction in certain types of petition including many petitions to the *nobile officium*—the inherent power of the court to grant a remedy where none is otherwise available.

04.11　The Court of Session has a general power to review the judgments of inferior courts and tribunals on the ground that they have exceeded their jurisdiction or have failed to observe fundamental rules of justice, such as the rule that both parties must be heard before a decision is given.

The House of Lords

04.12　In civil cases, unlike criminal, there is an appeal from the Court of Session to the House of Lords. An appeal must be lodged within three months of the judgment appealed from.

PROCEDURE IN CIVIL CASES IN SCOTLAND

04.13　What follows is merely an outline designed to give a general picture of the steps involved in getting a case into court. The person who brings an ordinary civil action is called the pursuer, the person against whom it is brought, the defender.

04.14　In the case of ordinary actions in the Court of Session, the first step is for the pursuer's solicitor or counsel to prepare a summons.

This is, in essence, a document summoning the defender to appear at court, setting out the pursuer's claim and asking the court to give judgment in his favour. A copy of the summons is served on the defender, usually by recorded delivery or registered post. There is then a period of grace, known as the *induciae*, to give the defender time to take legal advice and decide on his course of action.

When this period expires, the pursuer's solicitor lodges in the **04.15** court offices what is known as the process, which consists of the summons and various other documents which will be needed later in the proceedings.

The next stage is that the case appears in the calling list of the **04.16** Court of Session. This is the first public announcement of the action. The only details given are the names and addresses of the parties and the names of the pursuer's solicitors.

If the defender does not defend, the court will give judgment for **04.17** the pursuer—a decree in absence. In divorce and other actions affecting status, however, decree will not be given until the grounds of action have been proved by sufficient evidence. If the defender does wish to defend, he must enter appearance and lodge defences containing his answers to the pursuer's allegations.

After the parties have completed their adjustments, the court **04.18** makes an order closing the record. A closed record is then printed and added to the process.

The next steps in the procedure vary. There may be a prelimin- **04.19** ary dispute about further procedure and this may have to be decided by a judge. In the normal course of events, the case will eventually be heard by a judge alone or, more rarely, by a judge and jury. An action for damages which involves difficult questions of fact and law may be regarded as unsuitable for a jury. In civil cases, the jury numbers 12 and may return a majority verdict (see later in this chapter).

To sum up, the procedure in an ordinary civil action in the Court **04.20** of Session is, in rough outline, summons—lodging of process—case in calling list—appearance—defences—open record—closed record—proof or jury trial.

At a proof there are no opening speeches. Counsel make **04.21** submissions at the end of the evidence. The judge may give an immediate decision, or, more likely, take time to consider the case and produce a decision in writing at a later date.

There is an important distinction between cases which are **04.22** dismissed and those in which decree of absolvitor are granted. If the defender is absolved that is a higher degree of success than dismissal since it prevents the pursuer from suing the same defender again over the same case. In the case of dismissal it is possible for the pursuer to find another remedy against the same defender.

04.23 Apart from damages for financial loss or loss of property (commonly referred to as patrimonial loss) a court may make an award for the pain and suffering (*solatium*) endured by an injured pursuer, and a loss of society award to compensate a bereaved relative for the death of someone who has died because of the defender's negligence. A loss of society award is intended to compensate for the loss of companionship and guidance. Following a change in the law in 1993 a pursuer can now also claim for the distress and anxiety they endure in contemplation of the suffering of a loved one before their death. In one of the first cases of its kind a jury at the Court of Session in 1998 awarded £50,000 to a mother who kept a vigil by the beside of her teenage son after he suffered appalling burns in a road accident. He died 16 days after the accident.

04.24 The procedure in an ordinary civil action in the sheriff court is broadly similar. The pursuer's solicitor draws up an initial writ instead of a summons and a copy is served on the defender. There is no calling list as such and the defender must, if he wishes to defend, enter appearance within the *induciae*. Thereafter he must lodge defences. Adjustments are now exchanged between parties only. They are not lodged in court. When adjustments are complete the sheriff closes the record and the case will proceed to debate or proof.

04.25 Anxiety about the length of time being taken for ordinary actions to reach their conclusion in the sheriff court, led to the introduction of a new set of rules as from January 1994. Basically, the aim is to cut down the length of proceedings by allowing the sheriff a greater managerial role over the conduct of actions. The "Options Hearings" introduced by the new rules may well prove a rich source of copy for court journalists, as they will often contain a brief discussion of the essential elements of the case.

Optional procedure

04.26 Following criticisms of delays in personal injury cases, a committee chaired by Lord Kincraig recommended reforms aimed at simplifying procedure and giving the court more control over the conduct of litigation. The result was the introduction in the Court of Session in 1986 of an optional procedure in such cases. The written pleadings are in a short, simplified form and a closed record is not obligatory. At an early stage the case is sent to a diet roll where a judge decides what course it will take. For example, he may order a hearing on the amount of damages alone, or, if the law is not in dispute, an inquiry only into the facts of the case.

The Commercial Court

In September 1994 Lord Penrose was appointed for a three-year **04.27** period as a full-time judge in commercial cases in the Court of Session. This followed a report by Lord Coulsfield in 1993 which reported a reluctance on the part of the business community in Scotland to litigate in the Court of Session. This was said to be based on a feeling that the Court of Session was slow and lacking in expertise, leading to people using arbitration or the English courts instead. The Coulsfield Report concluded that this situation was prejudicial to the development, perhaps even the survival, of Scots law. By early 1999 four judges had been nominated as commercial court judges, one full-time.

Petitions

There are, of course, special procedures in special types of case. **04.28** The points of most interest to journalists are dealt with later in the section on court reporting. For the present, it is worth noting that the procedure for cases brought by petition differs from that outlined above. The person presenting the petition is called the petitioner and the person opposing it is known as the respondent.

There is an important distinction between the standards of proof **04.29** demanded by the law in criminal and in civil cases. In criminal proceedings generally proof must be beyond reasonable doubt. In civil cases the court has to be satisfied merely on a balance of probabilities—in other words, the judge or jury has to decide which of two conflicting stories is more probable.

Judicial Review

A simplified procedure for dealing with petitions for judicial **04.30** review of administrative decisions came into operation in the Court of Session in June 1985. The first case under the new procedure, dealt with by Lord Ross in July 1985, concerned a girl aged 16, who left home as a result of being assaulted by her father, and applied successfully to the court for reversal of a decision of Monklands District Council rejecting her claim for accommodation as a person with a priority need under the Housing (Homeless Persons) Act 1977. She had no assets and no income, nowhere to go and had attempted suicide. The judge held that no reasonable authority could fail to conclude she was vulnerable, and ordered that she be given accommodation under the Act. She was also awarded damages against the council. Judicial review has proved a frequent source of copy. It has been used to test such diverse questions as the ownership of assets of the Trustee Savings Bank in Scotland, the nature and extent of Crown immunity in building a fence at a submarine base and the policy of the DSS on the payment of special cold-weather allowances. It is frequently used to challenge deportation decisions by the Home Office.

04.31 Judicial review was described by Lord McCluskey in the Reith Lectures in 1986 as one of the old forms of remedy now rediscovered by the judges to enable citizens to challenge infringements of their rights, especially infringements by public officials—a process by which, he said, the judges had armed the citizen with rights he did not know he had. If so, then clearly such cases deserve close attention from the journalist for their potential news value. (For a fuller discussion, see Chapter 14.)

Trust variation

04.32 The Trusts (Scotland) Act 1961 gave the Court of Session the power to vary or "break" trusts which formerly were inflexible. It also resulted in a departure from the accepted rule applied to the reporting of court proceedings generally—that the press was entitled to have access to, and to publish fair and accurate excerpts from, the pleadings put before the court.

04.33 To take an example, the most usual kind of petition brought before the court under the Act is aimed at getting round a provision in a trust which restricts a beneficiary to the income and puts the capital of the trust beyond his reach. The court may under the Act, where satisfied as to the interests of other beneficiaries, authorise payment of the capital of a trust to a person who previously was entitled only to the income. A variation of this kind will usually be designed to enable the interested parties to save tax. This is legitimate tax avoidance, and must not be referred to as tax evasion. The court has taken the view that the figures contained in this type of case must not be made public. For this reason reporters are not usually allowed access to documents containing figures.

04.34 The only means of reporting such cases—which from time to time produce copy of considerable interest, especially where the estates of well-known public figures are concerned—is to sit through the proceedings, and obtain the names and addresses of the parties from the clerk of court or solicitors.

04.35 In some cases solicitors for the petitioner will allow the press to see the petition, and this happened in a case in 1963 in which the petitioner, Lord Sorn, was a judge. But, in the first case under the 1961 Act to be reported in the media, the parties complained to the court about publication of figures not actually disclosed in court. The then Lord President (Lord Clyde) took the view that, since the court in such cases was performing what was in effect an administrative act on behalf of the parties, the figures should not be published. This is still the attitude of the court, except where the particulars in question actually emerge in court.

Civil juries

Although civil jury trials have virtually disappeared in England, it is **04.36** still a statutory right in certain important cases in Scotland. In 1988 the Lord Advocate of the day issued a discussion paper on whether civil juries should be abolished in the Court of Session, but they survived despite opposition from some judges and from lawyers acting for defenders, who felt that juries were expensive, unpredictable and made awards which were too high.

The right to jury trial in Scotland in both criminal and civil cases **04.37** appears to date from the fourteenth century, but fell into disuse in civil cases during the seventeenth century and was not revived until the passing of the Jury Trials (Scotland) Act 1815. It was already in operation in England and was brought to Scotland experimentally and, at first, for a limited period only. The Scottish civil jury in modern times is based on the English model, which explains why there are 12 jurors and not the traditional Scottish figure of 15. The Law Reform (Miscellaneous Provisions) (Scotland) Act 1980 abolished civil jury trial in the sheriff court.

Meanwhile in England it was eventually decided by the courts **04.38** themselves that jury trial in civil cases would not in future be permitted except by specific authority of the court. In Scotland, on the other hand, the position remains that, if a party with a statutory right to jury trial insists on this form of procedure, unless there is some "special cause" why it should not be allowed, there must be a jury trial.

"Special cause" usually consists of difficult questions of law or **04.39** mixed fact and law which would be difficult for a jury to deal with, or undue delay in raising the action, resulting in special problems in assessing the reliability of evidence given by witnesses whose recollection is dimmed by the passage of time. For example, in the case of *Shanks v. BBC*, a defamation action arising out of a TV programme, the BBC successfully asked the Court of Session to have the case conducted before a judge sitting alone without a jury. The case involved allegations about share dealings, which, the court felt, a jury would have difficulty in understanding.

A virtue of the old Scottish jury was that it had (and still has in **04.40** criminal cases) 15 members, making it possible to achieve a majority verdict. The traditional Scottish attitude in favour of majority verdicts is based on the idea of deciding the "sense of the meeting" rather than coercing every member of the jury to reach the same result. In civil cases with a jury of 12 derived from England there is always the risk of a "hung" jury with the vote equally divided. This happened in one case in the Court of Session in 1973 when a jury was discharged after failing to reach a verdict after three hours.

04.41 In practice civil juries are most often used to decide claims for damages for injuries caused by accidents of various kinds—for example at work or on the roads. Recent cases have shown, however, that juries are becoming equally popular for dealing with defamation cases. Since the Interest on Damages Act 1971 the verdicts of juries in civil cases are easier to understand than they used to be. Juries now have to return a verdict, if they make an award of damages, divided into separate sums for each element of damages—for example past and future loss of earnings and pain and suffering.

04.42 Perhaps reflecting its English ancestry, the procedure in a civil trial is different in several important respects from cases dealt with by a judge sitting alone. The hearing is opened by an address to the jury by junior counsel for the pursuer who outlines the circumstances of the case and explains the basis of his client's claim. The jury then hears the evidence for the pursuer before being addressed by junior counsel for the defender, who, in turn, introduces the evidence for his client. At the end of the evidence senior counsel for each side sums up the case for the jury and the judge completes the hearing by directing the jury on questions of law. As in a criminal case the judge makes it clear that the jury are judges of the facts.

04.43 Sometimes during a trial the jury are taken from the courtroom while counsel make submissions to the judge on a question of law. If the case is not ultimately withdrawn from the jury, care must be taken not to publish reports of statements made by counsel which could be read by jurors before the case is finished. It could be argued that such a report amounted to an interference with the course of justice or that it is a contempt of court because it prejudiced the case of one side or the other. If the judge does not make an order reporters will have to exercise their own judgment. The safest course is to assume that what was said outwith the jury's hearing should not be reported, at least until the end of the trial.

04.44 Appeal against the verdict of a civil jury is taken by way of a motion for a new trial. This is heard in the Inner House and may be on a variety of grounds such as misdirection by the trial judge, insufficiency of evidence or because of a perverse verdict by the jury. The appeal may be against the amount of damages awarded, either as too high or to low. The appeal judges may order a new trial before a fresh jury or, if they agree unanimously that the jury was not entitled to find in favour of the pursuer and that there is no fresh evidence to put before a jury, find in favour of the defender.

Until recently the number of cases dealt with each year by civil **04.45** juries had greatly diminished, but a jury award of £50,000 to a woman clerical officer who sued the *Sun* newspaper following an allegation published in 1988 that she had sex with a prison inmate was instrumental in leading a revival for juries. The action by Mrs Lilian Winter was said to be the first dealt with by civil jury in a defamation case in Scotland in living memory, and the award was by far the highest won by an individual in a case of its kind. In 1991 three Court of Session judges refused to interfere with the award despite an appeal by the newspaper that the jury award was too high.

The £50,000 record was shattered in another case in 1998 in **04.46** which a Court of Session jury awarded a former schoolteacher £125,000, again against the publishers of the *Sun*. The jury upheld Miss Annie Clinton's claim that a story in the newspaper had defamed her by falsely alleging that she had been involved in a secretive sexual relationship with a Roman Catholic priest. The priest, Father Noel Barry, was awarded £45,000. An appeal was marked in the case but did not go ahead.

The issue of the role of civil juries and the level of awards was **04.47** discussed and clarified by the House of Lords in 1997 in the case of *Girvan v. Inverness Farmers Dairy*. A jury at the Court of Session awarded Mr Girvan, a sheep farmer and former champion clay pigeon shooter, damages of £193,080 after he suffered a disabling elbow injury in a road accident. Of that total, the jury awarded £120,000 for pain and suffering which was successfully challenged as excessive. A second jury awarded £165,530 pounds, including £95,000 for pain and suffering. That £95,000 pound award was again challenged as too high and the case went to the House of Lords.

Lord Hope, the former Lord President, said it was very unusual **04.48** for a jury's award to be challenged twice in the same action and if the second challenge was successful the case would have to go back to a jury for a third time on the issue of damages. He added that the case highlighted the unease among lawyers in Scotland about the relationship between pain and suffering awards by juries and those made by judges.

The House of Lords judges decided that the proper approach **04.49** was still the same as adopted by the Court of Session in the case of *Landell v. Landell* as long ago as 1841—the award of damages must be so excessive that the court could say the jury had committed a gross injustice or reached a palpably wrong result. An award for pain and suffering could not be precisely worked out and reasonable and fair-minded jurors might quite properly arrive at widely differing figures.

04.50   Lord Hope added

> "If there is any justification for preserving the present system it lies in this fact: that judges may . . . take quite a different view from 12 ordinary men and women on the jury as to the current money value of the pursuer's claim. . . . In this case we now have the benefit of two jury awards and the award by the second jury is £25,000 less than the first. I find it quite impossible to say that no other jury would award such a large sum."

The court decided that the award for pain and suffering could not be described as excessive.

04.51   Lord Hope observed that there were signs of a small increase in the number of civil jury trials and accepted that the discrepancy between awards by judges and juries was not likely to disappear. However, he thought it inappropriate for the House of Lords to recommend any change in Court of Session practice—such as providing guidance for juries on the level of awards or to give appeal judges in the Court of Session the right to assess damages after a successful motion for a new trial. In his opinion these issues were best left to the Scottish Law Commission.

Judicial Committee of the Privy Council

04.52 The Judicial Committee of the Privy Council is a body of distinguished lawyers, including senior judges and former judges, acting as a court of appeal from the supreme courts of Commonwealth countries. It was formerly the final court of appeal in the British Empire, and still decides appeals from New Zealand, Singapore, the Channel Islands and most of the Caribbean countries. In June 1993 seven law lords sat to consider an appeal from Jamaica involving two men who had been on death row awaiting execution since 1980. The condemned men argued that this long delay breached the Jamaican constitution. In 1999 the judicial committee unanimously rejected death row appeals by nine convicted murderers in Trinidad and Tobago.

04.53 Within the United Kingdom, the Judicial Committee hears appeals from the decisions of English ecclesiastical courts and various professional disciplinary bodies such as the Disciplinary Committee of the General Medical Council.

The Judicial Committee was also provided with a new role with **04.54**
the birth of the Scottish Parliament. In the event of a dispute
between the Scottish Executive and the United Kingdom government over whether proposed legislation is within the power of the
Scottish Parliament, it will be referred to five law lords in the
Judicial Committee. In effect the Judicial Committee has become
the court of final appeal for the United Kingdom in questions as to
the functions and/or legal competence of the devolved legislative
and executive authorities in Scotland (as well as Wales and
Northern Ireland). Cases can be referred to the Judicial Committee by one of the United Kingdom law officers including the
Lord Advocate or the Advocate General for Scotland. The law
officers can also require any court or tribunal to make a reference
and appeals against decisions on devolution issues lie to the
Judicial Committee from the Court of Session and High Court of
Justiciary.

EUROPEAN COURT OF JUSTICE

The court's powers are laid down in the European Economic **04.55**
Community Treaty, and one of the consequences of the United
Kingdom joining the Community in 1972 was that the court
assumed jurisdiction to give preliminary rulings on any question
raised before a Scottish or English court, criminal or civil. A
domestic court may in certain circumstances request the European
Court to give a preliminary ruling. The national court must be
satisfied that a decision by the European Court is necessary to
enable it to give a judgment in the case before it.

The national court or tribunal may take this course either at the **04.56**
instance of any party in the case or on its own initiative. Once the
ruling has been given the case returns to the court or tribunal
where it began. The procedure is likely to be adopted in situations
where the national law appears to be incompatible with Community law. The proceedings before the originating court are
halted meantime.

The first case referred from a Scottish court under this pro- **04.57**
cedure was a claim for a student's grant made by a Frenchman
which had been refused by the Scottish Education Department. A
question requiring an interpretation of Community law was
referred to the European Court from the Court of Session by Lord
Clyde in 1986. The applicant, born in France of an English father
and a French mother, claimed he was entitled to a grant in light of
certain provisions of EU law.

HUMAN RIGHTS

04.58 Not to be confused with the European Court of Justice, which deliberates in Luxembourg and is part of the apparatus of the European Union, is the European Court of Human Rights which sits in Strasbourg. Whereas the Court of Justice is concerned with the interpretation of European Community rules, often of a highly technical nature, the Court of Human Rights handles a broad range of cases frequently of great significance for the life and liberty of individual citizens. A list of some of the cases referred from the United Kingdom confirms this. The court has been asked to rule on issues such as corporal punishment in schools, the closed shop, pensioners' rights, contempt of court, the use of "plastic bullets" and telephone tapping. For journalists the *Lingens v. Austria* decision in 1986, is of interest as it recognised that public figures (such as politicians) must expect and accept vigorous criticisms. Domestic Scots law, however, has not been so generous to journalists at least until now.

04.59 The court is part of the machinery set up under the European Convention on Human Rights which was drawn up as long ago as 1950. Since then United Kingdom citizens have had the right to apply to the European Commission on Human Rights if they felt their rights had been infringed by the State. If the commission decided that the case was admissible it could refer the case to the Human Rights Court for a judgment. In practice, even getting to the two-stage system in Strasbourg was often a lengthy and laborious process which could be resorted to only after the all remedies in domestic courts had been remedied. The whole process normally took years. However, there have now been dramatic changes in the procedure. The commission and the court have been merged and the Human Rights Convention is now part of our domestic law.

04.60 Following its general election victory in 1997 the new Labour Government, in line with its manifesto commitment to incorporate the Human Rights Convention as part of our domestic law, published a White Paper "Rights Brought Home: The Human Rights Bill" in October 1995. The intention was that the Convention would be woven "far more powerfully" into United Kingdom law. The Human Rights Bill, guaranteeing rights such as freedom of speech and the potentially conflicting right to privacy, family life, home and correspondence, received the Royal Assent in November 1998. The Human Rights legislation provides that all courts and tribunals must interpret Westminster legislation in a way which is compatible with Convention rights. It will also be unlawful for public authorities, such as government departments, local authorities and the police, to act in a way which is incompatible with human rights.

If the Court of Session or the High Court in Scotland decides **04.61** that something in a Westminster Act is not compatible with a Convention Right they will be able to make a declaration to that effect. Since the Westminster Parliament is regarded as sovereign, however, the courts will not be able to strike out parts of Westminster legislation as they can do with an Act of the Scottish Parliament if it is ruled to be beyond the powers of the legislature and therefore of no effect.

The introduction of the Human Rights provisions effectively **04.62** took place in two stages in Scotland. As we have already seen in Chapter 1, even before the Human Rights Act applied across the United Kingdom the Scotland Act provided that an Act of the Scottish Parliament could not include any measure incompatible with Convention rights as defined in the Human Rights Act. The human rights provisions of the Scotland Act applied for most purposes from May 20, 1999.

The right to apply to the Strasbourg Court will still be available **04.63** even after the introduction of the Human Rights Act into Scots law. The significant difference will be the possibility of enforcing Convention rights in proceedings in Scotland first. (For a more detailed discussion on Human Rights, see Chapter 25.)

CIVIL CASES IN ENGLAND

In England most civil cases are heard by some 250 county courts **04.64** where legally trained circuit judges, referred to as, for example, Judge Jones, preside. More important cases and specialised cases are dealt with by the High Court of Justice. Following major procedural changes introduced in April 1999 the practice followed in both courts is pretty much the same. There are more than 80 High Court judges who sit in three Divisions—Queen's Bench, Family and Chancery. Apart from its civil functions, the Queen's Bench Division deals with some criminal appeals from magistrates' courts. As its name suggests, the Family Division deals with issues such as divorce and adoption and the Chancery Division with matters such as tax, wills and companies. The Court of Appeal (Civil) is headed by the Master of the Rolls and hears appeals from the High Court and County Courts. Again, there is an appeal to the House of Lords.

KEY POINTS

04.65 Civil cases are dealt with in the Court of Session and sheriff court. Sheriffs can now deal with divorce cases. The Inner House of the Court of Session (three judges) hears appeals, and there can be a further appeal to the House of Lords. The opposing sides in a civil action are the pursuer and defender. The Scottish system is based on written pleadings and the main documents involved are the summons or initial writ, open record and closed record. Civil cases are heard by a sheriff or judge sitting alone and, more rarely in the Court of Session, by a jury of 12. In a civil case the pursuer has to prove his case on a balance of probabilities, a lower standard than in criminal cases which have to be proved beyond reasonable doubt. In a civil case the pursuer is entitled to a jury trial unless the other side can persuade the court there is a special reason (such as the complexity of the case) why a jury is not suitable. Following the Scotland Act and the Human Rights Act, rights under the European Convention can now be enforced in United Kingdom courts. The right to apply to Strasbourg is still available.

CHAPTER 5

MISCELLANEOUS SPECIAL COURTS

Journalists should be aware that they run the risk of contempt in **05.01** the reporting of some of the miscellaneous special courts listed here just as much as in the reporting of the normal criminal and civil courts. The Contempt of Court Act 1981, s. 19, applies the law of contempt to "any tribunal exercising the judicial power of the State".

This vague phrase was inserted by Parliament when it was found **05.02** to be impossible to draw up a list of the tribunals and other courts to which contempt law should apply. Deciding whether or not a court or tribunal has the power to punish for contempt can be a complex issue and the journalist writing a controversial story based on the proceedings of an inferior court or tribunal should take legal advice.

The issue was discussed in the case of *Attorney-General v. BBC* in **05.03** 1981 when the House of Lords decided that the Lands Valuation Court was not a tribunal within the meaning of the 1981 Act and did not have contempt powers.

It should also be noted that even if a court or tribunal does not **05.04** itself have the power to punish for contempt, a contempt power may still be exercisable over a report of such a court or tribunal. It could be exercised by the High Court or the Court of Session which have a supervisory jurisdiction over all inferior tribunals and courts.

The Lands Valuation Appeal Court

The local valuation appeal committee deals with appeals against **05.05** the valuation of property for rating purposes. There is a further right of appeal on a point of law by way of stated case to the Lands Valuation Appeal Court which consists of three judges of the Court of Session.

Restrictive Practices Court

All restrictive agreements between manufacturers or traders must **05.06** be registered with an official known as the Registrar of Restrictive Trading Agreements. If he thinks they are not in the public interest he may bring them before the Restrictive Practices Court. The burden is then on the parties to the agreements to show that they are in the public interest. An example of the kind of case the court deals with arose in 1999 when the Office of Fair Trading (OFT) brought a case in the Restrictive Practices Court against the Premier League, Sky and the BBC arguing that the collective selling of television rights for football matches was against the public interest and should be banned. The OFT also argued that Sky's exclusive contracts for showing live matches and BBC's right to show edited highlights should be outlawed as anti-competitive.

05.07   When sitting in Scotland the Restrictive Practices Court usually consists of one judge of the Court of Session and at least two lay members qualified by experience in, or knowledge of, industry, commerce or public affairs. There is appeal to the Court of Session on points of law by way of stated case.

05.08   When sitting in other parts of the United Kingdom the court is similarly composed of a judge and two or more laymen. The 1999 Sky TV case, for example, was heard by Mr Justice Ferris and two lay judges—a publisher and a chartered accountant. There is appeal on a point of law to the Court of Appeal or the Court of Appeal of Northern Ireland.

Election courts

05.09   The function of these courts is to hear petitions, rare now, but at one time common, complaining against irregularities in the conduct of elections. In Scotland the election court in the case of a parliamentary election consists of two judges of the Court of Session. In the case of a local government election, it consists of the sheriff principal of the sheriffdom in which the election took place.

05.10   Election courts can try prosecutions for corrupt and illegal practices. Corrupt practices are the more serious and include bribery and treating, that is, treating people to "meat, drink or entertainment" to influence votes. One glass of beer may not justify the charge but a large number may, and "giving drink to women that they may influence the votes of their fathers, brothers or sweethearts" has been held to be treating. It is also a corrupt practice to exert undue influence on voters—by force or threats of force or injury. Illegal practices include such offences as paying or receiving money to transport electors to or from the poll, voting when disqualified or inducing a disqualified person to vote.

In England election courts consist, in the case of a parliamentary **05.11**
election, of two High Court judges and, in the case of a local
election, of a senior barrister.

Registration Appeal Court

Appeals over the registration of voters can be taken in the first **05.12**
instance to the sheriff and from there to a special Registration
Appeal Court consisting of three judges of the Court of Session.
The type of case which the court deals with can be illustrated by its
decision that a minister of the Church of Scotland who had been
summoned to the General Assembly and who would accordingly be
unable to vote at the polling station allotted to him, was entitled to
be registered as an absent voter.

The Scottish Land Court

The Scottish Land Court, established in 1911, resolves disputes **05.13**
over agricultural holdings. The Chairman of the Land Court enjoys
the same rank and tenure of office as a Court of Session judge. The
court operates on two levels—a divisional court where cases are
heard by a court member and a legal assessor, or a full court with a
quorum of two members and the chairman. The decision of the
court is issued as an order and is binding on the parties involved
but there is an appeal to the Court of Session on a point of law.
The court's approval is often necessary, for example, before a
landlord can serve an effective notice to quit on a farm tenant. The
Land Court also deals with the exercise by the Government of its
powers under the Agriculture Acts. If a person is aggrieved by a
proposed exercise of these powers he may have the matter referred
to the Land Court.

The Lyon Court

The Lyon Court is held by the Lord Lyon King-of-Arms to deal **05.14**
with questions of heraldry and the right to bear arms in Scotland.
No armorial bearings may be used in Scotland unless they are on
record in the Public Register of all Arms and Bearings in Scotland.
There is appeal to the Inner House of the Court of Session and
from there to the House of Lords.

Licensing boards

Licensing boards sit quarterly and comprise members of the district **05.15**
or islands council. Their functions include making decisions (after
considering objections) on applications for certificates for the retail

sale of alcohol, and on complaints, as well as imposing and revoking conditions, giving consent to and ordering alterations to licensed premises. Certificates normally last three years. There is a right of appeal to the sheriff by either an applicant or objector or by a licence holder or a complainer, and a right of appeal to the Court of Session against the sheriff's decision.

Church courts

05.16 The courts of the Church of Scotland have a statutory jurisdiction going back to 1592 and extending over the whole range of church affairs, including discipline. So long as matters are within the jurisdiction of the church courts, the civil courts cannot interfere.

05.17 The Courts of the Church of Scotland are the Kirk Session consisting of the minister and elders of a particular church, the Presbytery consisting of the ministers and representative elders from the parishes within its bounds, the Synod consisting of the members of the several Presbyteries within its bounds and finally the General Assembly with representatives from the whole church. Certain appeals concerning character and conduct are heard by a Judicial Commission of the General Assembly, which can decide at any stage of the proceedings whether they will be heard in public.

05.18 The courts of other churches in Scotland, including the Episcopal Church, have no statutory powers, their jurisdiction, like that of a club committee, dependant on agreement between the members. The civil courts can intervene if there is a breach of this agreement affecting property interests just as in any other case of breach of contract. The courts can intervene also where there has been a denial of natural justice within the courts of a church in dealing with a complaint against a minister or a member or where those courts have exceeded their powers.

05.19 In 1986 the Court of Session ruled that the Synod of the Free Presbyterian Church of Scotland had erred in suspending two ministers for life on grounds of contumacy (wilful disobedience). In his judgment in favour of the ministers, Lord Ross, the Lord Justice-Clerk, said that the court had a limited jurisdiction to interfere with decisions of the governing body of a church. There could be no question of the court reviewing the merits of the synod's decision, but it would entertain an action where a religious body had acted clearly beyond its constitution or where procedure was grossly or fundamentally irregular. In this case, the church had failed to show that the two ministers were ever given an order they had disobeyed. The ministers were also entitled to know what the case against them was; they were convicted of contumacy before being given any hearing and without any charge being put to them.

THE SERVICE COURTS

Courts-Martial

The Royal Navy and the Army and the Royal Air Force all have **05.20**
separate courts for dealing with crime and disciplinary problems
involving service personnel. Many of these matters dealt with as
disciplinary offences have no counterpart in civilian life. These
courts, collectively known as courts-martial, have no jury in the
conventional sense. The facts of a case are decided upon by officers
selected to do so. The prosecutors are generally service lawyers or
lawyers from civilian life or from amongst other officers who have
been asked to represent the person to be tried.

Many servicemen charged with minor offences are dealt with **05.21**
under an informal system of summary justice. The proceedings are
not a trial, the normal rules of evidence do not operate and lawyers
are not allowed to be present. Proceedings are normally conducted
by a commanding officer who has power to impose up to 60 days'
detention. Since the Armed Forces Act 1996, however, any service-
man being tried for a summary offence has the right to elect for
trial by court-martial where the procedure is the equivalent of a
trial at an English Crown Court.

There are three types of military courts-martial—a general **05.22**
court-martial which consists of at least five officers and can try
officers as well as other ranks, a district court-martial which
consists of at least three officers and cannot try an officer or award
more than two years' imprisonment and a field general court-
martial which normally consists of at least three officers and is, in
effect, an emergency general court-martial for the trial of offences
committed on active service.

A Judge Advocate from the Office of the Judge Advocate **05.23**
General officiates at all courts-martial. His role is to advise the
court on matters of law and summarise the facts. He does not take
part in the actual decision of the court although he does have a
vote on sentence. The Judge Advocate is a legally experienced, full-
time judicial officer, for example an advocate, barrister or solicitor
of at least five years' standing. He plays an independent role in the
system, neither being paid by nor responsible to the Ministry of
Defence.

Courts-martial are conducted in accordance with English law **05.24**
and the procedure closely follows that in the Crown Court even
when a court-martial sits in Scotland to try a Scottish soldier. The
prosecutor opens his case and calls his witnesses, who can be cross-
examined by the defence. At the end of the defence case the
advocates make closing speeches, the Judge Advocate sums up and
the court retires to consider its verdict.

05.25　　A finding of "not guilty" is final but for many years a guilty finding was subject to confirmation by a senior officer before it could be regarded as legally valid. However, the confirmation procedure has now been abolished and conviction and sentence are legally binding from the minute they are announced.

05.26　　Air force courts-martial are very similar and in the navy the great majority of offences are tried summarily by the Commanding officer. The right to elect trial by court-martial is much more limited in the navy than in the army or RAF. It is confined to offences which could result in the alleged offender being dismissed, detained or punished by disrating. A naval court martial is basically the same as in the other forces. The court must consist of not less than five and no more than nine officers of, or above, the rank of lieutenant.

05.27　　A person who has been tried by an ordinary court is not liable to be re-tried by a court-martial. Under the Armed Forces Act 1966 a person who has been tried by a court-martial cannot be tried later by an ordinary court for the same, or substantially the same, offence.

05.28　　Courts-martial meet as required. The practice regarding notice varies. In some cases, the media are sent notice of pending trials but usually notice is simply posted at the service headquarters. Courts-martial are, however, public courts and anyone may attend.

05.29　　There is appeal from the findings of a court-martial to the Courts-Martial Appeal Court, which consists of the judges of the English Court of Appeal together with nominated judges from the English High Court, the Scottish High Court of Justiciary and the Supreme Court of Judicature of Northern Ireland. The Lord Chancellor can also appoint other persons of legal experience to be judges of the court. Three judges normally sit but there may be a larger uneven number.

05.30　　Application for leave to appeal must first be made to the Courts-Martial Appeal Court. There is no appeal against sentence, but the court may vary the sentence incidentally if, for example, it finds that the accused was wrongfully convicted on one charge but that he was properly convicted or should have been convicted on another. Where a point of law of general public importance is at stake there can be a further appeal to the House of Lords. This is the only case where the decision of a criminal court sitting in Scotland may eventually be heard by the House of Lords and is very rare.

05.31　　The whole system of courts martial came under challenge in the 1990s when a dossier of 12 cases was presented to the European Human Rights Commission. It was alleged in these cases that the courts martial operated by the army and the RAF were in breach of Article 6 of the European Convention on Human Rights which guarantees the right to a fair trial before an impartial tribunal. The leading case was brought by Peter Elliot, a former RAF sergeant from Humberside who was sentenced to nine months imprisonment after being found guilty of using threatening, abusive and insulting behaviour. He denied the charges but was found guilty and lost his pension and career. Leave to take the case to a Courts-Martial Appeal Court was refused. Mr Elliot argued that the courts-martial system was unjust on the basis that it discriminated against the accused person. He contended that the system did not provide the same standards of fairness or burden of proof as the criminal courts and that there was no proper and full independent right of appeal against sentence. He argued that the system should be changed to give service personnel the right to trial by jury. Among the other 11 cases were a RAF squadron leader dismissed because of a conviction for shoplifting, an RAF corporal dismissed after a conviction for false accounting, an army signalman convicted of malicious wounding and an RAF corporal convicted of forgery.

Another European challenge was mounted by Falklands veteran **05.32** and former Scots Guardsman Alex Findlay who was sentenced to two years in a military prison for threatening to kill fellow soldiers after suffering a nervous breakdown. Mr Findlay had earlier sued the Defence Ministry and been awarded £100,000 after he claimed the Army had failed to diagnose that he was suffering from stress after the Battle of Tumbledown during the Falklands conflict in1982. During a second tour of duty in Northern Ireland in 1990 a colleague opened a can of beer and the noise triggered off memories of a bullet whizzing past him. Mr Findlay pulled out a pistol and put it to the head of a colleague before taking two other soldiers hostage and firing two shots. He was disarmed and no one was injured. Mr Findlay complained that he had not been tried by an independent and impartial tribunal and the European Commission of Human Rights decided that he had not been given the fair hearing to which he was entitled. Subsequent legislation has changed the detail of military pre-trial procedures to bring them into line with modern views.

Standing civilian courts

These operate outside the United Kingdom for the trial of people **05.33** employed by the armed forces or accompanying them but not subject to military law. A magistrate who is a member of the Office of Judge Advocate General has power to imprison for a maximum of six months in these courts.

KEY POINTS

05.34 The law of contempt of court applies to reports of any tribunal exercising the judicial power of the State. Scotland has a number of special courts to deal with disputes over, for example, heraldry and the right to bear arms, rateable values, the conduct of elections and the registration of voters. There is usually an appeal against their decisions to the Court of Session on a point of law. Special courts known as courts-martial deal with offences and disciplinary matters involving service personnel. They follow English criminal procedure even when a Scottish soldier is being tried in Scotland.

CHAPTER 6

OTHER BODIES

TRIBUNALS

There are a large number of tribunals which exercise judicial-type **06.01** functions but which are not courts. Tribunals are designed to achieve a quicker, cheaper and more informal kind of justice in specialised areas than the ordinary courts. Tribunals enable individuals to seek independent rulings on administrative decisions with which they disagree. While the operation of tribunals varies considerably, the system is based on the principles of openness, fairness and impartiality. In all there are scores of different types of tribunal dealing with a huge variety of subjects including complaints against doctors and solicitors, national insurance, immigration, fair rents, social welfare and war pensions. Some are open to the public while others are normally held in private. There is space here to mention briefly only a few of the more important ones to which the media normally have access.

Since 1958 most tribunals have operated under the supervision **06.02** of the Council on Tribunals and the Council's Scottish Committee has direct supervision over the operation and procedure of about 25 tribunals. The Tribunals and Inquiries Act 1971 introduced important reforms in this area of law by providing for the possibility of appeal to the courts on points of law from the most important tribunals. The Act also provided that tribunals should, if requested, give reasons for their decisions. In its report "Tribunals Their Organisation and Independence" published in 1997 the Council on Tribunals stated:

> "Since tribunals are established to offer a form of redress, mostly in disputes between the citizen and the State, the principal hallmark of any tribunal is that it must be independent. . . . Equally importantly, it must be perceived as such. That means that the tribunal should be enabled to reach decisions according to the law without pressure from the body or person whose decision is being appealed, or anyone else."

06.03 Since most tribunals are set up under the authority of Parliament, a fair and accurate report of tribunal proceedings will normally be protected by qualified privilege. However, many tribunals are, as they are intended to be, informal, with the result that witnesses or parties are frequently allowed to make allegations which would not be allowed in a court of law. For example, hearsay evidence is admissible and it is not normal practice for people involved in tribunal hearings to be placed under oath.

06.04 The journalist should always consider whether some wild allegation made in tribunal proceedings would form part of a fair and accurate report, bearing in mind that the protection of privilege does not cover anything which is not of public concern and the publication of which is not for the public benefit.

06.05 It is not always easy to answer the question of whether a journalist can be in contempt of a tribunal. It depends on the tribunal. The Contempt of Court Act states that a court includes any tribunal or body exercising the power of the State. An industrial tribunal would probably come under this category. Judges in England have held that the purpose of a local valuation court is essentially administrative and not therefore protected by the law of contempt. However, a mental health review tribunal has been held to be a court. Lord Donaldson, the Master of the Rolls, stated that the power of mental health tribunals to affect a person's liberty was a classic example of the exercise of judicial power. (See Chapter 10.)

Employment tribunals

06.06 Employment tribunals (formerly known as industrial tribunals) are a regular source of copy. They deal with questions of redundancy, equal pay, sexual and racial discrimination at work, contracts of employment, trade unions and labour relations and health and safety at work. In particular, they deal with complaints by employees of unfair dismissal and have power to order the reinstatement of the employee or an award of compensation.

06.07 The tribunal normally consists of a legally qualified chairman and two other members selected from a panel with specialist knowledge or experience. The Employment Protection Act 1975 provided for the setting up of a special Employment Appeal Tribunal to hear appeals on questions of law from employment tribunals. This consists partly of nominated judges, at least one being from the Court of Session, and partly of members having special knowledge or experience of industrial relations.

Employment tribunals normally sit in public but can take **06.08** evidence in private in the interests of national security or to prevent a breach of the law, a breach of confidence or to stop information being revealed which would damage the interests of an employer.

Since the Trade Union Reform and Employment Rights Act **06.09** 1993, employment tribunals have had the power in cases involving allegations of sexual misconduct to make an order preventing the media from naming certain witnesses. The rule states that in sexual misconduct cases an order may be made "specifying the persons who may not be identified". The definition of sexual misconduct is contained in the Industrial Tribunals Act 1996 and includes sexual offences, sexual harassment and "other adverse conduct of whatever nature relating to sex". It also includes behaviour based on the sex of the person against whom the behaviour is directed or the sexual orientation of that person. The tribunal can make a restricted reporting order on its own initiative or on the application of a party to the case in question, including the party against whom the allegation is made. The order can be made at any time before the tribunal decision is promulgated—the date on which the notice announcing the tribunal's decision is sent to the parties. The order stays in force until promulgation of the decision, unless the tribunal has revoked it earlier.

The restrictions were apparently an attempt by the Department **06.10** of Employment to halt what it considered to be "sensationalist" reporting of tribunal cases which had a "sex angle". It felt that reports of that kind deterred people wanting to bring cases alleging sexual misconduct. Some newspaper editors took the view, however, that the power would be used to protect employers. In a case in England the Employment Appeal Tribunal has ruled that a "person" is not necessarily an individual but could include a company. In another English case the *East Anglian Daily Times* was banned from identifying a local council on the grounds that the local authority was a "person". The power was first exercised in Scotland in December 1993 in a case brought against Aberdeen Journals Limited by a woman employee. It is good practice for journalists to check with the tribunal clerk as to whether such a restricted reporting order has been made.

In 1995 the High Court in London ruled unlawful an attempt to **06.11** exclude the press and public from hearing "sensitive and salacious" evidence in a sexual harassment case. Mr Justice Brooke said that an industrial tribunal in Hampshire had exceeded its powers by seeking to exclude reporters from "sensitive" parts of the hearing.

The case involved a waitress who was accusing her employer of offering her £60 a week and a steak meal in exchange for sex. Upholding a challenge to the exclusion order by a news agency and Express Newspapers, Mr Justice Brooke ruled that the hearing should continue under the order already made banning identification of the parties involved in the case. The judge accepted that there was great anxiety about the case and a fear that witnesses would be inhibited from giving evidence if it was reported in a salacious way. Under the statutory rules of procedure, however, tribunal hearings had to be in public except in certain limited circumstances which did not apply in this case.

06.12 In 1997 the Court of Appeal in England warned that tribunals should not make orders restricting reporting automatically, even if both sides requested it. The court stressed: "The tribunal still has to consider whether it is in the public interest that the press should be deprived of a right to communicate information to the public if it becomes available. It is not a matter to be dealt with on the nod, so to speak." In 1999 the *Daily Record* succeeded in blocking an attempt to impose a restricted reporting order requested by both sides in a sexual harassment case due to be heard by an employment tribunal. The case involved a former topless model who claimed she was being sexually harassed by the owner of a cash-and-carry warehouse in Glasgow. The *Record* argued that the case was already in the public domain following a series of articles in the newspaper earlier in the year and claimed that both sides had willingly given information to the press. The tribunal chairman agreed that both parties had co-operated with or manipulated the press to a certain extent and took the view that in light of the publicity already surrounding the case a restricted reporting order would be "largely useless".

06.13 Employment tribunals can make broadly similar orders where they are dealing with complaints about unlawful discrimination in employment on the grounds of disability. Disability is defined in the Disability Discrimination Act 1995 as physical or mental impairment which has a substantial and long-term effect. A tribunal has power to make an order in a case it is likely to hear "any evidence of a medical or other intimate nature which might reasonably be assumed to be likely to cause significant embarrassment to the complainant if reported". The tribunal can make an order if the person making the complaint asks for one, or on its own initiative. The person or company against whom the complaint is being made cannot apply for an order (unlike in sexual cases) but the tribunal does have an unlimited discretion as to the people named in the order.

National Health Service tribunals

The National Health Service (Scotland) Act 1947 provided for the **06.14** setting up of a tribunal to investigate cases where it is claimed that a doctor, dentist, pharmacist or optician should be removed from the National Health Service list.

The tribunal consists of a legally qualified chairman and two **06.15** other members. If it decides that the practitioner should not be removed from the list, the matter is at an end. There is no appeal. If it decides for removal, the practitioner can appeal to the Secretary of State and has also an appeal to the Court of Session on a point of law. The tribunal meets in private unless the practitioner otherwise requests but its decisions are generally made public.

Transport

The Traffic Commissioner for Scotland is appointed by the Secre- **06.16** tary of State for Environment, Transport and the Regions. The commissioner has responsibility for licensing operators of heavy goods vehicles (HGVs) and of buses and coaches (public service vehicles or PSVs). He is also responsible for the registration of local bus services and considers the suitability of drivers who hold or apply for large goods vehicle (LGV) and passenger carrying vehicle (PCV) licences. Another of the commissioner's respon- sibilities is to deal with appeals against decisions of Scottish local authorities on taxi fares. He appoints the adjudicators who con- sider appeals against parking fines imposed by local authorities in Scotland.

The traffic commissioner may consider at a public inquiry **06.17** applications for operator licences or disciplinary action against operators, including the revocation of a licence. Appeals against decisions taken by the commissioner on the issue of or action against operator licences go to the Transport Tribunal. Appeals against decisions made by the commissioner on drivers' licences are heard by a sheriff.

The Transport Tribunal consists of a legally qualified president **06.18** and four other members experienced in finance, commerce or transport. Appeals on road haulage issues are heard by the Road Haulage Division of the Tribunal, which consists of the president and two of the members. The Transport Tribunal sits in public and sits in Scotland when considering a Scottish case. There is an appeal to the Court of Session on a point of law.

Lands Tribunal

06.19 The Lands Tribunal for Scotland, established in 1971, deals with disputes over compensation for the compulsory acquisition of land, with the variation and discharge of certain obligations contained in the titles to land, and with the valuation of land for certain tax purposes. It deals with appeals under the Land Registration (Scotland) Act 1979 and disputes concerning council house sales. Valuation Appeal Committees can refer complaints about non-domestic rating assessments. Parties may also voluntarily refer a matter to the tribunal as an arbiter. The tribunal consists of both lawyers and valuers, with a legally qualified president. Appeal on a point of law lies to the Court of Session. The tribunal sits in public, except when it is acting as arbiter under a voluntary reference, when it may, if requested, sit in private.

INQUIRIES

06.20 Inquiries into matters of national importance can take three forms—a tribunal of inquiry, a committee of inquiry or a royal commission.

Tribunals of inquiry

06.21 Tribunals of inquiry are appointed by Parliament to inquire into matters of "urgent public importance". Their findings are laid before Parliament and published by the Stationery Office. Tribunals of inquiry sit in public, unless they think privacy is in the public interest in view of the subject-matter of the inquiry or the nature of the evidence to be given. They can exclude the public for part only of the proceedings,

06.22 They have power to order witnesses to attend and give evidence. There is also power to refer cases of contempt of the tribunal to the High Court in England or Court of Session in Scotland for consideration and, if necessary, punishment. The threat of contempt proceedings was raised prior to the inquiry held by Lord Cullen into the massacre of children at Dunblane Primary School in March 1996. The Lord Advocate issued a note to editors expressing his concern at media "harassment" of potential witnesses. For a full discussion of the issues raised see Chapter 10.

Committees of inquiry

06.23 Either House of Parliament may set up a committee of inquiry to investigate any matter of public importance. The committee may include people who are not members of Parliament. Committees of inquiry were widely used at one time but have now been super-seded in practice by tribunals of inquiry. Their main disadvantage is that it is difficult to exclude the suspicion, or indeed the actual presence, of political bias.

Royal commissions

Royal commissions are often set up where the object is not so **06.24** much to find out facts as to consider a situation with a view to reform. There have been royal commissions on, among other things, the press, capital punishment, the law of marriage and divorce and legal services in Scotland, England and Wales. The Royal Commission on Criminal Justice in England and Wales under the Chairmanship of Lord Runciman reported in July 1993. Commissioners are appointed by the Crown and given power to summon witnesses and demand information. Their report is gener-ally published as a Command Paper.

In practice royal commissions often sit in public but may hear **06.25** evidence in private and may receive written evidence which need not be published. The bodies submitting such evidence may send it to the media for publication.

Local inquiries

Local inquiries are held, generally in public, under various statutes. **06.26** Planning inquiries are among the most common and deal with questions such as proposed motorway routes and the building of "superstore" developments. Local inquiries are also held when there are objections to a proposed Private Act of Parliament.

In Scotland inquiries are held by reporters who are often **06.27** practising advocates. The reporter makes his findings and recom-mendations to the appropriate Minister who then gives his decision.

Fatal accidents and sudden deaths inquiries

The law on these inquiries is contained in the Fatal Accidents and **06.28** Sudden Deaths Inquiry (Scotland) Act 1976. Public inquiries are held (a) in the case of fatal accidents at work, (b) in the case of deaths in legal custody (for example in a police station or prison) and (c) in any case in which the Lord Advocate considers that it is in the public interest that an inquiry should be held on the ground that the death was sudden, suspicious or unexplained, or occurred in circumstances such as to give rise to serious public concern.

Even in cases (a) and (b) an inquiry will not be held if the Lord **06.29** Advocate is satisfied that the circumstances of the death have been sufficiently established in criminal proceedings. The inquiry is held by the sheriff, without a jury. The fact that a person is examined as a witness at an inquiry does not prevent criminal proceedings later being taken against him but the sheriff's determination as to the cause of death and other relevant facts is not admissible in evidence in any judicial proceedings arising out of the death or accident.

06.30   The sheriff may ban publication in any newspaper or broadcast of any identifying particulars (including a picture) of any person under 17 involved in the inquiry in any way. (See Chapter 13.)

Shipping and railway inquiries

06.31   There is statutory provision for inquiries into deaths at sea, shipping casualties and railway accidents. These are again in no way trials or civil actions. Their sole purpose is to find out the facts.

06.32   Where there is a death on board any foreign-going British ship, an inquiry is held, generally in public, by a Department of Transport superintendent at the next port of call if in the United Kingdom or by a British consul if in a foreign port. If it is thought that death was caused by violence or other improper means the department can if need be take steps for bringing the offender or offenders to justice.

06.33   Department of Transport shipping casualty inquiries are held when a ship is lost, abandoned or materially damaged if at the time of the casualty the ship was registered in the United Kingdom or was in the United Kingdom or its territorial waters.

06.34   A preliminary inquiry may be made by a person appointed by the Secretary of State for the Environment Transport and the Regions. If a formal inquiry is considered desirable it is held by a court of summary jurisdiction (the sheriff court in Scotland) assisted in each case by one or more assessors who are experts in nautical engineering or other relevant matters. In practice shipping casualty inquiries in Scotland are held in public. The questions for the opinion of the court must be stated in open court. In practice the rest of the proceedings are also in public. After hearing the case the court must report to the Secretary of State. The court has power to cancel or suspend the certificate of a master, mate or engineer, if it finds that the casualty was due to his "wrongful act or default". Its decision on this matter must be announced in open court.

06.35   The Secretary of State for the Environment Transport and the Regions has power to order inquiries into train accidents. As with marine accidents, railway safety policy is an area reserved for the Westminster Parliament. Independent formal investigations into railway accidents are carried out by the Health and Safety Executive (HSE) using the powers available under the Health and Safety at Work Act 1974. For all serious railway accidents the Health and Safety Commission consults the Transport Secretary on the most suitable form of investigation.

Accident investigations by the HSE and HM Railway Inspecto- **06.36** rate are carried out under section 14 of the Health and Safety at Work Act. The Act also provides for the Health and Safety Commission to order a special investigation into any accident and to require a report to be published. The public are admitted to these inquiries but can be excluded if, for example, evidence would be likely to prejudice an accused at a subsequent criminal trial. HM Inspectors of Railways have wide-ranging powers under the Health and Safety at Work Act. They can compel witnesses to co-operate with their investigations and examine all the relevant evidence.The findings of Health and Safety Executive Investigations are made public in an annual report or in specific accident reports.Internal railway industry investigations are carried out by Railtrack with the train operating companies concerned and the results are passed on to the Health and Safety Executive to assist in their independent investigation.

The Ombudsman

On the model of the Scandinavian Ombudsman, the office of **06.37** Parliamentary Commissioner for Administration was created in 1967, to investigate complaints by the public against actions of the Executive or of bureaucratic incompetence giving rise to injustice. Appointed by Parliament, the commissioner is independent and his duty is to act impartially between government and the individual. A separate commissioner with particular and similar duties in relation to the administration of the National Health Service came into being in 1973. The journalist is most likely to be concerned, however, with the work of the Local Commissioners for Administration—one for England and Wales (created in 1974) and another for Scotland (1975). As in the case of the Parliamentary Commissioner, the local ombudsmen are entirely independent, their main function being to investigate complaints by members of the public who consider they have been victims of injustice as a result of maladministration by a local authority.

The majority of complaints are concerned with matters of **06.38** housing, planning and building control, education and environmental health. The commissioner issues an annual report, which is published, and his report on each individual complaint is also made public through the media. The identity of the complainant is not usually disclosed, but the local authority concerned is named.

06.39 Complaints are normally made in the first instance through a councillor, but in the event of his failure or refusal to pass it to the commissioner, the complainant may submit his grievance direct, provided it is made in writing. The commissioner will not usually look into any complaint which can be taken to a court, tribunal or Minister, unless for some reason the person who feels aggrieved is unable to follow that course. In carrying out his inquiries, the commissioner has the same powers to compel attendance of witnesses and insist on production of documents as has the Court of Session.

06.40 The procedure is informal and private, and he prepares a draft report for the chief executive of the local authority concerned, for comment. In this way any dispute on the facts is established before the formal report is prepared and published. If there is a finding of maladministration resulting in injustice the local authority has to indicate to the commissioner what action they propose to take to rectify matters. If he is not satisfied (as happens in a small minority of cases) he presents a further report.

06.41 The weakness of the system is that, apart from issuing his finding and pointing the direction in which he holds the remedy lies, the commissioner is powerless to do more. But the pressure his efforts bring to bear on defaulting authorities through the publicity his reports receive in the media should not be underestimated. His functions are seen as concerned with settling questions of principle rather than dealing with disputes involving issues of compensation. Even without powers of enforcement, his watchdog and investigative role for the most part achieves its essential purpose in producing a solution without recourse to law.

PROFESSIONAL DISCIPLINARY BODIES

06.42 There are various bodies set up under statute to supervise discipline in the professions. Broadly speaking, they all have power to strike members off the respective registers if (a) they have been convicted of a criminal offence or (b) they have been guilty of "infamous or disgraceful conduct in a professional respect". In the case of doctors, it used to be said that conduct of this type was usually one of the five As—adultery, abortion, alcohol, addiction or advertising.

06.43 The professional disciplinary bodies dealing with doctors, dentists, opticians and pharmacists should not be confused with the National Health Service tribunals dealt with earlier. The former are concerned with discipline in the profession, the latter with breach of the terms of employment in the National Health Service. The former can remove a name from the register of members of the profession, the latter only from the list of those members of the profession employed in the National Health Service.

The general rule is that proceedings of these bodies take place in **06.44** public, but that they may exclude the public in the interests of justice or for other special reason.

Professional disciplinary bodies fall into two classes, those from **06.45** which appeal is to the Privy Council and those from which appeal is to the Court of Session. Reports should always state that the name will be removed "failing the entry of an appeal to the Privy Council within twenty-eight days" or as the case may be. Even where the name is removed it is generally possible for the person concerned to apply after a suitable period for restoration to the register.

Bodies from which appeal lies to the Privy Council within 28 **06.46** days are the Disciplinary Committee of the General Medical Council, the Disciplinary Committee of the General Dental Council, the Disciplinary Committee of the Council of the Royal College of Veterinary Surgeons and the Disciplinary Committee of the General Optical Council all of which generally meet in public.

Bodies from which appeal lies to the Court of Session or the **06.47** High Court in England within three months are the Statutory Committee of the Pharmaceutical Society which must open in public and announce its decisions in public but can if it thinks fit hold any other part of the hearing in private, and the Disciplinary Committee of the Architects Registration Council which appears to have discretion as to meeting in public.

The Scottish Solicitors' Discipline Tribunal can strike a solicitor **06.48** off the roll, suspend him and, in cases of professional misconduct, fine him up to £10,000. There is a right of appeal to the Court of Session within 21 days.

The tribunal meets in private but under the Law Reform **06.49** (Miscellaneous Provisions) (Scotland) Act 1990 the decision, including the name of the solicitor, is made public whether or not professional misconduct is established. The only exception is where, in the opinion of the tribunal, publicity might damage the interests of someone other than the solicitor against whom the complaint was made, his partners or their families. The Law Society must keep available for inspection without payment a copy of every decision of the tribunal.

The tribunal is an independent body, not an offshoot of the Law **06.50** Society of Scotland. The majority of its members at any hearing are solicitors but lay members make up not less than 25 per cent of the numbers. Members of the tribunal are appointed by the Lord President of the Court of Session. Complaints are prosecuted by fiscals, who are private practitioners independent of the Council of the Law Society. Although the majority of complaints are brought by the society, private prosecutions may be taken.

06.51 In July 1991, Scotland's first Legal Services Ombudsman was appointed. The appointment was made under the Law Reform (Miscellaneous Provisions) (Scotland) Act 1990, with the intention of strengthening procedures for dealing with complaints against members of the legal profession.

06.52 The new post replaced that of the Lay Observer but the Ombudsman was given a wider remit. His basic function is to consider the way that professional bodies providing legal services in Scotland handle complaints against their members. The bodies include the Law Society of Scotland and the Faculty of Advocates.

06.53 The work of the Ombudsman includes examining written complaints from, or on behalf of, members of the public who are unhappy with the way in which a professional body has dealt with a complaint about alleged professional misconduct or inadequate legal work. The Legal Services Ombudsman produces an annual report which is laid before Parliament.

06.54 Disciplinary measures against members of the Scottish Bar are normally taken in private by the Dean of the Faculty of Advocates. Rarely, a disciplinary body chaired by a retired judge is used in serious cases. Robert Henderson, Q.C., was disciplined in 1993 for releasing confidential information from a client to others. In 1994 Raymond Fraser was fined for bringing the Bar into disrepute because of flippant remarks he made to the media after his conviction for drink driving at Haddington Sheriff Court. He was also suspended from practice for a time.

06.55 In 1999 the Dean of the Faculty, Mr Nigel Emslie, Q.C., instigated a complaint against Mr Donald Findlay, Q.C., one of Scotland's leading criminal defence counsel, alleging "serious and reprehensible conduct bringing the Faculty into disrepute". Mr Findlay had resigned as vice-chairman of Rangers Football Club after being captured on video singing anti-Catholic songs at a celebratory social event after the Scottish Cup Final. He accepted that his behaviour amounted to professional misconduct and was fined £3,000 by the Dean of Faculty. Mr Findlay had earlier been given a formal written censure by the Dean for making critical remarks to a jury after they took just half an hour to find his client guilty of murder after a trial at the High Court in Glasgow. The Dean ruled that this amounted to professional misconduct.

06.56 In another case in 1999 the Dean rejected a complaint that a member of the bar, Mr Jock Thomson, had brought the Faculty into disrepute over a jocular remark he had made to a coloured macer at a Christmas party. The macer himself did not regard the remarks as racially offensive and was not the source of the complaint. The Dean ruled that although the remarks were clearly inappropriate, he was satisfied that Mr Thomson did not harbour any racist attitudes and that the remarks fell "well short" of professional misconduct.

Appointment and removal of judges

The Scotland Act 1998 made changes in the way that High Court **06.57** and Court of Session judges are appointed. Section 95 of the Act provided that the Prime Minister would continue to recommend to the Queen the appointment of the Lord President and Lord Justice-Clerk. Now, however, the name has to be nominated by the First Minister of the Scottish Executive who in turn consults the Lord President and Lord Justice-Clerk (unless either office is vacant). As far as other High Court judges, sheriffs principal and permanent sheriffs are concerned, the First Minister recommends a name to Her Majesty after consulting with the Lord President.

The procedure for removing judges of the High Court and Court **06.58** of Session judges was uncertain and became a matter of controversy during the passage of the Scotland Bill through the House of Lords towards the end of 1998. The Bill contained a proposal to allow the removal of High Court and Court of Session judges if two thirds of the 129 Members of the Scottish Parliament voted in favour. This proposal was attacked by Lord McCluskey, Scotland's longest serving judge at the time. He argued that putting the fate of judges in the hands of politicians was a threat to the independence of the Bench. His basic complaint was that it would become possible for a judge to be removed on the basis of alleged rather than proven unfitness for office. Lord McCluskey's concerns found strong support in the House of Lords and the Government agreed to amend its proposals.

Section 95 of the Scotland Act provides that a judge of the Court **06.59** of Session and the Scottish Land Court may be removed from office only by the Queen on the recommendation of the First Minister following a motion approved by the Scottish Parliament. The Act makes provision for a tribunal of three chaired by a member of the Judicial Committee of the Privy Council to investigate and report on whether a Court of Session judge is unfit for office because of inability, neglect of duty or misbehaviour and for the report to be laid before the Scottish Parliament. The First Minister can make a recommendation to remove a judge only if he has received a written report from the tribunal concluding that the judge in question is unfit for office. The report must give reasons for its decision. If the judge in question is the Lord President or Lord Justice-Clerk, the First Minister has to consult the Prime Minister.

06.60 Under the Sheriff Courts (Scotland) Act 1971, the Lord President of the Court of Session and the Lord Justice-Clerk have power, either on their own initiative or at the request of the First Minister, to carry out a joint investigation into the fitness for office of any sheriff principal or sheriff. A sheriff may be deemed unfit for office by reason of inability, neglect of duty or misbehaviour. Two sheriffs in Scotland have been removed from office under this power. Hamilton Sheriff Peter Thomson's offence was to publish a pamphlet advocating the holding of a plebiscite on Scottish home rule. This was held to amount to political activity incompatible with the holding of judicial office and he was removed in 1977.

06.61 In 1992 Highland Sheriff Ewen Stewart was held to be unfit for office because of a "character defect" which meant he was completely unable to confine his attention to the evidence led in court and decide cases on that basis. Sheriff Stewart's appeal against his dismissal was rejected. His argument that "inability" meant physical incapacity and did not involve consideration of a sheriff's competence was rejected. Before the passing of the Scotland Act an order for the removal of a sheriff had to be laid before both Houses of Parliament at Westminster. Now the order is laid before the Scottish Parliament.

06.62 In England, High Court judges under the Act of Settlement hold office during good behaviour, subject to removal on an address to both Houses of Parliament. The Lord Chancellor, a political appointee, is not subject to this procedure. He has authority to remove a circuit judge on grounds of incapacity or misbehaviour.

KEY POINTS

06.63 Tribunals are designed to achieve speedier and less formal justice than courts. They deal with a wide range of social issues, generally sit in public, and a fair and accurate report of proceedings is normally protected by qualified privilege. However, care must be taken with wild allegations that would not be allowed in a court of law. Privilege protects only matters of public concern, publication of which is for the public benefit. A journalist can be in contempt of a tribunal which is exercising the judicial power of the State (Contempt of Court Act 1981). Fatal Accident Inquiries are held by a sheriff sitting without a jury. He has power to ban identification of anyone under the age of 17 involved in the inquiry. The

1998 Scotland Act introduced a new procedure for the removal from office of a High Court or Court of Session judge if the judge is deemed unfit for office because of inability, neglect of duty or misbehaviour.

CHAPTER 7

THE COURT REPORTER

RIGHTS AND RESPONSIBILITIES

07.01 The aim here is to present a guide, for quick reference, to cover the situations most likely to cause difficulty or raise doubts for journalists reporting the courts in Scotland. Over the years, there have been statements by judges on many important aspects of the court reporter's work, but these are only pieces in the jigsaw. Decisions of the courts and Acts of Parliament leave unanswered vast areas of difficult and dangerous territory. Common sense is as important as a detailed knowledge of the law.

07.02 Few members of the public have the time to attend and see for themselves that justice is being done. In the civil courts in particular—including the Court of Session, the supreme civil court in the land—the public are often entirely absent. The desire to ensure that justice is not only done, but seen to be done, can hardly be achieved if the only people present in court are counsel and solicitors and the judges themselves.

07.03 Perhaps no one has expressed the role of the court reporter and the need for open justice better than the distinguished English judge, Lord Denning. He said it was fundamental that proceedings in courts of justice should be public unless there were overwhelming reasons to the contrary. A judge, when he tried a case, was himself on trial to see that he behaved properly, conducted the case properly, and that his reasons, when given, justified themselves at the bar of public opinion. How could that be done if the case was heard in private?

07.04 Lord Denning added: "The great principle should always be that cases must be heard in open court when . . . reporters are there to represent the public and there to see everything is rightly done. They are indeed, in this respect, the watchdogs of justice, but a free press has its responsibilities. Its freedom must not be abused".

07.05 Where so much is at stake—not only the reputations of people named in the journalist's reports but possibly also the journalist's

80

own career—the court reporter must have a sound grasp of what information can be safely used. This is preferable to muddling along, hoping to pick up bits of advice from court officials or lawyers. The reporter will find it difficult to insist on his rights if he does not know what they are.

Fairness and accuracy

The essential ingredient of a court report is that it is fair and **07.06** accurate. This is important not just from the point of view of fair play to everyone involved in the case—parties, witnesses, counsel and the judge. A fair and accurate report of proceedings held in open court is also protected from a defamation action even though it contains defamatory information. It also cannot be a contempt of court.

The reporter must not fall into the trap of believing that as long **07.07** as his report is accurate it is safe—that is, protected by privilege. It must also be fair. Fairness implies not only that there should be a proper balance between the claims of both sides, but also that there should be no unfair allegations about third parties who are not present or represented in court and therefore have no opportunity to reply.

The classic example is the plea in mitigation made by counsel on **07.08** behalf of an accused person, based on information from the accused. Counsel has no opportunity himself to check the truth of these statements, and it is part of his duty to his client and to the court to bring them out. One example is what has become known as the Portsmouth defence, where the accused alleges that the victim of an assault made a homosexual advance. If there is a guilty plea the victim may not be in court to and find out about the allegation for the first time when he sees his name in the paper. Where statements of this kind form an essential part of the story and must be published, it should be made clear in any report that they are allegations and not necessarily statements of fact.

Denials made out of court by someone offended by the plea, or **07.09** demands for a right to reply, must be treated with great care since publication of these would not be protected by privilege.

Although Scotland has so far been spared legislation on the **07.10** subject, the Criminal Procedure and Investigations Act 1996 (s. 56) was introduced in England in an effort to ban the reporting of derogatory claims made in pleas in mitigation. The Act would of course apply to Scottish newspapers and broadcasters when they are reporting English proceedings. Section 58(4) states that a banning order may be imposed where there are substantial grounds for believing: (1) that an assertion forming part of the speech or submission is derogatory to a person's character (for instance because it suggests that his conduct is or has been criminal, immoral or improper) and (2) that the assertion is false or that the facts asserted are irrelevant to the sentence. The power to ban reporting does not cover derogatory statements made in the prosecutor's statement and an order cannot be made if the claim made during mitigation was previously made at the trial at which the accused was convicted.

07.11   The *News and Star* in Carlisle was the first newspaper to run into problems with the new power. A reporter from the newspaper was attending a trial at Carlisle Magistrates' Court in July 1997. The accused, Alison Laird, admitted a charge of assault and was jailed for four months. The magistrates consulted the clerk of court and announced that the restrictions in section 58 applied, preventing any derogatory remarks about the victim. At the hearing the court had been told that James Murphy, the victim of the assault, had gatecrashed a funeral, claiming to be the dead man's long lost father. The prosecutor told the court that a witness saw Miss Laird, the dead man's cousin, throw the contents of her half-pint glass at Mr Murphy before smashing the glass over his head. He was left bleeding from a head wound. The plea in mitigation was to the effect that Mr Murphy's claim to be the father of the deceased had annoyed the funeral party. Mr Murphy was said to be "ferociously drunk" and to have suggested to Miss Laird in vulgar terms what he would do to her sexually.

07.12   In a note to the magistrates who imposed the ban, the *News and Star* reporter argued that it was unfair that the woman who had been jailed had been denied her right to a public airing of her side of the story, which was that she had struck the victim after he had claimed falsely in public that she had agreed to have sexual intercourse with him. In the event, the ban in this case was lifted after it was discovered that the offence was committed three months before the Act came into force. However, the potential problems caused by the Act are all too obvious.

07.13   The Guild of Editors pointed out that the banning power would be available in all cases where a guilty plea had been tendered. Its effect would be to prevent the public from receiving full information as to the reasons why a sentence was passed, an area of legitimate public interest. Regional newspaper editors suggested that the proper balance between open justice and protection of the individual against whom the derogatory statement was made would be better achieved by allowing the individual the opportunity to make a statement in open court at the conclusion of the proceedings. This would allow full, fair, accurate and contemporaneous reporting of the case while permitting a form of public redress to the individual which could be safely reported without the fear of proceedings for libel or contempt. However, this proposal was rejected by the Government in the House of Lords, apparently on the view that editors could not be relied upon to give adequate prominence to rebuttals.

The great majority of civil cases are argued in the presence of **07.14** both parties and their lawyers. Normally, claims made by one side against the other will be answered, and the reporter has the opportunity (which he will miss at his peril) of giving the reply where one is given. But if one side makes an allegation in the presence of the other, and there is no reply, the newspaper is as free to publish the allegation as if a reply had been made. The point is that there was an opportunity to reply which was not taken. In that situation, justice would be on the side of the journalist, provided, of course, that the report was fair and accurate. It would probably be appropriate to indicate in the report that no reply was made.

Balance

A court report should also include more than information which **07.15** makes it a good hard news story, amusing or out of the ordinary. It should leave out nothing which is essential for a balanced report, viewed from the position of both sides in the case. To achieve this balance, the court reporter may have to include in his story dull or uninteresting information. For example, it may be important to say in an interim interdict hearing that one side was not represented in court, otherwise it may look as if he has no defence to put forward.

The reporter should always remember, however, the important **07.16** distinction between details which could lead to a court action and information which merely causes annoyance or irritation. Many complaints about press reports have no merit, and the journalist has to be ready for, and to recognise, the groundless protest when it arises. He should also remain detached, because if he falls into the trap of feeling sympathy for one side he will be in danger of causing prejudice to the other.

Depending on the kind of organisation the reporter works for, **07.17** he may not always find it necessary to report every piece of information the law allows. As a matter of taste rather than law it might, for example, be preferable in certain circumstances not to identify someone who was insane or mentally defective. When the reporter does decide to omit from a report information which would normally be regarded as newsworthy, whether the name of a party or an allegation, he must be able to justify his decision.

Otherwise, he may be accused of suppressing information without good reason.

07.18 If a reporter is approached by someone involved in a court case with the suggestion that details of the case should not be published, he should inform the news editor. In the meantime the report should be written up as if no approach had been made. The duty to write the story is the reporter's, that of deciding whether to publish it is the editor's. Requests by interested parties to publish an explanation or correction in a case before the court should be treated with great caution. This might suit the interests of one side but interfere with those of the other. It would also not be privileged if it was not part of the court proceedings.

Closed doors

07.19 While proceedings are sometimes held behind closed doors in special circumstances, it is one of the fundamental principles of the Scottish system that the judicial process is public. It is only in this way that justice may not only be done but may be seen to be done. Two Acts of the Scottish Parliament—the Evidence Act 1686 and the Court of Session Act 1693—are still in operation. The first of these lays down that there shall be "publication of the testimonies of witnesses". The second provides that "in all tyme comeing all bills, reports, debates, probations, and others relating to processes shall be considered, reasoned, advised, and voted by the Lords of Session with open doors . . . but with this restriction, that in some speciall cases the said Lords shall be allowed to cause remove all persons except the parties and their procurators".

07.20 The types of "special cases" that are in practice taken in private are few. In criminal law, for example, bail appeals, although they may be heard in court, are usually heard in chambers because the judge deciding whether to grant bail may be given information such as details of previous convictions. Since such applications precede trial, it is in the interests of justice that details of this kind are not made public at this stage. Appearances by an accused on petition in solemn criminal cases, both first appearance and the subsequent full committal diet, are held in private.

07.21 Cases brought in the sheriff court or the Court of Session involving the adoption of children are, with rare exceptions, heard in private. Referral hearings before a sheriff are held in the sheriff's chambers. The press can attend but the sheriff has a discretion to refuse to admit the media if he thinks it proper.

07.22 Actions of declarator of nullity of marriage sometimes involve evidence which can only suitably be given in private, since it would often be difficult to persuade witnesses to speak freely on matters such as sexual perversion or impotency in the presence of spectators.

The doors may be closed in any case on the order of the judge **07.23** for part of the hearing where it appears to him that this is necessary for the doing of justice, but it should not be a decision which is reached lightly. He may decide on this for reasons other than the particular character of the evidence, for example, where he has reason to anticipate a demonstration in the courtroom which might disrupt the proceedings, or any conduct among members of the public which would distract the attention of the court, counsel or witnesses. It is not usual for the media to be excluded in cases of this kind.

The decision to close the doors, where not provided by statute, is **07.24** a matter for the discretion of the judge, and some judges are likely to exercise it more freely than others.

The media are also admitted to sittings of the Court of Session, **07.25** when it sits during court holidays. The judge and counsel do not normally wear wig and gown, and the court deals with urgent business, often custody and access cases.

Summary trial procedure

There is a kind of short-cut procedure in the Court of Session **07.26** known as summary trial provided for by section 10 of the Administration of Justice (Scotland) Act 1933, by which parties, by agreement, may bring their dispute before a Court of Session judge of their choice for a speedy decision, and without right of appeal. In the great majority of such cases the procedure, so far as reporters are concerned, does not differ significantly from that of a proof under the ordinary procedure—evidence and counsel's speeches are heard, and the judge delivers a judgment (which, however, is final).

In 1967, however, a petition was brought before the court to **07.27** determine who was the heir male of the late Lord Sempill, and the procedure appears to have been unique in that it took place entirely in secret. The decision of the case depended on the sex of Ewan Forbes-Sempill, who was registered in infancy as female but underwent a change of sex as an adult. The petition, which was brought under the section 10 procedure, was heard by Lord Hunter in a solicitor's office, no decision or judgment was ever issued, and no press report of the case was therefore possible.

Following press reaction to this unusual method of avoiding **07.28** publicity, the Lord Advocate said that under section 10(3) of the 1933 Act the course taken by the court was justified in view of the "purely private" nature of the matter being dealt with. It seemed to him that somewhat similar considerations to those operating in nullity cases justified the secret hearing. The view of Lord Kilbrandon, then Chairman of the Scottish Law Commission, was that section 10 was intended to provide a kind of judicial arbitration, whereby people could take their private disputes before the judge they had selected and get a final decision. The judge's opinion need not be published, any more than the deliverance of an arbiter. The Commission, he said, saw no reason to amend section 10.

07.29 Subsection 3 of section 10 provides that the judge may, on cause shown, hear and determine in chambers any dispute or question submitted for his decision under the section. Subsection 8 lays down, however, that the section shall apply to any dispute or question "not affecting the status of any person". In other words, actions of divorce or nullity of marriage cannot be dealt with by summary trial procedure. Perhaps the most remarkable aspect of the procedure, as applied to the Forbes-Sempill case, is that the choice (with the judge's consent) lies with the parties themselves. It is a device for maintaining secrecy in judicial proceedings which one would like to believe would be rarely if ever invoked since it is so directly in conflict with the principle that justice should be seen to be done.

07.30 The public are normally excluded from court when the alleged victim gives her evidence in a rape trial. Reporters are allowed to stay, on the understanding that they do not disclose the woman's identity.

07.31 Section 11 of the Contempt of Court Act 1981 gives the courts power to direct non-publication of a name "or other matter" which it was already able to allow to be withheld from the public during the hearing of a case. This extension of courts' powers is more fully dealt with in Chapter 10.

The reporter's privilege

07.32 While the privilege of reporting judicial proceedings in England is provided by statute, the right in Scotland originated in the common law. Lord President Inglis, put it this way in the case of *Richardson v. Wilson* in 1879.

> "The publication by a newspaper of what takes place in court at the hearing of any case is undoubtedly lawful; and if it be reported in a fair and faithful manner the publisher is not responsible though the report contains statements or details of evidence affecting the character of either of the parties or of other persons; and what takes place in open court falls under the same rule, though it may be either before or after the

proper hearing of the cause. The principle on which this rule is founded seems to be that as courts of justice are open to the public, anything that takes place before a judge or judges is thereby necessarily and legitimately made public, and being once made legitimately public property may be re-published without inferring any responsibility".

But, as was pointed out in the case of *Macleod v. Lewis Justices* in 07.33 1892, it is only what takes place in open court which may safely be published. Examples will be given later of situations in which it is not always entirely safe even to publish everything that passes in open court. Following the case of *Cunningham* in 1986, reporters may be able to claim qualified privilege to publish passages from a summons founded on in open court although these have not actually been read out in court.

Lord Clyde held that a summons founded on in this way is made 07.34 public—a ruling of importance to court reporters as it may be applied also to documents other than the summons, although not, as the judge observed, to court productions. An important distinction between this case and *Richardson*, quoted above, is that in *Richardson* the action had appeared on the calling list but there had been no hearing of any kind in court.

The importance of reporters keeping their notebooks for a 07.35 reasonable period is of particular importance in court cases. What is a reasonable period will vary with the circumstances, but experience suggests that one year would not be excessive.

In one Court of Session case, a newspaper report quoted counsel 07.36 as stating in court that a director of a company had been trying to sell the company's assets. Eleven months after the item appeared, a director of the company, although he was not named in the report, apparently recognised himself as the person referred to in it. He wrote to the editor of the paper, alleging he had been defamed and threatening to sue the paper for damages. Fortunately the reporter was able to find his notes, which showed that the statement complained of was indeed made by counsel in court and was accurately reported. Nothing more was heard of the matter.

A report based upon a statement made in court which is 07.37 privileged may lose that protection if it is not clearly attributed to the speaker. If a statement from court proceedings is quoted in a press report without attribution, the newspaper itself will bear responsibility for the statement, and if it should prove to be actionable the defence of privilege will not be open to the paper.

The *Daily Record* reported a bigamy case in Edinburgh Sheriff 07.38 Court in 1971 under the headline "Unlucky bigamist gets nine months". The report opened with the bare statement: "Robert

Hogg was unlucky in his two attempts at a happy marriage. His first wife ran off with another man—and his second had a child to another man". The statement that Mr Hogg's second wife had had a child to another man was based on a submission made in court by Mr Hogg's solicitor, but it was denied by the woman in question, who sued the *Daily Record* for £2,000, alleging she had been defamed.

07.39 Her complaint was that the passage in the report stood by itself as a statement of fact by the paper and was not attributed to anyone taking part in the sheriff court proceedings.

07.40 At a legal debate in the Court of Session, Lord Brand rejected an argument by counsel for the paper that the passage, if read by itself, did not identify the woman. Sending the case for trial by jury, the judge said it was one thing for a solicitor to say in court on his client's instructions that the woman had had an illegitimate child, but it was quite another matter for a newspaper to make such a claim on its own authority. In his view, the bald statement that the pursuer had a child to another man was, on the face of it, defamatory.

07.41 He accepted that the remainder of the paper's report, duly attributing to Mr Hogg's solicitor in court the statement that the pursuer had had an illegitimate child, was privileged, but said it would be for the jury to decide whether the opening passage was a fair and accurate summary of the fuller, privileged passage which followed.

07.42 The case in fact never went to trial, but Lord Brand's judgment provides a useful warning on the care to be taken in publishing possibly defamatory statements without attributing them.

Party litigants

07.43 Special care has to be taken in reporting statements made by people conducting their own case, either because they do not wish or can not afford to be represented by counsel. This is always a very difficult situation for a layman, and the judges invariably are less strict in enforcing rules of procedure than they would be with a lawyer.

07.44 The difficulty is that party litigants tend to bring in irrelevant statements and sweeping allegations which have no direct bearing on the questions before the court. The reporter may have to exclude these from his report. Where these statements or allegations implicate third parties who have not the opportunity to reply, or are patently irrelevant to the issue under consideration, they will form no part of a fair and balanced report of the proceedings.

07.45 The need to preserve a fair balance between prosecution and defence in criminal cases and between the opposing sides in a civil action, is especially important for evening papers. Where the report is incomplete in one edition and presents an unbalanced picture of the case, particular care should be taken to ensure that the balance is restored in later editions or in the issues of the following day. Statements rebutting earlier assertions by the other side must be reported.

A proper balance between opposing sides does not necessarily 07.46 require the publication of equal space to each. A lengthy argument advanced by one party may be completely demolished in a single sentence.

The reporter who has some background knowledge of a case 07.47 from an outside source should remember that if that information is included in his report, it will not be protected by privilege.

Interpretation

The court reporter has to be especially careful in interpreting, 07.48 condensing, or translating into lay language passages from legal proceedings. It may be relatively simple to copy accurately and reproduce what a speaker says, but the exact reproduction of language used in court would rarely be acceptable, particularly for the tabloid press or for radio and television reports.

In "translating" legalese into lay terms the reporter must first be 07.49 certain that he understands the meaning of the information he is dealing with and uses precisely the words which will convey the idea intended by the speaker. For example, a trust disposition and settlement can simply be called a will, and someone who alienates his heritable subjects can normally be said to be selling his house. There are many other expressions, more or less baffling to the ordinary mortal, that crop up from time to time, and the most common are included in the glossary at the end of this book.

Apart from offering a kind of translation of legal jargon, the 07.50 reporter will often find it necessary to condense the normal verbosity of legal terminology, especially when his report is based upon written pleadings in a civil action. Written judgments of the court may have to be condensed from 40 or 50 or even 100 or more pages to a few hundred words or less before they appear in print or on a news bulletin. Again, the reporter must understand what the judge's decision means and the reasoning by which he reached it.

Where the judge has had to wrestle with difficult legal questions, 07.51 perhaps involving lengthy citation of cases, the reporter's job will vary according to the kind of organisation for which he works. In many cases the paper will be satisfied with the bare result, but other newspapers will wish to give their readers some sort of explanation of the reasoning which lies behind a decision. For the bald decision in a case may sometimes seem, on the face of it, unjust or unfair. A report of the reasoning which led to the decision may explain the apparent anomaly.

07.52   Journalists should also remember that they are subject to the ordinary law of the land and can be prosecuted for offences such as breach of the peace, assault and harassment. In 1998 a reporter and photographer from the *Daily Record* stood trial at Edinburgh Sheriff Court for breach of the peace. The reporter was fined £1,500 and the charge against the photographer was found not proven.

07.53   Both men had denied committing a breach of the peace by pursuing and photographing two women, uttering threats and placing them in a state of fear and alarm. The reporter was also alleged to have placed his foot in the door of a house and prevented it from closing. One of the women was due to be married to a man called Archie McCafferty, who had been deported from Australia to Scotland after serving 25 years for multiple murder. The case aroused tremendous interest in the media who referred to McCafferty as "Mad Dog". Sheriff Peter McNeill, Q.C. at Edinburgh was told that the *Record* reporter thought he had arranged an exclusive interview with McCafferty and his pregnant fiancée. The reporter and photographer turned up for the interview but McCafferty and his girlfriend did not.

07.54   According to the *Record* reporter, when he tracked down the fiancée to her friend's house he called through the letterbox, asking why the interview had not taken place. He denied putting his foot through the door, shouting or swearing or threatening the women. The women claimed that the reporter and photographer had come "storming up" and chased them to the door. They alleged that the reporter had been "very aggressive and intimidating" and had put his foot in the door to prevent it closing. The procurator fiscal submitted that the behaviour of the journalists had gone beyond their legitimate duties as reporter and photographer and that it had been made clear to them that their presence was unwanted. Defence solicitors argued that both journalists had been carrying out their lawful business and that the Crown had failed to prove that the taking of pictures had caused fear and alarm.

KEY POINTS

07.55 It is a fundamental principle of Scots law that unless there are exceptional circumstances the courts sit in public. A fair and accurate report of legal proceedings held in public is protected against defamation or contempt of court actions. This privilege may be lost if a statement that would be defamatory outside the courtroom is not clearly attributed to the person who makes it. Special types of cases, such as adoption hearings are conducted behind closed doors. By agreement, the media does not name victims in rape cases.

Special care is also needed in reporting statements of people **07.56** conducting their own cases. It can also be highly dangerous to mix up background knowledge with what is said in court. Journalists are subject to the ordinary law of the land and can be prosecuted for offences such as assault and breach of the peace.

CHAPTER 8

ACCESS TO INFORMATION

COURT DOCUMENTS

08.01 In reporting the civil courts one of the most common problems for the journalist is gaining access to documents. In principle, the practice in the sheriff courts should be the same as in the Court of Session; although relatively few civil cases appear to be reported from the sheriff courts, which is unfortunate since this may be a rich source of news. The lack of reporting may also make it more difficult to persuade court staff to allow access to documents when an important story does come along.

08.02 The most important documents which a reporter may have to refer to before he can write a fair, accurate and balanced report of a case at its various stages are the Calling List, Court Rolls, petitions, records and judgments. The list is not exhaustive because a wide variety of other documents may come, with the permission of lawyers or court authorities, into the hands of reporters. These include copies of wills, contracts, letters and minutes. In general these may be seen and quoted only where their contents have been referred to and seen by the judge in open court, and the reporter wants to see them only to check the accuracy of his notes.

The Rolls of Court

08.03 The Rolls of Court show the allocation of civil and criminal cases in the Court of Session and High Court of Justiciary in Edinburgh. There is (1) a "long" Roll published at the beginning of each Session (usually in September, January, and April) showing in advance the dates for hearings on the evidence such as proofs and jury trials, and procedure rolls (legal hearings); (2) a weekly Roll, showing next week's business in the Supreme Court; and (3) a daily Roll, showing tomorrow's business in the Supreme Court. The first part of the daily Roll is the Calling List.

Calling List

The Calling List is published daily during the sittings of the Court **08.04** of Session and on certain dates during vacations, and is an official document. It is usually the first public notice of a court action being raised, and a copy is displayed on the wall in Parliament House. It is now available, along with the rest of the Rolls of Court, on the Scottish Courts website (http://www.scotcourts. gov.UK/index1.htm). It contains intimation of actions just raised, and is worth careful daily scrutiny. Each entry contains only the names and addresses of the parties to the action, and the names of the solicitors acting for the pursuer.

The Contempt of Court Act 1981 relaxed restrictions on publica- **08.05** tion of reports at the Calling List stage (see Chapter 10) and has made it possible to prepare a report based on information in the Calling List without falling foul of the contempt law.

At this stage, however, there is still the risk of defamation and **08.06** unlike coverage of a case being heard in open court, a report based on inquiries at the Calling List stage will not have the protection of privilege. And, since any report at this early stage may involve access to particulars contained in the summons, special care is needed to avoid publishing defamatory allegations from that source.

The reporter in the Court of Session can use the Calling List as a **08.07** guide to the cases likely to be available for reporting in the future. It is important to keep track of the major news stories of the day because many of them end up in the Court of Session and the first sign may be in the Calling List.

A major court action which first came to light in the calling list **08.08** involved an AIDS virus victim who was suing the Blood Transfusion Service, the Secretary of State for Scotland and a health board over his condition.

Summons

The appearance of a case on the Calling List is the public signal **08.09** that the pursuer in the action has served a summons on the defender. The journalist must treat a summons with great caution, particularly before a hearing of any kind has taken place in court.

In the case of *Richardson v. Wilson* (1879) the Court of Session **08.10** rejected the argument that once an action appeared on the Calling List the contents of the summons could be made public. The court said that would not be a report of judicial proceedings, but of the contents of a writ which were at the time unknown even to the court.

08.11   The *Edinburgh Evening News* published a passage from a summons which had appeared on the Calling List. No further step in procedure had taken place and a party mentioned in the report sued the paper for libel. The newspaper argued, unsuccessfully, that the paragraph which was published was a bona fide and correct report of the claims in an action called and pending in the Court of Session and they were entitled to publish it. The pursuer in the libel proceedings maintained that statements contained in the report (reproduced from the summons) were untrue and libellous. The report was not said to be in any way unfair as a representation of the statements in the summons.

08.12   Lord Craighill said the principle, stated generally, was that what might be seen and heard in court could be published. The courts were open and accessible to all. It did not follow, however, that every step of process in a cause from the calling to the final judgment was an occasion on which everything which could be discovered from an examination of the process might be published to the world. Were this so, the world would get to know the contents of writs and productions before the court.

08.13   The public, he said, had no right and no interest to know more than could be learned by attendance in court. The public could not demand to know, and newspaper reporters who catered for the public could not insist on knowing, what was not intended to be published merely because a writ or production had been made the subject of judicial procedure. The right and the interest of the public were concerned not with the statements which one party in a cause might make against his adversary, but with the proceedings in open court, by which justice was to be administered.

08.14   The *Edinburgh Evening News* appealed unsuccessfully to the First Division. Lord President Inglis said the duty of the clerk in charge of the process was plainly not to part with the summons or give access to it, except to the parties to the case or their agents. If they made the contents of the summons public at this stage, they would undeniably be subject to an action of damages if it contained defamatory statements. If the agent of either party were guilty of publishing it in any way he would also be answerable to the court for his misconduct. At the stage where no defences had been lodged, no one except the parties or their agents could lawfully obtain access to the summons.

08.15   In the much more recent case of *Cunningham v. The Scotsman Publications*, 1987, where there had been a hearing in open court and the contents of the summons were known to the judge, Lord Clyde decided that reporters might be able to claim the protection of qualified privilege in quoting from the summons although the summons had not been read out.

Mr David Cunningham, a former advocate, sued *The Scotsman*, **08.16**
Dundee Courier & Advertiser and the *Herald* for £600,000 damages,
alleging they had defamed him in reporting a hearing in the Court
of Session in 1984, when interim interdict was granted in his
absence to ban him from dealing in certain shares. (That action
was later abandoned.)

Mr Cunningham complained that the reports contained passages **08.17**
from the summons which had not been read out in court and were
thus not covered by privilege. He argued that privilege protected
only reports of the factual details of what went on in court—the
identity of the parties and the judge, the nature of the proceedings,
what was said by counsel and the judge and what the court actually
did. Putting a document before a judge did not amount to
publishing it in open court.

The newspapers argued that the summons was before the court, **08.18**
it was referred to by counsel, the allegations in it were founded on
by counsel and the court granted an interdict in terms of one of the
conclusions in the summons.

Lord Clyde, upholding the newspapers' plea that their reports **08.19**
could be protected by qualified privilege, said that previous Scottish cases (including *Richardson*) did not support the argument that
a report must always be limited to what was said and read aloud in
open court. Courts sat to hear cases and give judgment "with open
doors", and it was evident that for public confidence in the
administration of justice to be maintained the public must be able
to see and hear proceedings for themselves.

The proceedings must also be intelligible. Lord Clyde added: **08.20**

"The public must have at least the opportunity of understanding what is going on and if they do not have the opportunity I
do not consider that the hearing is a public one. If the hearing
is a public hearing then it does not seem to me that that
characteristic is destroyed simply because for perfectly proper
reasons of convenience a document is referred to and not read
out in full. Where a document has been incorporated into
what counsel has said, the proceedings cannot be said to be
open to the public unless the terms of the document can be
seen by the public".

The danger of secrecy was regarded as so great that publicity was **08.21**
considered preferable even at the cost of private hardship.

There was also a clear advantage in enabling the public to know **08.22**
with certainty and accuracy what had passed in court rather than
leaving them to rely on rumour or speculation, and the reporting of
proceedings might be found to be unfair or misleading if access to

the pleadings which had been founded upon in open court was not allowed. To make a realistic application of the principle to the circumstances of the *Cunningham* case, Lord Clyde said he could not restrict the availability of privilege to a report of what was actually read out in court. Lord Clyde continued: "The test is not what is actually read out—although all that is read out is published—but what is in the presentation of the case intended to be published and so put in the same position as if it had been read out. If it is referred to and founded upon before the court with a view to advancing the submission which is being made, it is to be taken as published".

08.23   To decide the scope of privileged reporting by reference to the method of communication between counsel and judge seemed to Lord Clyde to involve adopting a standard which could be fixed by "chance, caprice or idiosyncrasy". One advocate might prefer to read passages of pleadings while another would summarise or merely make reference to them. Making publication depend on whether or not a document founded on in open court was or was not read out by counsel or judge might more easily invite suspicion of secrecy and the broad purpose which lay behind the principle of openness might be put at risk of frustration.

08.24   Lord Clyde's judgment was obviously a significant one for the media but its limits should be carefully noted. The decision was not appealed and the case never went to proof. This meant that the question of whether the allegations published in the newspapers were in fact privileged in this case was never decided. All that was decided was that they might be. Lord Clyde also pointed out that it might well be that documents other than pleadings, such as productions, were in a different position. The newspapers defending Mr Cunningham's action agreed that productions could not be published unless they were led in evidence.

08.25   Lord Clyde also made it clear that not all parts of a document would necessarily be safely used in a court report: "I should not wish to exclude the possibility that cases could arise where a document contained matter which was quite distinct and separable from the point in issue before the court and neither relevant to it nor necessary for its determination and where such matter might not necessarily be published where other parts were founded upon".

08.26   An example might be a preliminary procedural step such as continuing a case to allow pleadings to be amended. It seems to follow from what Lord Clyde said in *Cunningham* that a report based on the pleadings and containing defamatory allegations, for example of criminal conduct, would not be protected by privilege unless read out in open court (which is highly unlikely at that stage of the case).

Adjustment roll

After the summons has been served and defences lodged—all of which is done in private—an action appears on what is known as the "adjustment roll". The allegations that each party intends to prove will be made into an open record and at intervals fixed by the court, the action appears on the case-list of a particular judge who has to decide whether a continuation should be allowed for one side to answer claims put by the other. At some stage he will decide that no further adjustment of the pleadings is to be allowed and order that the record be closed. **08.27**

The distinction between an open record and a closed record is important for the safe reporting of civil actions. The record (containing the parties' written pleadings) remains open so long as the case is on the adjustment roll. The court reporter must check from the front cover that it is in fact a closed record before he uses extracts from it. In the sheriff court the cover of the record may not indicate whether it is open or closed and a check must be made with court officials or lawyers as to whether it has in fact been closed. **08.28**

The closing of the record means that the pleadings of the parties to the action are in their final form, subject to anything that might be added by a minute of amendment. The reporter should be mindful of the fact that even when the record is closed and both parties have therefore stated their case fully he cannot necessarily quote from the record with impunity. The safest view is to regard statements contained in a record as covered by privilege only if they are supported by evidence led at a proof hearing. It should also be remembered that the closing of a record has the effect of making proceedings active in terms of the Contempt of Court Act 1981. **08.29**

Open record

It was decided in the case of *Young v. Armour* (1921), that publication of the contents of an open record was an interference with the administration of justice. The action was one for damages for breach of promise of marriage and extracts from the record were published in certain English newspapers and by one Scottish paper, the *Weekly Record*, before it had been closed. Under the heading "Love on the Golf Course", the report gave a detailed account of the facts stated in the open record. Both sides agreed **08.30** there had been an interference with the due course of justice, because the case might have been settled without any of the facts having been made public.

08.31 Lord Blackburn said that the appearance of the article amounted to contempt of court since the record, while still open, was not public property. The editor was ordered to appear in court personally to give an explanation.

08.32 He apologised and explained that, although he knew that the contents of an open record should not be published, he had seen the article in certain English papers and had assumed, wrongly but quite honestly, that the case had been heard in court. The apology was accepted, but the judge said that if the explanation had not been satisfactory, the fine inflicted would have been severe. The court considered that "the contempt which resulted from publication of this sort was a serious offence and one which should be met with a severe penalty".

08.33 While that case sounded a warning about the dangers of publishing details from an open record, the reporter should not take fright at the very mention of the words open record. The Contempt of Court Act has relaxed the *Young v. Armour* rule. It is now contempt to publish from an open record only when proceedings are active under the Act, for example at a preliminary hearing (see Chapter 10), although publication from the open record could still be contempt at common law if intended to prejudice the administration of justice.

08.34 Important points of law are often debated before the closing of the record, and if a full-scale hearing takes place in open court a report of the proceedings can be published. On the basis of the *Cunningham* decision, information from the open record could be used if it is referred to in court and the court is being asked to make a decision on it. A report based on information in the record which had nothing to do with the particular hearing would probably not be privileged.

Closed record

08.35 A closed record is sometimes referred to as a public document, but this does not mean that its contents can be freely published at any stage in the proceedings. It was made abundantly clear in a decision in 1892 that, until a case has come into open court, excerpts from even a closed record should not be published. In particular great care must be taken over information from a closed record which might in itself be actionable.

08.36 The privilege which protects a newspaper from an action of defamation over what it publishes from a closed record operates only from the time the action has come into open court.

In the case of *Macleod v. Lewis Justices* (1892), it was decided **08.37** that publication in a newspaper of a closed record containing defamatory statements not referred to publicly in discussion in open court was not privileged. The record contained in that case, statements about two justices of the peace which, if untrue, were grossly libellous. The justices, who were the defenders in the case, answered the statements with a general denial.

Immediately after the record was closed an agent for the pursuer **08.38** handed to a reporter for the *North British Daily Mail* a record containing pursuer's contentions but not the defenders' general denial. A summary of the record was published in the paper and also in the *Scottish Highlander*. The papers later published a letter from the justices stating the allegations about them in the record were "a tissue of libellous falsehoods". The pursuer complained to the Court of Session that the publication of these letters was contempt of court. The court ruled that there was no contempt, but made some observations which provide useful guidance on this aspect of court reporting.

Lord Justice-Clerk MacDonald said it might be a practice to **08.39** hand complete records to the newspapers, but it was not one to be looked on with favour, and certainly to hand an incomplete record to anyone for the purpose of publication was a very gross irregularity. That was quite different from the publication by newspapers of what took place in a case when it was in open court.

Lord Young, agreeing, said it was clear that statements made in **08.40** pleadings were privileged, however libellous they might appear, but there was no privilege whatever in the publication of pleadings. Reporting of proceedings was simply an enlargement of the audience which heard them in court, but which was limited by the size of the courtroom. It was therefore quite right to report, for example a debate on the relevancy of a case, and the report would be privileged if it was fair. While a litigant was privileged in the statements he made on record, he was not privileged if he sent his pleadings (whether the record was closed or not) to a newspaper for publication. If the pleadings published were slanderous, then the paper publishing them, and the person sending them for publication, were liable in damages for slander.

It is not surprising, therefore, that reporters sometimes find **08.41** solicitors reluctant to hand over to them closed records in cases which have not reached the stage of a hearing in open court. Yet, where a closed record is made available, and contains nothing which could reasonably be regarded as libellous, or the reporter is careful not to reproduce such statements if they do appear to be slanderous, there is still scope for the safe reporting of cases from this source.

08.42   The effect of the ruling in the case of *Macleod* seems to have been modified by practice in the intervening years. For example, when an action of damages opens before a judge or jury in the Court of Session it is usual for solicitors willingly to let the press have a copy of the closed record without any reservations as to which passages may be published. They do so although at a proof or jury trial the whole, or even a major part, of the closed record may never be read out in open court. A literal reading of *Macleod* in such cases would make adequate reporting impossible.

08.43   Since the closed record is the only reliable and practicable means of preparing a complete, fair and balanced report, it is not surprising that solicitors engaged normally hand over a copy to the press at the opening of the evidence and often at a preliminary legal debate. Indeed, it would surprise many of them to learn that by so doing they were providing the media with something they had no legal right to publish.

08.44   The case of *Macleod* seems to assume that in all cases the closed record will sooner or later be read out in open court. In fact this rarely happens, since the judge has a copy, as do counsel and instructing solicitors. There may be no need for counsel to read it out, except to draw attention sometimes to a particular passage. If the reporter had to depend solely upon such desultory readings, often out of context, from one side of a case, he would have great difficulty in ever achieving any semblance of fair or balanced reporting.

08.45   It seems a fair interpretation of the position, taking *Macleod* into account, that there is a risk in publishing the contents of a closed record if the case has not yet come into open court. From the moment a hearing has begun (whether legal debate, proof or jury trial) the journalist can safely use the record as a basis for reporting the proof hearing, even though the contents of the record itself may not be read out in open court. This must apply particularly when the judge, because he has already read the closed record in preparation for the hearing, tells counsel expressly that he need not trouble reading it out in court. In that situation the record may properly be "taken as read".

08.46   The journalist should always check, however, that the record is up to date. It is important to ensure that the amount sued for has not changed and that there has been no major change in the allegations and defences put forward by the parties to the action. For example, are the parties to the action still the same and is the pursuer still insisting on a plea of contributory negligence?

Common sense

As in so many other aspects of court reporting, the journalist needs **08.47** to exercise a high degree of care and common sense in deciding which passages, if any, it is safe to reproduce from the record before the case is heard in open court. He must remember that if he publishes something that is libellous he cannot rely on the protection of privilege. Where the pleadings are read out by counsel during the proceedings, these passages, when published, are of course privileged, no matter how defamatory the statements they contain might be if uttered outside the courtroom.

It is safe to assume that a lawyer who hands over a closed record **08.48** to a reporter without reservation is tacitly conceding that the statements, so far as his client is concerned, may be published without fear of reprisals. But the reporter has to keep in mind the interests of other parties to the case.

Open court

Once the case is in open court the situation is entirely different, **08.49** and the reporter can normally expect to obtain a closed record from the solicitor for one party or the other. If he fails to do so, and the case is worth the trouble, his next step will be to approach the clerk of court. If the clerk is unable or unwilling to provide a copy, the reporter's next line of approach is to the Principal Clerk of Session. In the unlikely event of his refusal to help, he will have to ask to see the Lord President.

This situation did occur in a case where, not only did both **08.50** parties to a large property dispute refuse to hand over a record, and the clerk feel unwilling to supply one to the press, but one of the parties offered a journalist a sum of money for not publishing anything about the case. As it was impossible to report the case without access to the pleadings Lord President Cooper was approached and instructed the Principal Clerk that the court staff should provide the press with a closed record. Otherwise, he said, the parties would be enforcing a closed-doors hearing at their own hand.

The Lord President intervened when evidence was being heard **08.51** and it cannot be assumed that he would have taken the same decision had the case been at a preliminary stage, such as a hearing of debate on relevancy or competency.

Journalists should also be aware that in cases where the media **08.52** have asked for eminent counsel's opinion on this issue, the view has been expressed that the provision of a closed record to reporters by the court or solicitors does not mean that every allegation in the record is covered by privilege.

08.53 The transcript of evidence taken on commission (where a witness is unable to attend court) is in a similar position to the closed record when evidence is being heard. Although the evidence may not be read out because the judge will have the actual transcript, it should, for press purposes, be taken as read, and treated as being covered by the same kind of privilege as spoken evidence. The reporter is entitled to have access to a copy of the transcript, unless it contains the type of evidence which the court would ordinarily hear behind closed doors.

Petitions

08.54 There are a wide variety of cases which are started by a petition rather than a summons. The procedure is different, and there is a separate petition department in the Court of Session.

08.55 While an ordinary action is begun by the pursuer serving a summons on the defender, who in turn replies (if he proposes to contest the case), a petition is addressed to the court which orders notification to other parties having a potential interest to lodge answers to the petition. Interdict, custody of children, authority to vary trusts, confirmation of reduction of capital of a company, presumption of death of some missing person and company liquidations or amalgamations are brought by petition.

08.56 When (and if) answers are lodged to a petition, these go through the kind of adjustment which occurs in an ordinary action, and eventually a document equivalent to a closed record (usually entitled "petition and answers") is drawn up. The journalist can normally treat this in the same way as a closed record.

Interim interdicts

08.57 An interim interdict may be granted on the basis of a summons or a petition. The only practical difference for reporting the case is that the documents are handled by a separate department.

08.58 There are also certain changes of wording. With a summons the parties are pursuer and defender, not petitioner and respondent, and time may be allowed for lodging defences, not answers, as to a petition. In cases where the court makes an *ex parte* order (in the absence of the party interdicted) a report should indicate, in the interests of fairness, that the other party was not present or represented in court and was allowed time to answer.

08.59 The use of the expression "temporary order" or "temporary ban" is not always a satisfactory way of referring to an interim interdict. "Interim" does not necessarily mean "temporary". An interim order is made to restrain someone from doing something until some further development in the case. That may not take place for weeks or for months or may never happen at all. The interim interdict could continue in operation indefinitely and could not properly be called temporary. It is also attributing to a court more power than it has, to say in a report of interdict proceedings that it has issued an order to prevent some specific act. An interdict can only prohibit it.

Because interim interdicts come to court as a matter of urgency, **08.60** the summons or petition is often in a fairly basic state. Sometimes it will be in handwriting because there has not been enough time to have it typed. There is also often no opportunity for the alleged wrongdoer to be represented at the application for an interim order against him. The court's decision has to be reached upon an *ex parte* statement which, for the reporter, requires special care. Only as much of such a statement as is necessary to explain the basis of the court's decision may be safely published.

If someone has reason to think an interim interdict will be taken **08.61** out against him he can, in Scotland, lodge in court what is known as a *caveat*. A *caveat* obliges the clerk of court to contact the person against whom an interdict is sought and ask whether he wishes to appear and make submissions before the judge decides whether the interdict should be granted.

Most newspaper and broadcasting organisations in Scotland **08.62** lodge *caveats* which last for a year.

If the court refuses to grant an application for interim interdict, **08.63** the case for publishing no more than is absolutely necessary is even stronger. Unless there is some compelling reason why the result should be reported—for example where the case has been reported at an earlier stage and there is an obligation to publish the result— petitions for interim interdict which fail on an ex parte application should be reported with extreme care. It is possible that in refusing the application for interim interdict the judge has taken the view that the allegations contained in the writ lodged by the pursuer are unfounded, but there are a number of reasons why the court might refuse interdict at this stage.

For example, the judge might feel there is a lack of specification **08.64** in the pleadings or that the test of "balance of convenience" has not been satisfied. The existence of such a variety of possibilities illustrates the difficulties and dangers of reporting interim hearings.

If there is a compelling reason why the decision refusing an **08.65** interim order should be published, the decision alone should be given, and it would generally be unwise to go into the detail of the allegations made by counsel in seeking the order. On the other hand, where, in refusing to grant an interim interdict, the court reaches a decision which is in itself important the reporter is justified in asking court staff for enough information about the case, including names and addresses of parties, to prepare a report.

08.66 It is not unusual in an interim interdict application for counsel to put before the court a string of allegations in the hope that one of them at least, will tilt the case in his favour. The judge may uphold only one or some of the claims and reject others, and this should be made clear in any report of the case. It may be necessary to consult the clerk of court or counsel or solicitors in the case to find out precisely which part of the claim has been sustained.

Court Rolls

08.67 Cases which have come to court by way of a petition are usually indicated by "Pet" before the name of the petitioner. The name of the party who is suing comes first. Parties' names are followed by the names of junior counsel and solicitors for all parties represented in the case. Where a defender is appealing to the Inner House, this is indicated by: "Appeal for defender in causa . . ." An appeal from a single judge is known as a "reclaiming motion" and this is indicated by the initials "R.M.".

08.68 Only in a few cases do the Rolls give a clue as to what the case is about. Where, for example, the pursuer's and defender's surnames are the same, the case is likely to be a divorce action.

08.69 In the Outer House incidental motions are marked with an asterisk if counsel are due to appear to make submissions in open court. Where there is no asterisk, there is no public appearance, and the entry in the Roll indicates a formal step in procedure which is not usually reportable at all. In the Inner House motions are called "single bills" and the same asterisk rule operates. Although the two Divisions are concerned largely with appeals from the Outer House and from the sheriff courts, they also deal with a wide variety of petitions.

08.70 At the appeal stage the court will have before it not only the closed record, or petition and answers, but also usually an appendix containing a transcript of the evidence from the court below and a copy of the judgment delivered by the judge or sheriff, which is under appeal.

08.71 Where the evidence has been given in open court, it may be useful to refer to this and the judgment of the inferior court where necessary to prepare a report of the appeal.

Avizandum

08.72 After the hearing of evidence or legal debate the court may give an immediate decision or may "make avizandum", which means that it will take time to consider the case before issuing a written judgment. Occasionally the court will give its decision and produce reasons in writing later.

Strictly speaking, the judgment of the court comprises two **08.73** documents—the interlocutor and the opinion of the judge(s). In practice the opinion is the source of news. The interlocutor is a minute kept by the clerk of court recording in formal style the precise terms of the decision. This is normally not of the slightest use for publication and the reporter should refer to it only as a guide to the true effect of a decision if this is not clear from a reading of the judgment.

Decisions do not come into force until the interlocutor is signed **08.74** by the judge. In certain circumstances a judge will grant a decree but for specific reasons will agree to delay operation of his decision for a stated period. He does this by "superseding extract" of the decree, in other words, delaying the process by which the successful party can obtain the extract copy of the decree which will enable him to enforce it. In these circumstances, reports of the case should make it clear that the decision does not become effective immediately.

Criminal cases

In criminal proceedings the document with which the reporter is **08.75** mainly concerned is, in cases dealt with in solemn procedure, the indictment, and in summary cases, the complaint or charge-sheet. In the district court the complaint contains the name and address of the accused person as well as the charge against him. In the High Court where bail has been allowed the address of the accused is normally on the indictment, and where he is in custody his address, if known, can usually be obtained from court officials.

In the case of indictments, the first point at which the media are **08.76** fully entitled to publish the whole contents of the document is when it is read out to the jury at the opening of the trial, or when the accused pleads guilty to the charge(s) contained in it.

Where charges are dropped against an accused person without **08.77** trial he may feel sufficiently aggrieved to threaten proceedings against the papers which published the charge at an earlier stage, for example when he appeared on petition, but there is no record of a successful complaint of this kind. The fact that proceedings have been dropped should of course be published.

When someone appears on petition the procurator fiscal will **08.78** normally inform the media of the name of the accused and provide brief details of the charge for publication. Where no plea is taken from the accused and his case is continued for one reason or another, normally for further examination, these facts should be included in any report. On the question of bail, the journalist may come to have details of the submissions made to the court (*e.g.*, the P.F. opposing bail on the grounds of previous convictions). Although he may have access to this information such details must never appear in a report. All that can be said is that bail was granted or refused (see para. 14.26).

08.79 The general practice is not to name an accused person before he appears on petition. The charge may be dropped and he may not appear in court at all and, if he does, it may be on a different charge from that originally preferred by the police.

08.80 There do not seem to be any general difficulties for the media in getting hold of indictments and complaints once a case has come into court for a trial or a guilty plea. This has not always been the case and on one occasion, when the media were refused access to a complaint at the old Burgh Court in Edinburgh, the Lord Advocate of the day, Mr John Wheatley, Q.C., was approached. His opinion was that, although reporters had no statutory right of access to complaints, it was a matter of public policy that they should have this facility in the interests of accurate reporting of cases.

08.81 The position on documents in general seems to be that while a journalist has no greater right than any member of the public to attend legal proceedings, it is recognised that the reporter requires access to certain court documents at the appropriate stage in proceedings if he is to carry out his job properly. As a matter of public policy the media are allowed access to certain papers, both in criminal and civil cases, or at least to some of the information contained in them. Where access to documents necessary for the fair and accurate reporting of a case heard in open court is refused, the reporter should raise the matter with the appropriate court authority.

Data Protection Act 1998

08.82 The Data Protection Act 1998 replaces the earlier Data Protection Act 1984. It aims to regulate the processing (including collecting) of personal information, set preconditions for data to be processed, and to increase the individual's right to control how information about him or her is used.

08.83 The 1984 Act required data users to register with the Data Protection Registrar, to handle data in accordance with certain principles (to do with keeping the data safe, accurate and using it for defined purposes only) and to give individuals access to information about them. The new 1998 Act is similar, but wider.

08.84 Related regulations, to do with unsolicited telephone calls and faxes (possibly also Internet "spamming") came into force in

March 2000 and may severely restrict the build-up of marketing profiles.

Manual files

From the journalist's point of view the major changes in the new **08.85** Act are that it covers manual records forming part of a "filing" system. This potentially covers journalists' notebooks but there is an exception, discussed below, for "journalistic activity". For manual records to be covered they have to form part of a "system" sufficiently structured to allow efficient retrieval of information about the particular individual. Existing manual filing systems do not need to comply with the Data Protection principles until October 2001, and in some respects until 2007. A system being newly set up will have to comply straight away. So will new personal data added to structured manual files.

Sensitive data

In relation to "sensitive" data—*e.g.* information about a person's **08.86** ethnic origin, politics, trade union affiliations, criminal record, religion, sexuality or health—you will normally need explicit consent before processing. Data may include sound or image data, *e.g.* digital programming. "Processing" is widely defined. It covers organising, holding, adapting, altering, retrieving, using, disclosing, blocking, erasing and destroying information!

Processing of non-sensitive data without consent

Even in relation to information which is not "sensitive" the subject **08.87** should agree, expressly or by implication, to the processing. If he or she does not, you have to show that the processing was necessary for the performance of a contract; for compliance with another legal obligation; to protect the vital interests of the individual (a stringent requirement); for the exercise of a public function in the public interest, or for the processor's or someone else's legitimate interest.

New rights

As well, the 1998 Act gives people increased rights to be informed **08.88** about information held on them, including its source. Under the 1998 Act, individuals can act directly to enforce those rights and they can also seek compensation for breach.

They have a right to prevent certain types of damaging, distress- **08.89** ing or annoying processing; to be advised if a decision which significantly affects them is taken solely by automated means—credit checks, for example; to claim compensation if the Act is breached and to amend or erase inaccurate information.

08.90   An opt-out must always be offered in the case of direct marketing.

Criminal Offences

08.91   It is a criminal offence unlawfully to obtain or to sell unlawfully obtained data. In some cases, compensation may be payable to individuals who have suffered from inaccuracy or unauthorised disclosure.

08.92   It is also a criminal offence to require "enforced subject access", *e.g.* for an employer to make an employee or interviewee consent to the handing-over of data re criminal records, unless one of the two statutory exemptions (authorisation by law/public interest justification) applies. The public interest justification does NOT cover an argument that this would assist in preventing or detecting crime.

Security

08.93   Once processed, data must be kept secure. What amounts to adequate security depends in part on the sensitivity of the data.

08.94   Data will not be regarded as lawfully obtained unless certain criteria are met. These include informing the data subjects of who is using the information and why.

08.95   Where the data is processed automatically, and will form the sole basis for any decision significantly affecting the individual, the logic involved in the decision-making has to be revealed.

08.96   There is also a ban on transfer of personal information outside the European Economic Area if the country to which the information is going does not have an adequate level of protection for personal data (unless the subject consents or the transfer is absolutely necessary). The U.S. takes a very different, and more minimalist, approach to data protection. There is scope for a clash here and attempts are ongoing to resolve it.

Data Protection Commissioner

08.97   The Data Protection Registrar is now to be called the Data Protection Commissioner, and is given significant new powers including entry and inspection. Data users are those who control the contents and use of a collection of automated information, including opinions, about living, identifiable individuals. Data users have to "notify" themselves to the Commissioner.

Journalistic activity

There are a number of exemptions to the requirement to comply **08.98** with the Data Protection principles. The most important for the journalist is the pre-publication exemption for processing for journalistic, artistic and/or literary purposes. This exemption only applies if the processing is solely for these "special purposes" and (1) the information is processed with an intention to publish; (2) the journalist, etc. ("data controller") has a reasonable belief that publication of the information is in the public interest; and (3) there is a reasonable belief that compliance with Data Protection would be incompatible with journalistic, artistic and/or literary purposes. The journalists still requires to keep the data secure.

In any litigation by an individual to enforce his rights or claim **08.99** compensation, the journalist or other data controller claims the exception and the Commissioner decides whether it applies. It is important for the journalist to show compliance with any relevant code, *e.g.* the PCC or BSC Codes. The journalist can appeal to the Data Protection Tribunal if the Commissioner decides against the exemption's applying.

The protection covers pre-publication processing and all process- **08.100** ing up to 24 hours after the first publication, in order to prevent prior restraint. Each data controller benefits from its own 24-hour period, so there can be independent publication of the information.

Journalistic problems

Despite this exemption, some lawyers think this Act is the end of **08.101** the self-regulation of the press. All publications, true or not, effectively have to be justified by a reasonable belief that publication is in the public interest. Yet compelling public interest justifications tend to emerge after investigation, not in advance of it. As with the privacy element of the Human Rights Act, a major concern is the scope for interference in investigative journalism at the investigation stage, not through publication bans. The existing, nominally voluntary, codes have been given some legal force by the back door. The other major difficulty for journalists is that the Act may be used as a reason on the part of the police and local authorities to withhold information from the media. There is considerable leeway for the police to disclose even sensitive information, in terms of the exemptions contained in the Act, including a "Crime and Taxation" exemption; however, compelling such disclosure will be far from simple.

Freedom of information

08.102 On November 18, 1999, a Freedom of Information Bill was introduced in the House of Commons. (At the time of writing, it has passed the House of Commons stage and is before the Lords.) It was intended to supersede the Code of Practice on Access to Government Information so as to create a statutory right of access. The activities of local government, National Health Service bodies, schools, colleges and other public bodies were to be open to scrutiny. Access was to be given to documents, as well as to the information itself.

08.103 However, the Bill was felt by many to be a watering down of the White Paper on which it was based, both because of the number of exemptions created from the duty to disclose information and because the test for refusing to reveal certain types of information was reduced from "substantial harm" to merely "harm". (Given the interpretation accorded to "substantial risk" in the Contempt of Court Act 1981, one might not think that a very significant amendment.) The original draft Freedom of Information Bill for the U.K. had 21 exemptions which would allow information to be withheld. In the wake of the protests, the Home Secretary agreed a number of amendments to tighten up the proposals.

08.104 There are two types of exemption which may be claimed: class-based and content-based. Information which cannot be disclosed for reasons of national security is exempt. A ministerial certificate to the effect that the information is exempt is required. It can be appealed, however, to the Information Tribunal which will be set up if and when the Bill is enacted.

08.105 Class-based exemptions (where the question of prejudice does not have to be raised) include any information held at any time by a public authority for the purposes of a criminal investigation or proceedings. Another such blanket exemption relates to information held by the department relating to the formulation of Government policy, ministerial communications, law officers' advice or the operation of a ministerial private office. Information provided in confidence, legal professional information and trade secrets are all exempt as a class.

08.106 The Campaign for Freedom of Information, together with the Society of Editors and also the Newspaper Society, reacted badly to the Bill as drafted. They regarded some of the tests—such as the authorities being able to withhold information which "in their opinion" would "prejudice the effective conduct of public affairs"—as vague and difficult to overturn by judicial review; other tests, such as "harm" as being too weak. The Campaign was concerned about the width of the exemption for police information and the workings of Government. They also felt that the Information Commissioner proposed to be created under the Bill had too little power. The Campaign points out, also, that the refusal of consumers to buy a product which they believe to be dangerous would "prejudice the commercial interests" of its producer. The Government is under considerable pressure by such groups to give the Bill, and the Information Commissioner, more teeth in relation to exemptions.

Freedom of information in Scotland

In the meantime, there are proposals for separate legislation by the Scottish Parliament for freedom of information in Scotland in the areas of Holyrood's competence. Such legislation would not cover governmental information held within Scotland. A consultation document was produced by Jim Wallace, Q.C. which may in certain respects be an improvement upon the English draft Bill. However, even allowing for the fact that the question of Scottish legislation is at a preliminary stage, concerns have been raised about the consultation document. It avers that decisions on releasing information will be based on a "presumption of openness", but it is felt that this does not square with the idea of a class exemption; there is no balancing test where the presumption may apply. **08.107**

The Scottish Executive's proposals for Scotland envisage a Scottish Information Commissioner who would be able to order the disclosure of information in the public interest, adjust charges levied and resolve disputes through mediation. The regime proposed would cover all public bodies and public service providers in Scotland, including information relating to the services performed by contractors working for Scottish public authorities. Enquirers would not have to say why they wanted the information. Documents of any age could be requested. Responses should be made within 20 working days as a general rule. The "harm test" would be "substantial prejudice". Background information used to develop policy would have to be published. **08.108**

Although the police would be included under the Scottish freedom of information proposals as presently envisaged, the Campaign for Freedom of Information in Scotland are sceptical about this, since only administrative matters would appear to be covered. Everything else to do with policing would fall under "investigations" and thus be potentially exempt. The proposals also allow Scottish Ministers to overrule the Information Commissioner where the Commissioner believes that the release of documents relating to policy development would be in the public interest. **08.109**

The Scottish Parliament could be covered by the new system, but would not be if the Executive decided to opt out. Cross-border **08.110**

bodies operating in Scotland would fall under the United Kingdom
freedom of information regime, not the Scottish one. This would
include the Department of Social Security and the Ministry of
Defence. The proposals make it clear that they intend to protect
"the independence of the Lord Advocate in his capacity as head of
the systems of criminal prosecution and investigation of deaths in
Scotland".

REGULATION OF INVESTIGATORY POWERS ACT 2000

Regulation of Investigatory Powers Act 2000

08.111 This Act deals with the interception of telecommunications, surveillance use of covert human intelligence sources and encryption.
It repeals the Interception of Communications Act 1985 and
creates a new statutory framework for telephone and email
monitoring and interception, with a view to making the latter
comply with the Human Rights Act 1998.

08.112 The Act makes unauthorised interception of telecommunications
a criminal offence. It creates also a civil liability for interception
over a private system. Emails, pagers and mobile 'phones are all
covered. Interception is only permissible: (a) under a warrant; (b)
with the consent of the sender and recipient; (c) where necessary
by reason of provision or operation of the service (*e.g.*, at certain
"firewalls" messages may be decrypted for virus checking); (d) for
monitoring or recording business communications. Operators,
including ISPs, may have to maintain interception capability.
Where information has been encrypted, one may be asked to
disclose it in intelligible form, or more unusually, to provide the
key, *e.g.* where encrypted documents are gathered in a "dawn raid"
under the Competition Act 1998.

08.113 Interception of communications is lawful if a warrant has been
issued. Such warrants or notices must also be justified in terms of
the Human Rights Act, *i.e.* they must be necessary and proportionate, not used merely for convenience where alternative means of
achieving the same end would be available.

08.114 The main concern for the media arising from the Regulation of
Investigatory Powers Act 2000 is that it allows for the interception,
surveillance and disclosure of journalistic sources without prior
judicial authorisation, and indeed, without the journalist even
knowing that the interception has taken place. Whether this will
survive challenge in the European Court of Human Rights in
Strasbourg still remains to be seen.

Regulation of Investigatory Powers (Scotland) Act 2000

This Act of the Scottish Parliament deals with similar issues. It **08.115** seems to impose controls on, in particular, the police's use of intensive surveillance in people's living accommodation and private vehicles. Only the chief Constable can authorise this, and the authorisation must be approved by a Surveillance Commissioner. The Act also seeks to create greater protection for "covert human intelligence sources", *i.e.* undercover agents and the like. In order to be authorised under the Act, any surveillance, has to be necessary for particular purposes and proportionate to the ends to achieved by it.

KEY POINTS

The most important documents in a civil action are the summons, **08.116** calling list, court rolls, open and closed record and opinion of the court. Reports based on information from a calling list, summons or open record are not privileged and could lead to a defamation action. There will, however, be instances where a case can be safely reported in some detail at the calling list, summons or open record stage. The closed record can be used as the basis for a fair, accurate and balanced report once a case has come into open court. The record is not normally read out and it is important to check that it is up to date.

The Data Protection Act 1998 radically extends the protection **08.117** afforded to personal data. Structured manual files now come under protection. Sound and image data are covered. In principle, one needs explicit consent to organise, hold, adapt, retrieve, use, disclose, block, erase or destroy "sensitive data" such as political or medical information. There is an exemption for journalistic activity in certain circumstances, but it is likely that the "public interest" element in any story will be subject to increased security. The Act seeks to put adequate safeguards in place against prior restraint of publication, but there are concerns that it will impede investigation.

Controversial freedom of information legislation is proposed by **08.118** both the Westminster and Holyrood Parliaments. Access to information about oneself is still, however, likely to fall under the Data Protection regime.

CHAPTER 9

NEWS GATHERING

09.01 Generally, journalists expect to find any legal challenge to their work at the post-publication stage. However, the courts and other regulatory bodies have in recent years been dealing more often with objections to journalists' news-gathering techniques. Journalists should remember that they may find themselves open to legal challenge prior to the publication date. In fact, it would be perfectly competent for a challenge based on news-gathering techniques to proceed in a case where at the end of the day there was no publication at all. We now consider areas which the working journalist should bear in mind when gathering information for a story.

Privacy

09.02 Journalists must respect the privacy of individuals when gathering information. Privacy has been mentioned in statute since 1990 when it was included in the list of matters to be regulated by the Broadcasting Standards Council. The Broadcasting Standards Council's Code makes it clear that the privacy of individuals can only be breached by journalists in circumstances where there is an overwhelming public interest in obtaining the information. In the case brought by the high street retailers, Dixons plc, against the BBC's "Watchdog" programme the BSC upheld the argument from Dixons that a company as well as private individuals has a right to privacy. The English Court of Appeal ultimately agreed with this decision. Thus, journalists will have to take care when news-gathering, even if no private person is involved. There is a similar provision in the PCC Code for print journalists. To date there have been no court proceedings arising out of the interpretation of that Code.

Breach of Confidence

09.03 Prior to the incorporation of the European Convention on Human Rights into domestic law, breach of confidence was seen by those wishing to prevent publication of a story as an alternative basis to a right of privacy to obtaining an interim interdict. The Scots law of confidence was fully examined in the case *Lord Advocate v. Scotsman Publications and Others* in 1988. In essence, if a journalist comes into possession of information which is clearly confidential, a court may grant an order preventing publication of that material. However, for a pursuer to succeed, it is necessary for the pursuer to show that the information had the "quality of confidence" attaching to it. It is not possible for individuals or organisations to keep embarrassing information secret by agreeing that the information is confidential; the 1999 Court of Session case of *Dr Avril Osborne v. BBC* established this in relation to "gagging clauses" in employment termination agreements. If journalists publish confidential information, it is possible for a party damaged by the publication to sue for recompense. In this way, in the *Spycatcher* case the *Sunday Times* were ordered to pay the Government a sum equivalent to their profit from increased circulation when they included an excerpt from the memoirs of Peter Wright in their final edition. Similarly, the *Daily Mirror* settled with the late Princess Diana in respect of its increased profit when it published pictures of her exercising in the Chelsea Harbour Club Gym in London. Information does not become confidential automatically because it is obtained from private premises. The English courts have recently refused an injunction against Channel 4, who sent an undercover journalist in to film in a funeral parlour, on the basis that the journalist had become an employee of the funeral parlour and so owed it a duty of confidence. Similarly, in 1998 an English judge refused an injunction against showing film which had been shot undercover in a private house, owned by a woman who had been convicted of animal neglect.

Deception

Investigative journalists in particular often find that they have to **09.04** use a degree of deception as part of their news-gathering techniques. The Codes for both print journalists and broadcast journalists recognise that there are circumstances in which deception is a necessary tool as long as the public interest is being served. However, journalists would be well-advised to realise that, quite independent of the terms of these Codes, the common criminal law may intervene. For example, a journalist who obtained access to a hospital in Kilmarnock by pretending to be a relative of the person he wanted to interview, was convicted of fraud. Obtaining documentation by deception could lead to a prosecution for theft. Broadly speaking, the journalist has to weigh up the degree of deception being used with the degree of public interest in the story which is being pursued. This is a delicate matter which may well require an editorial decision at a high level.

Use of hidden cameras and microphones

09.05 With the progress of miniaturisation technology, it has become increasingly easy for journalists to conceal hidden microphones and cameras about their person for the purpose of information-gathering. The use of these techniques is by no means confined to television journalists. For example, in September 1999 the *Observer* newspaper used a hidden camera to record interviews with staff of the Beattie Media Group PR company. The *Observer* journalist posed as an agent for American businessmen who were supposed to be interested in obtaining direct access to Scottish Ministers. Although the *Observer* story caused embarrassment to the Scottish Executive, no complaint to the Press Complaints Commission appears to have been made.

Data Protection Act

09.06 The Data Protection Act of 1984 appears to have had little impact on the conduct of journalism. The Data Protection Act of 1998, however, following on a European Directive, is expected to have a greater impact. That legislation, which came into force on March 1, 2000, has the effect of extending the data protection regime to all indexed data whether stored on computer or manually. An individual has the right to see what information is stored about him or her by a "data controller". There is no doubt that a newspaper or a broadcaster would be considered a data controller in light of the information storage methods they employ. However, there is an exemption for information held for journalistic purposes. This exemption on the face of it means that requests from individuals whom journalists are investigating for details of the data held on them can be resisted on the basis that the information is "held for journalistic purposes". It should be noted that there are various conditions which have to be satisfied before the exemption applies. It should also be noted that the Data Protection Commissioner (soon to be called "the Information Commissioner") has indicated during the debate on the terms of the legislation and subsequent to its passage that she intends to construe the journalistic exemption as narrowly as possible. As this is a highly complex area of law, it is recommended that journalists seek legal advice when faced with an application under the data protection legislation. For a more detailed discussion of Data Protection Law, see paragraphs 08.82 to 08.101.

Looking at that legislation from the other side, as it were, it may **09.07** be that journalists, like other individuals, could use the data protection legislation to access information from bodies which are "Data Controllers". The Data Protection Commissioner might be able to be of assistance to journalists in this respect. Her office address and website are as follows:

The Office of the Data Protection Commissioner
Wycliffe House
Water Lane, Wilmslow
Cheshire SK9 5AF
http://www.dataprotection.gov.uk/dprhome.htm

Freedom of information: the United Kingdom

At the time of writing, the Freedom of Information Bill is still **09.08** progressing through the House of Commons. There has also been an announcement that there will be separate freedom of information legislation in Scotland in respect of public authorities which deal with devolved matters. An *Open Scotland: Freedom of Information Consultation Document* was issued in November 1999. The concept of freedom of information has been the subject of legislation in a good number of European countries and, most famously, has been in place in America for many years. Freedom of information legislation basically entitles the citizen to obtain information from a "public authority". The aim behind the legislation is to allow the citizens of a democratic country to find out what public authorities are doing in their name. It follows the principle that in a democratic society openness is a necessary part of government. Freedom of information was promised by numerous opposition parties but never followed through when that party became the Government of the day. However, in November 1999 Jack Straw, as Home Secretary, introduced the Freedom of Information Bill. This followed on the previous year's White Paper "Your Right To Know". Critics pointed out that the Bill introduced by the Home Secretary was a much watered-down version of the bold sentiments found in "Your Right To Know". In particular, they noted that refusal by a public authority to divulge information which previously would have had to satisfy the test of "substantial harm" now only had to satisfy the much lesser test of "harm".

The only journalistic organisations which are subject to the **09.09** Freedom of Information Bill are the BBC and Channel 4. That is on the basis that they are publicly funded and fall within the ambit of a "public authority". However, the BBC and Channel 4 Corporation will be comforted by the fact that, as in the data protection legislation, there is a journalistic exemption. Accordingly, they should not find themselves bombarded with freedom of information requests by those seeking to ascertain details of journalist activity being carried on by these broadcasters.

09.10 All other journalistic organisations are likely to use freedom of information legislation to obtain detail for stories from public authorities. The Information Commissioner (this position to be held by the former Data Protection Commissioner according to the Bill introduced into the Commons by the Home Secretary in November 1999) will be responsible for operating the freedom of information regime. He or she will intervene on behalf of the individual requesting the information should it not be forthcoming, on payment of an appropriate charge. There will also be an Information Tribunal, which will hear litigation arising out of disputes on access to information held by the public authority. For a more detailed examination of the proposals on freedom of information see paragraphs 08.102 to 08.109.

Freedom of information: Scotland

09.11 In the Consultation Document, "An Open Scotland", it became clear that the Scottish Executive was of the view that there should be a separate Scottish Information Commissioner. The proposal is that that Information Commissioner will deal with public authorities which are responsible for devolved matters. When using the Freedom of Information Act in the Scottish context, journalists will therefore have to decide if they are dealing with a United Kingdom matter, in which case they will apply to the Commissioner in Cheshire, or a Scottish matter.

09.12 The Scottish Consultation Document makes it clear that the information regime in Scotland is to be quite different from that covering the rest of the United Kingdom. This may reflect the fact that it is introduced by a Liberal Minister for Justice, who sets great store on openness. The harm test in Scotland, it would appear, is to be higher than that in the United Kingdom legislation. This will mean that information is more likely to be forthcoming from a Scottish public authority than from a United Kingdom public authority.

09.13 Scottish journalists may find themselves confused as to whether a particular public body is subject to the United Kingdom freedom of information regime or the Scottish freedom of information regime. Put simply, if the body is dealing with a devolved matter, the Scottish freedom of information regime will apply. If it is not a devolved matter, the United Kingdom freedom of information regime will apply. Probably the quickest and easiest solution in cases of doubt will be to contact the United Kingdom or Scottish

Freedom of Information Commissioners and ascertain from their offices which regime applies.

Most surprisingly, the Consultation Document proposes that the **09.14** Lord Advocate's office, procurators fiscal and the police will be covered by the freedom of information regime. However, there will be two major kinds of exemptions (a combination of which will apply to "law enforcement and legal proceedings"). In the first place, class-based exemptions will apply to information which falls within the identified class without any necessity for the application of the harm test. In the case of contents-based exemptions, the argument will centre on whether the actual contents of the document would cause harm were they to be released. There is also the possibility of ministerial certificates preventing release of information. Such a certificate will only cover information which falls within a class-based exemption. See also paragraphs 08.110 to 08.114.

The Human Rights Act 1998

Section 12 of the Human Rights Act of 1998 anticipates conflicts **09.15** between the right of freedom of expression (Art. 10 of the Convention) and other legal rights. Section 12, which was produced after much media lobbying, suggests that the right to freedom of expression will be of considerable importance. However, it may be wondered if at the end of the day the court would always find in favour of the journalist if there had been a flagrant breach of individual rights, for example personal privacy. Generally speaking, the courts look rather unfavourably on invasions of personal privacy and this is clearly an area which journalists will have to monitor as human rights law in Scotland develops in the coming years.

Applicability of the Human Rights Act

There is presently debate as to whether the Human Rights Act **09.16** applies only as against public authorities or if it can be enforced between individuals. Leading constitutional lawyers have disagreed about this point. If the Human Rights Act is enforceable only against public authorities, the only journalistic organisations against which it could be enforced would be the BBC and Channel 4, and that only in respect of certain of the functions which they carry out. However, courts themselves are public authorities in terms of the Human Rights Act. Many commentators feel that this obliges the court to enforce the legislation in cases with which they deal even where a public authority is not involved as a party to the proceedings. Accordingly, the Human Rights Act would apply against private individuals and organisations such as newspapers and independent broadcasters. It would be a strange result of the human rights legislation if a right of privacy could be enforced against Channel 4 but not against tabloid newspapers. Until the courts have determined this matter, no one can be entirely clear on the extent of applicability of legislation. However, it is suggested that the correct approach for journalists working in all organisations is to take the view that the human rights legislation applies to their activities and they may expect to be challenged in the courts by individuals and organisations enforcing their rights under the ECHR.

CONCLUSION

09.17 The purpose of this short chapter is simply to raise awareness amongst journalists of the possibility of challenge, not to what they broadcast or publish, but to the techniques they use when gathering information for publication. Journalists must be mindful of their obligations under the Human Rights Act, Data Protection Act, Freedom of Information legislation, the Broadcasting Standard Commission's Code and the PCC Code if they are to avoid challenges on their news-gathering activities. Unfortunately, clear guidance on the courts' approach cannot be given at this stage. The law, however, is likely to develop in the coming years.

CHAPTER 10

CONTEMPT OF COURT

Contempt of court can take several forms, but for the journalist the **10.01** area that causes the greatest danger is the risk of compromising an accused person's right to a fair trial by publishing prejudicial information.

Legal systems adopt entirely different approaches to the ques- **10.02** tion of balancing the often conflicting interests of freedom of speech and the right to a fair hearing. In the USA, for example, a mass of detailed information about a case is often published before and during a trial. This can even extend, as it did in the *John de Lorean* case, to the accused being shown on television, apparently accepting a consignment of drugs. The result was that 200 potential jurors had to be asked 100 questions to decide whether they could return a fair verdict despite the pre-trial publicity. Similarly, before former American footballer O.J. Simpson appeared for trial on a murder charge, there was extensive and detailed publicity about the strength and weaknesses of both prosecution and defence cases. The pre-trial publicity included nationwide screening of Simpson's arrest, following a lengthy car chase.

Historically, Scots law has adopted almost exactly the opposite **10.03** approach, as expressed by Lord Emslie in the case of *Vinko Sindicic* in 1988. The Lord Justice-General said:

> "Our system of criminal justice in Scotland depends essentially upon the proposition that jurors called to try an accused person should arrive in the jury box without knowledge or impression of facts, or alleged facts, relating to the crime charged on the indictment."

In a later case Lord Hope, Lord Emslie's successor as Lord Justice-General, put it this way: "The court must do what it can to minimise the risk of prejudice because it is in the public interest that proceedings for the detection and punishment of crime should not be interrupted by the effect on the course of justice of publicity."

10.04   Whether these statements still represent an entirely accurate picture of how Scots law strikes the balance between the administration of justice and freedom of speech must be open to doubt following a decision by three senior judges in a case in 1998 involving the *Daily Record*. The full details of the case can be found later in 10.134. In the *Record* case, the judges, led by Lord Justice-General Rodger, were prepared to give a significantly more prominent role than Scottish courts had in the past to freedom of speech as defined in Article 10 of the European Convention on Human Rights.

10.05   They also stressed the robust ability of jurors, under appropriate guidance from the trial judge, to ignore outside publicity and bring in a verdict based solely on the evidence in the case regardless of outside publicity. One judge described juries as healthy bodies who did not need to operate in a "germ-free" atmosphere. The approach in the *Daily Record* case was followed by Lord Rodger when he dismissed an attempt by the Lord Advocate to find the *Evening Times* in contempt over a story about a well-known Scots actor. Another important factor in the *Evening Times* case was the introduction of the Scotland Act which provided that from May 20, 1999 the Lord Advocate had no power to do anything which was incompatible with any of the European Convention rights. Again full details of the case can be found later in this chapter.

10.06   Until 1981 the law of contempt could be found in a series of decisions by the courts, but it is now largely contained in the Contempt of Court Act 1981 (see Appendix 1). According to Lord Hailsham, the Lord Chancellor at the time, the aim of the Act was to make the law clearer and more liberal. Journalists may be forgiven for thinking that neither of these aims has been entirely achieved.

Scotland and England

10.07   The Act was also designed to harmonise the law north and south of the border but experience has shown a wide divergence of interpretation, even allowing for the different pre-trial procedures in Scotland and England. Several stories that would have seen a Scottish editor at least heavily fined, have passed without adverse comment in England.

10.08   In the *Sindicic* case, for example, the *Daily Express* was fined £30,000 for what Lord Emslie described as a disgraceful contempt. He described the story, about a shooting in a street in the Fife town of Kirkcaldy, as painting a lurid picture of an attempted murder and giving the clear impression that the man who had been arrested by the time the article appeared had committed the crime.

Counsel for the *Express* explained that the story had been **10.09** checked in Manchester by an English barrister. Lord Emslie said: "It is perhaps unfortunate, since our system depends so much on the absence of pre-trial publicity, that advice about publication should be given ultimately not by a Scottish lawyer but an English one."

A cynical journalist might think that however "disgraceful" the **10.10** contempt, it was not so severe as to prevent the Lord Advocate (who brought the case against the *Express*) from later prosecuting Sindicic (and securing his conviction). What some would see as an application of double standards seemed to become an established part of Scots law following the case of *Stuurman* (see from 10.112 onwards).

While the *Daily Record* judgment might be seen as bringing the **10.11** approach of the two systems closer together, another case in 1997 involving a notorious sex offender illustrated that differences in interpretation still remain.

The publishers of the *Daily Record* and the *Sun* were each fined **10.12** £5,000 in May 1997 for stories about a man called John Cronin. The *Record's* editor and the *Sun's* Scottish editor were both fined £250. The petition for contempt was brought by the Crown in the High Court after stories were published following Cronin's appearance at Haddington Sheriff Court charged with making nuisance telephone calls to women political workers.

That day the *Record* ran a story saying that Cronin was due to **10.13** appear in court and informing readers of his background, including the fact that he had been jailed for six years for an appalling sex attack on a woman who became known as Judy X. Following his court appearance, the *Record* and the *Sun* both carried similar stories which again went into Cronin's previous history and referred to him as "a sex beast". At that stage he had appeared on petition which meant that he was facing a jury trial although shortly afterwards the charge was reduced to summary level and Cronin pleaded guilty.

Mr Roy Martin, Q.C., counsel for the *Record*, tendered an **10.14** unreserved apology to the court and explained that there had been no deliberate intention to interfere with the course of justice. The newspaper had taken legal advice before publishing both stories and the advice had been that the publication would not create a substantial risk to Cronin's prospects of a fair trial. Mr Martin told the court:

"The Daily Record took the view that, given the nature of Cronin's public *persona*, given the widespread knowledge of his identity through photographs both in newspapers and on television of his whereabouts and his previous criminal activities, any risk created by publication of an article which repeated these elements would not be sufficiently substantial to result in contempt."

10.15 Mr Martin said that this reasoning had been based on the English case in which a court had aborted a trial involving Geoff Knights, the boyfriend of actress Gillian Taylforth because of pre-trial publicity. The saturation coverage had made frequent references to Mr Knights' "violent past". In 1996, however, the Queen's Bench Divisional Court refused to hold five papers in contempt over stories they carried after the arrest of Mr Knights on a charge of wounding a taxi driver. The reports quoted witnesses stating in graphic terms that Knights had committed the offence—"Knights beat me to a pulp". "Knights went berserk with an iron bar"—and referred to his previous convictions. In an unprecedented decision the court said that it was taking account of the saturation coverage given over previous years to the relationship between Miss Taylforth and Mr Knights. In particular, there had been reference to Mr Knights' previous convictions and his violent behaviour in the past.

10.16 Mr Martin argued that the Cronin reports could be seen as falling into the same category. Both Cronin and Mr Knights had become notorious in the public eye because of widespread media publicity. Mr Martin did not press the comparison, however. He said that the *Record* had now taken further legal advice and was prepared to accept that the articles had given rise to a more than minimal risk of prejudice to a fair trial. Mr Michael Jones, Q.C., for the *Sun*, accepted that what had been published amounted to contempt. He added that the *Sun*, too, had taken legal advice before publishing, which was to the effect that the story did not constitute contempt.

10.17 Another interesting aspect of this case was that the judges dismissed the case against the reporters who had written the stories. Lord Rodger, the Lord Justice-General, who heard the case with Lords Sutherland and Marnoch, decided that since the journalists had submitted the stories for legal scrutiny they were not responsible for what had happened after that.

Strict liability rule

10.18 The 1981 Act lays down a "strict liability" rule which means that a journalist can be guilty of contempt even although he did not mean to interfere with the course of justice. The risk of committing contempt under the strict liability rule applies only to a publication which creates a substantial risk that the course of justice in legal proceedings will be seriously impeded or prejudiced. A publication is defined as any speech, writing or broadcast or other communication in whatever form addressed to the public at large or any section of the public. The phrase "communication in whatever form" would include, for example, pictures, headlines and cartoons.

Active proceedings

The risk also arises only when proceedings are active, which in a **10.19** criminal case in Scotland is from the moment of arrest without warrant, the grant of a warrant to arrest or the service of an indictment or summons setting out charges against an accused person, whichever comes first. Both of these measures in the 1981 Act—the kind of risk needed to constitute contempt and the starting point for contempt—were broadly in line with the position the Scottish courts had arrived at a few years earlier.

In the case of *Atkins v. London Weekend Television Ltd* (1978) **10.20** the High Court said the question for the court was whether the contents of a London Weekend Television programme gave rise to a "real risk" of prejudice to a fair and impartial trial. The test of substantial risk of serious prejudice laid down in the Act is basically the same, if more precise. Lord Lane, the Lord Chief Justice, put it this way in an English case in 1983: "A slight risk of serious prejudice is not enough; nor is a substantial risk of slight prejudice".

Lord Diplock has expressed the view in the House of Lords in **10.21** the case of *Attorney-General v. English* (1982) that the word "substantial" in section 2 of the 1981 Act is to be equated with "not remote". Lord McCluskey seemed to adopt the same approach in the trial of Paul Ferris at the High Court in Glasgow in March 1992 when he said a substantial risk meant a risk which was not negligible.

This would appear to mean that it would be very easy to fall foul **10.22** of the Contempt of Court Act, but textbook writers have expressed doubts as to whether Lord Diplock's approach is consistent with the intentions of Parliament when it passed the 1981 Act.

It is impossible to give an exact definition of what the courts will **10.23** regard as a substantial risk of serious prejudice, but obvious examples are the revealing of previous convictions or publication of any inference that the person charged committed the offence. For example, you could report a bank robbery and say that "a" man had been arrested but not "the" man.

The publishers and editors of the *Milngavie and Bearsden Herald* **10.24** were each fined £250 for contempt in 1977 over a report about two men who appeared on petition at Dumbarton Sheriff Court on charges of assault and robbery. The newspaper reported that the two men, whom they identified, had both been wearing masks when they had been caught. The Crown submitted that this was a "fair indication of their guilt" and the court accepted that there had been an interference with the administration of justice.

10.25   In 1998 the High Court decided that *The Scotsman* had committed contempt by stating that two witnesses in a pending election fraud trial against Glasgow Govan M.P. Mohammed Sarwar had asked for police protection because they feared intimidation. Lord Marnoch said he was in no doubt that that the ordinary reader would be left with the impression that two "key witnesses" had asked for protection because they feared intimidation from Mr Sarwar or his associates.

> "In my opinion, where, in the context of a criminal prosecution, particularly one involving charges of election fraud and attempting to pervert the course of justice, there is reference to feared intimidation, the ordinary reader is likely to assume that the accused is ultimately the person whose intimidation is to be feared. . . . He, after all, is the person with the most obvious interest in the outcome of the trial. . . . If I am right so far then I have to say that in my opinion there could hardly be a more prejudicial suggestion in advance of a trial than the one in question. . . . The fact that an accused should stoop to intimidating witnesses is one which many readers, including the ordinary reader, would regard as almost tantamount to guilt."

Once the ordinary reader had formed that impression it was an impression that was likely to "stick", particularly when applied to someone as well known as Mr Sarwar.

10.26   Lord Rodger, the Lord Justice-General, said that looking at the date of publication, the likely date of the trial and the very small readership of *The Scotsman* in the west of Scotland, he had found it harder than Lord Marnoch to be satisfied that the risk of serious prejudice to the proceedings was other than remote. However, particularly because of the high profile of Mr Sarwar which might make the story stick in a reader's mind, he had decided that it would not be right to dissent from Lord Marnoch's view.

10.27   Lord Caplan agreed that the prominence of the accused was an important factor in deciding that the article had amounted to contempt.

> "If he had been a relatively anonymous accused then I should have found it difficult to conclude that the import of the

article would have been retained in the mind of a juror participating in any trial which occurs some months hence. . . . However, because of the publicity which has surrounded him, an adverse impression of his character, which a reader might derive from the article, could readily be retained in his or her mind until the trial. . . . What are the odds of this happening I do not know but the risk is certainly a serious one."

We have seen that in the case of *Atkins* the court decided that **10.28** the test for contempt was whether publication had created a real risk. In the case of *Hall v. Associated Newspapers Ltd* in the same year the High Court also decided that the starting point for contempt was arrest or issue of a warrant for arrest. This confirmed the traditional view of the Scottish courts as set out in the case of *Smith v. Ritchie* in 1892 when it was stated: "A prisoner has the right to ask the court to secure him against anything which might prejudice the public mind so as to endanger his prospects of a fair trial". The court took the view that from the moment someone was a prisoner he was entitled to the protection of the court to safeguard a fair trial.

The *Hall* and *Atkins* decisions restored some common sense to **10.29** the law which had been thrown into confusion for a number of years by Lord Clyde in the case of *Stirling v. Associated Newspapers Ltd* in 1959. Lord Clyde stated that the risk of contempt began, not when someone was a prisoner, but as soon as a crime was suspected and being investigated by the criminal authorities. The media in Scotland rightly felt that this interpretation of the law made their legitimate role in the investigation and exposure of crime well-nigh impossible.

Detention powers

One complication for the media is that since the Criminal Justice **10.30** (Scotland) Act 1980 police have the power to detain a suspect for up to six hours. Section 14 of the Criminal Procedure (Scotland) Act 1995 contains the current statutory provision. This is not an arrest and proceedings are technically not active under the Contempt Act, but any story at the detention stage would have to be written with extreme care. By the time the newspaper was published or the item broadcast the suspect might either have been released or arrested, which could lead to problems with defamation or contempt of court. The possibility of contempt at common law would also have to be considered. This covers conduct intended to prejudice the administration of justice.

Defences under Contempt Act

10.31 There are several sections of the 1981 Act which come under Lord Hailsham's definition of liberalising the law, at least in theory. For the first time in Scotland the journalist is afforded a defence of innocent publication. The Act provides that the publisher of information will not be guilty of contempt if, having taken all reasonable care, he does not know and has no reason to suspect that proceedings are active. The burden of proving this defence lies on the publisher of the information and it will not be enough simply to say that he did not know the case was active. Some positive steps, such as checking with the police and the procurator fiscal or Crown Office, would be necessary.

10.32 Section 5 provides a public interest defence and was included in the Act following the judgment in the European Court in favour of the *Sunday Times* in the thalidomide case. A publication made as, or as part of, a discussion in good faith of public affairs or other matters of general public interest, is not to be treated as contempt if the risk of prejudice to legal proceedings is merely incidental to the discussion.

10.33 This has proved a useful defence on several occasions, notably for the *Daily Mail* in the case of Dr Leonard Arthur, a paediatrician charged with the attempted murder of a Down's Syndrome baby. During the trial, the *Daily Mail* published an article by Malcolm Muggeridge in support of a pro-life candidate in a forthcoming by-election. The House of Lords decided that although the article, which did not specifically mention the *Arthur* case, did create a risk of prejudice to the trial, it was a discussion of public affairs written in good faith. Any prejudice was merely incidental. To decide otherwise would have meant that all media discussion of mercy killing would have been stifled from the time Dr Arthur was charged in February 1981 until his acquittal in November.

10.34 The following year, the *Mail on Sunday* also successfully pleaded a public interest defence in the case of Michael Fagan, who became notorious as the man who managed to get into the Queen's bedroom. Lord Lane described the references in the newspaper to the appalling state of security at Buckingham Palace as a matter of the gravest public concern and an excellent example of the kind of information section 5 was designed to cover.

10.35 The test seems to be how close a link can be established between the trial in question and the publication. In 1989, TVS Television was fined £25,000 and the publishers of the *Reading Standard* £5,000 after Lord Justice Lloyd rejected the argument that they were protected by section 5. The TV station broadcast a programme about sham bed and breakfast accommodation in Reading and the newspaper ran an article about the programme. As a result, a trial in Reading had to be aborted after nearly a month at a cost of £215,000. The case involved a local landlord who was charged with defrauding the DSS over bed and breakfast accommodation, and his picture featured in the TV programme. Lord Justice Lloyd said that the common sense test was to look to see how closely the subject matter of the discussion related to the particular legal proceedings. In this case the relationship between the two was very close.

In a case at Durham Crown Court in April 1991 Judge Jowitt **10.36** took the highly unusual step of warning a jury not to watch a "World in Action" programme. The jury had heard a week of evidence in the trial of three prison warders charged with beating up inmates at Armley Jail, Leeds, and the TV documentary highlighted alleged brutality throughout Britain's jails. Granada Television would no doubt have argued that they were covered by section 5, but the judge said that if any of the jury watched the programme he might have to consider restarting the trial with a fresh jury.

Journalists' sources

On the face of it section 10 of the Act protects the confidentiality **10.37** of journalists' sources. It states that no court may require the disclosure, nor will a person be guilty of contempt for refusing to disclose the source of information contained in a publication, unless it is established to the satisfaction of the court that disclosure is necessary in the interests of justice, national security or for the prevention of disorder or crime.

Early experience of the section suggested that the exception was **10.38** wider than the rule. In a number of cases the English courts declined to interpret the phrases national security, the interests of justice and the prevention of crime in the media's favour. However, more recent decisions indicate that the United Kingdom courts are being influenced by more liberal decisions in the European Court of Human Rights, particularly in the *Goodwin* case (see below).

In 1983 *The Guardian* came into possession of a secret Govern- **10.39** ment memorandum about publicity surrounding the arrival of cruise missiles in the United Kingdom The Government asked the courts to order the return of the memo so that they could examine markings on it to try to discover who had leaked it. *The Guardian* claimed protection under section 10, but this was rejected by the House of Lords.

The court said that although there was no threat to national **10.40** security in this particular case, the leaker might strike again, this

time with more serious consequences. The result was that Sarah
Tisdale, a Foreign Office Clerk, was identified as the informant
and jailed for six months under the Official Secrets Act. This could,
of course, have been avoided had the newspaper destroyed the
document before any order for its return was made (*Secretary of
State for Defence v. Guardian Newspapers Ltd*).

10.41   In 1988 *The Independent* newspaper was fined £20,000 after
financial journalist Mr Jeremy Warner refused to answer questions
put to him by inspectors appointed under the Financial Services
Act to identify the source of suspected leaks from Government
departments. The inspectors claimed this information was necessary for the prevention of crime and that two articles written by Mr
Warner suggested he was in possession of leaked information.

10.42   Lord Griffith said in the House of Lords that the word "necessary" in section 10 had a meaning somewhere between "indispens-
able" and "useful". The nearest paraphrase was "really needed".
The court's view was that Mr Warner's evidence was really needed
by the inspectors for the purpose of their inquiry, which was the
prevention of crime. The judges also rejected the argument that
the phrase "prevention of crime" was limited to the situation in
which identification of the journalist's source would allow steps to
be taken to stop a particular, future, identifiable crime from being
committed [(*Re* an Inquiry under the Company Securities (Insider
Dealing) Act 1985).]

10.43   In 1990 William Goodwin, a young trainee reporter on *The
Engineer* magazine, was fined £5,000 after refusing to hand over the
notes of a telephone conversation with his source. After he
received information about a private company's plans for refinanc-
ing, the company went to court to stop publication and compel
disclosure of the source. At least one judge took the view that the
phrase "interests of justice" did not necessarily have to refer to
legal proceedings. Lord Bridge said that it might refer to a
company's wish to discipline a disloyal employee, even although
legal proceedings might not be needed to achieve that (*X Ltd v.
Morgan-Grampian (Publishers) Ltd*; *Re Goodwin*). However, in
May 1994, the European Commission of Human Rights ruled that
fining Mr Goodwin and threatening to jail him for refusing to
reveal his source breached his right to freedom of expression under
the Convention. Protection of journalistic sources was one of the
basic conditions for press freedom and an order for sources to be
disclosed must be justified by an overriding requirement in the
public interest. The Commission stated:

> "Protection of the sources from which journalists derive
> information is an essential means of enabling the press to

perform its important function of 'public watchdog' in a democratic society. . . . If journalists could be compelled to reveal their sources, this would make it much more difficult for them to obtain information and, as a consequence, to inform the public about matters of public interest."

In 1996 the Human Rights Court reached the same conclusion— that an order for a journalist to disclose his or her sources could not be compatible with Article 10 of the Convention unless it was justified by overriding public interest.

On an equally encouraging note, Daniella Garavelli, then chief **10.44** reporter of the *Newcastle Journal*, successfully pleaded a section 10 defence in a case in 1996 over her refusal to reveal to a police disciplinary tribunal the sources of a story. Lord Justice Beldam, sitting with Mrs Justice Smith in the High Court, said that Ms Garavelli had put before the public fully and fairly a question of considerable public importance. The police had failed to show that the interests of justice outweighed her right not to disclose her source and the court dismissed an application for her committal to prison for contempt. The story involved allegations that senior police officers in Northumbria might be massaging crime figures. A senior police officer was later suspended on suspicion of passing information from the police national computer and Ms Garavelli was questioned under caution. She refused to answer all questions. She was later *subpoenaed* to the suspended officer's disciplinary hearing and again refused to provide details apart from stating that the suspended officer was not the source of her information. The Chief Constable of Leicestershire, who presided over the tribunal, then made the unsuccessful attempt to have Ms Garavelli jailed.

There has been a scarcity of decisions by the Scottish courts on **10.45** section 10 but in the case of *Daily Record* journalist Gordon Airs in 1975, the High Court took the view that a journalist witness who refused to answer a competent and relevant question was guilty of contempt. Lord Emslie took the view that it was hard to imagine any circumstances in which a relevant question could be judged unnecessary.

The *Stair Memorial Encyclopaedia of the Laws of Scotland* states **10.46** that it is difficult to see what difference section 10 has made to Scots law and practice. The authors say: "a Scottish court will rarely, if ever, hold that a competent and relevant question is unnecessary in the interests of justice if the answer to that question would consist of relevant, admissible evidence".

Reports of court proceedings

10.47 The 1981 Act states in section 4 that a fair and accurate report of legal proceedings, held in public, published contemporaneously and in good faith, will not be contempt of court.

10.48 In 1986 at the High Court in Edinburgh Lord Sutherland refused to hold the *Herald* newspaper in contempt over a story about Thomas "TC" Campbell, who was serving 20 years in Peterhead prison after being convicted of murder in the Glasgow "ice-cream war" trial. He was later charged with mobbing and rioting in the jail and the *Herald* carried a story of a preliminary court hearing before the trial. The story was headlined: "Killer accuses prison officers" and defence counsel objected in the strongest possible terms to jurors being told that his client was a killer. He described the report as grave contempt.

10.49 Lord Sutherland pointed out, however, that the references to Campbell's murder convictions had been made in open court at the preliminary hearing and what the *Herald* had done was to report the proceedings in court. Given the terms of section 4, there was no contempt.

10.50 As far as reports of the Scottish Parliament are concerned the Scotland Act 1998 provides that a fair and accurate report made in good faith in proceedings of the Parliament in relation to a Bill or subordinate legislation will not amount to contempt under the strict liability rule. As we have noted in chapter one, this is a limited protection which would not apply, for example, to the reporting of prejudicial comments about an active case made during a general debate, say, on law and order.

Legal debate in jury's absence

10.51 The question of whether this defence would be available where a newspaper published, before the end of a trial, legal debate in the absence of a jury has not been conclusively decided in Scotland.

10.52 In February 1985, Mr Justice McCowan, the judge trying the case of civil servant Mr Clive Ponting, asked the Attorney-General to consider a prosecution for contempt against the *Observer* newspaper. During the trial of Mr Ponting, who was charged with a breach of the Official Secrets Act, the newspaper published the contents of a legal debate outwith the presence of the jury.

10.53 The judge said he had made no order banning publication, because, "I assumed that the greenest reporter on his first day on a provincial newspaper with a circulation of 1,000 would know that he should not report remarks made in the absence of the jury". However, the Attorney-General later confirmed that he would not prosecute the newspaper.

In March 1991 the publishers of the *Evening Times* were fined **10.54** £5,000 and the editor £500 at Paisley by Sheriff James Spy. The sheriff said the newspaper had given details "for all the world to see" of information which had been kept from a jury. The jury in the trial had been reduced to 14 after one of their number claimed to know one of the accused. This had been the subject of a legal debate outwith the presence of the jury where the accused's lawyer said his client did not know any of the jurors, and that if one of the jurors knew his client, it could only be "by reputation".

The *Evening Times* reported what had happened outwith the **10.55** jury's presence and the sheriff halted the trial after ruling that the report had created a substantial risk that the two accused would not receive a fair hearing. This was disputed by the newspaper, which also argued that despite the absence of the jury the proceedings were in public.

On appeal, the findings of contempt and the fines were set aside **10.56** after the Crown said it did not support them. Unfortunately, since no reasons were given for the Crown's view and no written judgment was issued by the court, it is difficult for the journalist to obtain any guidance from the appeal. It is suggested that the practice of not reporting anything which takes place outwith the presence of the jury should still be followed and that the appeal court decision in the *Evening Times* case should not be taken as authority to the contrary.

Restrictions on court reports

Section 4(2) has proved troublesome, particularly in England, **10.57** where it seems to have been used much more frequently than in Scotland to postpone the reporting of court cases, sometimes for many months. A court may order that a report of proceedings, or any part of them, should be postponed for as long as the court thinks necessary to avoid a substantial risk of prejudice to the administration of justice. The risk can involve the proceedings in question or any other proceedings, pending or imminent.

Postponements in Scotland are sometimes ordered when one **10.58** accused pleads guilty to a charge and a co-accused is to stand trial in the near future. This happened in a case where a solicitor admitted charges of fraud and embezzlement in July 1986. Because of an order under the Contempt Act, this could not be reported until September. A co-accused had been due to stand trial on associated charges in August but after it became clear that the trial would not go ahead because he was ill the Scottish Daily Newspaper Society instructed counsel to appear in the High Court to apply, successfully, for reporting restrictions on the July hearing to be lifted.

10.59 Reporting was also postponed in a case at the Court of Criminal Appeal in Edinburgh in 1991 where the judges ordered a retrial after a successful appeal by a convicted murderer.

10.60 One of the most interesting uses of a section 4(2) order in Scotland involved a case in which a 15-year-old girl stood trial for the murder of her 18-year-old sister. She was convicted of murder in September 1998 but the media was banned from reporting anything about the case until the end of the trial of her 14-year-old brother, who was also accused of having taken part in the murder. It was not until he was acquitted in March 1999 that details of the earlier case could be published. By that time she was 16 and her name could be published. Defence counsel for the 14-year-old boy also agreed that the usual restrictions on naming him in press reports should be lifted.

10.61 In the case of *Kim Galbraith* in September 2000 L.J.G Rodger provided welcome guidance on section 4(2) orders. He said courts must ensure that such orders were no wider than necessary to avoid a substantial risk of prejudice and stressed that they covered only the postponement of reports of court proceedings, publication of which were fair and accurate but nevertheless posed a substantial risk of prejudice to the administration of justice. An order to postpone reports of prejudicial comment not contained in a fair and accurate report of proceedings in open court would be an abuse of the power contained in section 4(2).

10.62 Ms Galbraith had been convicted of murdering her husband, a policeman, and one of her grounds of appeal was that she had not received a fair hearing because of adverse publicity during the trial about her senior counsel Mr Donald Findlay, Q.C. One possible outcome of the appeal was a retrial and Margaret Scott, Galbraith's counsel, argued that there should be no reporting of the appeal proceedings, possibly until the end of any retrial. Miss Scott argued that much of the reporting of the original trial had been hostile and it could be anticipated that the appeal would be reported in much the same way if no section 4(2) order were granted. A barrage of hostile media comment would be likely to poison the minds of potential jurors at any retrial. Lord Rodger pointed out, however, that comment of that kind would not be protected as a fair and accurate report of court proceedings and the publisher could be punished:

> "The court's power in section 4(2) is not intended to be used to deal with such publications but to deal, rather, with reports of its proceedings which are fair and accurate but should nonetheless be postponed.
> "It would accordingly be an abuse of the this particular power to pronounce an order not for the purpose of warding

off an anticipated consequence of the fair and accurate reporting of the appeal proceedings but for the purpose of warding off prejudicial comment which those proceedings might prompt."

Dealing with Miss Scot's other argument that even a fair and **10.63** accurate report of the appeal proceedings would substantially prejudice the right to a fair trial, assuming there was a fresh prosecution, Lord Rodger said the court was aware of other cases in which the reporting of appeal proceedings had been postponed under section 4(2). In this case the order sought was in the widest terms and would exclude reporting of legal arguments that would be unlikely to have any bearing on the jury's assessment of evidence at any retrial. Lord Rodger added:

"The position might be different if the appeal court were dealing with prejudicial and inadmissible material such as previous convictions.

"These considerations merely serve to underline the need for the court to consider carefully the scope of any order which it is asked to make and to ensure that it is no wider than necessary to avoid the relevant risk of prejudice.

"Even if we examine those parts of the evidence which might relate to the evidence led at the trial we see no reason to anticipate at present that a fair and accurate report of the appeal hearing would create a substantial risk of prejudice to the fairness of any possible retrial.

"This court and courts in other jurisdictions have frequently had occasion to express their confidence—based on accumulated experience over many years—in the ability of jurors, when properly directed, to reach their verdict on the evidence led at the trial unaffected by any extraneous considerations.

"We are confident that . . . jurors who had read and remembered reports of the appeal proceedings would still be able to reach an impartial verdict at any retrial. That being so there is no basis upon which the court could properly make an order under section 4(2)."

Lord Rodger also pointed out that journalists wishing to discover whether a section 4(2) order had been made in a particular case should check the Scottish Court service website (http://www.scotcourts.gov.uk).

The Contempt of Court Act also provides (s. 11) that where a **10.64** court has the power to allow information to be withheld from the public in court proceedings, it may also ban the publication of the information. The thinking behind this section is to prevent the purpose of the court order being frustrated by the publication by the media of the names of, for example, blackmail victims.

When contempt risk ends

10.65 In criminal proceedings, the risk of contempt under the Act ends when the accused is acquitted or sentenced or with the return of any other verdict, finding, order or decision which puts an end to the proceedings. Proceedings may also cease to be active because of some other process causing them to be discontinued or by other "operation of law". Proceedings are discontinued when they are expressly abandoned by the prosecutor or deserted *simpliciter* (*i.e.* absolutely or without qualification).

10.66 As the *Scottish Daily Express* discovered to its cost in 1999 the risk of contempt still runs when proceedings are deserted *pro loco et tempore* (for the time being). In a case which also confirmed that the media can appeal against a contempt finding by way of a petition to the *nobile officium* (which exists to provide a remedy in extraordinary or unforeseen circumstances) the *Express* was fined £50,000, one of the biggest amounts in Scotland for many years.

10.67 The circumstances were that the *Express* published a front page article about a case four days after it had been deserted temporarily by the Crown. The article dealt with the evidence in the case. The fine was imposed by three judges at the High Court and the *Express* appealed to a larger court against the size of the penalty.

10.68 In a hearing before five judges at the High Court in Edinburgh, Lord Rodger, the Lord Justice-General, said the newspaper now accepted that the case had still been active under the 1981 Act but had originally published on the opposite and wholly mistaken view. The reporter involved in the case had spoken to the procurator fiscal who advised that the Crown reserved the right to re-indict the accused. A firm of solicitors who had advised the newspaper for many years gave advice that the proceedings were now at an end. Lord Rodger said the *Express* had been misled. Counsel for the newspaper now accepted that the legal advice was "completely indefensible" and did not try to explain how solicitors experienced in this area of the law had tendered the advice they did. Lord Rodger added:

> "The only question for us is whether the fine can properly be regarded as excessive, given all the circumstances of the case. ... We note that the Express gave considerable prominence to the article. We note also that, even though the Express took legal advice, it is well established that where sections one and

two of the Contempt of Court Act apply, the duty of publishers is actually to avoid publishing articles which create a substantial risk of serious prejudice to the course of justice. ... The Express have acknowledged that they failed to discharge that duty and so did indeed create that risk of serious prejudice. . . . Having regard in particular to the level of fines imposed in some recent cases, we accept that the fine imposed in this case may be considered to be high. . . . On the other hand, it appears to us that in some at least of the recent cases, the fines were lower than fines imposed in comparable cases in the past. . . . We have reached the view that the fine selected by the judges in this case was within the range of fines which they were entitled to impose to mark their serious view of the publication of the article which, as the Express admitted, created a substantial risk that the course of justice would be seriously impeded or prejudiced in a case which merited proceedings on indictment."

Ironically from the point of view of the newspaper the prosecution eventually became time-barred after a year elapsed from the first appearance of the accused on petition. **10.69**

An accused is sentenced when he or she is made subject to any order or decision following on conviction or finding of guilt which disposes of the case, either absolutely or subject to future events. Where a sentence is deferred for two or three weeks to enable the court, for example, to obtain background reports on the accused the proceedings remain active during that time. **10.70**

Criminal proceedings are also no longer active if the accused is found to be under a disability rendering him or her unfit to be tried or to plead or is found insane in bar of trial. **10.71**

Contempt and appeals

For reasons which are not entirely obvious, the Act extends the contempt law to cover cases at the appeal stage, as if judges were as susceptible as jurors to influence from what they may read in the press or see on television. **10.72**

This has made the media in Scotland more wary than before about the terms of background articles published at the end of criminal trials. It is worth remembering, however, that there has to be a substantial risk of serious prejudice and that senior judges rather than a jury will be hearing any appeal. It was also made clear in Parliament during the debate on the Contempt Bill that there would normally be a "free for all period" for the media between the end of a case and an appeal being lodged. **10.73**

10.74   A case does not become active for contempt purposes merely because a lawyer says at the end of a case that his client intends to appeal. There must be a definite starting process such as a notice of appeal or an application for leave to appeal or some other originating process. Appeal proceedings are active until disposed of, abandoned, discontinued or withdrawn. However, if the appeal court grants the Crown authority to bring a fresh prosecution, the risk of prejudicing the new proceedings begins from the end of the appeal.

10.75   All this is against a background where the High Court in Scotland has stated in the case of *Bernardi* in 1984 that lay magistrates, far less legally-trained sheriffs and High Court judges, should be incapable of being influenced by the media.

10.76   The issue of contempt and appeals was discussed in the unreported case of *Forbes Cowan* in 1998 in which the BBC's "Frontline" programme planned to broadcast "The Skipper's Tale", the story of the detection and arrest of the crew of a ship which had been seized by customs officers at Troon in Ayrshire. Four accused were convicted after trial and, after they were sentenced to a total of 32 years, lodged appeals, some against both conviction and sentence. Before the appeal came to court, the BBC announced its intention to broadcast "The Skipper's Tale", even although it knew that appeals were pending. The BBC was also aware that if the appeals against conviction were successful there was the possibility of fresh prosecutions. One of the accused, Forbes Cowan, applied to the High Court claiming that the broadcast would amount to contempt. His petition specifically addressed the possibility of the case being heard by another jury in a second trial. The High Court dismissed Mr Cowan's petition without asking the BBC to present an argument. In effect, the court was saying that he had not made out even a prima facie case worthy of consideration. Without a written judgment it is not easy to work out the reasoning behind the decision but it may be that, having been convicted, Mr Cowan was not given the full protection of the law of contempt.

10.77   The court did seem to be concerned about the possibility of the media not being able to discuss a much publicised case until all appeals had been exhausted, perhaps years in the future. It may be that they were anticipating the incorporation of the European Human Rights legislation and its protection for freedom of speech. It can be taken from this case that the launching of an appeal is unlikely to prevent the media from discussing a case in a fair and balanced way.

10.78   The English courts, however, discovered a different reason for extending contempt to appeals. In 1987, Lord Chief Justice Lane banned the showing of a Channel 4 re-enactment of hearings in the Birmingham pub bombings appeals. The programme was based on daily transcripts of what had already been said in court, but Lord Lane decided that showing it was likely to undermine public confidence in the legal system. With all due respect, this seems to show little faith in the robustness of the legal system or the common sense of the public.

The Lockerbie case

This approach was rejected in Scotland in the case of two Libyan **10.79** nationals accused of conspiracy to murder after Pan Am flight 103 exploded over Lockerbie, killing 270 people. They petitioned the High Court in July 1999 asking it to hold the *Sunday Times* in contempt. The newspaper had run a story headlined: "Official: Gadaffi's Bomb Plot". The story alleged that the Libyan leader had personally instructed the head of his External Security Organisation to organise the Lockerbie bombing as revenge for an American air raid on Tripoli. The article detailed alleged links between the head of the ESO and one of the accused and concluded: "It would be an odd sort of justice that found his cat's paws guilty of murder and let the real villain off the hook." The accused argued that a fair and dispassionate reader of the articles would be left with the impression that their guilt could be taken for granted.

Lord Cullen, the Lord Justice-Clerk, said he had no doubt that it **10.80** was as true today as it was in the days of *Smith v. Ritchie* more than 100 years ago (see above) that anyone who had been committed for trial was under the protection of the court. However, as the court had pointed out in the *Daily Record* case the 1981 Contempt Act had been passed to change United Kingdom law and bring it into line with the European Convention on Human Rights. "The Act represented a distinct shift in favour of freedom of expression", Lord Cullen emphasised.

If the Libyans had been in custody in Scotland awaiting trial by **10.81** jury he would have little difficulty in accepting that the *Sunday Times* article raised a serious question over the effect on minds of potential jurors. However, special arrangements had been made for the men to stand trial in the Netherlands before three judges and at the date of publication it was unrealistic to consider the effect on potential jurors in Scotland. Counsel for the two men maintained however that the *Sunday Times* had still committed a contempt. They argued that the court should take action to prevent public confidence in the course of justice from being undermined and that the accused were entitled to be assured that they would be tried by an impartial tribunal. In support of their argument they relied on the Channel 4 decision (above) in which Lord Chief Justice Lane had said that the broadcasting of a TV reconstruction of a current appeal might affect the public's view of the judgment of the court and leave the accused in doubt about the effect of outside influences.

10.82 Lord Cullen said it seemed clear that this approach was an attempt to establish a general rule in the law of contempt that it was offensive for the media to "pre-judge" issues in pending cases and usurp the function of the court. The problem with that was that it could not stand alongside sections 1 and 2 of the Contempt of Court Act in which Parliament had adopted a different test.

10.83 "There is nothing in the Act which enjoins the court to apply as the test the perception of others as to whether the course of justice may be affected," Lord Cullen stressed.

> "The administration of justice has to be robust enough to withstand criticism and misunderstanding. . . . I do not consider that liability for contempt of court should depend on the viewpoint of the party to the proceedings whether that is based on his actual attitude or upon some objective assessment of his position. . . . It is one thing to say that it is good law that a party to proceedings should be able to rely on there being no usurpation by any other person of the court to decide the case according to law. . . . That is saying no more than that such a person has a right to complain about that as being contempt of court. . . . It is quite another thing to say that what is contempt of court should be judged by reference to the perspective of that party."

10.84 Lord Cullen added that even if it had been correct to use the test of whether public confidence in the administration of justice had been undermined, he would have decided that the test had not been met in this case.

> "In this country the public and those who are the subject of criminal proceedings enjoy the benefit of an independent judiciary, the members of which are well used to concentrating on the evidence, and only the evidence, which is put before them in the proceedings, and to arrive at decisions in an impartial manner."

10.85 He refused go as far as to rule out absolutely the risk of a professional judge being influenced by something he had read about a case with which he was dealing. But he quoted the words of Lord Bridge of Harwich in the *Lonrho* case in which the judge had said this was a "very much more remote" possibility (than in a case involving a jury).

Lord Coulsfield agreed, pointing out: **10.86**

> "I think one can detect in the pre-1981 cases . . . a feeling that once an issue has been taken to the courts, the courts should be left alone to deal with it without further comment. . . . It seems to me, however, that that must be one of the areas in which a shift in the balance between freedom of expression and regard for the administration of justice has occurred."

He also rejected the reasoning of the court in the Channel 4 **10.87** case, stressing that it was for the court to decide whether there was a substantial risk of prejudice to proceedings. "If the court decides there is no such risk, the perception of other persons as to the fairness or otherwise of the proceedings is, so far as I can see, neither here nor there for the purposes of section 2(2) of the 1981 Act."

He said it would only be in an exceptional case that a single **10.88** publication, like the *Sunday Times* in the present case, would be regarded as so damaging that a trial could not go ahead. He warned, however, that repeated publication either by one or several newspapers over a period of time might create an atmosphere in which it would be extremely difficult for either a judge or jury to reach a proper conclusion. "Such repeated publication might properly be described as 'trial by newspaper' and might be capable of being regarded as prejudicial to the course of justice."

Another point emphasised by the Lockberbie case is that **10.89** criminal proceedings are no longer active 12 months after a warrant has been issued unless the person in question has been arrested within that period. If he or she is arrested after the expiry of the 12 months, the proceedings become active again. In the Lockerbie case the sheriff in Dumfries originally issued warrants for the arrest of two Libyans in December 1991. The strict liability rule ceased to operate in December 1992 as no arrests had been made, although the possibility of common law contempt remained. The proceedings became live again when the two Libyans surrendered themselves in April 1998 for trial in the Netherlands.

Under the strict liability rule, criminal proceedings before a **10.90** court-martial or standing civilian court are not concluded until the completion of any review of finding or sentence.

Juries and tape recorders

Section 8 of the Act protects the confidentiality of the jury room **10.91** and changes the law following the decision in England that it was not contempt for the *New Statesman* to interview a juror in the Jeremy Thorpe case. It is now contempt to obtain, disclose or solicit any particulars of statements made, opinions expressed, arguments advanced or votes cast by members of a jury in the course of their deliberations in any legal proceedings. A journalist who interviewed a juror about a particular case would be guilty of contempt even although nothing was ever published. In 1994 the House of Lords decided that the prohibition applied not just to jurors but to anyone who published information they revealed. They dismissed an appeal by the *Mail on Sunday* against a finding of contempt after it published interviews with jurors revealing details of jury room discussions. Lord Lowry said section 8 was aimed at keeping the secrets of the jury room inviolate in the interests of justice. The paper, editor and a journalist were fined a total of £60,000. However, a general discussion about the merits or otherwise of the jury system would not be contempt.

10.92 It seems clear that, at the very least, section 8 has not made it any easier to carry out genuine research into how juries approach their job. This is regrettable in an area like contempt where the whole approach of the courts hinges on how jurors are thought to be affected by publicity.

10.93 Section 9 makes it contempt to use a tape recorder in court, or bring one into court for use, without the court's permission. It would also be contempt to publish a recording of legal proceedings by playing it in public or to dispose of a recording with a view to publication. The section gives courts a discretion to allow tape recording under such conditions as they think fit. The courts also have power to order forfeiture of a tape recorder and any recording.

Common law contempt

10.94 It is still possible to commit contempt of court at common law, outside the provisions of the 1981 Act, if the court decides that the conduct involved was intended to impede or prejudice the administration of justice. Section 6 of the Act specifically leaves that possibility open. The kind of behaviour that the courts might regard as serious enough to amount to deliberate contempt can be seen in a case in 1988 in which the publishers of the *Sun* newspaper were fined £75,000 in England.

10.95 The authorities had decided there was not enough evidence to prosecute a doctor accused of raping an eight-year-old girl. The *Sun* financed a private prosecution and published a number of articles describing the doctor as a "beast" and a "swine". They also published his name and his picture on the front page. The doctor went to trial at Chelmsford Crown Court and was acquitted.

10.96 In later proceedings taken against the publishers, Lord Justice Watkins agreed with the Attorney-General that the *Sun* had been guilty of contempt, although not under the 1981 Act. The court said that where a newspaper gave practical help to stage a private prosecution then published a series of articles intended to prejudice a fair trial, it was guilty of contempt at common law (*Attorney-General v. News Group Newspapers* [1989]).

10.97 In May 1991 the editor of *The Sport* newspaper was cleared of contempt after the Attorney-General brought proceedings against him at common law. North Wales police had issued a picture of David Evans, a man they wished to interview in connection with the disappearance of a schoolgirl. They asked that his previous convictions for rape and a history of sex attacks should not be published. Two days before a warrant was issued for Evans' arrest (which meant the case was not active under the 1981 Act) *The Sport* published a story headlined "Evans was given ten years for rape".

10.98 Evans was later jailed for life for the girl's murder, and in subsequent proceedings, the High Court decided that the Attorney-General had failed to show that the editor of *The Sport* had intended to prejudice a fair trial. In court, the editor, Mr Peter Grimsditch, defended the decision to publish Evans' record on the basis that "he was on the run and a danger to other women".

10.99 In the course of his decision, Mr Justice Hodgson was strongly critical of the decision in the *Sun* case. He said the decision was wrong and were it necessary to do so, he would refuse to follow it. He warned that to find a newspaper guilty of contempt in these circumstances could impede investigative journalism. He added: "Many of the targets of investigative journalism are rich and powerful and who is to say that they, when attacked, will not respond by seeking leave to move for contempt?"

Sunday Times case

10.100 In a decision with wide-ranging implications for the media, the House of Lords decided in April 1991 that the *Sunday Times* had been guilty of contempt at common law by publishing extracts from the book *Spycatcher* while an injunction was in force banning publication by a number of other newspapers. There was no injunction restraining publication by the *Sunday Times* and the newspaper argued that it would be an unwarranted extension of the law to find it guilty of contempt. The newspaper maintained that although it knew of the existence of the orders against other papers it was not bound by them nor was it assisting a breach of the injunction by those newspapers which were caught by the injunction. The *Sunday Times* had received legal advice that to publish in these circumstances would not amount to contempt.

10.101   The Attorney-General, who brought proceedings against the *Sunday Times*, accepted that the newspaper could not be bound by a court order to which it was not a party. His argument, which the court accepted, was that by publishing *Spycatcher* extracts, the paper had knowingly destroyed the whole point of the injunctions, and that was a deliberate interference with the course of justice. Lord Ackner pointed out that *Sunday Times* editor Mr Andrew Neil knew of existing injunctions against the *Observer* and *Guardian* and regarded *Spycatcher* as "banned in Britain". To avoid the risk of an injunction against his own paper, Mr Neill kept the *Spycatcher* extracts out of the first edition.

10.102   Lord Ackner said that since the whole point of contempt was to prevent interference with the course of justice, it would leave a remarkable gap in the law if it could not deal with a situation of this kind. "Whatever would be the point of a court making an order designed to preserve the confidentiality of material, the subject matter of a dispute between A and B, pending the trial of the action, if, at the whim of C, the protection afforded by the court by its order could be totally dissipated?"

10.103   Lord Jauncey, one of the Scottish judges in the appeal, said he was quite satisfied that a person who knowingly acted to frustrate the operation of a court order could be guilty of contempt even though he was neither named in the order nor assisted anyone who was named to breach it. He did not accept that this necessarily converted every injunction from an order against a named person to one against the world. It was only in a limited type of case that independent action by a third party would interfere with a court order in which he was not named.

10.104   However, Lord Oliver recognised the wide-ranging implications of the decision and the potential for gagging the media for a lengthy period. He said he had reached his decision with "a measure of disquiet" not because he doubted its validity, but because of the possibilities that it opened up. He stressed the importance of the courts keeping a vigilant eye on the possibility of the law of contempt being invoked in support of claims which were, in truth, insupportable. This was because a plaintiff seeking an injunction never had to show more than a fairly arguable case to succeed. Lord Oliver added:

> "The effect in a contest between a would-be publisher and one seeking to restrain the publication of allegedly confidential information, is that the latter, by presenting an arguable case, can effectively through the invocation of the law of contempt, restrain until the trial of the action, which may be two or more years ahead, publication not only by the defendant by anyone else within the jurisdiction".

By this means, what might turn out to be perfectly legitimate comment could be stifled until it was no longer important or had any public interest. (*Times Newspapers v. The Attorney-General* [1992]. See also Chapter 30, Official Secrets.)

The European Court of Human Rights considered the use of **10.105** injunctions in the *Spycatcher* cases. It decided that although the Human Rights Convention did not ban the use of prior restraints on publication, the dangers involved called for the most careful consideration by the court, particularly in cases where the media was involved. The 1998 Human Rights Act included special measures to deal with the situation where a court is considering granting an interdict affecting freedom of expression. (See Chapter 25.)

Right of Appeal

Any doubt that existed about the right of a publisher to appeal **10.106** against a finding of contempt in criminal proceedings was removed by a judgment of the High Court in 1982 setting aside convictions against the *Herald* and *The Scotsman* following reports of a High Court trial in Glasgow in July 1981. The case involved 11 accused charged with conspiring to further the aims of the Ulster Volunteer Force by illegal means.

The reports of the case included reference to a Mrs Gibson and **10.107** her husband (witnesses at the trial) being surrounded by police as they left the building and taken in an unmarked police car to a secret address. Lord Ross, the trial judge, held there was a risk that jurors might be influenced in their consideration of the credibility of the two witnesses, and admonished both papers after finding them guilty of contempt.

They appealed by way of a petition to the *nobile officium*, to a **10.108** Bench chaired by Lord Emslie, the Lord Justice-General, which decided there had been no contempt. It was understood to be the first case of an appeal by any newspaper against a conviction for contempt in Scotland.

The judgment stated that Gibson was a self-confessed accom- **10.109** plice in the crime, who admitted being a commander of the UVF and implicated several of the accused. The appeal judges agreed with the newspapers' submission that it was mere speculation to say the jury might be influenced by what the newspapers had said about the two witnesses. The reports had to be read in the context of the particular trial and of the extraordinary security precautions obviously being taken throughout its course, which were a matter of public knowledge (*Kemp, Petrs,* 1982).

The case in which the *Daily Express* was fined £50,000 in 1999 **10.110** (see para. 10.63) raised the question as to whether it was competent for someone who had been found in contempt and punished by three High Court judges to appeal to a larger bench by presenting a petition to the *nobile officium*. The *Express* sought an appeal on the basis that the fine was excessive. Lord Rodger, the Lord Justice-General, said that the petition for contempt brought by the Lord Advocate could have been heard by a single judge, rather than a bench of three. Since the court was being asked to entertain an appeal against a decision of three judges, the court had decided that it was appropriate for the appeal to be heard by five judges.

Background information

10.111 Apart from establishing the procedure for appeal in a contempt case, Gibson provided some useful guidance for the media over the publication of outside information which is not part of the evidence in court. Although references to an unmarked police car and a secret address were not based on evidence that had come out in court, Lord Emslie was satisfied that their mention was not prejudicial. However, it would be highly dangerous to assume that it is always safe to include information from outside the courtroom in reports of criminal cases. As in Gibson, there will usually be no substantial risk where the information consists simply of facts which are already known to members of the jury and will not therefore influence their minds in reaching their verdict. And it should always be made clear that it is a statement of known fact and does not form part of the proceedings as such.

10.112 The dangers of using background knowledge were well illustrated by a case in 1989 in which the *Alloa Advertiser* admitted contempt. At the end of a report of an ongoing trial at Alloa Sheriff Court, the newspaper stated that all the accused were released on bail, except two (who were named) "who are serving sentences for drugs offences imposed at the High Court in Edinburgh". The result of revealing the previous convictions was that the Crown had to desert the case and serve a fresh indictment.

10.113 It is also highly dangerous to mix together background with what is said in court. In December 1991 the BBC were fined £5,000 over a television news report on a drugs trial in Shrewsbury, a report described by Lord Justice Watkins in the High Court as "strewn with error". Counsel for the BBC told the court: "There was a series of mistakes, in no small measure due apparently to the inability of this reporter to distinguish what he had heard and seen in court on the one hand, and what he had been told some time before in briefings by Customs and Excise."

Attitude of courts to contempt complaints

In Scotland a complaint of contempt against the media in a **10.114** criminal case can be brought from three separate sources—the Crown, the defence, and the judge who is hearing the case in question. It is also worth remembering that prejudice can affect the prosecution as well as the defence. In the case of Michael Fagan, the man who broke into the Queen's bedroom, the High Court in London took the view in 1983 that inaccurate statements in a newspaper story to the effect that certain charges against Fagan had either been withdrawn or dropped created a substantial risk of serious prejudice to the prosecution.

The classic example of contempt proceedings being brought by **10.115** the Crown is the case of *Stuurman* in 1979 which underlines several important points—most importantly, that there can be contempt even although the court decides at the end of the day that there was no actual prejudice. The test is whether there was a substantial risk at the time of publication. *Stuurman* also makes clear that anyone who publishes prejudicial material cannot plead as a defence that the information came from police sources nor that the story was passed as safe by a lawyer.

In *Stuurman*, the *Herald* was fined £20,000 and the then editor **10.116** £750 for publishing a front-page story about a major drugs operation in the Scottish borders. The headline read: "Armed raids smash big drugs ring in Scotland", and the accompanying story provided details of how a "huge illicit drugs operation" had been smashed by police. It also informed readers that three of the Dutch nationals who had been arrested were believed to have escaped from prison in Holland. A police spokesman said the four people under arrest had been operating the biggest laboratory ever found in Scotland.

The Lord Advocate presented a petition for contempt to the **10.117** High Court and, given the tone of the story, the *Herald* had little option but to admit its guilt. Lord Justice General Emslie described the offence as being of the gravest character and well-nigh incomprehensible. The court was appalled to learn that publication had been checked by a legal adviser.

The court was also informed that the story had been sent out by **10.118** the Press Association and was based on information released by police in England. Lord Emslie said: "There can surely be no lingering doubt that if information, even from police sources, about a person who has been charged with criminal offences and arrested, is such that, if published, it would constitute contempt of court, the source of the offending material cannot be relied upon in mitigation of the offence."

10.119 The defence then presented a petition to the High Court, arguing that since the pre-trial publicity was so blatantly prejudicial a fair hearing was now impossible. Having previously instituted the contempt proceedings against the *Herald* (and Radio Forth) the Lord Advocate now informed the court that in his opinion there was not such a risk of prejudice that the trial should be aborted and the court agreed.

10.120 Following their convictions, three of the accused appealed on the ground that their trial should not have been allowed to go ahead because of the prejudicial publicity. The Court of Criminal Appeal rejected this argument. Lord Emslie said the question for the court was whether the risk of prejudice was so grave that even the careful directions of the trial judge could not reasonably be expected to remove it. "In our opinion, that question falls to be answered in the negative. The publications occurred almost four months before the trial diet was called. In considering the effect of these publications, the court was well entitled to bear in mind that the public memory of newspaper articles and news broadcasts and of their detailed contents is notoriously short." That being the case, the residual risk of prejudice to the prospects of a fair trial could reasonably be expected to be removed by careful directions such as those which were given by the trial judge.

10.121 In the light of Lord Emslie's remarks, the media could be forgiven for wondering why the contempt was treated so seriously in the first place if the public's memory is short and the problem could be cured by a careful direction by the trial judge. While one can appreciate the desire of the Crown Office and the courts not to see the prosecution of serious crime thwarted by pre-trial publicity, the *Stuurman* case left the distinct impression of the authorities having their cake and eating it.

10.122 In May 1994 the High Court in London regarded a lapse of nine months between publication and trial as being of "overriding importance" in rejecting contempt complaints against ITN and four newspapers. They had referred to a previous conviction of IRA terrorist Paul Magee—the murder of an SAS captain—when Magee was arrested in June 1992. Magee was later jailed for 30 years for the murder of special constable Glenn Goodman. Following the conviction, the Attorney-General brought contempt proceedings, but his case was rejected by the High Court. Lord Justice Leggatt said the media organisations involved might be thought to be "extremely fortunate" but nine months was a long time to retain a story in one's mind. The court could not say with certainty that reports had created a substantial risk of prejudice to the trial.

Tom King case

There may be exceptional cases in which the courts will decide that **10.123** the risk of prejudice to a fair trial is so great that no direction by the trial judge can remove it. In 1990 the Appeal Court in England quashed the convictions of three Irish citizens who had been jailed for 25 years on charges of conspiring to murder Home Secretary Mr Tom King. Less than 24 hours after the three declined to give evidence at their trial Mr King made a statement in the House of Commons declaring his intention to curb the right to silence because, in his view, too many guilty people were being acquitted. He repeated his views in a number of TV news bulletins.

The following day, the trial judge rejected a defence plea for a **10.124** retrial and went on to direct the jury about the inalienable right of the accused to remain silent. The Appeal Court took a different view. Lord Beldam said: "We are left with the definite impression that the impact the statements on television and in the press may have had on the fairness of the trial could not be overcome by the direction to the jury".

Joseph Trainer case

One case in which a Scottish court has followed through a finding **10.125** of contempt by aborting a trial was that of Joseph Trainer at the High Court in Paisley in 1987. Trainer was on trial for the murder of his brother-in-law; his defence being that the fatal stabbing was an accident. After closing speeches, Radio Clyde reported that he had offered to plead guilty to a reduced charge of culpable homicide. This had not been said in open court and, in any case, was not consistent with a plea of accident.

Lord Allanbridge took the exceptional step of polling the jury to **10.126** see how many had heard the offending broadcast and it turned out that seven out of the 15 had. The judge fined Colin Adams, the news editor of Radio Clyde, £20,000 and Gavin Bell, the freelance who had sent out the story, £5,000. He also decided the prejudice was so great that the trial must be halted.

The case had two interesting sequels. Mr Trainer was retried at **10.127** the High Court in Edinburgh and acquitted. Mr Adams appealed against his fine which was quashed by three appeal court judges. Lord Emslie said that Mr Adams had relied on the expertise of a freelance journalist with 20 years' experience and it was difficult to attach any blame to him for what had happened. However, the court took the view that the culpability of Mr Bell, who, wisely, did not appeal against his fine, was of a high order.

The case is also interesting for anyone trying to answer the **10.128** question of who is liable for contempt. In many cases it will be the publisher and editor, but *Trainer* illustrates that freelance reporters and news editors can also be found liable and fined heavily. It will depend on the particular circumstances of each case. As we have already seen in the *John Cronin* case earlier in the chapter, the court decided that since the stories in question had been submitted for legal checking, the reporters could not be held responsible for what happened after that.

Mistakes in court reports

10.129 In a number of other cases, the Scottish courts have decided that the fact that a mistake has been made in a story will not necessarily lead to a finding of contempt. This should not however, be taken as a signal to relax standards of accuracy. As the *Trainer* case illustrates, mistakes can still be costly.

10.130 In a murder trial at the High Court in Kilmarnock in 1989, a reporter's story stated that the two victims had been "felled" by single blows. A sub-editor changed the word to "killed" and also used the word "killed" in the headline. Counsel for the editor of the *Daily Record* argued that any problem created by the story could be solved by a direction by the trial judge that the jury should concentrate solely on the evidence in court. Lord Kirkwood said that in the circumstances, he was not satisfied that the *Record* story had created a substantial risk of serious prejudice.

10.131 Lord Cameron reached a similar decision in a trial at the High Court in Glasgow in which the accused was alleged to have said: "I'll get life for it." The quote appeared in the *Herald and Evening Times* as: "I'll get life for what I've done". The second statement amounts to a confession, while the first may not.

10.132 This approach to reporting errors was summed up by Lord Cowie in the case of Daniel Pollock at the High Court in Airdrie in 1984 where the BBC reported details of charges which were no longer on the indictment before the jury. Lord Cowie accepted the argument that the realistic view of what a juror would think if he had heard the BBC report was that the reporter had got it wrong because the story did not coincide with the indictment. Any risk of prejudice could be cured by a simple direction to the jury to ignore the BBC report and decide the case solely on the evidence. The *Pollock* case illustrates the importance of checking with the clerk of court that the indictment in the hands of the reporter is the same as the one in the hands of the jury.

10.133 A reporter would be unwise to believe, however, that all judges will adopt the same approach when a mistake has been made. In the case of Alistair Keating at the High Court in Edinburgh in 1987, the publishers of the *Sun* were fined £5,000 by Lord

Mayfield. This was a case where a fireman was accused of trying to kill his wife by wiring explosives into her car. The *Sun* ran a story in the middle of the trial giving the impression, wrongly, that the accused had admitted putting the explosives in place.

It is also possible to commit contempt through a simple misun- **10.134** derstanding of criminal procedure. In 1990 the *Aberdeen Press and Journal* was found guilty of contempt over a report of a murder trial which was headed: "Husband decides on no defence in wife-murder trial". This was based on the first paragraph of the story which stated that the accused had decided not to defend the charge. In fact all that had happened was that his defence counsel had decided not to call any witnesses in support of his not guilty plea. After an unqualified apology by the editor, Lord Cameron decided that the contempt had been purged.

Journalists must also be wary of reporting trials at an early stage **10.135** when all that has happened is that an indictment has been read to the jury. Scottish judges tend to disapprove of phrases such as "The court was told" or "The court heard" at this stage. They take the view that this gives the impression that evidence has been led, when in fact, it has not.

If basing a story simply on allegations in the indictment it is safer **10.136** to use a phrase such as "The Crown alleges" or "The indictment states". To a journalist the distinction may seem artificial and pointless but the courts regard it as important and it could avoid a finding of contempt.

The *Daily Record* case

As indicated earlier in the chapter, one of the most significant **10.137** decisions on the law of contempt since the passing of the 1981 Act followed a story published in the *Daily Record* in April 1998. The story related how a number of "high risk" prisoners were moved from one jail to another under "a massive armed police guard". The story quoted a police insider as saying: "We are taking no chances with this lot. It was an impressive sight and part of an intricate plan to ensure these heavy-duty guys got to their destination. They are facing a lot of heavy charges."

When the case called at the High Court in Edinburgh a week **10.138** later counsel for one of the accused argued that the article created a substantial risk that the course of justice would be seriously prejudiced. Lord Bonomy agreed and imposed £1,500 fines on Peter Cox, the duty editor of the *Record*, and Stuart Griffiths, the reporter who wrote the story. The judge said he was in no doubt that the terms in which the accused were described and the description of the arrangements made for their transfer amounted to a contempt of court.

10.139   The journalists appealed and in his report to the appeal court Lord Bonomy said: "This article would, in my opinion, cause any objective reader to conclude that organised criminals were being put on trial.

> "It contained language which was designed to give the reader the impression that each of the accused fell into that category. . . . While references to tight security arrangements do not on their own justify an inference that those to whom they relate are criminals or of bad character, in this article these have to be read in the context of referring to the prisoners being transferred as 'this lot' and 'these heavy duty guys.'"

10.140   In the appeal by the journalists Lord Rodger, the Lord Justice-General, said the article appeared in a paper with a wide circulation in the Edinburgh area and he had no hesitation in deciding that it was quite likely that some of the jurors would have read the article. He also considered it likely that any juror who had read the article might well have still remembered it when the trial began and made the connection between the story and the case which he was being asked to decide. The question was whether, in these circumstances, the publication of the article created a substantial risk of impeding the course of justice.

10.141   Lord Rodger said that at times counsel for the journalists had appeared to ask the court to accept that readers of tabloids did not really believe what they read in their paper and that stories were written more to entertain than inform. The judge added: "I reject any suggestion that that, because the article appeared in a tabloid newspaper, the court should apply a different (and apparently higher) standard in judging its potential for impeding or prejudicing the course of justice."

10.142   He agreed with Lord Bonomy that in themselves references to high security arrangements did not amount to contempt.

> "Juries will often see that some accused are on bail, while others are held in custody, while still others are taken to and from court under conditions of particular security. There is nothing to suggest that jurors' awareness of these particular facts affects their ability to return a proper verdict based on the evidence which they have heard in court. . . . There is similarly no reason to suppose that an article in a newspaper referring to security precautions will interfere with a juror's ability to judge the case properly."

10.143   Lord Rodger noted that the trial judge had attached importance to the references to "this lot" and "these heavy-duty guys" but, having read and re-read the article, he took the view that it did not amount to a contempt.

"It seems to me that an attentive reader of the article would be likely to carry away an abiding impression that the prisoners concerned, as a group, were facing very serious charges and were people who, for that reason and perhaps for other reasons, the police considered had to be kept under tight security conditions in case someone engineered their escape."

A reader who had formed that impression might also wonder whether the prisoners on trial were people with underworld contacts who might try to arranger their escape.

"Further than that I do not think a juror would go on a fair reading of the article. If a juror's speculation went that far, I consider that there would be a risk of the article causing some prejudice to the course of justice in the proceedings: from the point of view of the administration of justice it would be better if these thoughts were not stimulated in the juror's mind.

"It is important, however, to recall that the due course of **10.144** justice is only one of the values with which the Contempt of Court Act 1981 was concerned. The other value was freedom of expression. Parliament passed the 1981 Act in order to change the law of the United Kingdom and so to bring it into conformity with the interpretation of Article 10 of the European Convention on Human Rights ... the Act was designed to regulate the boundary which had always, of course, existed between freedom of expression and the requirements of the due course of justice. ... That boundary may have been displaced from the familiar place where once it ran. ... Parliament may have re-drawn the boundary at a point which would not have been chosen by people looking at the matter primarily from the administration of justice. ... But these factors simply make it all the more important that the courts faithfully observe the boundary which Parliament has settled in order to meet the international obligations of the United Kingdom.

"Approaching the matter in that spirit, while I consider that **10.145** the article may indeed have created a risk of some prejudice to the course of justice, I cannot say that there is a risk that the course of justice in the proceedings being seriously impeded or prejudiced. ... On the contrary, it seems to me that a juror who had heard and concentrated on the evidence in the trial, who had heard the submissions for the Crown and the defence and who had been directed by the judge in the usual way to consider only the evidence in the case, would not be likely to be significantly influenced in his conclusion by any recollection of the article which he might have."

10.146   If anything, Lord Prosser's opinion was even more "media-friendly." He also emphasised that the 1981 Act was concerned not only with the due course of justice but also with freedom of expression and pointed out that the need to delineate a boundary was not new. He quoted from a case in 1974 in which the great Scottish judge Lord Reid said: "Freedom of speech cannot be allowed where there would be real prejudice to the administration of justice." But Lord Reid had added that freedom of speech "should not be limited to any greater extent than necessary".

10.147   Lord Prosser said:

"I think it worth emphasising that quite apart from the 1981 Act and quite apart from the European Convention on Human Rights, there was in my opinion never any excuse for the courts extending the boundary, and diminishing freedom of speech, on the basis that some wider boundary is more convenient, or simpler, or provides a useful cordon sanitaire or the like. . . . Just as Parliament, in defining the boundary, denies freedom of speech only where necessary, so the courts in applying the limitation on freedom need have no qualms about going to the boundary. . . . On the outer side of the boundary, and right up to it, it seems to me that the press and public are entitled to express themselves as they wish, and I would regret it if they felt that the courts were discontented or critical, or felt entitled to tell them to keep further away."

10.148   As far as juries were concerned the law was not so foolish as to assume that no juror would ever entertain a suspicion that an accused was violent or dishonest or criminal in various ways. It was largely because the law realised that jurors might well have such suspicions that they were told to stick to the evidence they heard in court and exclude other considerations from their minds. Lord Prosser quoted with approval the words of Mr Justice (later Lord Justice) Lawton who said in an English case: "I have enough confidence in my fellow countrymen to think that they have got newspapers sized up . . . and they are capable in normal circumstance of looking at a matter fairly and without prejudice even though they have to disregard what they may have read in a newspaper."

10.149   As far as the *Daily Record* article was concerned, Lord Prosser said:

"Anyone reading this particular article can see an element of drama, or indeed melodrama, in the way the whole events are described. One might add that it would be extremely boring if this were no so.... At all events, it is not merely the language but the essence of the report that is telling the reader not merely that there is to be a serious trial, or that there are perhaps security problems, but that there are 'goings-on' surrounding the trial which are of popular interest in a very familiar way.... The atmosphere created, or re-created by the article seems to me to be fairly typically (and acceptably) 'tabloid'—but it is an atmosphere very familiar from television and indeed an atmosphere created in the first place (deliberately or otherwise) by the way in which 'high-risk' prisoners are normally conveyed to court by the police."

Lord Prosser said he had read the article a number of times. **10.150**

"On no reading have I seen anything which I would regard as creating any risk of any prejudice, far less a substantial risk of seriously impeding or prejudicing the course of justice in the proceeding.... Juries are healthy bodies. They do not need a germ-free atmosphere. Even when articles in the press do contain germs of prejudice it will rarely be appropriate, in my opinion, to bring these to the attention of the court, far less for specific directions to have to be given, far less for the issue to be treated as even potentially one of contempt.... I do not see this article as even near to the crucial boundary. The whole matter seems to me to be a harmless piece of perfectly ordinary reporting."

Lord Coulsfield agreed that the finding of contempt should be quashed.

On any reading this seems to be an extremely liberal approach to **10.151** contempt, certainly by previous Scottish standards. The decision seemed to take defence lawyers by surprise because there had been a general assumption that Lord Bonomy's approach was an accurate reflection of the law. Given that the chairman of the three judges in this case was the Lord Justice-General and that the other two judges were vastly experienced, the decision carries a great deal of authority. The law on contempt in Scotland can safely be said to be completely unrecognisable from its condition in the days of the late Lord Clyde.

The *Evening Times* case

The *Daily Record* decision was reinforced in June1999 when the **10.152** High Court, again with the Lord Justice-General in the chair, dismissed a contempt petition by the Lord Advocate against the *Evening Times*.

10.153   Scots actor Ian McColl, of "Rab. C. Nesbitt" fame, appeared on petition at Glasgow Sheriff Court on a charge of threatening sheriff officers with an axe when they arrived at his home to execute a warrant over unpaid debts. On the same day the *Evening Times* published an article detailing how Mr McColl spent a night in the cells after allegedly brandishing an axe when sheriff officers arrived at his flat. The Crown argued that the article created a substantial risk that the course of justice would be seriously impeded.

10.154   Lord Rodger pointed out that the Lord Advocate now held his appointment on the recommendation of the First Minister under the Scotland Act 1998. He was now a member of the Scottish Executive and since May 20, 1999 had no power to ask the court for any remedy which would not be compatible with the European Convention on Human Rights. The Contempt of Court Act itself, which the *Evening Times* article was alleged to contravene, had been passed by Parliament to bring our law into line with Article 10 of the Convention.

10.155   Lord Rodger said the court had to assess the risk of prejudice at the time the article was published, adding:

> "In assessing the risk we have to take account of the time which would elapse between publication and the likely date of the trial. . . . Here, in a case where Mr McColl was released on bail, trial would be likely to take place within 12 months but, realistically, would not be likely to take place within the first three months. In fact we know that it is unlikely to take place until around nine months after publication. . . . We must also assume that a jury will hear and pay attention to the evidence led in the case, that they will be addressed by the procurator fiscal depute and by the agent for Mr McColl and that they will then be given the standard directions by the trial sheriff, including the direction that they are to consider only the evidence which has been laid before them in court. . . . We then have to ask ourselves whether we are satisfied beyond a reasonable doubt that, when published, the article created a substantial risk that the deliberations of the jury would be so affected as to give rise to serious prejudice to the course of justice."

10.156   In the court's view it was impossible to say that the article was in contempt of court. Lord Rodger went on: "We consider it rather unlikely indeed that anyone cited to serve as a juror would even recall the article." The case was unusual since it involved someone who might be known to jurors as an actor on television and where personalities from the world of politics, sport or entertainment were tried by a jury, the jurors might often know more about their way of life and the background to any charge than in the normal case. That might lead the presiding judge to give a more pointed direction about the need to reach a verdict based solely on the evidence. Lord Rodger said that in this particular case "we have no reason to believe that, even if a juror or jurors did happen to remember what the article said about Mr McColl and the supposed background to the alleged offence, this would diminish their ability to reach a proper verdict on the evidence".

Julian Danskin case

The growing influence of the European Human Rights Convention **10.157** on our law of contempt was again emphasised in the case of Julian Danskin in November 1999. The previous year, Mr Danskin, a solicitor and a football club chairman, had appeared as a Crown witness in a particularly unsavoury blackmail case in which there had been considerable adverse comment about his conduct. Some of the criticism came from the trial judge. When Mr Danskin appeared at Kirkcaldy Sheriff Court in 1999 on charges of sexual misconduct involving children, Sheriff Frank Keane at first imposed a total reporting ban on the proceedings until the end of the trial. He took the view that there might be reference in the evidence of what had taken place in the previous case and a substantial risk that the previous adverse comments about Mr Danskin might find their way into reports of the current case, prejudicing a fair trial. The reporting ban was challenged by several sections of the Scottish media and the sheriff accepted that he had to balance the media's right to freedom of expression as envisaged by Article 10 of the European Convention against the right of the accused to a fair trial under Article 6. He was referred by lawyers representing the media to the *Daily Record* case and invited to follow the reasoning of the judges. Sheriff Keane stated:

> "The requirement is that the proceedings be in public and the reporting of those proceedings currently before the court should be fair and accurate. . . . If the reporting is done in these terms then to my mind it presents no substantial risk even though reference might be made in the evidence to the previous proceedings. . . . If the reporting goes beyond those bounds then it is liable to be treated as contempt. In such a situation the risk is one to the fair and accurate reporting of these proceedings. . . . In these circumstances I am prepared to recall the total prohibition on publication. Publishers will require to bear in mind that the reporting must be fair and

accurate and should not refer to previous proceedings or conduct involving the accused which has not formed part of the evidence before the jury."

The sheriff also took the view that there might be a difference between the "substantial risk" envisaged in section 2(2) of the Contempt Act and that in section 4(2). While the latter raised the question of potential risk section 2 concerned actual risk.

Penalties for contempt

10.158 Where a court imposes a prison sentence for contempt it must, under section 15 of the 1981 Act, be for a fixed term although the court retains its power to order discharge at an earlier date. The maximum prison sentence which may be imposed by the High Court or a sheriff court in cases taken on indictment is two years, but a fine (without statutory limit) may be imposed as well or as an alternative. Where the contempt is dealt with by a sheriff in summary or civil proceedings other than on indictment the maximum penalty is three months' imprisonment or a fine of £2,000 or both. In the district court the maximum is 60 days or £1,000 or both.

Civil proceedings

10.159 The Act also applies to civil proceedings which now become active either from the time arrangements for a hearing are made (in Scotland when the record is closed) or from the time the hearing begins, whichever happens first. This brought about an important change in the stage at which the contempt law began to operate under the strict liability rule in the Court of Session and civil cases in the sheriff court. Previously, it was possible to commit contempt from the much earlier stage of the case appearing in the Calling List of the Court of Session or in the official list of cases intimated in the sheriff court.

10.160 A hearing need not necessarily be the hearing of the case on its merits or for disposal of the main point. It can be a hearing to deal with an incidental or preliminary matter, such as interim interdict, interim custody or access, amendment of pleadings, appointment of curator, etc. As we have seen, a fair and accurate report of such a hearing would be protected under section 4 of the Contempt of Court Act.

10.161 The making of arrangements for a hearing is defined in the Act as meaning, in the case of an ordinary action in the Court of Session or sheriff court, when the record is closed; in the case of a motion or application, when it is enrolled or made; and in any other case, when the date for a hearing is fixed or a hearing is allowed. Again, it is the step which happens first that has the effect of deciding when the case becomes active.

Since some of the steps referred to—such as closing the record, **10.162** enrolment of a motion or allowance of a hearing—take place usually in the offices of the appropriate court without public intimation, the journalist will have to check with either court staff or lawyers in the case as to whether any of the stages in question has been reached.

The changes made in the Act on contempt in civil cases have an **10.163** important bearing on the summons as a possible source of information for journalists. Before the passing of the Act it was understood from the case of *Richardson v. Wilson* in 1879 that a summons was a private document. Publication of material from a summons in that case, which had only appeared on the Calling List, led to a newspaper being sued for slander. The First Division, in upholding a complaint against the paper, also ruled that it would be contempt for a lawyer to make the contents of a summons available to the press before the case had come into open court. Publication from a summons could therefore lead to a risk of contempt as well as proceedings for defamation. The 1981 Act appears to rule out the risk of contempt by the media by the publication of information from a summons. A summons will normally be issued before a date for a hearing has been fixed or any other relevant step under the Act has caused the case to become active.

But the Act does not alter the pre-existing law that it is contempt **10.164** to publish material intended to prejudice the proceedings. So far as clerks of court and lawyers in possession of summonses are concerned, it may still be contempt at common law for them to disclose the contents at that early stage.

There certainly have been cases since the Contempt Act was **10.165** passed where stories have appeared in the media based almost entirely on summonses which have been handed over either by lawyers or one of the parties involved in the case. This has happened, for example, in cases where prison officers have been suing the Secretary of State for Scotland over injuries received in prison riots. It has also happened in the case of haemophiliacs who have been diagnosed as suffering from the AIDS virus after receiving batches of contaminated blood. No objection was taken to these reports. Journalists should always bear in mind, however, that particularly where an individual is being sued rather than some public body such as a health board, the summons may include allegations which could lead to a defamation action, even although publication would not be contempt.

10.166   Civil cases remain active until they are disposed of, discontinued or withdrawn. It is also worth noting that when an action is adjourned or interrupted so that negotiations can take place, the case remains active in terms of the Act and until the proceedings are settled, disposed of or withdrawn. But section 5 of the Act is designed to ensure that this fact does not preclude comment on a case while active, provided it is published "as part of a discussion in good faith of public affairs or other matters of general public interest".

10.167   Some eminent judges have expressed the view that there is no need for contempt to protect civil cases, but it must be remembered that some civil cases are heard by juries. The editor and publishers of *Private Eye* were each ordered to pay £10,000 by the Court of Appeal in England for their "serious contempt" in publishing two articles about the wife of the Yorkshire Ripper while her libel action against them was pending. The allegations—that Mrs Sonia Sutcliffe had provided her husband with a false alibi and defrauded the DSS—were published three months before the hearing of the libel action. The Appeal Court took the view that apart from the possibility of influencing potential jurors by blackening Mrs Sutcliffe's character, the articles were intended to deter her by what were tantamount to threats. They posed a threat to the administration of justice and clearly created a substantial risk of serious prejudice.

Tribunals and other bodies

10.168 Tribunals and "bodies exercising the judicial power of the State" are now treated as courts for the purpose of applying the law of contempt under the Act. This measure met strong opposition during passage of the measure through Parliament. The Government could not undertake to provide a list of the tribunals and other bodies which fitted the definition. If the Government with its resources found the task beyond it, it is not one this book can be confident of achieving, given the great number and variety of bodies possibly involved. (The provision is understood to have been included in the Act because of a controversial English decision arising from a BBC television discussion of a valuation tribunal case while it was *sub judice*.)

10.169   The problem may be simplified to some extent by leaving out of the definition all those tribunals set up to deal with disputes or complaints over the conduct of members of professions, trades or specialised bodies where no judicial power of the State is involved. In most of these cases the body in question is deciding questions of discipline, ethics or practice within the profession or trade in question. The definition does, however, cover a judicial appeal from a tribunal which is not itself within the category.

It also covers tribunals of inquiry set up under statute or by **10.170** ministerial order, fatal accident inquiries, the Lands Tribunal for Scotland, industrial tribunals, rent tribunals, inquiries into deaths at sea, shipping casualties or railway accidents held under statutory provisions laid down for the purpose, local planning inquiries, inquiries into objections to Private Acts of Parliament, and inquiries held under statute dealing with safety in mines and collieries.

This list is not exhaustive, and in doubtful cases the journalist **10.171** may have to inquire into the nature of the powers of the tribunal in question before deciding whether the contempt law applies. If in doubt, the journalist should ask the advice of the Crown Office in Edinburgh on whether a particular tribunal or other body comes within the definition given in the Contempt of Court Act. During Parliamentary debate on the Bill the Attorney-General gave assurances, so far as England was concerned, that assistance of this kind would be provided, where possible, by his office.

Where there is a tribunal to which the Tribunals of Inquiry **10.172** (Evidence) Act 1921 applies, the risk of contempt runs from when the tribunal is appointed until its report is presented to Parliament. Such tribunals are extremely rare. However, the inquiry by Lord Cullen, the Lord Justice-Clerk, which followed the massacre of children at Dunblane Primary School in March 1996 was constituted under the 1921 Act and the publication of a number of newspaper articles prompted the Lord Advocate, Lord Mackay of Drumadoon, to warn of the dangers of contempt. The Lord Advocate issued a note to editors expressing his concern at the tone of articles which attacked the conduct of individuals, including police officers, councillors and local authority officials whose actings might be the subject of scrutiny at the inquiry and who might have to give evidence. Lord Mackay said that in some cases publication followed "intrusive personal approaches" to individuals. He raised his concerns with Lord Cullen who agreed that any further instances of harassment of potential witnesses by the media or publication of material which might impede the investigation or interfere with the giving of evidence should be referred to the Lord Justice-Clerk. This would enable Lord Cullen to consider certifying the conduct of those responsible with a view to contempt of court proceedings in the Court of Session.

The Lord Advocate said he recognised that the media wished to **10.173** discuss issues that might form the subject of recommendations by Lord Cullen and emphasised that he had no wish to inhibit such debate unless it amounted to contempt of court. By way of guidance he referred to the Salmon Committee on the law of contempt as if affected tribunals of inquiry which recognised that the publication of interviews with prospective witnesses raised difficult problems of contamination of evidence.

10.174   The Salmon Committee (which reported in 1969) stated that the media had always considered that once any type of tribunal was appointed it was inappropriate for them to conduct in the nature of a parallel inquiry and had never done so. "We regard it as of the utmost importance that this restraint should continue to be exercised." Whether the media would now exercise such "restraint" 30 or so years later must be open to doubt, but the warning issued over the Dunblane case was clear.

10.175   Salmon distinguished between the obtaining of background material for publication after the appearance of the tribunal's report and interviews which might contaminate evidence.

> "A witness could be bullied or unfairly led into giving an account which was contrary to or put a slant upon the truth. He could commit himself, particularly under the strain and tension of a television interview, to a badly expressed or inaccurately recollected version of events. . . . Witnesses might also be tempted to give a version of events which they thought most newsworthy, particularly if a fee were being paid for the interview. . . . When such witnesses come to be give evidence before the tribunal they would either have to stick to what they have already said, however inaccurate it might be, or reveal the true facts. . . . In the latter event, the weight of their evidence might be considerably shaken by the discrepancy between what they had said previously. . . . This might greatly hinder the tribunal and, in an extreme case, prevent it from arriving at the truth."

The only legal sanction to prevent evidence from becoming contaminated lay in the law of contempt.

Fatal accident inquiries

10.176   There have been attempts to bring contempt proceedings against the media over the reporting of fatal accident inquiries, although these are held by a sheriff sitting alone without a jury. In 1990 Sheriff Principal John Mowat, Q.C., ordered the editor of the *Sunday Telegraph* and the author of an article in the newspaper to appear before him in the inquiry into the Lockerbie disaster.

10.177   In an article headed "Lockerbie Whitewash Warning" the *Sunday Telegraph* suggested that lawyers acting for the bereaved families were trying to avoid bringing out evidence of security flaws at Heathrow airport so as not to damage a possible future compensation claim against Pan Am. Mr Brian Gill, Q.C., counsel for the relatives, complained that the article could influence the way in which legal representatives carried out their duties.

The Sheriff Principal said, however, that he was reasonably **10.178** confident that the implication in the article that he was conducting a whitewash did not impede the course of justice. He added that Mr Gill had some grounds for suggesting that he had been defamed in the article, although that was not a matter for the court.

In 1991 there were contempt hearings at Dunoon Sheriff Court **10.179** during an inquiry into the death of a Glasgow lawyer who had lost her life while hillwalking. There was a complaint by counsel for the dead woman's family that an article in the *Evening Times* previewing the inquiry had anticipated the outcome of proceedings by pointing out that the woman was an experienced hill walker who died in fair weather conditions. There was also a complaint that the *Herald* had committed contempt because inaccurate remarks had been attributed to a witness. Although it was accepted that the sheriff was an experienced professional who could dismiss the article from his mind, it was argued that witnesses could have their evidence influenced by what they had read.

Both newspapers submitted that there was no contempt since **10.180** there was no jury to be influenced at a fatal accident inquiry. To decide that witnesses might be influenced by something they had read in a newspaper was to suggest that they were not going to fulfil their oath to tell the whole truth and that would be a dangerous extension of the law. It was also argued on behalf of the *Evening Times* that the pre-inquiry publicity might in fact have had the desirable effect of bringing witnesses forward.

Sheriff William Palmer said he was not satisfied that there had **10.181** been a substantial risk of serious prejudice to the proceedings, but the question of influencing witnesses remains an interesting one. It has been decided in at least one sheriff court case (*Tudhope v. Glass* in 1981) that witnesses are not affected by pre-trial publicity. Also, in the *Stuurman* case Lord Emslie said: "We are not impressed by the supposed risk that the evidence of witnesses would or might be tainted by anything they had read or heard" (following the arrest of the accused). He pointed out that the basis upon which any witness's evidence or opinion was given or expressed was open to the test of cross-examination.

While it would be going too far to say that publicity in advance **10.182** of a fatal accident inquiry could never amount to contempt of court, it is clear that fatal accident inquiries are not in the same position as criminal trials. The crucial difference is the absence of a jury, but another important factor is that no one is on trial at a fatal accident inquiry. The authorities might, however, take a different view if the complaint was not merely that a witness had read something in a newspaper but that his evidence had been influenced by his being interviewed by a journalist shortly before the inquiry or trial. There could be an argument that this had changed the evidence the witness would otherwise have given. This was certainly the line taken by the Salmon Committee and raised by the Crown before the Dunblane Inquiry.

10.183   The question of whether witnesses might be influenced by something they had read was also at the centre of a case at Dumbarton Sheriff Court in November 1999 in which the publishers and acting editor of the *Daily Record* were each fined £500 for contempt. The journalist who wrote the story was also found guilty of contempt but escaped with an admonition because she had no say in how her report was presented. The young age of the witnesses involved seemed to pay an important part in the sheriff's decision.

10.184   Sheriff Tom Scott was told that the newspaper had published the offending article on the eve of a children's hearing into alleged ill-treatment and assault involving an eight-year-old girl. The girl was due to give evidence, along with two other family members aged under 16.

10.185   The Reporter to the Children's Panel argued that the evidence of the young girl was likely to be tainted by publication of the newspaper article at such a critical time. The *Daily Record* submitted that it was unlikely that an eight-year-old would have read the article or, even if she had, understood it sufficiently for it to colour her evidence in court. Their counsel also pointed out that the newspaper had received clear an unequivocal legal advice that the article was safe to publish.

10.186   Sheriff Scott was satisfied that the article had created a substantial risk of prejudicing the evidence of all three children. He accepted that the hearing was concerned with events that had taken place nine months previously but added: "On the very day before three children were due to give evidence one of them was branded a liar in the newspaper and that created a risk of prejudice."

Coroners' inquests

10.187   These are confined to England and Wales, but because the 1981 Act applies to the whole United Kingdom, it is important for journalists and publishers in Scotland, whose work may circulate elsewhere, to know the position of the inquest in the context of contempt law. In 1986 the English Court of Appeal upheld a ruling by a High Court judge that it would be contempt for London Weekend Television to screen a programme about the death of a man in police custody during an adjournment of an inquest into his death. The Police Federation and six policemen had successfully applied to the High Court of Justice to stop transmission of a TV programme dealing with events leading up to the death of John Mikkleson, aged 34, at Feltham police station. The inquest had been opened at Hammersmith and adjourned and police investigations were proceeding to discover whether there were grounds for criminal charges. Lord Justice Watkins said in the Appeal Court that there was a high probability that if the programme was shown there would be a substantial risk to the course of justice; proceedings which were "active" might well be prejudiced.

Contempt in court

If a party to a legal action or a witness or member of the public **10.188** commits contempt by his behaviour in court or makes offensive remarks amounting to contempt, it will not normally be contempt for a report of the incident to be published, including quotations of what was said by the offender, provided his remarks can be treated as relevant to the proceedings before the court. It may be a matter of degree to decide when remarks not relevant to the case are safe to publish, but proceedings for contempt against the publisher are unlikely where the report is accurate. No action was taken, for instance, against newspapers which published accurate reports of a litigant in the First Division of the Court of Session who called the judges "Nazis".

Dignity of the court

The media would be failing to meet their responsibilities if they did **10.189** not criticise the judiciary and court decisions where criticism is deserved. A court would be extremely reluctant, unless in the most exceptional circumstances, to treat this as contempt of court. Outspoken attacks on the legal system and individuals within it are now far more frequent than before, although the portrayal of appeal court judges as "the three wise monkeys" after a controversial ruling was not well received by the judges involved.

Proceedings for contempt are rarely taken unless there is a clear **10.190** infringement of the law and in the case of *Royle v. Grey* in 1973 the High Court made it clear that the power to punish for contempt should be exercised only with care and discretion. In their judgment the court quoted with approval what Lord President Normand had said in the earlier case of *Milburn* in 1946: "The greatest restraint and discretion should be used by the court in dealing with contempt of court, lest a process, the purpose of which is to prevent interference with the administration of justice, should degenerate into an oppressive or vindictive abuse of the court's powers".

10.191   Justified criticism of the system or individuals is one thing, but it would be highly dangerous to state or imply, for example, that a judge or sheriff had been guilty of dishonest or criminal behaviour. The most likely result would be an action for defamation.

Escaped prisoners

10.192   Care must be taken in publishing reports about prisoners who have escaped from prison or from custody, in case what is said will prejudice their subsequent trial or proceedings taken against them for having escaped. (See the case of David Evans earlier in the chapter.) It is by no means unknown for someone to plead not guilty to a charge of escaping from custody. An accused charged with attempting to defeat the ends of justice by escaping has the same basic right to protection from prejudice by publicity as any other person awaiting trial, but the extent of this right may be modified because of his own violent behaviour. Where the escaped prisoner has a record of violence he may be a danger to members of the public, and the media would feel entitled to publish details sufficient to warn them.

10.193   In deciding how much to publish, journalists should be guided by official sources—such as the Crown Office or the procurator fiscal—who may authorise publication of a fugitive's violent tendencies in appropriate cases. In certain instances, by authority of the Lord Advocate or Solicitor-General, the media may be allowed, or encouraged, to publish a photograph or photofit picture of a violent person at large.

10.194   Normally, official statements will not contain reference to the crime of which the escaped prisoner has been convicted, or the charge for which he awaits trial, except where a departure is justified by considerations of public safety. The basic information— name, home area, date and place of sentence and term of sentence—will normally be issued for publication.

10.195   In 1981 a man serving life for murder was allowed out of Saughton Prison to visit his family under escort, escaped and, while at large, raped a woman. At the time of his escape an official of the Scottish Prisons Department was quoted as saying he was not considered dangerous. Next day a public warning was issued through the media, along with his photograph, authorised by the Lord Advocate. After the man was caught and sentenced for the rape, the Scottish Home and Health Department stated that in future cases of the kind, their advice to the media would be that, although a person's behaviour in prison did not suggest he would be a danger to the public, his record involved violent crime.

KEY POINTS

Contempt law tries to balance the often conflicting interests of **10.196** freedom of speech with the right to a fair trial. The traditional approach of Scots law is that pre-trial publicity should be kept to a minimum, particularly where a jury is involved. However the recent decision in the *Daily Record* case indicate a relaxation of the strict approach and greater weight being given to freedom of speech in accordance with the European Convention on Human Rights.

The Contempt of Court Act 1981 says that anything which **10.197** creates a substantial risk of serious prejudice to legal proceedings is contempt, even although prejudice was not intended. Publication of previous convictions before a trial would amount to contempt, as would publication of the accused's picture if identification was in issue. The risk of committing contempt starts when someone has been arrested, a warrant has been issued for his arrest, an indictment has been served or a summons issued, whichever comes first. Bear in mind, however, the possibility of common law contempt which covers publication intended to prejudice legal proceedings. The risk ends when the accused is acquitted or sentenced or with the return of any other verdict or decision which puts an end to proceedings.

The risk of contempt starts to run again when an appeal is **10.198** lodged but publication must create a substantial risk of prejudice and the case will be heard by experienced judges rather than a jury, making the risk extremely remote. In civil cases the risk of contempt normally runs from the moment the record is closed.

Contempt law also applies to tribunals and other bodies **10.199** "exercising the judicial power of the State".

CHAPTER 11

PHOTOGRAPHY

11.01 The publication of a photograph is just as capable as a story or a headline of creating a substantial risk of serious prejudice in terms of the Contempt of Court Act. The Act makes no specific mention of pictures at all but lays down rules which apply to "publications" and goes on to explain that this includes "any speech, writing, broadcast or other communication in whatever form, which is addressed to the public at large or any section of the public". "Other communication in whatever form" will include photographs, as well as television pictures, videos, sketches, drawings or cartoons.

11.02 The Act does not, however, deal with the whole law of contempt as it affects photography, and it is still necessary to go back to the old common law for guidance, particularly over the restriction on taking or making pictures within court precincts.

11.03 It should certainly not be assumed that, although the Act is a United Kingdom statute, the Scottish courts will apply the same standards as the English in interpreting it. For example, English newspapers have always exercised much greater freedom than those in Scotland in publishing pictures of criminal suspects. Even since the passing of the 1981 Act they have continued publishing this kind of picture to an extent that would be inviting contempt proceedings in a Scottish case.

11.04 An outstanding instance was the case of Dennis Nilsen who, after the unearthing of parts of a number of human skeletons in London in 1983, appeared in pictures published in English newspapers handcuffed to two detectives. Lord McCluskey, the former Solicitor-General for Scotland, asked the Lord Advocate in the House of Lords whether Scottish newspapers were free to follow the example of the English press and to publish pictures of people accused of murder, allegedly committed in Scotland, without risk that the Lord Advocate would petition the High Court to treat publication as a contempt of court. Lord Mackay of Clashfern, the Lord Advocate, made it clear that they were not.

Lord McCluskey was also the judge who found the BBC guilty of **11.05** contempt in March 1992 for broadcasting footage of Paul Ferris, a murder accused on trial at the High Court in Glasgow, being led from a police van to the court. The judge made it clear that the duty of the court was to ensure that those accused of serious crimes received a fair and impartial trial. He added:

> "It is clearly essential that witnesses are not materially influenced in any way. It follows that in any case where the question of identification may arise it is clear that the publication in the press or television of any film, photograph, or even an artist's likeness during a trial or after a warrant has been issued, causes a potential risk to the administration of justice."

There might be circumstances where the risk was small, for **11.06** example if the accused was well known to the public as a sports or showbusiness personality, but such cases would be rare. The judge added, however: "There is only one safe route for the media to follow and it is this—do not publish any picture of an accused person in Scotland until a trial is finished or the charge has been dropped by the Lord Advocate. It has been made clear in many cases that any breach of this rule is liable to be dealt with by this court as contempt".

The BBC submitted that viewers saw only a fleeting glimpse of **11.07** Ferris for two or three seconds and not at a peak viewing time, but Lord McCluskey said the accused had been clearly identified and there was a substantial risk that the course of justice might be seriously prejudiced.

The kind of picture that would invite trouble, even in England, **11.08** can be illustrated by the case of Peter Hain in 1976. The *Evening Standard* was fined £1,000 for printing a picture of Mr Hain on its front page on the day he was due to attend an identification parade. Even although the caption read "Hain, he's no bank robber", the court ruled that the picture prejudiced his trial by making it more likely that someone would pick him out at the identification parade.

It would be wrong, however, to treat it as a total certainty in **11.09** every case that the publication of a picture would bring contempt proceedings. As Lord McCluskey suggested in the *Ferris* case, there will be circumstances in which the identification of the accused will not give rise to a risk of prejudice. To give one example, if a celebrated television chat show host appeared on a speeding charge there would be unlikely to be any objection to his picture being published. His identity would already be well-known and a speeding case would not be tried by a jury. Even in that kind of case, however, it would be sensible to take legal advice before publishing.

11.10 On the basis of several decisions by the Scottish courts before the 1981 Act, contempt could be committed by the publication of a picture of an accused person during his trial although there was no possibility of any issue of identification arising in the case and no question of prejudice.

11.11 Common sense was restored to the law in the case of *Atkins v. London Weekend Television Ltd*, in 1978, when the High Court accepted that there was no hard and fast rule that the publication of a photograph of an accused person would always constitute contempt. The court added: "We accept, too, the further proposition that the publication of a photograph of an accused person will constitute contempt only where a question of identification has arisen or may arise and where the publication is calculated to prejudice the prospect of fair trial."

11.12 Pictures of witnesses who have completed their evidence are normally permissible, but the safest course is to check whether the identification of a witness is still relevant. In a case where there is a defence of incrimination (where the accused blames someone else for the crime), if the person being incriminated gives evidence his picture should not be used until the trial is complete.

Care with captions

11.13 Even although a picture is regarded as safe, great care has to be taken to avoid a substantial risk of serious prejudice in writing the caption. At the risk of stating the obvious, there must be a check that the caption matches the picture. In a libel case before the High Court in London in December 1986 Dr Abdel Yassine, director of research at the Arab Institute for Socio-Economic Studies in Jordan, won undisclosed damages after a picture linking him to a notorious terrorist organisation was published in *The Times* and the *Guardian*. Both newspapers and the Press Association, who distributed the picture, agreed to pay substantial damages and costs. The court was told the photograph had been distributed and published in good faith.

Civil cases

11.14 While contempt cases stemming from publicity in civil proceedings have been extremely rare, it should not be assumed that no risk exists. It is still possible, for example, for a jury to be involved in a damages action in the Court of Session.

Inside the court

The precise aim and scope of the law of contempt not covered by **11.15**
the 1981 Act, for example, where there has been no publication
and possibly none is intended, are by no means clear. While it is
easy to understand the desire to prevent prejudice by publicity, it is
less obvious why, for example, it should be contempt merely to
bring a camera into a courtroom without actually using it or
possibly even intending to do so.

There is no statute specifically dealing with the taking of **11.16**
photographs, or having a camera in court. The Criminal Justice Act
1925, which bans the taking of photographs and the publication of
photographs taken in court, applies only to England and Wales,
although the attitude towards photography in and around the
courts in Scotland was similar. Photographing court proceedings in
the Supreme Courts was permitted only with the permission of the
Lord President and permission was always refused.

However, as we shall see, this policy was reversed in 1992 when **11.17**
Lord President Hope paved the way for court proceedings in
Scotland to be televised.

English Act

The 1925 Act provides that no one shall take or attempt to take in **11.18**
any court any photograph or, with a view to publication, make or
attempt to make in any court any portrait or sketch of any person,
either a judge or a juror or witness or a party to any proceedings,
civil or criminal. The Act also bans the publication of any
photograph, portrait or sketch taken or made in contravention of
the Act. The Act covers a photograph, portrait or sketch taken or
made in the courtroom or in the building or in the precincts of the
building in which a court is held.

There were two examples in 1986 of how the English and Welsh **11.19**
courts deal with this situation. One involved a member of the
public who took a flash photograph of Judge Malcolm Ward during
a sitting of Wolverhampton Crown Court. Mrs Joan Maynard,
recently married to a solicitor, had been taken to the court by her
husband to see justice being administered and gain experience
before starting work in her husband's office. Mrs Maynard, who
said later she had no idea she was breaking the law, was detained
in the cells until the judge later dealt with her, fining her £500
(later reduced to £100 on appeal) and confiscating her camera.

The publishers of the *Merthyr Express* were fined £200 for **11.20**
contempt when a staff artist was discovered sketching during a trial
after permission to do so had been refused by Judge Lewis Bowen.

The editor, Graham Jones, who was ordered to appear, told the judge he had sent the artist to sketch from memory and not during the case. Judge Bowen said he had refused permission to sketch in court because he felt it might make the jury uncomfortable and because it was unfair to the defendant (a hospital consultant) who had already had widespread publicity. He conceded the editor acted in good faith.

11.21 In a case in Glasgow Sheriff Court in 1975 a Mr Peter Sweeney admitted being in contempt of court in that, during the proceedings in a criminal case in the court, he was in possession of a camera and took photographs in the court. His solicitor said Mr Sweeney had wanted a souvenir of his first visit to a courtroom, but, after being told by an attendant to leave, which he did, he had been pursued by a detective, apprehended and detained in custody overnight. The following day the photographs he took were produced in court and Sheriff Archibald Bell, Q.C. admonished Mr Sweeney for contempt of court and confiscated the camera. He stated: "Proceedings in court cannot and should not be subject to any interruption", although Mr Sweeney's solicitor had said what his client had done was so quiet and unobtrusive that even the sheriff was "unaware and not troubled by the matter".

11.22 It is difficult to see why the taking of a photograph should amount to contempt when it does not interfere with the proceedings before the court. It would be a different matter if the photography disturbed the judge or counsel or a witness or jurors. Obviously, the taking of a photograph with flash equipment in a courtroom during the hearing of a case would invite swift retribution. At the other end of the scale—without implying that such conduct would be approved by the court—there can be no doubt that tourists visiting our courts have taken photographs with miniature cameras and the court has been none the wiser nor the worse for it.

11.23 The Criminal Procedure (Scotland) Act 1975 (which came into operation after the *Sweeney* case) provides, that "any person who interrupts or disturbs the court (in solemn procedure) shall be liable to imprisonment or a fine or both as the judge thinks fit" and no maximum is specified. In light of the decision in *Sweeney*, it would appear that a photographer might be held in contempt of court even though the judge was unaware that the camera had been used in court, or even that there was one in the courtroom at all, and there could therefore have been no actual interference with the progress of proceedings as a result.

Precincts of the court

In a case in which official guidance was sought in 1964, the then **11.24**
Lord President issued a ruling which stated: "No photographing is
permitted within the precincts of the Law Courts. The precincts of
the Law Courts are defined as the areas occupied by the car park
and the piazza". The reference was to the portion of Parliament
Square, Edinburgh, lying between St Giles' Cathedral and Parliament House, and offered no guidance as to the precincts of any
other law court in Scotland. Neither did it define the extent of the
precincts at other exits from Parliament House which have been
used in some cases to help parties escape the attentions of the
Press.

It was probably the first formal attempt to define the precincts of **11.25**
any Scottish court over restrictions on photography. When invited
to supply a definition of precincts of the court in an earlier case,
the Lord Advocate of the day, Lord Wheatley, stated that a
definition was not possible because the extent of the precincts must
vary with the circumstances and requirements of each case.

Over the years the precincts rule was relaxed to the extent that **11.26**
cameras (including television cameras) were allowed into Parliament House to take pictures or film of, for example, a judge who is
to appear in some future programme or feature article. The inside
of Parliament House was also filmed to provide background shots
·for a TV series about lawyers. This was, of course, always done
after asking the permission of the Lord President.

Televising the courts

A significant breakthrough came in the summer of 1992 when Lord **11.27**
President Hope announced that he no longer thought it in the
public interest that there should be an absolute ban on televising
court proceedings.

Lord Hope stated: **11.28**

"The rule hitherto has been that television cameras are not
allowed within the precincts of the court. While the absolute
nature of the rule makes it easy to apply it is an impediment
to the making of programmes of an educational or documentary nature and to the use of television in other cases where
there would be no risk to the administration of justice. In
future the criterion will be whether the presence of television
cameras in the court would be without risk to the administration of justice."

Lord Hope felt that technology had now reached such an **11.29**
advanced stage that certain court cases could probably be televised

without undue interference with the proceedings, much as had happened in Parliament. He felt that there was sufficient support for the change within the judiciary and the Scottish legal profession in general.

11.30   He added:

"It is also in the public interest that people in Scotland should become more aware of the way in which justice is being administered in their own courts. There is a risk that the showing on television of proceedings in the courts of other countries will lead to misunderstandings about the way in which court proceedings are conducted in our own country."

11.31   The Lord President issued a series of guidelines under which requests by broadcasting organisations to televise proceedings in the Court of Session and High Court would be dealt. The televising of current proceedings in criminal cases at first instance, for example trials or preliminary hearings, were not be to be permitted under any circumstances "in view of the risks to the administration of justice". The same rule was to apply to civil cases at first instance. Although juries are not normally involved, Lord Hope felt there were risks in televising civil cases while witnesses were still giving their evidence.

11.32   However, cameras were to be allowed into the courtroom to televise appeal cases, both civil and criminal, subject to satisfactory arrangements being made about the placing of cameras and provided there was no additional lighting which would make courtroom conditions intolerable. The cameras will be allowed in subject to the approval of the presiding judge and under such conditions as he chooses to impose. Subject to the same conditions ceremonial occasions may be televised in the courtroom for use in a news bulletin. The taking of television pictures (without sound) of judges on the Bench, as a replacement for still pictures, will be allowed with the permission of the judge concerned. Requests by television companies to film proceedings, including proceedings at first instance, for later showing in educational or documentary programmes, will be given favourable consideration. However, the consent of all parties involved in the proceedings will be needed as will the approval of the presiding judge before the final product is screened. Similar guidelines were introduced by the sheriffs principal for sheriff courts as from November 1992.

11.33   The first ever broadcast of a Scottish criminal trial was seen in April 1994 when BBC Scotland screened "Focal Point—The Trial" a case in Glasgow before Sheriff Brian Lockhart and a jury. In November 1994 BBC2 began showing a six-part series filmed in the

Scottish courts. The first programme featured a murder trial. The programme was broadcast only after the accused's trial and appeal had been completed and there was no risk of prejudice to the proceedings. Cameras were also allowed into the Court of Criminal Appeal in 1997 to film the judges issuing their opinions in the case of T.C. Campbell and Joseph Steele who alleged that their murder convictions were a miscarriage of justice. BBC Scotland unsuccessfully petitioned the *nobile officium* of the High Court in 2000 to be allowed to televise the Lockerbie trial after the Court agreed to relay television pictures from the Camp Ziest Courtroom to bereaved American relatives in New York and Washington D.C.

The attitude of the court to pictures being taken of people **11.34** arriving at and leaving court may depend on the particular circumstances of the case. A picture of a convicted murderer being led away to begin his sentence might be treated completely differently from a photograph of a witness in a custody case who later complained of press harassment.

In the open

When the judge, jury, clerk and counsel leave the courtroom, for **11.35** example to go outside to inspect a piece of evidence such as a car, the place where the inspection takes place becomes, for the time being, the equivalent of the courtroom.

Parties or witnesses or counsel walking along the street, either **11.36** going to or leaving the court buildings, are in a different position and there is no danger in taking pictures provided nothing is done that would amount to obstructing or molesting them. Any conduct by photographers which discouraged a witness from coming voluntarily to court to give evidence might be regarded as an interference with the course of justice and punishable as common law contempt.

Invasion of privacy

Unlawful interference with the person is assault. This may result in **11.37** a criminal prosecution or a civil action for damages. The law on assault should not be of concern to the journalist but there have been instances of mobbing and manhandling by reporters on the trail of a story. To photograph a person is not by itself assault, even if he or she does not consent, but to force him to submit to being photographed in a certail place or in a certain pose probably would be assault.

Traditionally, the mere invasion of privacy has not in itself been **11.38** actionable. It is not unlawful to photograph a person and expose his features to the public gaze even if the photograph is a bad one. Nor is it unlawful to expose a person's private life to the glare of publicity. But the courts do not look favourably on conduct of thes kind and if there is any actionable wrong involved, such as defamation, infringement of copyright or breach of confidence, they are quite likely to take the invasion of privacy into account in assessing damages.

11.39 In the notorious *Argyll* divorce case (*Argyll v. Argyll* [1967]), the Duke of Argyll and *The People* were restrained from publishing certain intimate matters communicated to the Duke in confidence by his former wife during their marriage.

11.40 And in the case of *Williams v. Settle* [1960], where a man's wedding photograph was published because it included a picture of his subsequently murdered father-in-law, it was said with reference to the amount of damages awarded against the photographer who had sold the picture:

> "[I]t is the flagrancy of the infringement which calls for heavy damages because this was a scandalous matter in the circumstances ... It is sufficient to say that it was a flagrant infringement of the right of the plaintiff, and it was scandalous conduct and in total disregard of not only of the plaintiff's legal rights of copyright but of his feelings and his sense of family dignity and pride. It was an intrusion into his life deeper and graver than an intrusion into a man's property".

11.41 We have seen too that the defence of fair comment in a defamation action may not be available if the comment is on a man's private life. The position can be summed up by saying that the courts at present give no redress for invasion of privacy by itself but they do not like it and are apt to take it into account if it is an element of a case before them. Journalists should also be aware of a case in 1989 in which a newspaper reporter in Scotland admitted a charge of fraud. She had gained access to a hospital pattient by pretending to be his neice. The causing of distress to the patient would not be necessary to constitute the offence but could be regarded as an aggravating factor by the court.

"Assault by photography"

11.42 In 1975 proceedings were begun, but later abandoned against two press photographers who took pictures of a solicitor in the street outside the sheriff court at Dunfermline. The solicitor was appearing on behalf of a client at an inquiry into a suspicious death and the picture was taken during an adjournment. The solicitor complained to the procurator fiscal, on whose authority the photographers were later charged with assault and had their films confiscated. The case was unprecedented.

Researches could produce only a civil case in 1916 in which a **11.43**
boy aged 17, charged with a minor offence, had his fingerprints and
photograph taken by the police without his parents' consent. He
brought proceedings against the chief constable for defamation,
claiming that his reputation had been damaged by having his
fingerprints and photograph filed by the police along with those of
notorious criminals.

In the Dunfermline case, the Crown Office intervened and **11.44**
instructed the procurator fiscal not to proceed with the case against
the photographers, whose films were returned to them. The case
establishes only that there has been no instance in Scotland of a
successful prosecution for assault by photography. It is possible,
however, that a photographer could be charged with breach of the
peace—the scope of which has been gradually extended over the
years—if he persisted in photographing someone in public against
his wishes with results which led to a complaint by them or some
kind of disturbance.

In March 1992 at Kilmarnock Sheriff Court a photographer was **11.45**
warned by police that if he tried to take a picture of a witness at a
fatal accident inquiry he could be charged with breach of the
peace. The case concerned the death of the witness's five children
in a house fire, and he had made it clear to police that he did not
wish to be photographed.

Children

There are special provisions to protect from publicity children **11.46**
under 16 involved in court proceedings. This is an area of
particular importance to photographers and anyone involved in
television journalism. The law is contained in section 47 of the
Criminal Procedure (Scotland) Act 1995 and a full account of the
section is contained in Chapter 13.

An important point to remember is that the ban on identifying a **11.47**
child will also mean that the picture of an adult involved in the
case cannot be used if this would lead to the identification of the
child. The ban could also extend to pictures of a school or any
other area that could lead to the child's identification. In one case
a 12-year-old boy appeared at the High Court in Edinburgh and
admitted firearms offences. He had arrived at school one morning
armed with a shotgun. Reporting restrictions were not lifted and
neither the boy nor his school could be named. Reports referred
only to the general area of Scotland in which the incident took
place. After the case was dealt with a photographer took pictures
as the boy was driven away from court to a secure school. The boy
himself could not be seen in the pictures and at least one

newspaper published the picture on the understanding that the adult who was visible in the car was a social worker accompanying the boy to court. In fact it was one of the boy's parents and the newspaper had committed an offence by unwittingly identifying the child by publishing a picture of his parent.

11.48 There is an automatic ban on publishing anything that could lead to the identification of any child concerned in a children's hearing, or an appeal in such a case before the sheriff or Court of Session. An appeal court decision in 1993 seemed to suggest that all pictures of children are banned even though the picture is taken from behind or the child's face is blanked out and he or she cannot be identified. (see para. 13.25).

Fatal accident inquiries

11.49 The sheriff presiding at a fatal accident inquiry has power to order non-publication of a picture of any person under 17 in any way involved in the inquiry (see Chapter 13).

11.50 The Civic Government (Scotland) Act 1982 makes it an offence to take any indecent photograph of a child under 16, to distribute or show such a photograph, or to possess one with a view to its distribution. The prohibition covers also video recordings and films (see also para. 26.08). Contravention can result in a fine of up to £2,000 or a jail sentence of not more than two years, or both. It is a defence to prove there was a legitimate reason for distribution or possession of the item in question or that there was no knowledge or suspicion it was indecent.

Official secrets

11.51 There is a voluntary system administered by a joint committee representing the media and civil service to restrict publication of sensitive material, and matters which are subject to restriction are listed under a series of "D-A Notices". These are dealt with in more detail in Chapter 30; the aspect most likely to concern photographers covers pictures of defence establishments, installations, dockyards and factories.

KEY POINTS

11.52 Publication of the picture of an accused person before or during a criminal trial will almost certainly be treated as contempt of court if identification is in issue. Cases where identification is not in issue will be rare. Pictures of witnesses are normally permissible after their evidence is complete, but take legal advice before publishing. The taking of pictures in court is not banned by statute in Scotland but has been held to be contempt even although the proceedings were not disrupted. In 1964 Lord Clyde ruled that no pictures should be taken within the precincts of the law courts. In 1992 Lord President Hope announced that the absolute ban on pictures within the precincts was to end. Televising of appeal court cases, under strict rules, was to be allowed. Bear in mind the special rules designed to protect children from being identified in court proceedings, children's hearings and fatal accident inquiries.

CHAPTER 12

MATRIMONIAL PROCEEDINGS

12.01 Media reports of divorce cases in Scotland are rare for several reasons. First, the Judicial Proceedings (Regulation of Reports) Act 1926, imposes strict limits on what the media can publish about divorce, nullity and separation actions. Secondly, the overwhelming majority of divorces in Scotland are undefended and since 1978 are not normally heard in open court at all. It is also undoubtedly the case that the breakdown of marriage is now so commonplace in Scotland—about one marriage in three fails—that the average case is not in the least newsworthy.

12.02 The legal profession expressed concern that divorces would be conducted in the glare of publicity after the Divorce Jurisdiction, Court Fees and Legal Aid (Scotland) Act 1983, which gave power to sheriff courts as well as the Court of Session to deal with divorces but there has in fact been no explosion of publicity for divorce cases from sheriff courts around Scotland. Reports of sheriff court divorces have been rare and local newspapers did not follow the practice of some of their English counterparts of publishing weekly lists of names of people who have been divorced in undefended cases. There have also been few reports of judgments of the courts in defended cases. It is important, however, that journalists should be familiar with the terms of the 1926 Act, particularly since 1999 saw the first ever attempted prosecution under the Act. The Crown Office had already made it clear that, despite the complete lack of prosecutions since 1926, the Act was still very much in force.

12.03 The Act is unusual because, rather than banning the publication of specific details of matrimonial cases, it says that reports are prohibited altogether except for four limited categories of information. Section 1(i)(a) is not restricted to divorce cases and applies to judicial proceedings of any kind. It bans the publication of any indecent material or any indecent medical, surgical or physiological details, publication of which would be calculated to injure public morals.

History of the 1926 Act

It is clear from evidence which was led at public inquiries before **12.04** Parliament passed the 1926 Act that much concern was being voiced at the time about the effects on public morals of unrestricted reporting of full details of some scandalous divorce cases.

The background to the 1926 Act was explained by Lord Simon **12.05** of Glaisdale in the *Ampthill Peerage* case in 1977 when he said:

> "[I]if ever there was a family, seemingly blessed by fortune, where the birth of a child was attended by an evil spirit bearing a baneful gift to frustrate all the blessings, it was the Ampthill Russells. Its curse was litigation. . . . In the early 1920s there were two long hearings in the Divorce Division of the High Court, in the first of which the jury disagreed. . . . Some of the most famous and expensive counsel of the day were briefed for the petitioner, for the respondent and (ultimately) for no less than three named co-respondents. . . . The most private and embarrassing marital intimacies were investigated and extensively regaled to a salacious public; Parliament was apparently so disturbed as in consequence to pass the Judicial Proceedings (Regulation of Reports) Act 1926."

Terms of the Act

The part of the 1926 Act which has most relevance to the working **12.06** journalist is section 1(i)(b) which affects reports of any judicial proceedings for dissolution of marriage, nullity of marriage or judicial separation. Nothing may be published about these types of case except:

(a) the names, addresses and occupations of the parties to the action and of witnesses;
(b) a concise statement of the charges, defences and counter-charges in support of which evidence has been given;
(c) submissions on any point of law arising during the proceedings including the court's decision on the legal point;
(d) the judgment of the court and any observations made by the judge in giving judgment.

The maximum penalty for each contravention of the Act is four **12.07** months' imprisonment or a £5,000 fine or both, liability lying with the proprietor, editor, and printer or publisher. The Act applies to both defended and undefended divorces and undefended cases are by far the more frequent.

Procedure in divorce cases

12.08 In undefended cases an important change in procedure affecting the working practice of journalists was introduced in 1978. Anyone seeking a divorce in an undefended case no longer has to attend court personally with his or her witnesses. Written evidence in the form of sworn statements has replaced evidence in court, and these cases are now normally dealt with by a judge in chambers.

12.09 A list of the divorces granted in undefended cases in the Court of Session is published in the court rolls once a week. A similar list is published in at least some sheriff courts. These lists do not contain enough information in themselves to provide the reporter with a story and a check to confirm details would have to be carried out with the relevant court department.

12.10 To comply with the terms of the 1926 Act only the brief details permitted by the Act should be used from the court documents. The few reports published in newspapers of affidavit divorces have run to only a few paragraphs setting out who has been divorced, on what ground and which judge granted decree. To use further details from the court documents would run the risk of breaching the Act.

12.11 As far as defended cases are concerned the normal practice in the Court of Session has been to wait until the judge issues his decision in a case before carrying a report. This is likely to be several weeks after he has heard evidence. The decision is normally given in writing and a copy is made available to journalists. Divorce judgments are normally in very full terms and provide the journalist with more than enough information to present a complete picture of a case.

12.12 There may of course be defended cases which are seen as so interesting and important that a decision is made to report them before the judgment stage. Again, this can be done only within the terms of the 1926 Act. The basic point to remember is that unlike most other cases, a detailed account of the evidence as it unfolds cannot be given in a divorce, nullity or separation action. The Act talks about a "concise" report of claims on both sides "in support of which evidence has been given." In other words, the journalist must wait until he has heard enough of the evidence to produce a "concise" summary of the case.

12.13 The word "concise" could present some difficulty, since its exact interpretation will vary with the circumstances of each individual case. A recital of alleged incidents or allegations based on the evidence given in court would not come within the definition of "concise". Where there is doubt, or the case is complicated, the safest course is to err on the side of brevity and keep the summary to a single sentence for the charges and another for replies and countercharges.

The restrictions in the Act apply to reports "in relation to court **12.14** proceedings". In any follow-up story, such as an interview with one of the parties outside the court it would be sensible to avoid a mere rehashing of any evidence given in court, as this could arguably be caught by the terms of the Act. The dangers of defamation should also be kept in mind since a report based on information given outside the court would not be protected by privilege.

Points of Law

Submissions on a point of law which crop up during the proceed- **12.15** ings can provide a good source of copy. There have been several outstanding instances, for example the question of whether artificial insemination by a donor (AID) was a good defence to an action of divorce for adultery. In the notorious *Argyll* divorce case the issue arose as to whether a wife could be compelled to surrender as evidence passages in her diary containing references to her alleged association with men other than her husband.

In reporting this kind of submission the reporter must be careful **12.16** that what he is publishing is not in essence an argument on the facts but truly deals with a question of law. A legal argument must of course be based on a certain minimum amount of fact, but any report, to come within the Act, should contain no more factual information than necessary for a proper report of the legal submissions.

The next permissible category is "decision of the court" on the **12.17** submissions on any point of law. This brings in the judgment given by the court at certain preliminary stages in a case where the issue is a legal one, but the judge is not necessarily being asked to give a final decision on the case. In the AID case referred to above Lord Wheatley heard preliminary debate on issues of great legal interest and public importance. The arguments contained a great deal of reportable and permissible material although very few newspapers took advantage of the opportunity, and of course the judgment could be published.

In another case a wife made a preliminary application to the **12.18** court for an advance of a very large sum of interim expenses to enable her to bring witnesses from various countries to Scotland to help her defend a divorce action. The judge, Lord Guthrie, said that under the 1926 Act his judgment on the point could be legally reported provided that the only other information published was the parties' names and addresses as they appeared on the calling list.

12.19   In reporting such preliminary matters, as well as the judgment, the provisions of section 1(i)(a) mentioned earlier in the chapter should not be forgotten. This prohibits the publication of any material calculated to injure public morals.

12.20   The Act does not say that the media are allowed to publish in matrimonial cases the name of the judge or the court in which he is sitting or description of the parties or witnesses. But it seems a matter of common sense that the Act cannot have been intended to ban the publication of details of this kind provided any descriptive material does not amount to evidence.

12.21   The term "decree nisi" applies only in English law where, in divorce actions, decree becomes effective only after a certain period of time during which the authorities must be satisfied that no reason has arisen why decree should not be granted. Decree in Scotland becomes absolute when it is granted subject to a 21-day period to allow for any appeal to be lodged.

12.22   The granting of a decree is, however, delayed in certain cases where the court has to be satisfied about the circumstances in which the children of the marriage are being cared for before issuing decree.

12.23   The restrictions imposed by the 1926 Act upon the reporting of matrimonial cases apply to the appeal stages as well as in the court which first hears the case.

Presumption of death

12.24 In 1956 a newspaper published material from a petition for dissolution of marriage on the ground of presumed death at the stage when the document was displayed on the wall of Parliament House. The editor was required by the Lord Advocate to give a written undertaking that he would not allow a repetition, although the offence was a purely technical one.

12.25   The case was not a matrimonial one in the usual sense and publicity of this kind would more likely help than hinder the ends of justice being achieved. Parliament has since rectified the situation, however: section 14 of the Presumption of Death (Scotland) Act 1977 states that, for the avoidance of doubt, section 1(i)(b) of the 1926 Act does not apply to an action of declarator of death under the Act.

New cases under the 1926 Act

12.26 Any doubts over the continuing validity of the 1926 legislation were removed by a case in 1996 in which the procurator fiscal in Glasgow investigated claims that the *Evening Times* and the

Scottish edition of the *Daily Mail* had breached the Act over reports of a divorce action at Glasgow Sheriff Court involving a member of the Scottish Bar.

The reports recounted in detail what the *Daily Mail* described as "the drama of [a] bitter divorce action".

The deputy Crown Agent wrote to the director of the Scottish **12.27** Daily Newspaper Society confirming that following a complaint by the advocate involved, Strathclyde police had been instructed by the fiscal to look into alleged contraventions of section 1 of the 1926 Act. The letter stated that Crown counsel had considered the reports by police and the fiscal and concluded that there should be no criminal proceedings. No reason was given for the decision not to prosecute. The letter continued: "Crown counsel are concerned that there may be some apprehension as to the continued applicability of the 1926 Act. I have therefore been asked to write to you and the editors of the two newspapers pointing out that the 1926 Act remains in force."

As recently as July 15, 1996 in the case of *Re Moynihan* the **12.28** President of the Family Division of the High Court in England and Wales ruled in terms that the 1926 Act applied to proceedings in that case which was concerned with nullity of a decree of divorce granted in 1990. "As long as the provisions of the 1926 Act remain in force it will be necessary for the prosecution authorities to consider the question of prosecution in any case which may be referred to them on a case by case basis."

According to experts in media law in England, the *Moynihan* **12.29** case was the first in 70 years in which a judge had given guidance on the 1926 Act. Sir Stephen Brown adopted what appeared to be an extremely liberal interpretation of how the media should approach the Act but also pointed out that *Moynihan* was a very exceptional case. After the death of Lord Moynihan his fourth wife Editha raised a court action to have their marriage declared null and void. On the first day of the case the media attended en masse and Sir Stephen read out the relevant parts of the 1926 Act, pointing out that the effect was that in defended divorce cases the evidence could not be reported even although it was given in open court. The statement of the charges, defences and counter-charges in support of which the evidence was given could be published, but not the details of the evidence. That meant that nature of the charges could be published as could the final judgment of the court in full "without editing in any sense so that the full matter might be revealed in the course of the judgment".

Up to that point the judge's understanding of the law appears to **12.30** coincide with the views expressed so far in this chapter. However,

Sir Stephen went on to say that nobody in court (including the Attorney-General) had raised any substantial objections as to why details should not be made public as and when they arose. The judge said he had a great deal of sympathy with reporters but pointed out that the terms of the 1926 Act were mandatory and did not allow the court any discretion to lift reporting restrictions. He added: "The Attorney General has . . . indicated that he would not be very anxious to institute criminal proceedings if by some oversight there was a breach of the strict letter of the law." He warned, however, that until Parliament intervened the Act did apply. "Having said that, it is quite plain that there would appear to be ample scope in the context of the sub-paragraphs of sub-paragraph (b) (see above) for clear and full details of the proceedings to be given, though not necessarily a line by line account of what a particular witness says at any particular time."

12.31 If the judge meant that the general gist of a witness's evidence can be reported, even though not a line by line account, that provides greater scope for reporting divorce actions than had previously been understood. The judge also made it clear that he saw no objection to the reporting of closing submissions and the *Daily Telegraph* duly ran a report under the headline: "Wives fight for the Moynihan millions." The *Telegraph* report went into details of the evidence as rehearsed by counsel.

12.32 That was, of course, an English decision, and it remains to be seen whether a Scottish court would take a similarly relaxed view. The first prosecution of any kind in the United Kingdom at Paisley Sheriff Court in 1999 suggests not.

First prosecution

12.33 Proceedings for a breach of the 1926 Act were taken against the *Glasgow Evening Times*, the *Scottish Daily Mail*, the *Scottish Daily Express*, the *Paisley Daily Express* and *The Scotsman*. The charge stated that on June 17, 1998 the respective newspapers had published reports of judicial proceedings for an action of divorce at Paisley Sheriff Court containing particulars other than those permitted by section 1(1)(b) of the 1926 Act. In particular, the charge went on, material had been published which was not a concise statement of the charges, defences and counterclaims in support of which evidence had been given. The action had been settled without evidence being heard but newspapers published lurid allegations of a sensational nature from documents lodged in court. These included claims of homosexual encounters, violence and theft.

12.34 The sheriff dismissed the complaints on the argument that Paisley Sheriff Court had no jurisdiction to try the case. He said there was no dispute that the newspapers were circulating in the Paisley area, but in his view each was printed outwith the jurisdiction.

The submission for the newspapers was that publishing took **12.35** place at the place of printing. At that point the newspaper was sold to wholesalers for onward sale. Any offence was completed when printing was completed and anything done after that to bring the newspaper into the hands of the public was not part of publication. The Crown argued that it was wrong to say that publication stopped at the door of the printing press. There was a whole chain of events up to sale and they were all part of the process of publication.

The sheriff said, however: **12.36**

> "It seems to me that in the context of this criminal statute that 'publish' occurs at one point in time and place. . . . It seems wrong that although the accused does nothing more once the paper is handed over that nonetheless he is to be held to be criminally responsible for matters thereafter that are beyond his control. . . . It is my view that publication for the purposes of the statute takes place once and that is when the paper is handed over to the wholesaler at point of printing."

The sheriff said the fact that the *Paisley Daily Express* coincidentally sold the paper directly in the sheriffdom was irrelevant if the publishing was complete at an earlier point.

The Crown appeal against the decision was rejected by three **12.37** judges at the High Court in Edinburgh headed by Rodger, the Lord Justice-General. Lord Rodger said that even though the Act had been on the statute book for many years researches of counsel had turned up just one case—*Moynihan* (see above). He pointed out that by a "nice irony" the baby whose birth gave rise to the 1926 Act later became the distinguished deputy chairman of Express Newspapers. Lord Rodger added: "The origin of the Act in a desire to prevent a salacious public being regaled with accounts of unsavoury details from judicial proceedings is of some importance for present purposes." The Act had been introduced not to protect the privacy of those involved in the proceedings but to prevent injury to the morals of those who might read the reports in the newspapers. The Long Title of the Act stated that it was: "An Act to regulate the publication of reports of judicial proceedings in such manner as to prevent injury to public morals." Lord Rodger added:

> "The aim of the Act is therefore to prevent injury to public morals throughout Great Britain by the publication of unsavoury matters and details from judicial proceedings, wherever

> they may be held. . . . Nor is this surprising: in 1963, for instance, newspaper reports of Lord Wheatley's opinion in the Argyll divorce case were devoured just as eagerly in London as in Edinburgh where the action was heard."

Similarly, although the present divorce case was in Paisley, Parliament must have been just as concerned to prevent injury to the morals of readers in Morningside in Edinburgh.

12.38 In the appeal, the Crown argued that the sheriff had been wrong to rule that publication for the purposes of the 1926 Act took place once—when the paper was handed over to the wholesaler at the point of printing. According to the Crown the offence of publication involved the circulation for sale of a newspaper within the jurisdiction of the court. The argument was that publication should be regarded as a continuing offence, beginning at the printing works when the publisher handed the newspaper over for distribution to retailers and persisting when the public bought their newspapers from the retailer. A newspaper was published whenever and wherever it was offered to the public by the proprietor, the Crown maintained. In this case the publishers had offered the newspapers for sale in Paisley.

12.39 Lord Rodger said he was satisfied that the Crown approach must be rejected. In the context of the 1926 Act it appeared to him that an editor or publisher published a newspaper at the point where it had been printed and was offered for sale or distribution.

> "The publisher may allow members of the public to come to the premises and buy copies hot off the press. Most of the copies will, however, be out into the wholesalers' vans and will be driven off for distribution throughout the areas where the paper circulates. . . . By this stage the papers have been published and, where they contain offending particulars, the offence has been committed."

12.40 Lord Rodger said that interpretation of the Act was consistent with the statutory aim of preventing publication of reports calculated to injure public morals.

> "The aim must be to prevent ANY publication of newspapers containing such reports and so the bar on publication must be breached and the offence committed as soon as the newspapers are offered for sale or distribution. . . . Since the bar has been breached and a punishable offence has been committed at this stage, the legislation is effective if a prosecution can be based on what has occurred at this point. . . . There seems no reason why Parliament should have intended the

subsection to cover any later stage in the distribution process when it is being carried on by others."

It was not easy to see how an editor could properly be made criminally liable by the subsequent actings of wholesalers and others. "If any offences were committed they were committed when the papers were offered for sale or distribution at the publishers' works or offices. . . . They were not committed at the stage when the papers were circulating in Paisley; there is accordingly no basis for the Sheriff Court at Paisley having jurisdiction to try the alleged offences."

KEY POINTS

The Judicial Proceedings (Regulation of Reports) Act 1926 **12.41** places strict limits on what can be reported in divorce and related cases. Detailed reporting of evidence is not allowed. Legal argument can be reported. The safest way to report defended divorces is to wait for a written judgment. There is no decree nisi in Scotland. There was no prosecution under the Act in the United Kingdom until 1999 when the Crown took proceedings against five newspapers over reports of a divorce case at Paisley Sheriff Court. The sheriff decided that he had no jurisdiction to hear the case because the papers had not been published within the sheriffdom and his decision was upheld in the Court of Appeal. The decision means that, for the purposes of the 1926 Act publication takes place once—when a newspaper is handed over to the wholesaler at the point of printing. The 1926 Act also bans in any judicial proceedings the publication of indecent material the publication of which is calculated to injure public morals.

CHAPTER 13

CHILDREN

13.01 The law provides the protection of anonymity for children involved in legal proceedings on the basis that they may be harmed by publicity. The protection is provided in various ways in criminal and civil cases, children's hearings and fatal accident inquiries.

13.02 The law on identifying children in criminal cases is contained in section 47 of the Criminal Procedure (Scotland) Act 1995.

13.03 Section 47 applies to any criminal court in Scotland and forbids disclosure in court reports of a name, address or school, or any information calculated to lead to the identification of "any person under 16 years concerned in the proceedings". The section is intended to protect a child against or in respect of whom the proceedings are taken—an accused or victim—or who is appearing as a witness. The ban on identification applies to pictures as well as to newspaper, radio and television reports of cases. But see para. 13.25 below as to whether even "non-identifiable" pictures are allowed. Where the person under 16 is involved as a witness only and no one against whom the proceedings are taken is under 16, there is no bar on identification unless the court makes a direction to that effect.

13.04 A court may at any stage of the proceedings dispense with the ban on identification if satisfied that this is in the public interest. The First Minister for Scotland is also given power, after a case has been dealt with, to make an order lifting the prohibition or to overrule an order made by the court. It is believed that this power has never been used.

13.05 In a case before the High Court in Edinburgh in 1983 (*H.M. Advocate v. George Aitken*), in which the Crown asked for a ruling, Lord Brand held the section does not apply to dead children. He ruled that a "person" within the meaning of the section was a live person and someone who was dead could not be "concerned" in the proceedings. The judge added that, if he had decided the section did apply, he would have allowed identification in the particular case in the public interest. Had the defence submission that the section did apply to the child in the case been upheld,

190

reports of the case could not have identified the father, who was charged with culpable homicide of the child, since this would have been "calculated" to identify the child.

In deciding whether or not to allow identification, the court must **13.06** bear in mind the public interest and the decision will depend very much on the view of the individual judge. In a case in 1991 at the High Court in Edinburgh, Lord Sutherland decided that it would not be in the public interest to lift reporting restrictions in the case of a 13-year-old boy who had been convicted of culpable homicide.

The maximum penalty for contravening the section is a fine of **13.07** £5,000 at present.

The journalist must look at the child's age when the case is in **13.08** court. If the child becomes 16 on the day the case is before the court, the automatic ban on identification no longer applies. It is now the practice of the Crown Office in framing indictments to include the age of accused and victims under 16.

There may be a question about exactly when the section 47 **13.09** restriction takes effect. The section has to be read subject to its opening words—"No newspaper report of any proceedings in a court shall reveal. . . ". On a strict reading, this means that the ban on identification operates only when the proceedings are in a court and not, for example, at preliminary stages of a case before a hearing takes place.

This has led to some rather strange results. Cases have been **13.10** reported including the name of a child victim one day, only to be published anonymously the next, after someone has been arrested and appeared in court.

The Act makes no express provision for appeal against a court's **13.11** direction either allowing or banning publication in terms of section 47, but the power given to the First Minister to make an order dispensing with the requirements of the section may provide a means for the media to ask in individual cases for the automatic bar to be lifted in the public interest. This, however, would not be possible until the end of the case.

Some unforeseen results of section 47 have become apparent **13.12** only with experience. For example, in a child custody case, if either parent was charged with an offence connected with the dispute, such as assault or abduction, the reporting of these criminal proceedings might become subject to reporting restrictions to prevent identification of the child. Disclosure of the child's identity in the civil action would have to be withheld, since to disclose it would defeat the purpose of section 47 in requiring anonymity in the criminal case.

A case at the High Court in Edinburgh in 1990 illustrated the **13.13** unexpected problems the section can cause. A man was charged with murdering his wife, and the only person under 16 involved in the case was the wife's son by a previous marriage, who was an eye-witness to the fatal attack. The Crown asked for an order to prohibit the child's identification in media reports on the basis that he was now living with relatives at a new address and attending a new school where no one knew of his tragic background.

13.14   Lord Milligan acknowledged the wide public interest in the free reporting of our criminal courts, but decided that in this case the boy's identity should be protected by banning publication of his name, address, or school. Reporters present in court pointed out, through the clerk, that it would be difficult, if not impossible to report the names of the accused and the victim of the alleged murder without revealing the boy's identity. They argued that it was highly undesirable to report a murder trial anonymously.

13.15   Lord Milligan stressed that his intention was that there should be no publicity only as to the fact that the boy had given evidence, the content of the evidence or that he was present when the alleged murder took place. The compromise was reached that the trial was reported with the names of the accused and the deceased but no mention whatsoever was made of the boy or his evidence, although from the media's point of view, it would have been of great news value.

13.16   When Parliament bans publication of information "calculated" to lead to identification, that does not mean that the journalist will be excused if he did not actually "calculate" that identification would take place as a result of what he had written. The journalist must decide whether identification of the child would follow as a natural and likely result of publication. In 1982 the *Lothian Courier*, Bathgate, was fined £75 at Linlithgow Sheriff Court for naming a man in a report it carried of his conviction for assault on his 18-month-old daughter. The newspaper admitted a charge under section 47, that publication of the man's name was "calculated" to lead to the identification of the child, although that was not the paper's intention.

Incest cases

13.17   In reporting cases of incest or other sexual offences, the media in Scotland have followed the practice of not identifying young people who are innocently involved. Where the person in question is under 16 it is an offence to publish his or her identity under section 47, but over that age there is no statutory protection. Incest cases often come to light after many years when the victim has grown up although only a child at the time of the offences.

13.18   In 1966 the Press Council recommended a course which has been widely followed. The object is to avoid "jigsaw identification" where two or more reports, each protecting the anonymity of a child, may disclose his identity when read together. This could happen where one report names the accused but does not disclose his relationship to the victim, while another publishes an anonymous report indicating the accused's relationship to the victim. The Press Council proposed that editors should adopt a formula by which the accused is named (if an adult) but the relationship to the child involved is not specified.

In 1980 Scottish newspaper editors agreed that in such a **13.19** situation they would apply a formula on the following lines—where a case of incest is reported the adult is identified but the word "incest" is not used, the offence being described as "a serious offence against a young child" or the like; the child is not identified and the report excludes anything implying the relationship between the accused and the child.

Children's hearings

The Social Work (Scotland) Act 1968 abolished juvenile courts and **13.20** brought about important changes in the methods of dealing with children. It laid down that a child could be prosecuted for an offence only on the instructions of the Lord Advocate, and that no court, other than the High Court of Justiciary and the sheriff court, had jurisdiction over a child for an offence.

It requires every local authority to set up a children's panel—a **13.21** pool of suitably qualified citizens to hear cases involving children who may need compulsory measures of care, including children who have committed offences.

The Act also requires each local authority to appoint an officer, **13.22** known as a Reporter (who must be legally qualified) to arrange children's hearings. The hearings have, in effect, taken over from the old juvenile courts. Where the Reporter considers that a child may be in need of compulsory measures of care, it is his duty to arrange a children's hearing.

Cases of the kind are heard by three members of the appropriate **13.23** panel. This tribunal of three, consisting of a chairman and two other members, must include at least one woman. It is properly referred to in media reports as a children's hearing and not as a children's panel, which, as already explained, refers to the complete list of people from whom the members of any particular children's hearing are selected.

There is a right of appeal by a child or his parent, or both, to the **13.24** sheriff against a decision of a children's hearing, and the appeal is heard in chambers. The media can be present at such appeals, although attendance is rare. The sheriff has a discretion to exclude reporters, and, of course, the child cannot be identified in any report. Where the sheriff is not satisfied that the decision was justified he may send the case back to the children's hearing for reconsideration, and the normal rules then apply to reports of the proceedings.

13.25   The 1968 Act provided that these hearings take place in private but allowed bona fide representatives of a newspaper or news agency to attend. The present law is to be found in the Children (Scotland) Act 1995. It prohibits any newspaper, radio or television report of any children's hearing, or of any hearing before a sheriff or appeal before the Court of Session in such a case, to reveal the name, address or school, or include any particulars calculated to lead to the identification of any child concerned. The provisions apply also to pictures. The restrictions may be dispensed with wholly or partly by order of the First Minister in any case if he is satisfied this would be in the interests of justice; they apply also to reports of children's hearings published in England, Wales and Northern Ireland. The part of the section which prohibits the use of pictures of the child should be noted. The media have interpreted that provision for 25 years as meaning that only a picture which identified the child was prohibited. A rear view (for example) was thought to be permissible. Such pictures were used extensively by all newspapers and television broadcasters when reporting the proceedings before the children's hearing and the referral hearing before the sheriff in the Orkney case. Their use of such pictures was never challenged in the courts until February 1993 when in the case of Bette McArdle, the Editor of the *Highland News*, the Justiciary Appeal Court appeared to take the view that all pictures of children are prohibited by the 1968 Act (and so now by the Children (Scotland) Act 1995)—irrespective of whether the child could be identified from the picture or not. In this case the newspaper had published photographs of the children with their faces "blanked out". If that is the correct interpretation of section 58 of the Social Work (Scotland) Act 1968, presumably a similar interpretation must be put on section 47 of the Criminal Procedure (Scotland) Act 1995 which relates to reporting of criminal cases involving children under 16 as accused, victims or witnesses.

13.26   It was decided in 1991 in a case in which it was alleged that nine children in Orkney had been sexually abused, that when a case is referred from a children's hearing to a sheriff to determine whether the grounds of referral are established, a sheriff has the discretion to allow the press into chambers to report the proceedings. Of course reports must not contain any information which would identify any child involved.

In cases coming before children's hearings, "child" means a **13.27** person under 18 years, where a supervision requirement of a hearing is in force, and in other cases a person under 16 years.

List D Schools provide residential education and care for **13.28** children referred to them by children's hearings or sheriff courts. They are administered by local authority social work departments. Since June 1985 a person known as a safeguarder or curator may be appointed in certain cases where there appears to be a conflict of interest between parent and child in a children's hearing. He or she is usually a person, not necessarily a lawyer, qualified by knowledge of and interest in problems of children who can safeguard the interests of the child involved. This practice is becoming increasingly common in children's hearings, particularly in the situation where the case is referred to the sheriff for a proof hearing.

The Criminal Procedure (Scotland) Act 1995, section 50, states **13.29** that no child under 14, other than an infant-in-arms, can be in court during the trial of any other person charged with an offence, or during any preliminary proceedings, except when required as a witness or otherwise for the purposes of justice.

The Act provides that in any proceedings involving an offence **13.30** against or conduct contrary to decency or morality, where a person who, in the opinion of the court, is a child, is called as a witness, the court may direct that the courtroom be cleared. Bona fide reporters will be allowed to remain. This section does not affect the courts' ordinary powers to hear a case *in camera*.

Disclosure of the sex and age of a child in a named village or **13.31** small community or, for example that he is the son of a policeman or teacher, could well lead to his or her identity being disclosed. In cases of that kind it may be necessary to leave out a local name and give instead only the name of the county or region so that the child's identity is protected. The aim of the legislation is to prevent anyone being able to identify the child and it will not be a defence to say that the public at large without any special knowledge could not make an identification. The law will be breached if, for example, neighbours could identify the child from what is disclosed in the media.

Custody cases

Where a custody dispute is part of divorce proceedings, reporting **13.32** will be restricted under the Judicial Proceedings (Regulation of Reports) Act 1926 (see Chapter 12). After many years of confusion about the legal position, it has now also been decided by the Court of Session that the media may be banned from identifying children in any custody hearing even although it is not part of a divorce action.

13.33 In an international custody dispute in 1988, Lord Murray agreed that publicity would be harmful to the child involved and made an order directing the media not to publish anything calculated to lead to the child being identified. He made the order under section 46 of the Children and Young Persons (Scotland) Act 1937 (as amended).

13.34 The judge referred the case to three judges in the First Division of the Court of Session because of the doubts which had existed for many years as to whether this section applied to civil cases. Lord Emslie, the Lord President, said the court had not the slightest doubt that Lord Murray's order was competent.

13.35 Section 46 states that in relation to any proceedings in any court, the court may direct that no newspaper report shall reveal the name, address or school, or include any particulars calculated to lead to the identification of a person under the age of 17 concerned in the proceedings. It applies to a person by or against or in respect of whom the proceedings are taken, or who is a witness. The prohibition applies to pictures and would also now cover radio and television.

13.36 The long standing doubt over whether section 46 applied to civil cases came about because it was originally included in a section of the 1937 Act which referred expressly to criminal proceedings. However, in the 1988 case, the judges accepted the argument that, following a series of amendments to the 1937 Act, it now had a wider scope. Since the 1988 decision judges in the Court of Session have made orders banning the identification of children in custody cases on a number of occasions. The effect is that if the case is reported at all, it has to be done anonymously. Note, however, that it is only where the judge makes an order that the media are prevented from identifying the child involved. In criminal cases, identification is banned unless the judge makes a specific order to the contrary.

Adoption procedure

13.37 Under the Rules of the Court of Session, adoption proceedings are normally heard *in camera*, unless the court directs otherwise. Likewise, all documents lodged in court in adoption proceedings are treated as confidential. The reporting of adoption proceedings is therefore extremely difficult, if not impossible, except where the court permits the hearing to take place in public. This rarely happens in practice, but occasionally, the proceedings may be reported, provided, of course, the identities of the parties are not disclosed and no information is published from any of the documents regarded as confidential by the Rule of Court.

An example of this was a case in 1973 where an important point **13.38** affecting procedure to be followed in adoption cases in general was debated in the First Division. The proceedings were of sufficient importance to be reported in some newspapers, without names and addresses. Judgments of the court may sometimes be made available for publication by authority of the court, again subject to non-identification of the parties.

The anonymity rule applying to wardship cases in English courts **13.39** may sometimes apply in Scotland. In a case before the English High Court Family Division in 1984, Mr Justice Balcombe ruled that he had power to make an anonymity order "against the world at large", *i.e.* the entire media. He was dealing with the case of a Englishwoman aged 27, who had been convicted of the manslaughter with diminished responsibility of two boys, aged four and three, when she was 11 years old and living in Newcastle. She was released on licence in 1980, made a new life for herself under a different name, and had a baby daughter who had been made a ward of court. The judge issued an injunction to stop the *News of the World* revealing the woman's identity, that of her child or of the child's father, and extending his order to apply to all the media in the interests of the ward.

Fatal accident inquiries

The Fatal Accidents and Sudden Deaths Inquiry (Scotland) Act **13.40** 1976 states that inquiries under its terms should be held in public unless a person under the age of 17 is in any way involved (a provision open to wide interpretation). The sheriff may at his own hand, or on an application by a party, order that no report in any publication or broadcast shall reveal the name, address or school of that person or otherwise identify him.

The sheriff also has power to order that no picture of the person **13.41** under 17 may be published "in any manner", which must be taken to cover television as well as newspapers.

The wide scope of the Act can be seen from a fatal accident **13.42** inquiry at Dumbarton Sheriff Court in 1984 into the death of a six-week old baby boy. Sheriff Principal Philip Caplan, Q.C., agreed to a motion by counsel for the boy's parents that there should be reporting restrictions in the case. The result was that no one was named in reports of the inquiry, although the names had already been published in a statutory advertisement published in the *Herald*. The reason given in court for applying reporting restrictions was to protect the three-year-old sister of the dead infant. She

was said to be involved in the case because of the father's evidence
that he had dropped his baby son after the little girl pulled his arm.

13.43   At Forfar Sheriff Court in 1992, during a fatal accident inquiry
into the death of a 14-year-old girl from inhaling solvent, Sheriff
Stewart Kermack made an order purporting to ban the media from
naming everyone involved in the inquiry under the age of 17,
including the dead girl. It is difficult to see how this order could
properly be made insofar as it related to the dead girl. On the
analogy of Lord Brand's decision in the *Aitken* case (see para.
13.05), the dead girl was not legally a person.

KEY POINTS

13.44 Section 47 of the Criminal Procedure (Scotland) Act 1995 bans the
identification of an accused, victim or witness aged under 16 in
criminal cases. The ban can be lifted by the court and does not
apply where the child victim is dead. Unless the court directs
otherwise, identification is allowed where the child is a witness only
and no one against whom proceedings are taken is under 16.

13.45   The ban relates to court proceedings and does not come into
effect at an earlier stage. It may sometimes result in a guilty adult
being protected. To protect children in incest cases, the general
practice is to say that a named accused has been guilty of a serious
sexual offence. The term incest is not used.

13.46   Children's hearings are in private but the media can attend as
long as they do not identify the child (Social Work (Scotland) Act
1968 and now the Children (Scotland) Act 1995).

13.47   In custody cases the court can make an order banning the
identification of a child under the age of 17 involved in the
proceedings. (Children and Young Persons (Scotland) Act 1937, s.
46).

13.48   In fatal accident inquiries a sheriff can ban the identification of a
child under the age of 17 in any way involved in the proceedings
(Fatal Accidents and Sudden Deaths Inquiry (Scotland) Act 1976).

CHAPTER 14

JUDICIAL REVIEW

Judicial Review is increasingly used to challenge actions and **14.01** decisions where more common legal remedies are not available. It is often thought of as an action available to the citizen against the state and its administration, but one can take judicial review action against many types of body.

The Scottish judicial review system arose from the ancient **14.02** "supervisory jurisdiction" of the Court of Session to provide a remedy which would not otherwise be available. (The High Court of Judiciary also has a supervisory jurisdiction in criminal matters.)

Procedure

In Scotland, judicial review procedure was reformed in 1985 with a **14.03** view to providing a quick flexible remedy where citizens were suffering from wrong or unjust or unreasonable decisions. Experienced Judges are given wide powers to grant any orders which they consider appropriate. According to the leading 1992 decision of *West*:

> "The Court of Session has power, in the exercise of its supervisory jurisdiction, to regulate the process by which decisions are taken by any person or body to whom a jurisdiction, power or authority has been delegated or entrusted by statute, agreement or any other instrument ... to ensure that the person or body does not exceed or abuse that jurisdiction, power or authority or fail to do what the jurisdiction, power or authority requires".

Unlike England, the courts in Scotland have not been overly-concerned as to whether the problem in question has anything to do with "public law". Arbiters can be judicially reviewed, for example. Nonetheless, central Government and local Government are particularly likely to be subject to judicial review. Legal Aid is available.

Use

14.04 Areas where judicial review has been active on both sides of the border include homelessness cases; immigration decisions; licensing decisions; planning and land issues; and matters relating to social security. Judicial review applications have also been taken in Scotland in relation to education, employment, legal aid, taxes, transport and the position of prisoners. High-profile cases in Scotland have included the petitions to prevent the withdrawal of the Fort William sleeper service, and in 1983, to stop Strathclyde Regional Council from adding fluoride to the water supply, and the recent attempt by the Glasgow Rape Crisis Centre to prevent boxer and convicted rapist Mike Tyson from being admitted to Scotland.

14.05 Not all organisations with decision-making powers can be judicially reviewed. The Professional Golfers' Association was recently held not to be subject to it, for example, although some sporting bodies have been judicially reviewed.

Remedies

14.06 In judicial review, Scottish Judges can grant such remedies as interim liberation, *i.e.* bail, in immigration cases; interim interdict, *i.e.* temporary banning orders in relation to a particular activity; or an order to secure accommodation in the meantime, in the case of homelessness issues. Damages can be awarded, although this is extremely rare.

PCC/BSC

14.07 Judicial review has direct significance for the media in some areas. Recently, in England, the BBC successfully judicially reviewed the decision of the Broadcasting Standards Commission that Dixons, the electrical retailers, had a right to privacy in relation to undercover journalism. (The merits of the decision are under appeal to the Court of Appeal.) The Press Complaints Commission's decisions are also thought to be judicially reviewable.

14.08 Judicial review has occasionally been sought against the media in matters of less obvious importance. Status Quo unsuccessfully sought judicial review in England of an alleged decision by Radio One not to play any more than necessary of the band's new recordings. This failed for the lack of any evidence, but would, it is felt, have failed in any event, because of the discretion allowed to broadcasters in the matter of content.

Political Coverage

14.09 Broadcasters may be subject to judicial review by one political party or another in relation to their allocation of Party Election Broadcasts and their political coverage in other respects. In 1997, for example, the BBC successfully defended an English judicial review application in relation to its decision to cut a film showing aborted foetuses which originally formed part of the Pro-life Alliance Party's Election Broadcast. In April 1997, the SNP sought interdict against STV and Grampian against Alex Salmond's exclusion from a possible leaders' debate. This was unsuccessful for a variety of reasons, one of which was that judicial review, not interdict, would have been the right way to challenge ITC licence-holders.

Grounds of Review

The grounds of judicial review include: **14.10**

- Acting *ultra vires*, *i.e.* if the Council or other body makes a decision which it does not in law have the power to make;
- Abuse of discretion, including taking an unreasonable decision. This is sometimes known as "Wednesbury unreasonableness". The level of unreasonableness has to be high. In Scotland, this argument succeeded in relation to the decision by a local authority that a 16 year-old girl who had left home because of domestic abuse was not a "vulnerable" person with a priority need for re-housing;
- Fettering of discretion—this means too rigid policy-making by an organisation, so that it fails to look at each question on its own merits;
- Breach of legitimate expectations—for example, the withdrawal of a licence suddenly without a hearing could be a breach of legitimate expectation;
- Failure to observe natural justice, *e.g.* serious irregularities in procedure, a refusal to listen to the petitioner's side of the story, the appointment of a decision-maker with a direct personal stake in the outcome, failure to allow cross-examination, etc.

It is not possible to contract out of judicial review.

Scotland Act 1998

Acts of the Scottish Parliament will be subject to judicial review. **14.11** This is because the Scottish legislature has powers defined by statute. If any Act is beyond Holyrood's remit — for example, by attempting to legislate in reserved areas (such as abortion); to legislate in contravention of U.K. duties such as the European Convention on Human Rights; or to alter the Act of Union — the Scottish judiciary is entitled to strike down the legislation. Similarly, the Acts of the Scottish Parliament will be subject to judicial review if they are incompatible with European Union law.

KEY POINTS

14.12 Judicial review is a means by which challenges to unfair or unreasonable administrative and other decisions can be made in court. It is designed to be quick, and may be used in a variety of areas affecting the media. Holyrood legislation will be reviewable by this route if the Scottish Parliament oversteps its limits.

CHAPTER 15

TITLES AND TERMINOLOGY

The principal judge in Scotland holds the dual office of Lord **15.01**
Justice-General (in which capacity he is president of the High
Court of Justiciary) and Lord President of the Court of Session.
The Lord Justice-Clerk, who is next in order of precedence, holds
office in both courts and carries the same title in each. In the Court
of Session the Lord President presides over the First Division as
well as over sittings of the full bench (which are not common); the
Lord Justice-Clerk presides over the Second Division. He also
deputises for the Lord President in his absence as head of the
courts.

There are 30 other judges (including the Chairman of the **15.02**
Scottish Law Commission, who may perform his judicial function
also from time to time). Each bears the title of Lord Commissioner
of Justiciary when sitting in the High Court and Senator of the
College of Justice when performing the functions of a Court of
Session judge. In either capacity he is entitled to the courtesy title
"Lord", but he is not a peer, unless he is one of the few judges who
have been made Life Peers. There is no objection to the forms
"Lord President Smith" or "Lord Justice-Clerk Black", styles
which are in use in the legal textbooks. The term Lord Ordinary is
used frequently in court with reference to a judge of first
instance—the reporter will usually have to inquire or search in the
documents of the case for the particular judge's name. The Court
of Session sits only in Edinburgh, the High Court of Justiciary
deals with criminal business in Edinburgh and on circuit in various
parts of Scotland.

Sheriff court

When a sheriff principal or sheriff is a Q.C., this designation **15.03**
should not be omitted from the first mention of his name in a
report. Sheriffs principal and sheriffs in court or when discharging
their shrieval functions are addressed as "My Lord" or "My Lady".
They should be given their judicial titles only in reports of matters
concerning their discharge of these duties. When a sheriff is

reported as speaking or participating in any activity as a private individual, his shrieval title should be omitted. (This practice may be reversed in local papers, where "the Sheriff" tends to carry this style with him wherever he goes and whatever he does in the public eye.)

Faculty of Advocates

15.04 From the point of view of etiquette, to which the law attaches much importance, it may be as offensive to describe an advocate as a Q.C. as to call a Q.C. an advocate. This can be understood if it is realised that when an advocate takes silk his junior practice comes to an end. There have been instances of juniors losing briefs because they were prematurely described in the press as Q.C.s—and, of course, members of the Faculty of Advocates may not advertise themselves, even in order to rectify such inaccuracies. The former rule by which a Q.C. could not normally appear without a junior was rescinded in 1977. In the High Court an advocate-depute who is a Q.C. may appear alone. The title advocate-depute belongs to several members of the Bar who assist in the preparation and conduct of criminal prosecutions. They are deputies to the Lord Advocate, and not advocates' deputies (as the title might suggest).

Law officers

15.05 The Lord Advocate holds one of the most ancient and influential offices in the Scottish legal system. Assisted by the Solicitor General for Scotland, he is head of the criminal prosecution system, in which capacity he acts independently of other Ministers of the Scottish Executive. He also advises the Government on all questions of Scots and European law.

15.06 The Scotland Act 1998 which ushered in a devolved Parliament in Edinburgh brought about a fundamental change in the position of the Scots law officers who both became members of the Scottish Executive rather than members of the U.K government. Part of their responsibility is to advise the Scottish Executive over whether a proposed piece of legislation is within the legislative competence of the Edinburgh Parliament. Both law officers can take part in proceedings of the Scottish Parliament and answer questions on legal issues before the Parliament and its committees. They can decline to answer any question which might prejudice a prosecution or damage the public interest.

15.07 The Lord Advocate's long-established role in the selection of judges to the Scottish Bench seems to have been diminished to some extent following the Scotland Act. Appointments are now officially recommended to the Queen by the First Minister after consultation with the Lord President of the Court of Session, although it would be surprising if the Lord Advocate of the day did not retain an active behind-the-scenes role in the selection process.

Members of the Society of Advocates in Aberdeen, who are **15.08** solicitors, are not to be confused with members of the Faculty of Advocates. Unless they have qualified as solicitor-advocates, Aberdeen advocates do not share the right to plead before the supreme courts.

The term "counsel" applies only to members of the Faculty and **15.09** is not accurately used in reference to solicitors or solicitor advocates appearing in court.

It is necessary in the reporting of Scottish court cases to avoid **15.10** the use of English court terms. We use pursuer, not plaintiff; defender, not defendant. In England divorce proceedings are taken by way of a petition; in Scotland, by way of a summons in the Court of Session and by way of an initial writ in the sheriff court. The distinction results in quite separate terms being used for the parties concerned in the proceedings. Thus, while in England the person who institutes divorce proceedings is the petitioner and the opposing party the respondent, these in Scotland are respectively pursuer and defender. The term "respondent" is used in Scotland in reference to a party contesting a petition as well as to one resisting an appeal. A third party who comes into divorce proceedings to deny allegations implicating him or her may do so by lodging a minute and is known as a party-minuter.

A number of Scottish and English court terms are interchangea- **15.11** ble according to the particular requirements of the newspaper, having regard to its readership. For example, although in Scotland a court order prohibiting some act which is the subject of complaint is properly called an interdict, the reporter writing for an English paper might find it desirable to call such an order an injunction, the equivalent English term which would be more readily understood by his readers and is at the same time not entirely unknown in Scotland. The same might be said of such terms as aliment (English maintenance or alimony), arbiter (arbitrator) and expenses (costs).

CHAPTER 16

ESSENTIALS OF DEFAMATION

16.01 This chapter has begun for many editions with two quotations from the last century of Scottish courts, which have been asserted as accurate summaries of modern Scots defamation law. However, since the publication of the sixth edition, there have been significant changes in the position. In the first place, there has been the decision of the House of Lords in the case of *Albert Reynolds v. Times Newspapers*, 1998, which recognises that a communication to the public at large may attract the protection of qualified privilege at common law. Furthermore, the European Convention on Human Rights has been incorporated into Scots law by the Human Rights Act 1999.

16.02 Taking all that into account, it must be doubted if the quotes from Lord Kyllachy and Lord Dees quoted in previous editions now adequately state the law of Scotland. Although Scots law has not moved to a point where it recognises (as some jurisdictions do) a "report privilege" to afford journalists a degree of protection when reporting on matters of considerable public import, it can be said that the stark statement that a journalist has no better protection than any other member of the public is no longer a full statement of the true legal position.

16.03 However, as these quotations will be familiar to readers of previous editions of this book and will form a useful starting point for our consideration of the law of defamation, let us once again quote them here. They are as follows: "I do not for my part, consider that any privilege whatever attaches to a newspaper report as such. If a newspaper gives circulation to a slander, it is simply in the position of any other party circulating a slander and the general rule is that a person circulating a slander is answerable equally with the author of the slander". (Lord Kyllachy in *Wright & Greig v. Outram* (1890) 17 R. 596.) The law has changed slightly since Lord Kyllachy said this at the end of the last century and newspaper reports of certain matters are now privileged by statute. But apart from these special cases the principle remains the same. The law of defamation applies to journalists as to ordinary mortals. There is no general privilege of journalism.

"It would be a total mistake to suppose that the editor of a newspaper, who sits behind a curtain like another veiled prophet, is entitled to vote himself public accuser, to the effect of calling every member of society to account for his misdeeds and to confer upon every anonymous contributor whom he admits into his columns, the same privilege".

(Lord Deas in *Drew v. Mackenzie* (1862))

After a period of considerable stagnation, it appears that the law **16.04** of defamation, both in Scotland and in England, has been developing over the past few years. The *Reynolds* case suggests that journalists will be protected if they are reporting significant matters of public interest. Although the concept of the public figure defence has not been imported into United Kingdom law from America, it does appear that journalists are more likely to be able to plead the *Reynolds* style defence when producing copy on individuals such as politicians and civil servants in whom the public have a legitimate interest. The *Reynolds* approach follows the high value placed on freedom of speech by Article 10 of the European Convention on Human Rights. Convention jurisprudence recognises the public figure concept in such cases as *Lingens v. Austria*. So both the development of common law privilege and the importation of the European Convention point towards a more sympathetic approach to the publication of critical material by newspapers and broadcasters.

To return to the *Wright* case, the second part of Lord Kyllachy's **16.05** remark should also be noted. "A person circulating a slander is answerable equally with the author of the slander." This means that the author, publisher and printer of a book can be, and frequently are, all sued for the one slander. It means that both the writer of a defamatory article, report or letter and the proprietor of the newspaper in which it is published may be liable for damages and it means that the newspaper which merely repeats a defamatory statement already published in the columns of another is as liable to be sued as if it originated the slander. (By the Defamation Act 1952, section 12, however, a newspaper owner can prove in mitigation of damages that other newspaper proprietors have already paid damages in respect of the statement in question.)

For many years the courts have recognised that strict appli- **16.06** cation of this rule would have made innocent disseminators of defamatory material, such as librarians and newsagents, liable in damages to the party defamed. That equitable approach has now the force of law in terms of the Defamation Act 1996, which makes the defence of "innocent dissemination" statutory. Section 1 of that Act states that a person will not be legally responsible for the dissemination of defamatory material if he is only involved in printing, producing, distributing or selling printed material; films or sound recordings; information by electronic means; live radio or television programmes or access to the Internet. However, to use this section to escape liability, the person must also demonstrate the following: (1) he or she took reasonable care in relation to publication; and (2) he or she did not know and had no reason to believe that what they caused or contributed to the publication was a defamatory statement.

16.07 There are as yet no Scottish decisions on interpretation of this section but it appears reasonable to assume that the courts will follow the general equitable principles which were applied in the past when the question of "innocent dissemination" was left at common law. If that is followed, it may be reasonably expected that those who merely provide the means of publication will not be held responsible for defamatory statements. On the question of "taking reasonable care", there may well be arguments as to situations where a publication is well known for containing libellous comments or an individual is well known for making them. In such situations, the "innocent dissemination" defence may be more difficult to run.

16.08 It is sometimes thought that it is safe to publish a statement if it is stated clearly that it is merely being repeated for what it is worth. Nothing could be further from the truth. A newspaper is as legally responsible in these circumstances as when a statement is printed and endorsed by the newspapers. The good journalist should always try to have a balancing comment to a potentially defamatory statement. It is important to note that if the opportunity to comment is given but not taken, this is no defence whatsoever to an action of defamation.

Civil wrong

16.09 In Scotland defamation is a civil wrong giving rise to an action for damages and not a criminal prosecution. However, the Representation of the People Act 1983 makes it a criminal offence for any person before or during a Parliamentary election to make or publish for the purpose of affecting the return of any candidate any false statement of fact in relation to the personal character or conduct of such candidate—although the pressure of time makes it much more likely that a defamed candidate will raise civil proceedings and request an interim interdict against repetition of the defamatory statement. See, for example, *Fairbairn v. Scottish National Party.* In theory, too, a publication tending to cause a breach of the peace might render the publisher liable to prosecution for this common law offence—although such a prosecution can almost be discounted due to the importation of the European Convention into United Kingdom law.

Publication

You can shout a slander to the waves and write reams of libellous **16.10** invective—if nobody hears or reads there will be no defamation. Publication of some sort is essential. In this respect there is a difference between Scots law and English law. Scots law allows an action for injury to the feelings caused by an insulting and defamatory statement even if it is not made known to any third party—although there would be clear problems of proving this wrong, if only two parties were present at the relevant time. English law requires communication to a third party before there will be civil liability. From the journalist's point of view the difference is not important. In his case there can seldom be any doubt about publication. There is no technical distinction in Scots law between words published in writing and words spoken. The terms "libel" and "slander" are often used interchangeably.

Falsity

Only false statements are actionable. Truth, or *veritas*, is a com- **16.11** plete defence. But defamatory statements are presumed to be false and, if the defender relies on *veritas*, the burden of proving the truth of his statements rests on him. If he makes one allegation, he must prove that it is true and not merely that it is partly true or that something less is true. If a man has been called a liar, it is not enough to prove that he lied on one occasion (*Milne v. Walker* (1893)) and if a man has been called a thief it is no defence to prove that long ago, as a boy, he had two convictions for petty theft (*Fletcher v. Wilson* (1885)).

On the other hand, if the pursuer founds upon two separate **16.12** allegations, the defender can always prove the truth of one of them even although he may not also be able to prove the truth of the other—*O'Callaghan v. Thomson & Co.*, 1928. Before 1952 this had the effect of diminishing the damages. Under section 5 of the Defamation Act 1952, it may absolve the defender from liability altogether. The section provides that:

> "In an action for defamation in respect of words containing two or more distinct charges against the pursuer, a defence of veritas shall not fail by reason only that the truth of every charge is not proved if the words not proved to be true do not materially injure the pursuer's reputation having regard to the truth of the remaining charges".

It should be noted that, under the present law, a pursuer can choose to base his action on only one allegation out of several. If he does this, the defender has no opportunity to prove the truth of the remaining allegations so as to take advantage of section 5.

16.13 It was formerly the law, at least in England, that if a man was said to have committed a crime it was not a defence to a defamation action to prove merely that he had been convicted of that crime. It had to be proved that he had in fact committed the crime. However, in a defamation action, proof that a person stands convicted of an offence by a United Kingdom court or British court-martial is now conclusive evidence that he committed the offence (Law Reform (Miscellaneous Provisions) (Scotland) Act 1968, s. 12; Civil Evidence Act 1968, s. 13). These provisions were amended by section 12 of the Defamation Act 1996. The 1996 legislation narrows the application of the previous rule. Evidence of a conviction is now conclusive evidence that the convicted person committed the offence only where the convicted person is the pursuer/plaintiff. Proof of the conviction of any other person is still admissible but will no longer be conclusive. It appears that Parliament's intention in 1996 was to cover such cases as those in which investigative journalists who have criticised the conduct of police officers are then sued for defamation by these officers. Often such cases relate to the arrest of accused persons. If these accused persons have been convicted, the law as it stood prior to 1996 precluded the defence from giving evidence to the effect that the accused persons were innocent—because the police officers had fabricated the evidence against them. The 1996 legislation allows the defence to challenge the correctness of the conviction of a third party, *i.e.* a person who is not the pursuer in the defamation case before the court.

16.14 As we shall see later, the Rehabilitation of Offenders Act 1974 adds a new complication to *veritas* in relation to criminal offences. If the offence in question is the subject of a "spent conviction" the defender in an action of defamation by the rehabilitated person cannot rely on *veritas* if the publication is proved to have been made with malice.

16.15 The defence of *veritas* can be a very difficult one. Even where charges seem justified, they may not be easy to prove. It can also be an unwise defence if there is serious risk of failure as it means that the defamation is persisted in and this is a factor which can aggravate damages. Although Scots law does not recognise the concept of exemplary or punitive damages, it does recognise the concept of aggravated damages, which will be awarded when the defender persists in the defamation right up to the end of the court proceedings. See, for example, *Baigent v. BBC* (1999).

Defamatory

There is no clear rule on what is and what is not defamatory. **16.16**
Generally speaking, however, a defamatory statement involves
some imputation against character or reputation, including business or financial reputation. The best way of answering the
question "What is defamatory?" is to set out by way of example
various types of statement which the courts have regarded as
actionable. It must be emphasised, however, that this is only a
guide. The fact that a statement has been regarded as defamatory
in the past, does not necessarily mean that it will be regarded as
defamatory now. Fashions in defamation change. Accusations of
Sabbath breaking are less likely to be held defamatory today than
they were in the last century, but in particular local communities
such accusations might well still be considered defamatory. An
example of this arose in 1990 when the *Stornoway Gazette* published a reader's letter which criticised the local M.P., Calum
MacDonald, for not voting in favour of legislation intended to
prevent the promotion of homosexuality. While this incorrect
allegation might well not have been considered defamatory in most
parts of Scotland, in the Western Isles it was seen as a slur on the
M.P.'s reputation. Mr MacDonald successfully claimed against the
newspaper.

To call a man a criminal in general terms is clearly defamatory. **16.17**
To call him a thief or accuse him of some other serious crime is
also defamatory. The *Sunday Mail* once made an unfortunate
mistake. In reporting a murder of which William Harkness and his
wife had been found guilty, it said beside a photograph of the two
murderers, "John Harkness and his wife, both of whom were
condemned to die but the man alone paid the extreme penalty.
The woman is serving a life sentence". John Harkness and his wife
were allowed an action for defamation—*Harkness v. The Daily
Record Ltd* (1924). It would not normally be actionable for example
to say that a man had exceeded the speed limit. Probably the
majority of drivers do so and it is not generally regarded as
reprehensible. But to say this of someone who makes their living
from driving and so should observe the Road Traffic Act carefully
as part of their job, might give rise to an action. As stated above it
is simply impossible to draw up a definitive list of what is
defamatory and what is not. It all depends on the circumstances.

An unusual set of circumstances led to the case of *Leon v.* **16.18**
Edinburgh Evening News (1909). The *Evening News* reported a
police court case under the headline "The Edinburgh Licensing
Prosecution: Prisoners Acquitted". One of the accused referred to,
who had in fact never been in custody but had simply appeared in

court in answer to a citation, sued for defamation, pointing out, quite correctly, that he had never been a prisoner. It was held that in the circumstances of the case the statement was not defamatory. Lord Kinnear observed that:

> "the description was not technically exact. But a paragraph in a newspaper of this kind does not necessarily use technical language: and in ordinary language an accused person at the Bar of a court may not improperly be described as a prisoner. To an ordinary reader, the paragraph with its heading, would not in my opinion convey any more injurious meaning than that the pursuer had been accused and had been acquitted."

There were also observations that it would not necessarily be defamatory to refer to a man as a prisoner in any event as a person may be a prisoner quite innocently. But clearly the word "prisoner" is not one to be recklessly bandied about.

16.19   Imputations of sexual immorality are clearly actionable. There can be no doubt about accusations of adultery or prostitution but, depending on the standards of the time and the views of reasonable people generally, very much less may suffice. Accusations of want of womanly delicacy have been held actionable. *Blackwood's Magazine* carried a story describing life in a Fife mining village. The author said that in the course of a social evening in one house, a girl of seventeen grew tired and in the presence of more than a dozen people of both sexes prepared herself for bed and got into it. She showed no embarrassment and the company took no notice. "Now this", said the author, "might be called 'indelicate'. Delicacy, however, is a standard of the more complex world, and this girl knew nought of it". The girl in question thought differently and brought an action against the publishers. It was held that the passage was actionable—*A.B. v. Blackwood & Sons* (1902).

16.20   A more recent example arose out of an allegation of sexual immorality in the *Sun* newspaper concerning a female employee at Glenochil Prison in Tullibody. The newspaper alleged that the lady, a Mrs Winter, had an affair with a prisoner and that she had sexual relations with him while she was on duty. The *Sun* was duly sued in respect of these untrue allegations and the pursuer was awarded £50,000 by the jury in the Court of Session. An appeal by the defenders on the amount of damages awarded was unsuccessful. This case was important for two reasons. First, it shows that Scottish juries are willing to award damages not too far removed from the awards made by their counterparts in England. Secondly, it shows that in defamation cases normally the pursuer can insist on a jury trial. It is only if the court feels the case is too technical and would not be suitable for consideration by a jury that the defender can avoid having the case decided in this way. An example of a court rejecting a jury trial was the case of *Shanks v. BBC* where in 1991 at the interlocutory stage the court felt that as the matters involved related to company frauds it would be best if the case were to be considered by a judge rather than a jury.

Scottish journalists feared that Mrs Winter's success might lead **16.21** to a spate of pursuers requesting trial by jury in defamation actions. It can perhaps be cautiously stated now that in the main these fears appear to have been groundless. However, in 1999, Father Noel Barry and Annie Kerr Clinton sued the *Sun* newspaper, again over allegations of sexual impropriety. Despite The *Sun* newspaper proving that Father Barry had had a romantic relationship with a former nun, the jury found in his favour. They awarded Father Barry damages of £45,000. In Mrs Clinton's case they were even more sympathetic, awarding her £125,000.

Actions have often been based on imputations of drunkenness or **16.22** dishonesty—the latter covering anything from appropriating public funds to evading payment of rent. In one case two political lecturers engaged a hall. A newspaper commented later, "Now one of them has left the town. Any information as to his whereabouts will be thankfully received by a sorrowing landlord, the proprietor of the hall, who now concludes that a Tory Cleon is no more profitable as a tenant than a Socialist Boanerges"—*Godfrey v. W. & D. C. Thomson* (1890). An action was allowed.

To sum up, any charge of conduct which is usually regarded as **16.23** discreditable or dishonourable may be defamatory.

It has been held defamatory to call a man debauched, corrupt, **16.24** two-faced, a blackguard, "a low dirty scum", a coward, a calumniator, a scoundrel, a disquieting brute, a mansworn rogue, an infidel, a hypocrite, an informer, a glutton or a plagiarist, but it would be very much a question of circumstances whether any of these expressions standing alone would be regarded as defamatory today. The leaning of the law is now against actions based on words of mere general abuse.

Imputations on solvency are clearly actionable. They need not go **16.25** as far as to allege bankruptcy. It is enough if they imply financial embarrassment. Indeed, it is possible to imagine enormous damages being paid by a newspaper which makes unfounded or unapprovable allegations against a firm or company. If the pursuer can demonstrate that losses occurred as a direct result of these allegations (*e.g.* cancellation of contracts by customers), then such losses would be recoverable. Further, it is vital to remember that the companies are often quoted on the public Stock Exchange and the value of their shares is dependent on the confidence in which they are held in the financial community. If a company could prove that its share value had plummeted as a result of an erroneous story in a newspaper it might well be able to recover substantial damages from the newspaper.

16.26 Numerous defamation cases have been concerned with imputations on an individual's fitness for his or her occupation or profession. To give only a few examples, it is dangerous to accuse a minister of brawling with his parishioners (*Mackellar v. Duke of Sutherland* (1859)), a Christian missionary of being a Mohammedan (*Davis v. Miller* (1855)), a teacher of ignorance of his subject (*McKerchar v. Cameron* (1892)), a medical practitioner of cruelty to a patient (*Bruce v. Ross & Co.* (1901)), an accountant of being unfit to be a trustee in bankruptcy (*Oliver v. Barnet* (1895)) or a solicitor of conducting cases for his own advantage and without regard to the interests of his clients (*McRostie v. Ironside* (1849)).

16.27 False allegations of insanity are actionable. There is more doubt about physical disease but it would probably be defamatory to say that a person suffered from some obnoxious disease which rendered him repulsive in the eyes of his fellows. AIDS is perhaps the most obvious example as it carries with it in the public mind the suspicion of homosexuality or drug abuse. In this connection journalists should remember that the test in defamation cases is what is perceived by the public as being derogatory. For example, it may be questioned in the modern world if an allegation of homosexuality is *per se* defamatory. Many members of the gay community would, understandably, find it extremely offensive if this were the law of Scotland. Today, all court proceedings arising out of allegations of homosexuality have proceeded on the basis that the allegation in effect accuses the individual concerned of hypocrisy. It is clearly defamatory to call someone a hypocrite. For example, Jason Donovan the TV soap star successfully sued over statements in a magazine to the effect that he was homosexual. The damages awarded by the English jury in the High Court in London were £250,000. An example of an unsuccessful action arising out of an allegation of homosexuality was the case taken by MP David Ashby against the *Times*.

Innuendo

16.28 Journalists must be aware of the legal concept of a defamatory innuendo. This arises in two situations. First, it can arise where words are innocent on their face but, in reality, carry a defamatory meaning. It is a question of fact in each case as to what meaning a reasonable, right-thinking person would take from the article or broadcast.

The most extreme example of this is where the words are **16.29** conveyed in such a way as to mean precisely the opposite of their ordinary meaning. An example will illustrate the point. In 1993, on the BBC programme "Have I Got News for You", the panellists repeatedly made reference to the sexuality of a pop star who had successfully sued in the High Court in London over a magazine article which claimed he was gay. In the broadcast it was repeatedly stated for a number of weeks "X is certainly not a homosexual". It is suggested it would have been possible for that individual to plead that these words were conveyed in such a sarcastic manner as to bear the opposite meaning.

It will be seen then that the concept of innuendo can be very **16.30** problematical for journalists, particularly those working in television and radio. An innuendo can arise from a wink, a nudge, a facial expression or intonation of voice. It is, of course, necessary for the pursuer to plead very precisely what innuendo he is setting out to prove. The defender has to be given proper notice of the charge of innuendo against him. Secondly, a defamatory innuendo can be pled by the pursuer if the words have a special (derogatory) meaning for certain people. For example, to say that a Scottish solicitor paid promptly for office furniture by a cheque from his client's account might seem unremarkable to the general public. To other solicitors, however, it would mean that, at best, he was guilty of professional misconduct and, at worst, was a thief.

Private Eye phraseology it is suggested would, as a matter of law, **16.31** be held to carry defamatory innuendos. Thus "tired and emotional" means drunk, "Ugandan discussions" means sexual intercourse and so on.

It must be understood that a defamatory innuendo, like defam- **16.32** ation itself, can arise unintentionally. That is no defence. If the court is satisfied that an ordinary right-thinking person would draw a defamatory meaning from the words (and possibly pictures) used, then the test for defamation is satisfied.

It is not enough that the words could bear the meaning alleged. **16.33** It must be shown that they probably would bear that meaning when heard or read by a reasonable man. The innuendo must represent what is a reasonable, natural or necessary inference from the words used, regard being had to the occasion and the circumstances of their publication (*Russell v. Stubbs* (1913). With regard to newspaper articles, it has been said that the court must consider the meaning which the words used would convey to an ordinary reader reading them as newspaper articles are usually read (*Hunter v.*

Ferguson & Co. (1906); *Stein v. Beaverbrook Newspapers Ltd* (1968)). If they would not appear defamatory to such an ordinary reader, no action will lie. This, however, is subject to the qualification that the reader may have knowledge of special facts making an apparently innocent statement defamatory. It seems harmless to say that Mrs M gave birth to twins on a certain date but this becomes defamatory when read by those knowing that she had been married for only a month (*Morrison v. Ritchie* (1902) and see para. 17.27, below).

Statement

16.34 There must be a statement. It need not, however, be in words. It may be inferred from acts, as where a waxwork effigy of the pursuer was placed in a waxworks among the effigies of notorious criminals (*Monson v. Tussauds* [1894]) or where a boy's photograph was placed by the police in their "rogues' gallery" (*Adamson v. Martin* (1916)). Of more importance for the journalist is the possibility of inferring a defamatory statement from drawings and photographs. An issue of the magazine *Lilliput* contained on a left-hand page a photograph of an outdoor photographer called Sydney Garbett with his camera. On the opposite page was a photograph of a naked woman. Under Mr Garbett's photograph were the words, "Of course for another shilling, Madam" and under the other photograph, the words, "You can have something like this". Mr Garbett alleged that after these photographs appeared, his friends stopped calling him "Sydney" and began to call him "Smutty". The court held that the arrangement of the photographs and captions was quite clearly libellous (*Garbett v. Hazel Watson & Viney Ltd* [1943]). More recently in the High Court in London in 1994 the Chancellor of Glasgow University, Sir Alex Cairncross, successfully sued the *London Evening Standard* over the juxtaposition of his photograph and an article on the Blunt/Philby/McLean spy ring. This clearly gives rise to a duty by the sub-editor to take care when laying out his pages. It is wise for the sub-editor to look over the whole page to see if any defamatory innuendo might arise from the juxtaposition of photographs and stories.

About a person

16.35 The statement must be of and concerning the pursuer. He must show that reasonable persons would take the words to refer to him but need not prove that they were intended to refer to him (see paras 17.31 to 17.39, below).

16.36 Difficulties arise where a class of persons is defamed. The general rule is that members of the class can sue if and only if the class is sufficiently well defined for the defamation to be applicable to them individually. A particular minister could not sue on an attack against ministers generally but could sue on a charge of drunkenness against the ministers of his particular presbytery (*Macphail v. Macleod* (1896)). Journalists should take particular care when dealing with a small group of people. If that group is sufficiently small, it would be possible for all members of the group to sue for damages, even if none of them is named. To use a simple example, it would be perfectly possible for a journalist to write that "all Scottish customs officers are dishonest". Such a large group would not be allowed to sue by the courts. However, if the journalist restricted this statement to customs officers based at a particular locality in Scotland, it might transpire that there were only two or three officers serving there. These customs officers would have a claim in defamation against the journalists which could only be defended if the journalist could prove that the statement was true. In this way, 12 Banbury police officers successfully sued the *News of the World* in the English courts when an allegation was made against "CID officers based at Banberry".

Defamation after death

Only a person in life can sue (*Broom v. Ritchie & Co.* (1904)). It is **16.37** often said, quite rightly, "you cannot defame the dead". The death of Robert Maxwell in 1992 was followed by a spate of articles, books, programmes and even plays about him which would never have seen the light of day had he been alive, for fear of receipt of a defamation action—a technique used successfully by Maxwell to stifle much criticism of him.

If, however, a defamation action is raised and the pursuer dies **16.38** when the case is in court, it is perfectly competent for his trustees to carry on the proceedings—section 3 of the Damages (Scotland) Act 1993. In this respect defamation and verbal injury actions are distinct from all other damages actions for personal injury. In all other cases it has been possible since the Damages (Scotland) Act 1993 for trustees/executors to raise proceedings for both *solatium* and patrimonial loss even if the deceased had not raised the action during his lifetime.

Corporate pursuers

A company can sue for defamation relating to its business interests **16.39** but cannot, of course, recover damages for injury to feelings. As previously indicated above (at para. 16.18) the damages recoverable by a company could be substantial if it can prove loss of revenue caused by the defamatory statement. In the *Capital Life v. Sunday Mail* case the damages awarded in 1978 were a then record £327,000 (excluding interest and expenses!) where the newspaper had unjustly accused an insurance company of unlawful business practices. At the time although this was a Scots case this was the highest libel award in Great Britain. The main element in the award of damages in the *Capital Life* case was the substantial loss of business the pursuers could prove to have resulted from the articles.

16.40 Defamation proceedings in Scotland must be raised within three years of the defamatory statement being made. Somewhat controversially the Scots time-limit is much more generous to pursuers than that afforded to plaintiffs throughout the rest of the United Kingdom where, in terms of the Defamation Act 1996, proceedings must be raised within one year. The reasoning behind Parliament creating this disparity between Scotland and the rest of the United Kingdom is unclear. As many newspapers and broadcasters publish both in Scotland and other parts of the United Kingdom, it might well be the case that a pursuer could find himself or herself in a situation in which proceedings for defamation are competent only in Scotland being time-barred throughout the rest of the United Kingdom.

KEY POINTS

16.41 A statement about a person which lowers his reputation in the eyes of the general public is defamatory. A statement can be plainly defamatory on its face or defamatory only by reason of the innuendo which it carries. A statement which is defamatory is presumed in law to be untrue. The burden of proving the defence of truth (*veritas*) rests on the (journalist) defender.

16.42 A corporate body such as a firm or a company can sue for defamation. If they can prove that they have lost business as a result of the defamatory statement such a corporate pursuer could be entitled to very substantial damages.

CHAPTER 17

DEFENCES

This entire chapter must be qualified to the extent of taking note of **17.01**
a case presently before the European Court of Human Rights.
Scots law, like English law, proceeds on the basis that the onus of
proof on defamation action lies on the defender. If the European
Court of Human rights rules in favour of the argument presently
being put forward in the case brought by former bank robber John
McVicar, the onus may well alter. Basically, Mr McVicar's argument is that it is a breach of Article 10 of the European
Convention on Human Rights for the domestic law of the United
Kingdom to insist that defenders discharge the burden of proof in
a defamation action. In most other countries in Europe there is
some onus of proof on the plaintiff/pursuer. It seems possible that
the European Court of Human Rights will take the view that
Britain is once again in breach of its Convention's obligations and
will have to be corrected. Were that to occur, the whole emphasis
presently placed by our courts on the examination of the defence
to a defamation action rather than the examination of the pursuer's
case would be reversed. With the incorporation of the European
Convention of Human Rights into domestic law (see Chap. 25),
this kind of point will be able to be argued in the domestic courts
even if the European Court of Human Rights decides against Mr
McVicar.

In Scotland a pursuer can raise an action for defamation up to **17.02**
three years from the date of publication. Journalists should remember that repetition of the publication is a fresh publication and
starts the three-year period (triennium) running again. So, for
example, if a broadcaster repeated a television programme after a
lapse of two years, the potential pursuer could sue up to five years
after the original broadcast.

It should be noted that since 1996 in the rest of the United **17.03**
Kingdom defamation actions must be raised after the lapse of one
year from the date of publication. The rather strange situation
which now exists is that proceedings throughout the United
Kingdom are time-barred after one year but in Scotland only after

three years. This has considerable significance for cross-border publications and broadcasters, particularly in light of the increased generosity of the Scottish courts towards defamation pursuers in the late 1990s.

Parties to the action

17.04 Certain pursuers may be debarred from pursing an action for defamation, although they can clearly prove that the words used were about them and that the words used were defamatory. As a matter of public policy, the House of Lords decided in the case *Derbyshire County Council v. Times Newspapers*, 1993 that local authorities could not sue. This principle has now been extended to cover the former nationalised utilities, such as the National Coal Board. It has also been extended to cover political parties; *Referendum Party v. Business Age*, 1997. However, under the present law, public figures can continue to pursue actions for defamation. A recent example was the action brought by Jimmy Wray, the Labour M.P. against the *Mail on Sunday* newspaper over their allegations that Mr Wray had been violent towards his former wife. Lord Johnston, in his judgment of March 2000, made it clear that although Mr Wray was a public figure he was still entitled to a remedy from the court where defamatory allegations had been made about his private life. Interestingly, the judge made it clear that in defamation case where the "sting" of the allegations amounted to an accusation of criminal conduct (as they did here because in effect Mr Wray was being accused of the crime of assault) then although the standard of proof which the newspaper had to discharge remained "the balance of probabilities" the court would require very strong evidence before being satisfied that the newspaper had proved its case. Here Lord Johnston was not satisfied with the standard of evidence led by the newspaper, so it followed that Mr Wray must succeed. He was awarded damages of £60,000.

Defences generally

17.05 In defence to an action for defamation the defender may claim that one of the essentials of defamation is lacking—for example, that no statement was made, or that, if made, it is true, or is not defamatory or would not be taken by a reasonable man to refer to the pursuer. These points were considered in the last chapter. We must now deal with various other defences.

Rixa and vulgar abuse

17.06 Words spoken *in rixa* are words uttered in the heat of a quarrel. Even if apparently defamatory they will not be actionable, unless it would appear to third parties that a specific charge was being seriously made. This defence is properly applicable only to spoken words and is hence of little importance for the journalist. The defence of vulgar abuse is a different aspect of the same matter. If the words used are so clearly a crude and unthinking gross insult, they will not be taken seriously by third parties. Therefore, they will not damage the pursuers' reputation. The odd result of this is that extreme language may not give a good basis for a defamation action.

Fair comment

The defence of fair comment is of great importance to newspapers **17.07** and broadcasters but its limitations should be understood by journalists. The Press is perfectly entitled to comment on matters of public interest but the comment must both be fair and be based on fact not supposition. The defence is much more likely to succeed in features work rather than in news stories. Journalists regularly misunderstand this defence, saying for example to call someone "a rogue" or "a thief" is fair comment. Such an approach shows a complete misunderstanding of this defence.

Fair comment is a particularly relevant defence when dealing **17.08** with stories on public figures. There is a belief amongst many journalists that people in public life must accept that they will be criticised in the media.. The English courts have already accepted that journalists have a degree of privilege when commenting on the public actions of those who occupy a high position in society, *e.g.* a politician. The decision in *Reynolds v. Times Newspapers* from the House of Lords in October 1999 makes it clear that defamation law in the United Kingdom has not as yet recognised the public figure defence. There is no equivalent in Great Britain to the *Sullivan v. New York Times* case where the American Supreme Court decided that public figures had to accept a substantial degree of criticism in the media in the interests of freedom of speech as enshrined in the American constitution. The most recent committee on defamation (the Lord Chancellor's Supreme Court Procedure Committee) specifically recommended that *Sullivan v. New York Times* should not become a part of the law of defamation in this country (the Neill Report, July 1991). It is perfectly clear from the experience of the English courts over the past 10 years that politicians will now sue regularly over defamatory statements. Journalists should take great care that their facts are both accurate and provable.

Certain conditions must be present before the defence of fair **17.09** comment will succeed. First, the matter complained of must be comment—the defence does not protect defamatory statements of fact (*cf. Waddell v. BBC* (1973)). Secondly, the comment must be such as an honest man could have made. Comment, however, does not cease to be fair merely because it represents a stupid, partisan or eccentric point of view. Fools and cranks can have their say. Nor does comment become actionable merely because it is couched in strong or vituperative language (*Archer v. Ritchie & Co.* (1891)). Thirdly, the comment must be based on facts and, if these are set out, they must be set out accurately. Under the Defamation Act 1952, s.6, however, a defence of fair comment will not fail only because the truth of every allegation of fact is not proved, if the expression of opinion is fair comment in view of such facts as are proved. Fourthly, the comment must be on a matter of public interest. This allows the person making the comment plenty of scope. It clearly covers comment on affairs of central and local government, the administration of justice and the conduct of those holding or seeking public office. It also covers comment on sport and criticism of books, and of films, plays and other public entertainments. It does not, however, cover observations on matters regarded by the law as lying outside the legitimate sphere of journalism such as the private lives of private citizens. While it is in the public interest that the Press should exercise freely its right of criticism in regard to public affairs, it is equally important that the right of a private individual to have his character respected should be maintained, and that people should not as private persons be exposed to unjustifiable and arbitrary comment" (*per* Viscount Haldane in *Langlands v. Leng* (1916)).

Fair retort

17.10 A certain latitude is allowed to the person who denies charges made publicly against him. Even if his denial is not entirely true and is in strong terms it will not be actionable. But he must not pass from repudiation to the making of separate defamatory allegations against his accuser. The retort must be a shield and not a spear. The defence of fair retort is thus of very narrow scope. Its main practical effect is to prevent an individual being sued for saying his accuser lied.

Privilege

17.11 There are two types of privilege—absolute and qualified. If a statement has absolute privilege, no action can be based on it, however false, defamatory or malicious it may be. If a statement has qualified privilege an action can be based on it but the pursuer must prove that it was made with malice. The theory behind both types of privilege is that in some circumstances the public interest demands freedom to speak without fear of an action for defamation.

Absolute privilege

Absolute privilege applies to statements made in the Westminster **17.12** Parliament, the Scottish Parliament, reports authorised by Parliament and statements made in court with reference to the case in progress by judge, advocate, solicitor or witness. The litigant, however, has only qualified privilege: he cannot indulge with impunity in malicious defamation simply by raising an action. In contrast, in England a litigant enjoys absolute privilege. By statute, absolute privilege attaches to certain communications by, or to, or arising out of an investigation by the Parliamentary Commissioner (see Chapter 6) commonly known as the Ombudsman, the Local Authority Ombudsman, the National Health Service Ombudsman and the Pensions' Ombudsman. In terms of the Defamation Act 1996, fair and accurate reporting of a public court of justice in either England or Scotland is accorded absolute privilege. This legislation removes the peculiar anomaly between English and Scots law whereby English journalists enjoyed absolute privilege for such reports whilst Scots journalists only qualified privilege. Journalists would do well to study the list of bodies contained in the Schedule to the 1996 Act (see Appendix 4). Fair and accurate reports of the public proceedings of these bodies are accorded qualified privilege. It should be noted that this qualified privilege may be of one or two types as more detailed in the Schedule. There is also the power to the Lord Chancellor and Secretary of State for Scotland to produce an additional statutory instrument containing the names of further bodies whose public proceedings when reported fairly and accurately by journalists are to be accorded qualified privilege. It should be noted by journalists that such reports must be published contemporaneously. In the case of a weekly newspaper, this will be the next available edition.

Court reports—how to obtain the protection of privilege

It must be remembered that journalists are not accorded absolute **17.13** privilege for any report of court proceedings. It must be, first, contemporaneous reporting and, secondly, it must be fair and accurate. Fairness and accuracy should be the bywords of the working journalist. Excellent shorthand is a necessity to accomplish accurate work in the courtroom (remember that tape recorders are specifically prohibited under the Contempt of Court Act 1981). If the report is not both fair and accurate, not only will the journalist fail to achieve the protection of absolute privilege, and thereby resist any possibility of defamation proceedings, he or she will also suffer the danger of being held to be in contempt of court if the inaccuracy is sufficiently serious to prejudice the proceedings before the court.

17.14 It has been made clear above that the report must be both accurate and fair. However, it need not be verbatim or even complete. Where a newspaper merely purports to report the result of a case and does so accurately it cannot be liable in damages because it fails to narrate the steps leading up to judgment. "There is no duty on a reporter in a report of a law suit to make his report exhaustive. It is . . . sufficient if the reporter gives the result of the litigation truly and correctly" (*per* Lord Anderson in *Duncan v. Associated Newspapers* (1929)). When more than the result is reported, however, great care must be taken to see that the report is not one-sided. If one party's allegations are mentioned, the other party's replies should be given equal prominence (*Wright and Greig v. Outram* (1890)). If reported allegations are found unproved this must always be clearly stated as soon as possible. There is no objection to publishing daily accounts of a case lasting several days but the reports should be kept up to date. If both allegations and refutations are available there will be no privilege if the allegations are published one day and the refutations held over till the next. The burden of proving that a report is fair and accurate lies on the newspaper (*Pope v. Outram* (1909)).

17.15 Care should be taken with headlines in reports of judicial proceedings. If these take the form of comment on the case, they cannot be regarded as part of the report and will not be privileged. They should therefore always be fair and justified by the facts reported so as to be protected by the defence of fair comment. Sub-editors should be mindful of this. They may have to sacrifice clever or amusing headlines in the interests of observing the law. The courts take the view that a reader's approach to a story can be very much affected by the headline on it so a defamatory innuendo could be created in a story by the terms of the headline.

17.16 It is often impossible, however, to understand a case completely without reference to the various documents connected with it. How far are statements derived from this source protected? The answer varies with the circumstances. In civil cases a report of statements made in an open record is completely unprivileged and the same would seem to apply to reports derived from a closed record which has not yet been referred to in open court. In practice, of course, there are many circumstances where it may be judged safe to publish information from a closed record at this stage but the law seems clear. A litigant is not privileged if he sends his pleadings (whether the record is closed or not) to a newspaper for publication. "If the pleadings so published are slanderous, then the paper publishing them, and the person sending them for publication, are liable in damages for slander" (*per* Lord Young in *Macleod v. J.P.s of Lewis* (1892)). The same principles would apply to the indictment or complaint in criminal cases. Once the case comes up in open court the position is different. Publication of a document actually read out in open court is, of course, privileged and privilege may also protect statements derived from documents which are merely referred to expressly or impliedly in open court. The test here would seem to be whether the information in the documents is an essential part of the case and is merely referred to for the sake of convenience. The point arose in *Harper v. Provincial Newspapers* (1937). A man called James Harper appeared in the Edinburgh Burgh Court. The clerk of court read out his name but not his address. He was found guilty of a fairly minor offence. A reporter verified the name and took down the address from the complaint, which was shown to him for that purpose by the clerk of court. In fact the address given in the complaint was not that of the accused but that of his father who was also called James Harper. When the report appeared the father sued the newspaper and the question then arose whether the statement derived from the complaint was privileged. It was held that it was. The address was an essential part of the case which was omitted from the proceedings in open court simply for reasons of speed and convenience. But it was observed that different considerations might apply to information taken from documents which were merely productions in a case.

In the case of *Cunningham v. Scotsman Publications Ltd* (1987), **17.17** Lord Clyde held that privilege applies to a document which "is referred to and founded upon before the court with a view to advancing a submission which is being made", even if not read out in open court (see Chapter 8, paras 08.15 to 08.26).

No privilege attaches to reports of proceedings held in private. **17.18** It is a question of circumstances in each case whether proceedings are in private or in public. In *Thomson v. Munro and Jamieson* (1900), it was held that when a statutory examination of a bankrupt took place in public in the sheriff clerk's room this "was for the occasion a public court". An interesting question arises regarding children's hearings. They are not, strictly speaking, courts. They are not open to the public, but bona fide journalists are admitted. Do fair and accurate reports of their proceedings have privilege? The point has not been decided but it can hardly be doubted that such reports would enjoy qualified privilege. The journalists are there to represent the public. There would seem to be the strongest reasons for according privilege to the only source of information on the proceedings available to the public.

17.19 Situations may arise where there is doubt whether remarks form part of the proceedings. Thus in one English case (*Hope v. Leng Ltd* (1907)) a witness shouted from the well of the court that the plaintiff's evidence was "a pack of lies". It was held in this case that a report containing this statement was none the less privileged. It is clear, on the other hand, that a report of a conversation between two spectators at the back of the court would not be privileged. The journalist must exercise his discretion in deciding whether or not the interruptions can properly be regarded as part of the proceedings (see para. 10.128).

17.20 Of course, by no means all legal business is carried out in the civil and criminal courts of the land. There are many other bodies which enjoy the name "court". For example, there is the Lands Valuation Appeal Court, the Restrictive Practices Court, Election Courts, the Scottish Land Court, the Lyon Court. Similarly, there are bodies which exercise functions rather like a court but which do not bear the name "court". In this category we find Licensing Boards, Employment Tribunals, Medical Appeal Tribunals and Social Security Appeal Tribunals. Which bodies can the journalist report with absolute or qualified privilege? The answer is to be found in the Defamation Act 1996, s. 14 and the Schedule to the Act.

17.21 The position on the reporting of foreign courts was a matter of some difficulty. At the time of the writing of the last edition of this book, it was made clear that the position was somewhat confused. However, the matter is now resolved by the Defamation Act 1996. As might be expected, reporting of the proceedings of the European Court and the European Court of Human Rights are accorded absolute privilege, as is any international criminal tribunal established by the Security Council of the United Nations or by an international agreement to which the United Kingdom is a party (s. 14). Reports of legislatures and courts of foreign countries enjoy qualified privilege.

17.22 It is clear from the foregoing that journalists enjoy a substantial degree of protection in their reporting of the proceedings of courts, tribunals and other quasi-judicial bodies. The journalist should have to hand the Schedule to the Defamation Act (reproduced at Appendix 4) to ascertain the type of privilege applying. A fair and accurate and contemporaneous report will almost certainly enjoy a degree of privilege either absolute or qualified.

Other forms of qualified privilege—the common law

Qualified privilege not only arises due to the terms of the **17.23** Defamation Act 1996. The Scottish courts will also recognise that the protection of privilege arises when someone communicates information when under a social or moral duty to do so. Qualified privilege applies generally to statements made by a person in the discharge of some public or private duty or in matters where his own interests are involved. It applies, for example, to statements made by an employer in giving his employee a reference. No action can be founded on such statements unless there is proof of malice (or possibly negligence, according to the House of Lords decision in *Spring v. Guardian Assurance plc,* 1993). This type of privilege may be relevant for journalists. If a person has a duty to make a statement and can only make it adequately in a newspaper, then it seems that qualified privilege will protect not only him but also the journalist publishing the information (*Brims v. Reid* (1885); *Waddell v. BBC* (1973)). A recent case which shows the limitations of qualified privilege is *Fraser v. Mirza,* 1993 S.L.T. 527. In that case a Glasgow J.P. had written to the Chief Constable of Strathclyde, complaining of his treatment by Constable Fraser, whom he accused of being motivated by racial prejudice when he arrested the J.P. for reset. The House of Lords decided in March 1993 that although, normally a citizen writing to complain about a police officer would be protected by qualified privilege, Mr. Mirza had misused the occasion and so no privilege applied. The court awarded the constable £5,000 damages.

Unintentional defamation

As we have seen, a person can recover damages for defamation **17.24** even if the statement complained of was not intended to refer to him or was not intended to be defamatory. This has given rise to some hard cases.

In *Morrison v. Ritchie* (1902), *The Scotsman* printed "birth **17.25** notices" in August saying that Mrs Morrison had given birth to twins. This statement was false but was printed by the newspaper in good faith. It had no way of knowing that Mrs Morrison had been married for only a month. The person who inserted the notice could not be traced and an action was raised against the proprietors of *The Scotsman.* They maintained that they were not liable because the notices sent to them for publication were not defamatory on their face and they had no reason to suppose that they concealed a libel. The court rejected this defence. The defenders could not escape liability by saying that the slander was unintentional. In 1989 a spoof advertisement was sent to and then appeared in the *Herald* newspaper intimating that the company C.R. Smith had gone into liquidation. This was quite untrue and the newspaper quickly corrected the inaccuracy. But had any business losses been suffered by C.R. Smith they may well have been able to sue the newspaper for recovery. It follows that, in so far as possible, a newspaper should institute a system of checking that the person inserting any advertisement is bona fide.

17.26 The famous case of *Hulton v. Jones* [1910], illustrates another type of unintentional defamation. The *Sunday Chronicle* published an article describing recent motor races at Dieppe. The article contained this passage:

> " 'There is Artemus Jones with a woman who is not his wife. Who must be—you know—the other thing!' whispered a fair neighbour of mine excitedly into her bosom-friend's ear. . . . Really, is it not surprising how certain of our fellow country-men behave when they come abroad? Who would suppose, by his goings-on, that he was a churchwarden at Peckham? No one, indeed, would assume that Jones in the atmosphere of London would have taken on so austere a job as the duties of a churchwarden. Here, in the atmosphere of Dieppe, he is the life and soul of a gay little band that haunts the Casino and turns night into day, besides betraying a most unholy delight in the society of female butterflies."

17.27 Artemus Jones was a product of the writer's imagination. He thought that nobody could have such a name. Unfortunately for his paper, he was wrong. There was a barrister known as Artemus Jones who read the article, brought a libel action and recovered £1,750 damages. This was in spite of the fact that he had no connection with Peckham and was not a churchwarden. More recently in 1994, Mr. Alex Wilbraham, an Old Etonian, won substantial libel damages from the publishers Faber & Faber in the High Court in London. His name (which had been selected at random from a New York telephone directory) had been used in a work of fiction about Eton School. The fictional character took drugs and indulged in homosexual activity. Not only did Faber & Faber have to pay damages to Mr. Wilbraham, but they also had to reprint the book using a different name for that particular fictional character.

17.28 In other cases of unintentional defamation, statements referring truthfully to one existing person were held to be defamatory of another existing person. As a result of all these cases, the law placed writers and journalists in an intolerable position and encouraged "gold digging" actions. Section 4 of the Defamation

Act of 1952 was intended to alleviate injustice in the case of innocent publication. Its provisions were unsatisfactory and it is generally believed that it was never used in any case anywhere in the United Kingdom. It was replaced in 1996 by sections 2–4 of the Defamation Act of that year. Although the media were consulted by the proposers of the legislation, the final terms of these sections do not reflect the representations made by newspapers and broadcasters. Many writers have said that even the new provisions will to them be an unacceptable route to take.

The 1996 Act—Offer of amends defence

Under the new provisions, which were only brought into effect in **17.29** England Wales and Northern Ireland on February 28, 2000 if the defenders takes the view that they were wrong in the original publication, they can make an offer to make amends. Such an offer must be in writing, it must refer to section 2 of the 1996 Act and must state whether it is a qualified offer or not. If it is a qualified offer, that means that, although the defender accepts that the words used in the original article were defamatory, he does not accept the meaning attached to them by the potential plaintiff/ pursuer. An offer to make amends must offer to make a suitable correction and a sufficient apology. This must be published. The correction and apology must be published in a manner that is reasonable and practicable. Further, the defender must offer to pay the pursuer's damages and costs. It is strongly recommended that journalists take legal advice on these complicated statutory provisions before trying to use this defence. At the time of writing the "offer of amends" sections of the 1996 Act have not been brought into effect in Scotland—although the Scottish Executive have indicated that there will be action to bring Scots law into line with that in the rest of the United Kingdom at an early date. The present situation in which we have a defence available only outside of the Scottish jurisdiction is far from satisfactory—particularly for cross-Border publications and national broadcasters.

To establish that words were published innocently the publisher **17.30** must prove (a) that he did not intend them to refer to the person complaining and did not know of circumstances by virtue of which they might be understood to refer to him or (b) that the words were not defamatory on their face, and that he did not know of circumstances by virtue of which they might be understood to be defamatory of the person complaining. The publisher must also prove in all cases that he exercised reasonable care in relation to the publication and, where he is not the author, that the words were written by the author without malice.

17.31   If the publisher can satisfy these conditions, he can escape liability by making an "offer of amends", under the Act. This means an offer to publish a correction and apology and where documents or records containing the words complained of have been distributed, to take reasonable steps to notify the recipients that the words are alleged to be defamatory of the person concerned. There are technical rules as to the form of the offer. These are the concern of the lawyer and as the offer must be made as soon as practicable, it is important that he should be informed as soon as it is known that the words give rise to complaint.

17.32   The effect of these provisions is that if a case like Artemus Jones' arose today the newspaper could escape liability by making an offer of amends under the statute. The position is not so clear with regard to the birth notices case or the liquidation notice case. The newspaper might find it difficult to prove that it had exercised all reasonable care and impossible to prove that the words were written by the author without malice.

Minimisation of damages

17.33 Apart from the offer of amends defence, it is clearly sensible for the journalist who discovers that he has unintentionally defamed someone to minimise his losses by inserting an apology/clarification in the newspaper as soon as possible. In the case of the journalist who is pursuing the offer of amends course, their apology will be part of the overall legal process put in place by the newspaper's or broadcaster's lawyers. However, if that course is not being pursued it is undoubtedly sensible to state the correct factual position in print or on the radio or television as soon as possible in order to minimise the journalist's exposure to a claim for damages.

Lapse of time

17.34 Under the Prescription and Limitation (Scotland) Act 1973, as amended in 1985, no action for defamation may be brought unless it is begun within three years from the date when the publication or communication first came to the notice of the pursuer. The court has, however, power to extend this period if it seems to it equitable to do so. The one-year time-limit for the rest of the United Kingdom has already been noted.

Defences presently developing

17.35 As mentioned at the beginning of the previous chapter, there may be the beginnings of the recognition of a "public figure" defence in United Kingdom defamation law along similar lines to the American approach set out in *Sullivan v. New York Times*. Apart from the

European decision in *Lingens v. Austria* there is the House of Lords approach in *Derbyshire County Council v. Times Newspapers* and *Reynolds v. Times Newspapers*. As far as Scotland is concerned, it is at least arguable that there has always been a public figure defence recognised in our law. *Langlands v. Leng* in the House of Lords in 1916, *Waddell v. BBC* in the Court of Session in 1973 and most recently *Mutch v. Robertson* in the Court of Session in 1981 all give journalists cause for optimism that the Scottish courts may be more willing to accept that public officials and public figures can be fairly vigorously criticised in the media without having a right to raise defamation proceedings. It must be emphasised that this a grey area of law in which European considerations are likely to play an increasingly large part. It will be of considerable importance and interest to Scots journalists if at some stage an adequately funded media organisation sees fit to run a public figure defence through the Scottish courts and perhaps beyond.

The recent developments in England in the likes of *Arnold* **17.36** *Robert Reynolds v. Sunday Times* must give journalists cause for optimism that the public figure type of argument will be available to them in the future, albeit through the medium of an extension to the existing privilege defences. For present purposes it will suffice to say that in *Reynolds* the English courts seemed to accept that journalists were under a social duty to publish material about prominent public figures carrying out public functions in circumstances where the readership/viewership had a legitimate interest in the subject matter. This may not go as far as the likes of the American courts in *Sullivan v. New York Times*. Nevertheless, from a journalist's perspective it is a welcome development of the right to comment on public affairs and continues the trend begun in the *Derbyshire County Council* case which recognised that if journalists were not given some leeway there would be a "chilling effect" on public debate. The whole matter, as stated at the beginning of this chapter, is presently in the melting pot due to the United Kingdom's incorporation of the European Convention on Human Rights into domestic law. There can be little doubt that media organisations will use the terms of Article 10 of the Convention to argue that something akin to the public figure approach has, in effect, been incorporated into our domestic law by our incorporation of the Convention.

KEY POINTS

If a defamatory statement is complained of, the journalist may rely **17.37** on the defences of (a) *veritas* (b) fair comment (c) absolute privilege or (d) qualified privilege. Very rarely the defence of unintentional defamation may be of assistance.

17.38   The defence of qualified privilege can be argued to apply in a good number of situations. In addition to the common law occasions of qualified privilege there are the occasions of qualified privilege set out in the Schedule to the Defamation Act 1996. Care should be taken to ascertain into which part of the Schedule the occasion falls.

17.39   A Scottish defamation action has to be raised within three years or else it will be time barred.

CHAPTER 18

DAMAGES AND OTHER REMEDIES

Having considered defences to an action for defamation, we now **18.01** turn to the position where there is no defence. Here there will be either a settlement or an award of damages. The question of settlement will usually be in the hands of the newspaper's legal advisers but prompt action by the journalist or editor in publishing an apology may facilitate their task.

Scots law, as we have seen (para. 16.05), allows damages for **18.02** injury to feelings alone. Substantial awards may thus be made even although the pursuer has suffered no financial loss. An example of this was Sam McCluskey, the leader of the National Union of Seamen, obtaining an award of damages of £7,500 in respect of a defamation in a letter.

Extremely high damages were awarded in February 1999 by **18.03** temporary Judge Gordon Coutts, Q.C. in the *Baigent v. BBC* case. These included £20,000 per head to each of three children of the Baigent family who were not even mentioned in the television programme complained against. However, this decision appears out of line with all previous Scottish decisions on damages. There does seem to have been a recent trend in Scottish courts towards higher damages awards in defamation cases. The awards of £45,000 to Father Noel Barry and £125,000 to his co-pursuer, Mrs Annie Clinton, have already been noted. That case was decided by a jury. A single judge decision by Lord Johnston in March 2000 assessed damages due to Jimmy Wray, the Westminster M.P. at £60,000. Lord Johnston honestly described his level of award as "almost instinctive".

The alarming news for journalists may be that having held **18.04** defamation damages down to the kind of level which most European Courts and the European Convention would find acceptable, the Scottish courts may now be beginning to make exactly the same mistake as the English courts who had to be rescued from the mess of excessive awards by repeated intervention from the Court of Appeal.

In recent years the damages awarded by English juries have **18.05** become the subject of much public interest and are naturally of concern to journalists. Examples include the award of half a million pounds, obtained by Jeffrey Archer against the *Star* newspaper over allegations that he had consorted with a prostitute and the award of £400,000 pounds obtained by Koo Stark against a tabloid in respect of allegations concerning Prince Andrew and her private life. More recently Lord Aldington obtained an award of over £1m against Count Leo Tolstoy in respect of allegations made by the Count concerning the Lord's behaviour whilst a Commanding Officer during the last war. In Scotland due to the fact that until recently judges sitting alone have decided most defamation cases, damages have been relatively low (although see para. 18.02). But since the case of *Winter v. News International* there has been a growing fear amongst the Scottish media that substantial jury awards may become the norm north of the border as well as south. In *Winter* the jury's award of £50,000 was unanimously upheld on appeal. So the case could be the beginning of an escalating spiral of damages awards by juries. In the twentieth century jury trials in defamation cases have been rare. Increasingly however pursuers have seen the advantage of obtaining trial by jury and so have raised proceedings in the Court of Session where jury trial is available. The onus is very much on the defender to demonstrate to the court why a jury trial should not be allowed. It would appear from recent decisions that it will be necessary for the defender to demonstrate that there is some particular technical matter which the jury could not understand before he would succeed in his plea. Although it should be remembered that exemplary damages which are available to a plaintiff in England are not competent in Scotland, a jury will always take a somewhat subjective view of the amount of damages to be awarded. It is clear from *Winter* that on appeal the judges are unlikely to interfere with substantial awards.

Aggravation

18.06 The general rule is that anything which increases the loss or injury to the pursuer will aggravate damages. In *Stein v. Beaverbrook Newspapers Ltd* (1968) it was held that if a libel were actuated by malice, this fact would not by itself entitle a pursuer to greater damages. The court stressed that damages are intended to compensate the pursuer, not punish the defender (*cf. Cunningham v. Duncan & Jamieson* (1889); *Fielding v. Variety Inc.* [1967]). It is highly doubtful if juries heed the directions of judges on this point. An examination of the high awards in English cases suggests that juries are, at least on occasion, perfectly happy to ignore the directions of judges on the size of damages.

18.07 Persistence in, or repetition of, a defamatory allegation, will aggravate damages. If a defamation in one edition comes to light, immediate steps should be taken to ensure that it is expunged from later editions. Similarly, as already pointed out, persistence in defence of a defamatory allegation right up to the end of the court hearing will entitle the judge to award a higher sum by way of aggravated damages to the successful pursuer than would have been the case if the defender had admitted the defamation at an earlier point in the proceedings.

The extent of publication is a relevant factor in assessing **18.08** damages and a pursuer can bring evidence of a newspaper's circulation in order to aggravate damages. Boasts about circulation may backfire. Remember that mass circulation may not be necessary for the law to regard the publication as particularly damaging. A leaflet distributed to a few well-chosen individuals could ruin for example the reputation of a village minister. He would be entitled to substantial damages if the contents of such a pamphlet were held to be defamatory. An example of this kind of situation was seen in England in 1982 where a Greek ship captain obtained damages of £400,000 in respect of a defamation contained in a Greek newspaper which had a circulation of only 30 copies in London.

Mitigation

A prompt apology or explanation will tend to mitigate damages **18.09** (*Morrison v. Ritchie*). It was formerly thought that evidence of the defender's innocence or good faith in publishing the statement would also be admissible to mitigate damages (*Cunningham v. Duncan & Jamieson*), but the case of *Stein* throws doubt on this view and suggests that the defender's lack of fault will be relevant to damages only if and in so far as it affects the extent of the pursuer's injury.

It will, however, be competent to lead evidence of the pursuer's **18.10** bad reputation in mitigation of damages on the theory that if the pursuer has a bad reputation already, the defamation makes little difference. Evidence of this sort must probably be limited to the particular aspect of character involved in the defamation. Where a woman was said to have had an illegitimate child it was held to be relevant to prove in mitigation of damages that she was well known in the neighbourhood as a person of loose and immoral character. Proof of specific acts of adultery was, however, not allowed. As Lord President Clyde said, "The point of such a defence is not that she is a bad character, but that she has a bad character" (*C. v. M.* (1923)). This neatly summarises the maxim that the law of defamation protects the pursuer's reputation (whether deserved or not) and not his or her (true) character.

18.11   The Defamation Act 1952, s.12 provides that a defender may prove in mitigation of damages that the pursuer has already recovered damages or raised an action or settled or agreed to settle in respect of publication of words similar to those on which the action is founded. This is clearly of great importance for newspapers. It discourages "gold digging" actions against a series of papers in respect of one defamatory allegation. If libelled in a number of newspapers the wise pursuer will sue in respect of the most virulent article. On being successful he will then usually be able to settle out of court with the publishers of the less libellous material. This is what happened in the Jeffrey Archer case although Mr Archer at the time of writing faces criminal charges of perjury in relation to his evidence at the original trial.

Interdict

18.12 Instead of seeking damages the person complaining of defamation may seek an interdict or interim interdict to prevent publication of the defamatory matter. These are perfectly competent remedies in relation to defamation. Scottish journalists do not enjoy the same degree of support from the courts as their colleagues south of the Border who on the basis of the case *Bonnard v. Perryman* (1891) can virtually ensure publication by telling the court at the injunction hearing that their facts are correct and that they will prove their facts correct if called upon to do so. Although they risk exemplary damages if proved wrong, an English Judge will allow journalists to publish in such circumstances. In contrast there is no absolute "right of unrestrained publication" in Scots law (see *Boyd v. BBC* (1969); *Waddell v. BBC* (1973)). Nevertheless in deciding whether the balance of convenience lies in favour of granting an interim interdict the court will take into account the fact that the pursuer has the right to seek damages for defamation in a later action and that to this extent any harm resulting from the publication would not be irreparable (*Waddell v. BBC*). However in the Sheriff Ewan Stewart case Lord Penrose stated *obiter* that he did not think that damages were invariably sufficient remedy for defamation. In November 1990 Sheriff Stewart presented a petition to the Court of Session craving interdict against the broadcast by BBC Scotland of the programme "Focal Point". The case was completed only five minutes before the programme was due to be broadcast. Sheriff Stewart obtained interim interdict but this was recalled a few days later at a further hearing in the Court of Session.

18.13   Similarly in 1991 the chartered accountants Touche Ross applied for an interdict against the "Focal Point" programme concerning

Glasgow's Glasgow Exhibition during the year of culture. Touche Ross claimed that the programme defamed them in respect of their actings as auditors to the limited company which ran the "Glasgow's Glasgow" Exhibition. Their application for interdict was also heard just a few minutes before the programme was due to be broadcast. In this case the application failed. In these two cases as the BBC had lodged a *caveat* in court they were notified of the interdict application and were given the opportunity to oppose it. Undoubtedly, the present practice of the Scottish courts in granting interim interdicts in defamation cases will be challenged by the media as being in breach of Article 10 of the European Convention on Human Rights. The terms of section 12 of the Human Rights Act 1998 suggest that Parliament expects the courts to be very reluctant to grant pre-publication interdicts. It is likely that due to Article 10 of the Convention Scottish courts will adopt the *Bonnard v. Perryman* approach under which (since 1891) English judges have refused to grant pre-publication injunctions where the newspaper or broadcaster maintains that their allegations are true and that they will prove them to be true at trial/ proof.

It is clear from the above that the media, particularly television **18.14** broadcasters are in danger of being the recipients of interim interdict applications. The lodging of *caveats* each year in the Court of Session and the local sheriff court for the area of publication or broadcast may be precaution. The lodging of a *caveat* means that the court will give the *caveator* the chance to be heard before an interim interdict is pronounced. But section 12 of the Human Rights Act 1998 may remove the need for the media to lodge caveats. The section appears to require the court to give the media the opportunity to be heard in opposition to an application for interim interdict.

KEY POINTS

Damages can be awarded for hurt to feelings alone. Such general **18.15** damages are not likely to be as high as the special damages awarded when actual loss, such as business loss, can be proved. A jury trial in the Court of Session is much more likely to result in a higher award of damages than a case before a Court of Session judge or a sheriff. Exemplary damages are not competent in Scotland as they are in England. Aggravated damages are competent in Scotland where the defence persist in the defamation.

A journalist who finds he has defamed someone can reduce his **18.16** liability for damages by publishing an immediate apology.

18.17   As an alternative to claiming damages a pursuer can try to prevent publication by seeking an interim interdict. In Scotland in the past it has been much easier for a pursuer to obtain an interim interdict than it is for a plaintiff to obtain a similar order in England. It must be doubted if the Scots approach complies with the European Convention. It is likely to be brought into line with English law to avoid Convention difficulties.

18.18   All newspapers and broadcasters should lodge *caveats* annually in the Court of Session and in the case of local newspapers at the local sheriff court—at least until the interpretation of section of the Human Rights Act 1998 is clear.

CHAPTER 19

LETTERS, ARTICLES AND ADVERTISEMENTS

A defamation can be contained in any part of a newspaper. It can **19.01** lurk in a news item or editorial or it can be blazoned forth in a headline or even on a billboard. In these last two cases, however, the words in the headline or on the poster are regarded as simply drawing attention to a specific article and they will not usually be held to be defamatory if not so when read fairly along with the article (*Leon v. Edinburgh Evening News* (1909); *Archer v. Ritchie & Co.* (1891)). It is clear and just that a newspaper should be responsible for material produced in its own offices. It may seem less clear and less just that it should be responsible for material such as letters, articles or advertisements contributed by outsiders. This chapter deals with these matters. It is largely an application of the principles already explained.

An example of a dangerous advertisement was a "spoof" **19.02** inserted in the *Herald* purporting to announce the liquidation of double-glazing company C.R. Smith. It was particularly difficult to spot this hoax as the letter containing the notice was typed on what appeared to be lawyers' notepaper. Had this adversely affected that company's trading it might well have been possible for them to claim damages for loss of profit against the newspaper. In the event, a clarification was enough to resolve the matter. However, the case shows the need for newspapers to have some sort of checking system in place to avoid the possibility of publication of spoof advertisements.

Letters to the editor

A newspaper is liable for a defamation contained in letters to the **19.03** editor and the person defamed can sue both it and the writer. In the case of a hidden libel, the newspaper may well be able to rely on the defence of innocent publication and an offer of amends but as we have seen it must be able to prove that the words were not written with malice.

Anonymous letters give rise to further difficulties. The general **19.04** rule is that a paper will not be forced to disclose the name of the writer but this is a rule of practice not of law, and if the court orders disclosure, the newspaper must comply. Disclosure has been ordered when the pursuer alleged that a series of letters to the editor were in fact written by the newspaper itself as part of a systematic plan to ruin his reputation (*Cunningham v. Duncan & Jamieson* (1889)), and a disclosure has also been ordered when a newspaper put forward a defence which the pursuer could only meet by finding out the names of the writers of the letters in question (*Ogston & Tennant v. Daily Record*, Glasgow (1909)). While the courts are unwilling to compel disclosure there are strong reasons why a newspaper should reveal the names of contributors of defamatory articles. If it does not, it may find itself cut off from a number of important defences.

19.05   It may, for example, lose the defence of qualified privilege. If the name of the writer is not disclosed it cannot be known whether he had a duty to make the statement complained of or whether he was actuated by malice (*Brims v. Reid* (1885); *McKerchar v. Cameron* (1892); contrast *Egger v. Viscount Chelmsford* [1965]).

19.06   Although the law on the point is neither clear nor entirely satisfactory it seems that a newspaper may also in some circumstances lose the defence of fair comment if it will not or cannot disclose the name of the writer of a letter. This has been discussed in the previous chapter. And a newspaper will probably be cut off from the defence of innocent publication and an offer of amends if it does not disclose the author's name. It would obviously be very difficult or impossible in this case to supply the necessary proof that the words complained of were written without malice.

19.07   To sum up, the newspaper is in a much stronger position if it can reveal the name of the writer of letters appearing anonymously in its columns but it will not normally be compelled to make a disclosure.

19.08   Forged letters are a particularly insidious danger as so little can be done to guard against them. In 1963 the editor and proprietors of the *Daily Express* were sued for libel by the Orchestral Director of the Royal Opera House. The letter was a forgery. The defendants admitted that it was defamatory in that it suggested that the plaintiff was disloyal to his employers. They published a full explanation and apology, paid an agreed sum in damages and indemnified the plaintiff against his legal costs (*Smith v. Wood, The Times*, April 10, 1963).

19.09   Exactly the same considerations apply to articles contributed by a correspondent and published anonymously.

Advertisements

In the case of advertisements and notices of births, marriages and **19.10** deaths, the newspaper will again be in a weak position if it cannot disclose the name of the contributor and the rules discussed above apply. As advertisements are not usually associated with defamation it may be of value to mention two cases where they did lead to litigation.

In the first case a newspaper published an advertisement which **19.11** read:

> "A criminal information for conspiracy to defraud is being prepared re the estate of B. Malyon (deceased) 74 Argyle Street. All persons having made payments at the above address since September . . . should send immediate information to T. Bernstein, private detective, 84 St. John Street."

The pursuer was B. Malyon's trustee and executor and had **19.12** succeeded to his business which he carried on at 74 Argyle Street. He was allowed to bring an action against the newspaper as well as the private detective on the ground that the advertisement represented that he had been engaged in a fraudulent conspiracy in regard to B. Malyon's estate (*McLean v. Bernstein* (1900)).

In the second case a herbalist inserted an advertisement in a **19.13** newspaper disclaiming any connection with another herbalist's business and stating that he would not be responsible for any medicines sold at its address "or by any so-called herbalist". The pursuer was the herbalist at the address mentioned, and raised an action against the newspaper, claiming that the advertisement represented that her medicines were dangerous, that she was not a competent herbalist and that she falsely represented herself to be a herbalist. Her action was dismissed on the ground that the advertisement would not reasonably bear this meaning in the circumstances of the case (*Thompson v. Fifeshire Advertiser* (1936)).

Advertisements are sometimes seen which state that somebody **19.14** will no longer be responsible for another's debts or which warn the public against imitation goods. Such advertisements can be dangerous (see, *e.g., Grainger v. Stirling* (1898); *Webster v. Paterson & Sons* (1910)) and should be accepted with caution. Care should be taken to ensure that they are genuine and phrased so as to avoid unnecessary aspersions. In the second type of case, for example, statements which would identify particular traders should be excluded.

CHAPTER 20

ACTIONABLE NON-DEFAMATORY STATEMENTS: VERBAL INJURY

20.01 Not only defamatory statements give rise to exposure to actions for damages in the courts. Statements which are not themselves defamatory may allow a right of action on the ground of either (a) verbal injury or (b) negligence. It is hoped that the possibility of journalists and their employers being sued for negligence are remote. There is, however, a worrying decision on negligent statements by the House of Lords on July 7, 1994, in the case of *Spring*. This decision of the House of Lords, *Spring v. Guardian Assurance plc* [1994] appears to recognise, at least in English law, the possibility of actions being based on negligence as an alternative to defamation. This case is more fully discussed at para. 20.08.

Convicium

20.02 The most extreme form of verbal injury which was at one time recognised by Scots law is the old Roman law remedy of *convicium*. The essence of *convicium* was that the pursuer had been held up to ridicule by the defender. Perhaps the best modern day examples of such lampooning are to be found in the television programmes. For example, the former Channel 4 series "Spitting Image", and more recent programmes by the comedian Rory Bremner, are based at least in part on ridiculing well-known public figures. To succeed in a claim for *convicium* it was necessary for the pursuer to show that the defender had made the statement maliciously and that he had intended to bring the pursuer into public hatred, contempt or ridicule. It was also necessary to show that the pursuer had suffered some form of loss or injury (injury to feelings might be sufficient). For the journalist the most frightening aspect of the remedy of *convicium* was that truth was no defence.

20.03 It is submitted that if the remedy of *convicium* was ever one of the forms of verbal injury recognised by Scots law that this is no longer so, particularly taking into account the incorporation of the European Convention into our domestic law. In modern times there have been no Scottish proceedings based on the remedy of *convicium*. It is suggested that journalists should proceed on the basis that such a remedy is no longer open to pursuers in Scotland.

Malicious falsehood

Another form of non defamatory verbal injury is malicious false- **20.04** hood. The pursuer will have a right of action if he can prove three things:

(1) that the statement about him was untrue;
(2) that it was made spitefully, dishonestly or recklessly; and
(3) that it caused him financial loss.

An example from the English courts illustrates the point. Stefan **20.05** Grappelli, the jazz violinist, was due to appear at certain concerts in England. Due to illness he had to cancel these concerts. His agents put out a statement explaining to the public not only that he was ill but saying further that the illness was serious and that "it is likely Mr. Grappelli will never tour again". To say that someone is seriously ill is clearly not defamatory—it evokes sympathy rather than lowers his standing in the eyes of right-thinking people. But, clearly, such a statement could affect the individual's business. Mr. Grappelli was allowed an action for malicious falsehood; *Grappelli v. Derek Block Holdings Limited* [1981].

Slander of goods

Scots law will allow an action to a pursuer if the defender has **20.06** unjustifiably criticised the pursuer's goods or property. Perhaps the simplest example is criticism of a product which the pursuer is producing commercially. Again, as in the case of malicious false-hoods it is necessary for the pursuer to be successful that he show:

(1) that the statement was untrue;
(2) that it was made maliciously or recklessly; and
(3) that it caused him actual damage.

This form of action should give particular concern to journalists working in the area of consumer affairs. Criticism of particular brand names is an exceptionally risky area.

Onus of proof

As will have already emerged, the comfort for the journalist is that **20.07** these actions for verbal injury are the reverse of defamation actions in that the onus of proving falsity lies firmly on the pursuer's shoulders. It is not, as in defamation, necessary for the defender to prove his statements to be true. It is also necessary for the pursuer to show that the statements were made either maliciously or recklessly. He must then go on to show some loss or injury. It might, however, be easy in the case of an individual pursuer to prove some form of injury in the form of hurt feelings. It should also be remembered that in terms of section 3 of the Defamation Act 1952, if an action is raised for verbal injury it is not necessary for the pursuer to prove special damage (*i.e.* actual pecuniary loss), if the words on which the action is founded are calculated to cause pecuniary damage to the pursuer.

Legal aid

20.08 Legal aid is not available for actions based on defamation. But it may be available for actions based on malicious falsehood or slander of goods. The availability of legal aid increases the journalist's exposure to action for the simple reason that more people have the ability to sue.

Negligent statements

20.09 Since the case of *Hedley Byrne and Co. Limited v. Heller and Partners Limited* [1964] it has been accepted in both Scots and English law that a statement made negligently which causes the pursuer loss is actionable. From the journalist's viewpoint the problems are obvious. The journalist does not enjoy the possibility of the defences of fair comment or privilege which he can use in cases based on defamation. On the other hand, it is necessary for the pursuer to show that the statement was firstly, false and that it was communicated negligently. The legal principles involved in the *Hedley Byrne* case are complex. It will suffice for present purposes to summarise the law in the following simplified form:

  (a) A person making a statement on which others may reasonably be expected to rely has a duty to take care that the statement is accurate.
  (b) If he ignores his duty by making the statement negligently or recklessly then he can be liable in damages.
  (c) For the pursuer to succeed he must show that he relied on the statement was relied upon and that he suffered loss as a direct consequence.

The defender can, however, exempt himself from liability by issuing a disclaimer—which is precisely what had happened in the *Hedley Byrne* case itself. This is why it is good practice for editors in the likes of financial advice columns in newspapers to include a footnote stating that the editor, his staff and the publishing company are not liable for the advice given.

As stated at the beginning of this chapter, the House of Lords **20.10** have dealt with the question of liability for statements made negligently in the case of *Spring v. Guardian Assurance*. In this case the House of Lords decided that the terms of an employment reference were actionable under the law of negligence. As was observed above, normally an employment reference is protected by the law of qualified privilege. Accordingly, unless it were made maliciously, it would not give ground to an action in defamation. The Lords in the *Spring* case, however, were willing to accept the plaintiff's contention that he had a good ground of action on negligence. It is unclear as to how far the principles set out in *Spring* will apply. As yet, the *Spring* decision has not caused a flood of actions against the media based on negligence rather than based on defamation. It is, however, an area of law which journalists would be well advised to monitor closely. If pursuers in Scotland could proceed regularly by way of the law of negligence, journalists might find themselves unable to plead the usual defamation defences of privilege and fair comment. As Mr Spring only succeeded by a majority vote in the House of Lords, it may be that legal advisers to potential claimants have felt this an unsafe precedent to rely upon.

Breach of privacy

With the incorporation of the European Convention on Human **20.11** Rights into domestic law, as from October 2000 journalists must expect to have claims made against them on the basis of Article 8 of the Convention, which creates a right of privacy. To date, neither Scots nor English common law has recognised a right of privacy.

It should be noted that in countries which allow actions of **20.12** privacy the truth of the private facts revealed is not justification for publication. In this respect, an action based on privacy is similar to the ancient claim of *convicium* noted above at para. 20.02. It seems likely that, following European jurisprudence, Scots and English courts will recognise a right to privacy only in cases brought by individuals as opposed to corporate pursuers. This point was debated before the English courts in the judicial review action brought by the BBC against the decision of the Broadcasting Standards Commission upholding a complaint from the High Street retailers Dixons that the programme "Watchdog" had breached the company's right to privacy when secretly filming Dixons' employees engaged in questionable practices.

KEY POINTS

20.13 Some statements which are not defamatory are nevertheless actionable. In such an action it is necessary for the pursuer to prove that the statement made by the defender has been made with malice. In addition to proving malice, the pursuer must also prove that the statements were false. Finally, in most cases, the pursuer must also prove that actual pecuniary damage was caused to the pursuer. Remember, however, the terms of section 3 of the Defamation Act 1952 in terms of which the pursuer may be relieved of the obligation of proving pecuniary loss. Statements made by a journalist negligently which are relied upon by others causing them financial loss can be actionable.

CHAPTER 21

DIFFERENCES IN ENGLISH LAW

The broad principles of the law of defamation are the same in **21.01**
England as in Scotland but there are several differences on
particular points. The more important of these will now be briefly
considered.

Distinction between libel and slander

Roughly speaking, a defamation which is written, or expressed in **21.02**
permanent form is a libel in English law, while a defamation which
is spoken or communicated in some other transitory form is
slander. Under the Defamation Act 1952, however, a statement
which is broadcast by wireless telegraphy is treated as libel.

The importance of the distinction is that, with some exceptions, **21.03**
no action will lie for slander unless the plaintiff proves that the
words complained of have caused him actual pecuniary damage.
The exceptional cases where an action for slander will be allowed
without such proof are those involving imputations (a) of a crime
punishable by death or imprisonment, (b) of having a contagious or
infectious disease, (c) of unchastity in a woman or (d) calculated to
disparage the plaintiff in any office, profession, calling, trade or
business held or carried on by him at the time of publication.

Criminal libel

In English law, libel is a crime punishable by fine or imprisonment **21.04**
as well as a civil wrong giving rise to a claim for damages. A
criminal prosecution is rare, however, and tends to be discouraged
if the civil remedy is available. It should be noted that while in
England there must be publication to a third party before a civil
action will lie, this does not apply to a criminal prosecution. It can
be brought if the statement has been made to the defamed person
alone and is of a type calculated to provoke a breach of the peace.
The Supreme Court Procedure Committee reporting to the Lord
Chancellor in England in July 1991 recommended that Parliament
should consider whether the public interest required the retention

of criminal libel in English law. Their recommendation was that if it was to be retained as a legal concept at all proceedings of criminal libel should only be launched with the approval of the Attorney-General (the equivalent of the Scottish Lord Advocate).

Defences

21.05 Justification is the English term for *veritas*. The same principles apply as in Scotland.

21.06 As we saw, only contemporaneous reports of judicial proceedings have absolute privilege in English law. Non-contemporaneous reports, however, have qualified privilege provided they are fair and accurate. Reports of foreign proceedings (not coming under the Defamation Act) do not even have qualified privilege under English law unless they are of legitimate interest to the British public.

21.07 In England a litigant has absolute privilege with regard to statements he makes in written pleadings or instructs his counsel to make in court. In Scotland he has only qualified privilege (*M. v. H.*, 1908 S.C. 1130).

21.08 Formerly the period within which an action for defamation had to be brought was six years in England. It is now one year in terms of the Defamation Act 1996.

Injurious falsehoods

21.09 The statements referred to in Chapter 19 as actionable non-defamatory statements are generally known in English law as injurious falsehoods. Before 1952 the plaintiff had to prove falsity, malice and actual financial damage in each case. Since the Defamation Act of that year he need not prove actual financial damage in many cases where the words are calculated to cause him financial damage.

Frequency of actions/exemplary punitive damages

21.10 In England a libel court may award the plaintiff (now called the claimant) exemplary damages as well as compensatory damages. This has almost certainly encouraged libel actions in the High Court in London. Punitive or exemplary damages are rarely awarded in practice. The plaintiff must prove malice or recklessness on the defendant's part to obtain such damages. When exemplary damages are awarded, the figures can be dramatic as in the Jeffery Archer case against the *Star* newspaper and Lord Aldington's case against Count Leo Tolstoy. The Supreme Court Procedure Committee when reporting to the Lord Chancellor recommended that English law should be brought into line with Scots law by removing the right the English jury presently holds to award exemplary or punitive damages. This recommendation was not followed in the 1996 Defamation Act.

Chapter 22

INTELLECTUAL PROPERTY

22.01 The idea behind copyright is that people should be able to enjoy the benefits of their own original work, in the knowledge that it will not be pirated or exploited by others. Copyright is in essence a right to prevent copying (although this definition may come under strain in the context of the Internet). It does not give a monopoly. If two people by some remarkable coincidence were to write two identical books and it could be proved that they were in fact completely independent, the one who got into print first could not prevent the other from publishing his book. There would be no copying.

22.02 The law of copyright is the same throughout the United Kingdom and is now contained in the Copyright, Designs and Patents Act 1988 which made significant changes in the law. It is a lengthy and complex Act and there are several sections which are important to staff journalists, freelances and photographers in guiding them as to the use they may make of someone else's work.

22.03 The Act describes copyright as a property right which covers original literary, dramatic, musical or artistic works, sound recordings, films, broadcasts or cable programmes and typographical arrangements.

22.04 It is a person's work that is protected, not his ideas. This is an important distinction. Whatever the ethical questions, it is no infringement of copyright to lift the idea of another person's story and use it in a story of your own, expressed in your own words, although it may amount to a breach of confidence (see Chapter 32).

22.05 Copyright protects only original works but here again it is the form rather than the content which is important. The ideas need not be original provided the form in which they appear is. And this form will be original if it involves the use of some independent knowledge, skill, judgment or labour. There can be copyright in a list of football fixtures or Stock Exchange prices if skill was required in the selection or arrangement.

22.06 On the same principle there can be copyright in verbatim newspaper reports of public speeches. Neither the ideas nor the way of expressing them would be commonly regarded as the original work of the reporter, but the conversion of the spoken word into a written report involves the use of independent skill and labour on his part and the report is regarded as an original work for copyright purposes. If, however, the speaker hands the reporter a written copy of his speech and this is published verbatim by the newspaper then there would be no separate copyright in the report. There would be no conversion of the spoken to the written word and no exercise of independent skill or labour.

Another example will help to bring out the meaning of "orig- **22.07** inality" in copyright law. A translation is an "original" work for copyright purposes. The ideas and their arrangement are not original in the ordinary sense but the translation does involve independent knowledge and hard work on the part of the translator. It is therefore protected.

The type of copyright which is of most importance for journalists **22.08** is that existing in "literary works". This term is much wider than might be thought. It certainly does not mean that a work must have literary merit before it is protected. An examination paper has been held to be a literary work for copyright purposes, the judge remarking that if something was worth copying, it was worth protecting. Proceedings in both Westminster and the Scottish Parliaments, the courts and public inquiries may be reported without fear of copyright infringement.

Musical copyright is particularly well-organised and well- **22.09** policed. Twenty seconds' worth of "Colonel Bogey", played by a school band and incorporated into a film of the opening of a Suffolk school once resulted in a successful breach of copyright action.

In the case of "artistic works" too, paintings, drawings, engrav- **22.10** ings and photographs are protected irrespective of artistic quality. A tie-on business label has been held to be an artistic work for copyright purposes (*Walker v. British Picker Co.* [1961]).

It is clear that a "work" need not be very substantial, but a line **22.11** must be drawn somewhere and in some instances protection has been refused on the ground that there was no "work". Advertising slogans consisting of a few words have been refused protection on this ground. However, attitudes may be changing in this area to allow protection for slender pieces of writing. In a recent Scottish court action concerning the Internet, for example, the defenders conceded that there was copyright in newspaper headlines.

It is probably for the same reason that titles of newspapers, **22.12** books and periodicals are not generally regarded as copyright. An established newspaper can, however, prevent another paper being sold under the same or a similar title by means of an action for "passing off". It must be proved that the other paper is so similar that it would be likely to deceive the public. The owners of the magazine *Punch* once failed for this reason to prevent the publication of a much cheaper magazine called *Punch and Judy.*

22.13 "Could anyone", asked the judge, "be misled into buying this other paper instead, which has the words 'Punch and Judy' printed on it in distinct letters with a different frontispiece, and its price a penny? I am clearly of opinion that the mass of mankind would not be so misled" (*per* Malius V.C. in *Bradbury v. Beeton* (1869) 18 W.R. 33).

22.14 The same considerations apply to a *nom de plume*. There is no copyright, but if the name has become well known the author can bring a passing-off action to prevent its use in ways likely to deceive the public.

22.15 To sum up what has been said so far, copyright is a right to prevent copying, not a monopoly. It protects works, not ideas; form, not content. The works must be original, but need not be very original. In most cases, originality means the use of some independent skill, knowledge or labour. Merit is usually unimportant. Works can be small, but not too small. If, like newspaper titles, they are too small, they may nevertheless be protected by the law of passing-off.

Ownership and infringement

22.16 The owner of copyright in a work has the exclusive right to copy it, issue copies to the public, perform, show or play the work in public, broadcast the work and make an adaptation of it. Copyright is infringed by anyone who reproduces the whole or a substantial part of the work without the permission of the copyright owner, but there are various exceptions which allow journalists to make use of copyright material for review, criticism and the reporting of current events. Conversely, a newspaper or broadcasting organisation which owns copyright of material can prevent anyone else from reproducing it in public, recover damages and charge a fee for allowing the work to be published.

22.17 Under the 1988 Act, s.11(2), the person who first brings a work into existence is the owner of any copyright in it. However, where a literary (or dramatic or musical or artistic) work is made by an employee in the course of his work, the employer is the first owner of copyright unless there is some agreement to the contrary. Until the change in the law brought about by the 1988 Act, staff journalists retained residual copyright in their work which meant that it could be republished. For example, a columnist could publish an anthology of his best work in a book or use it for a broadcast or a film. Now the newspaper retains the entire copyright unless a special agreement has been reached. The newspaper also owns copyright in pictures taken by staff photographers.

The freelance journalist, not working under a contract of service **22.18** or apprenticeship, is in a different position and owns the copyright in his or her work. This will apply even if a newspaper has ordered the freelance to write an article or series of articles. The position can be altered by a written agreement under which the freelance assigns his copyright. An assignation is different from a licence. An assignation actually transfers copyright: a licence merely gives permission to do something in spite of the copyright, which remains in the hands of the person granting the licence. Thus, the late Robin Ray, the musicologist and broadcaster, was able to object to Classic FM's selling their database abroad. He had copyright in the documents and catalogue which made up the database and had given Classic FM only an implied licence.

Before the 1988 Act, where a newspaper commissioned a picture **22.19** from a freelance or commercial photographer the newspaper owned copyright in the picture. Now, unless there is an agreement to the contrary, copyright belongs to the photographer or his employer. If a member of the public submits a photograph for publication, he will retain the copyright, again subject to any agreement to the contrary.

However, under section 85 of the Act, a person who, for private **22.20** and domestic purposes, commissions the taking of a photograph or the making of a film, has the right not to have copies issued to the public or shown in public or broadcast. This applies only to pictures taken after August 1, 1989, when the 1988 Act came into force. It may well create problems for the newspaper which borrows a wedding picture from a relative after the bride, groom or best man becomes headline news, perhaps years after the wedding. By publishing, the newspaper could be infringing the copyright of the photographer and of the groom who may have commissioned it and would have the right under section 85 not to have it issued to the public. (Unauthorised use of photographs or photography can also amount to breach of confidence.)

The solution for newspapers may be, if they accept commissions **22.21** for pictures at weddings and christenings, to get a written under-taking that they can publish the pictures at any time.

An exceptional case where a man did object, understandably, to **22.22** the publication of his wedding photograph was *Williams v. Settle* in 1960. The bridegroom's father-in-law was found murdered. Two national newspapers obtained from a freelance photographer, and published, a photograph of a group at the wedding which included the murdered man. The groom owned the copyright in the photograph in this case and recovered damages and costs from one newspaper and an apology and undertakings from the other. He also recovered substantial damages from the photographer.

Fair dealing

22.23 As we have seen, the owner of copyright in a work has the exclusive right to copy it, issue copies to the public, perform, show or play the work in public, or broadcast it. However, the 1988 Act, s. 30, contains a provision on "fair dealing" which allows the journalist to reproduce extracts from the work for reporting current events and for criticism and review (but this does not cover a photograph used for reporting current events). The criticism and review can be of the work itself, or of another work altogether. In the case of newspapers the use of the material must also be accompanied by a sufficient acknowledgment. No acknowledgment is needed in reporting current events by means of a sound recording, film, broadcast or cable programme.

22.24 If too much of a work was reproduced (for example lifting another newspaper's story or quotes word for word) that might not be held to be fair dealing. It is not possible to lay down a hard and fast rule on this. To quote a small but crucial part of a book might be regarded as an infringement of copyright, while the use of a longer but less important passage might not. In one case, the use of four lines from a Kipling poem was held to be an infringement of copyright when they were used in an advertisement.

22.25 In January 1991, in the High Court, Mr Justice Scott dismissed a breach of copyright action brought by the BBC against British Satellite Broadcasting over the use of BBC football highlights from the World Cup. The judge ruled that BSB's use of clips recorded from the BBC's live coverage was protected by the fair dealing defence allowing limited use of copyright material in reporting current events. The BBC had contended that BSB's use of the "best bits" of its coverage was a breach of copyright. Carlton TV also successfully used the "fair dealing" defence to justify its incorporation of parts of a German TV programme in a documentary about chequebook journalism. However, *Hyde Park Residence v. David Yelland* in 1999, Mohammed Al Fayed's security services company tried, ultimately unsuccessfully, to use copyright to prevent the *Sun* printing video security stills of the Princess of Wales and Dodi Al Fayed in connection with speculation as to the car crash which killed them. Where copyright is used in an attempt to gag speech, section 12 of the Human Rights Act 1998 will come into play once it is in force.

There is a question as to how far back current events could be **22.26**
said to extend. What if evidence of some scandal emerged years
after the event, as frequently happens, and, in the course of an
investigation, a newspaper gained access to some documents
protected by copyright? Would it be able to quote from the
documents by saying it was reporting current events? The position
is not clear. The recent Court of Appeal authority in the Carlton
TV case suggests, however, that a relatively wide meaning is to be
given to "current events".

The spoken word

One of the most important provisions for journalists was the **22.27**
introduction by the 1988 Act for the first time of copyright in the
spoken word. Until then, if no notes had been made and the
speech was completely off-the-cuff, the speaker had no copyright in
his words. There was no "work" to which copyright could attach.
Copyright came into existence only when the words were taken
down by a reporter and it belonged either to the reporter or his
employer. This meant, for example, that although the *Daily Mirror*
could sue *Today* newspaper for allegedly "lifting" quotes from an
interview with the late showbusiness personality Marti Caine, Miss
Caine could not take action because she had no copyright in her
words.

The Act gives the speaker a copyright which comes into exis- **22.28**
tence as soon as the words are recorded by the journalist. Section
58 provides, however, that where a record of spoken words is made
in writing or otherwise for reporting current events or broadcasting
all or part of them, it is not an infringement of copyright in the
words, provided:

(a) the record is a direct record of the spoken words;
(b) the making of the record was not prohibited by the speaker;
(c) the use made of the material is not of a kind prohibited by
   the speaker; and
(d) the use is by or with the authority of the person lawfully in
   possession of the record.

It seems that if a speaker stands up before he makes his speech **22.29**
and makes it known that he does not wish it to be reported in any
shape or form, the publisher who chooses to ignore this could be
sued for breach of copyright. If the speaker decides after he has
made the speech that he does not wish it reported, that will be too
late. He must make it clear beforehand. The journalist may also be
able to rely on the legal principle that there is no copyright in facts
and ideas, and probably on a defence of fair dealing.

22.30   The terms of section 58 also suggest that a speaker might be able to dictate in what form he wishes his words to appear. The section talks about the use of the material not being of a kind prohibited by the speaker. Suppose an M.P. was delivering a speech and made it clear that he wanted it reported by certain newspapers and not others? Or that he wished only part of the speech to be reported? The Act appears to give him the means to sue for breach of copyright if his wishes are ignored.

Moral rights

22.31 The Act also gives the author of a copyright literary work the moral right to be identified, not to have his work subjected to derogatory treatment, and not to have work falsely attributed to him. The treatment of a work is derogatory if it amounts to a distortion or mutilation of the work or is otherwise prejudicial to the honour or reputation of the author. Treatment is defined as any addition to, deletion from, alteration to or adaptation of the work. The late Alan Clark succeeded against the London *Evening Standard's* spoof diary, using moral rights and "passing off" arguments, although it was the latter which appeared to convince the court—apparently, readers had found the spoof entirely convincing.

22.32   The right to be identified and not subjected to derogatory treatment does not apply to work by employees or reports of current events or to material made available to a newspaper or periodical by the author for publication.

22.33   You have to assert your moral rights of paternity. You do not, however, have to assert your right not to have your work treated in a derogatory fashion—this is automatic. The exceptions to an action for copyright infringement also apply to infringement of a moral right. Another moral right is "the right of privacy" (dealt with at para. 22.20), *i.e.*, not to have privately commissioned photographs, videos, etc, published or broadcast.

Rights in performances

22.34 There are also "rights in performances". A performer in a dramatic performance, including dance and miming musical performance, reading or recitation of a literary work, performance of a variety act and the like (but not live sporting events or public ceremonies) can object to recording, broadcasting or showing on cable of the performance without consent, except for private and domestic use. Amateur performers have these rights. The surviving Beatles and Yoko Ono recently used this to prevent the marketing of an unauthorised recording of a Beatles performance made in 1962.

There are various exceptions, *e.g.* recordings made for the **22.35** purposes of instruction or examination/recordings made by educational establishments for educational purposes, but only for private use. Persons having "recording rights", *i.e.* the benefit of an exclusive recording contract in relation to the performance, have similar rights. Trading without consent in such recordings may be a criminal offence.

Duration

Copyright lasts for a very long time. In the case of literary, musical **22.36** and artistic works, including photographs, copyright normally lasts for 70 years after the end of the year in which the author dies.This is a change made in 1995 from the previous position, which was only 50 years. Some works which were out of copyright have now come back into copyright as a result. In the case of film and sound recordings, copyright lasts for 70 years from the end of the year of the death of the principal director, screenplay author, dialogue author or musical composer, whichever dies last. If none of these people is identified, copyright lasts for 70 years from the end of the year the film was made or released. (In addition to this 70-year period, there is a separate right to a 50-year copyright in sound recordings, performances, broadcasts and cable programmes and the first fixation of a film. This is a somewhat complicated area.) Moral rights last as long as copyright does.

Copyright in a computer programme lasts for 70 years from the **22.37** death of its author. A computer database has a special 15-year copyright. Copyright in a typographical arrangement, for example a cut-out from a newspaper, lasts for 25 years from the end of the year of publication. After the expiry of copyright the work becomes public property and can be freely copied. Cable programmes in general attract copyright protection, but there are certain exceptions, *e.g.* in-house commercial communication systems. Protection of a cable programme lasts for 50 years from its being made, or being made available to the public. The same period applies to sound recordings, computer-generated works and broadcasts. It will be noted that the 50-year period applies only to the recording, programme or broadcast itself, not the underlying rights.

The copyrights involved in individual aspects of the work (*e.g.* **22.38** the author's in his screenplay or the musician's in his score) exist separately. In other words, a film is a copyright work; the screenplay it uses is also a copyright work, the score written for it is, as is the novel on which it was based.

22.39 The owner of copyright can sue for damages if his right is infringed, but the person alleged to have breached copyright has a defence if he can show that at the time of the infringement he did not know and had no reason to believe that there was copyright in the work. In that situation the copyright owner will not be entitled to damages but might still have some other form of remedy such as interdict or accounting of profits.

22.40 In an action for infringement, the court has power to award "such additional damages as the justice of the case may require"— looking at all the circumstances of the case, particularly the flagrancy of the infringement and any benefit gained by the guilty party.

22.41 It is not, of course, an infringement of copyright for a newspaper to print and publish letters or manuscripts sent to the editor. The fact that the author sends them implies a licence to publish. An interesting legal situation arises when a letter or article is sent to a newspaper for publication. In the absence of agreement, the position is that the author retains the copyright and the newspaper gets the property in the actual paper on which the words are written and, in addition, implied permission to publish. It is doubtful how far, if at all, the newspaper has implied permission to alter the letter or article. The view of the English courts is that in the absence of express or implied prohibition it has the right, as licensee, to make alterations. Also, a prohibition on reasonable alteration would probably not be implied in the case of ordinary letters and unsigned articles.

Other intellectual property rights

22.42 There are other I.P. rights, including patents, trademarks, design rights and know-how. Most of these are more relevant to commerce than journalism, but there are some exceptions. A name, title or device that may be too slight in itself to attract copyright may nonetheless be a registered trademark. Trademarks confer a monopoly right, *i.e.* there are no "fair dealing" defences or similar. Trademark protection has now been extended so as to cover sounds, smells, colours, shapes and packaging, *e.g.* Pirelli has registered its rose-scented tyres, and Direct Line its jingle. The greatest controversy has been over the new concept of a registered image. Most strikingly, there was the failed attempt to register the "image" of the Princess of Wales. Some "images" have been successfully registered as trademarks, however, notably of racing drivers and sporting personalities who clearly "trade off" their names in the matter of sponsorship. Trademarking does not prevent use of the name altogether in Scotland. The band "Wet

Wet Wet", having trademarked their name, tried to use the trademark to prevent use of it as the title of an unauthorised book by Mainstream publishers. This failed as this was use of the name not as a trademark, but as a title. Although the reasoning behind this decision was criticised in the 1996 English case of *British Sugar v. Robertson*, the English court there reached a similar result.

Unlike copyright, unregistered design and know-how rights, all **22.43** of which arise naturally, trademarks, patents and registered designs all require the owner to undergo a registration process and pay costs. Trademark registration requires to be renewed.

KEY POINTS

Copyright law exists to prevent original work such as literature, **22.44** drama and music from being exploited without the owner's permission. It protects the expression of an idea, not the idea itself. The law is now contained in the Copyright, Designs and Patents Act 1988.

Copyright in work produced by an employee such as a journalist **22.45** belongs to his or her employer, unless there is an agreement to the contrary. A newspaper would also have copyright in pictures taken by a staff photographer. Freelance journalists own the copyright in their own work. Where a newspaper commissions a picture from a freelance photographer, the copyright belongs to the photographer or his employer.

The owner of a work has the exclusive right to copy it, issue **22.46** copies to the public, show or play the work in public or broadcast it. However, the 1988 Act contains a provision on "fair dealing" which allows the journalist to reproduce extracts for reporting current events and for criticism and review.

Section 58 of the Act introduces copyright in the spoken word, **22.47** and the journalist will infringe this copyright if a speaker makes it clear beforehand that he does not wish his words to be recorded. The Act also gives the copyright owner the moral right to be identified and not have his work subjected to derogatory treatment.

Copyright in the written word and photographs normally lasts **22.48** for 70 years after the end of the year in which the author dies.

CHAPTER 23

RIGHTS OF ACCESS

23.01 With one or two exceptions, such as the right of admission to children's hearings, the journalist is in exactly the same legal position as any other member of the public. He can go to public places and public meetings. He cannot go to private places and private meetings. In many cases, of course, reporters are given special privileges such as reserved seats and free admission, but these are at the discretion of those who grant them and can be withdrawn at will. Privileges of this kind should not be confused with legal rights.

23.02 Certain meetings must be held in public; certain places, such as streets and various open spaces in towns, are public places; certain places are private places to which the public are invited and most places are private places to which the public are not invited.

23.03 Meetings and proceedings which must normally be held in public include court proceedings and certain local government meetings. Surprisingly, perhaps, they do not include proceedings in Parliament.

Court proceedings

23.04 The general rule is that proceedings in a court of law must be in public, unless justice demands otherwise. The Human Rights Act 1998 reinforces this approach. The principal applications of and exceptions to this rule have been considered elsewhere in this book.

Quasi-judicial proceedings

23.05 Most inquiries, tribunals and other quasi-judicial bodies must, as a general rule, meet in public, but there are numerous exceptions. These have been mentioned earlier when discussing the various bodies concerned.

Parliament

23.06 Both Houses of Parliament normally admit public and press to their meetings, but this is merely practice and there is no legal right of admission. Both Lords and Commons have full power to regulate their own procedure and can hold secret sessions when they think it necessary. For example, many such sessions were held during the 1939–45 war. It is a breach of parliamentary privilege to publish any report of, or purport to describe the proceedings at, a secret session.

Each House has power to punish for breaches of privilege. These **23.07** have been summarised as follows:

> "Disrespect to any member of the House, as such, by a person **23.08** not being a member; disrespect to the House collectively, whether committed by a member or any other; disobedience to the orders of the House or interference with its procedure, with its officers in the execution of their duty or with witnesses in respect of evidence given before the House or a Committee of the House,"

(Ansan, Law and Custom of Parliament (5th ed.), Vol. 1, p. 187).

Clearly, breach of privilege could be a real danger for news- **23.09** papers. "Disrespect" is a word of wide meaning and leading journalists have criticised the law of parliamentary privilege on the ground that it curbs unduly the publication of information the public should know about. A draconian use of parliamentary privilege would be likely to fall foul of the Article 10 right to freedom of expression, and thus of the Human Rights Act 1998 [see Chapter 25].

Technically, to publish reports of debates in Parliament at all is a **23.10** breach of privilege, and in the eighteenth century attempts were actually made to punish those who infringed. These led to such a public outcry that publication of reports has been allowed ever since. But false or perverted reports are regarded as punishable in practice as well as in theory.

To publish information derived from the reports of select **23.11** committees before they have been laid before the House is a breach of privilege. The committee is reporting to the House in the first place and only indirectly to the public. To reveal the contents of a report before Members of Parliament have had a chance of reading it is dangerous. The same does not apply to Green and White Papers. They are addressed to the public in the first instance and, while the Government in practice communicates important matters to Parliament before publication, this is a matter of courtesy alone.

Complaints of breach of privilege are raised in the House by a **23.12** member and are then usually referred to the Committee of Privileges for a report. The Commons can imprison an offender, although this is rare. The imprisonment can be during the pleasure of the House (*i.e.* for an indefinite period), but in this event the offender must be released at the end of the session. The House of Lords can imprison for a fixed term or impose a fine. Normally an offender is merely admonished or reprimanded. Proceedings were commenced in October 1994 against the *Guardian* editor Peter Preston over his sending of a fax which bore the House of Commons logo.

Local authorities

23.13 The Local Government (Access to Information) Act 1985 gives the public and duly accredited reporters of newspapers (which include any organisation "systematically engaged in collecting news for radio or television or for cable programme service") rights to attend meetings of regional, district and islands councils and their committees and sub-committees, with certain prescribed exceptions. These rights do not, however, extend to the taking of photographs at meetings or the recording of proceedings for later communication to anyone not attending. The meeting has a discretion to decide whether to permit taping or photography.

23.14 Press and public may be excluded for either of two reasons. First, that it is likely confidential information will be disclosed at the meeting or secondly that the subject-matter of discussion is exempt from public access.

23.15 Confidential information is defined as information which has been furnished by a Government department on terms forbidding its disclosure or which is prohibited from being disclosed by any enactment or court order.

23.16 Exempt information is defined under a list of specific subjects, including such matters as adoption or fostering of particular children, financial affairs of named individuals, details of council contracts for acquisition or supply of goods or services, details of tenders for contracts and information about counsel's advice.

23.17 The list also includes "any protected informant", which means any person giving the local authority information about a crime or offence. Exclusion of press and public on the ground of exemption can take place only where a resolution to that effect has been passed identifying the particular subject on the list. The Act provides a right to challenge exclusion by application to the Court of Session for judicial review. The Secretary of State for Scotland has power to extend or curtail the exemption list.

23.18 A meeting also has power to exclude anyone to suppress disorder or other misbehaviour.

23.19 Press and public have a right to see copies of agendas, reports and other papers relating to meetings (but not those relating to confidential or exempt items). Papers must be supplied on request to the media and made open for public inspection for three days before a meeting, or, if it has been called at short notice, from the time it is convened. The papers remain open for public inspection for six years after a meeting. Where confidential or exempt information is concerned, an official of the local authority must provide instead a written summary indicating the nature of the matters considered in private without actually disclosing the confidential or exempt information. The authority is entitled to charge for the provision of these services and also for the supply of photocopies of extracts of documents.

Anything contained in any document supplied to the media **23.20** which is defamatory is privileged under the Act unless published maliciously.

The Act leaves intact the rights of access by the media in **23.21** Scotland to meetings authorised by earlier legislation. Admission to certain other bodies is covered by the Public Bodies (Admission to Meetings) Act 1960, as amended by the Local Government (Scotland) Act 1973.

The only bodies left in the 1960 Act so far as Scotland is **23.22** concerned are health boards set up under the National Health Service (Scotland) Act 1972 (so far as their executive functions are concerned). NHS Trusts were included in the Schedule to the 1960 Act by the Public Bodies (Admission to Meetings) (National Health Service Trusts) Order 1997. Joint committees of two or more local authorities, and their sub-committees, are covered by the 1985 Act.

According to English case law, there is an implied right in the **23.23** 1960 Act to exclude unruly members of the public, even if they appear to be making a political protest: *R v. Brent Health Authority, ex p. Francis and Community Rights Project* [1985].

Other public meetings

In the case of meetings held in public places the journalist has the **23.24** same right to be present as any other member of the public—a right which may be limited by bye-laws as well as by the law on such matters as breach of the peace. He cannot be singled out for exclusion by the organisers of the meeting. He has as much right to be in a public place as they have.

In the case of meetings or other proceedings, such as most sports **23.25** meetings, to which the public are invited but which are held on private property, the journalist's rights depend on the terms of the invitation. The organisers of such meetings may choose to exclude the media or impose conditions on entry, such as a ban on cameras. The whole question is really one of contract between those granting and those seeking admission and the terms of the contract may be express or implied. There may, for example, be an implied term that a person can be excluded if he does not behave in a proper manner. The Court of Session has upheld a right to exclude a known criminal from an enclosure at a race meeting. One of the judges observed that "there was an implied condition attaching to the right of entry that his character was such as warranted his presence in the enclosure".

Trespass

23.26 As a general rule no one is entitled to enter private property without the owner's consent, but there are exceptions. Statutes give certain people, such as police officers with search warrants, rights of entry. And generally entry is allowed if it is necessary in the public interest—to put out a fire, for example, or continue the hot pursuit of a criminal. These exceptions will not normally benefit the journalist—and so for him the normal rule applies. He is infringing the owner's legal rights if he enters his property, whether it is enclosed or not, without permission.

23.27 Trespass is an infringement of rights, but until the Criminal Justice and Public Order Act 1994, was not normally a criminal offence in Scotland. The Act made some types of trespass criminal, for example for the purpose of holding a "rave" or setting up a "New Age" encampment.

23.28 This does not mean, however, that the property owner has no remedies. He can order an intruder to leave. If met by a refusal, he can probably remove him by the use of reasonable force although there is some doubt about this in the case of property other than private houses. If the intrusion is likely to be repeated he can apply to the court for an interdict, which it is contempt of court to ignore. If the intruder has caused actual damage to the property, the owner can also sue for compensation.

23.29 In the past, then, where a trespasser is unlikely to repeat the trespass and has caused no damage, all that the owner could lawfully do was ask him to leave and, if he refused, remove him by reasonable force. If too much force is used the trespasser can sue for assault, but he starts with the scales weighted against him.

23.30 The law in this area is likely to change imminently, in part because of the furore over the English householder, Tony Martin, convicted of murder for shooting a burglar, but more importantly because of the Article 8 privacy right now brought into domestic law by the Human Rights Act 1998. (See Chapter 25.) The European Court of Human Rights in Strasbourg took a dim view of police even standing in the garden of a dwelling-house to prevent an anticipated breach of the peace whilst matrimonial property was transferred following a divorce, for instance.

KEY POINTS

Generally, the right of the journalist to attend meetings is the same **23.31** as any other member of the public. The Local Government (Access to Information) Act 1985 provides the right to attend meetings of councils and sub-committees. The media may be excluded if "exempt" information is to be discussed, but this can be done only after a resolution to that effect has been passed. Copies of agendas and reports must be made available for inspection.

CHAPTER 24

BROADCASTING

CONTEMPT AND DEFAMATION GENERALLY

24.01 The legal principles governing the activities of journalists outlined in this book apply also to television and radio broadcasters, particularly in relation to contempt of court and defamation. Indeed, broadcasters, particularly television broadcasters, might expect more severe treatment from the courts than newspaper journalists in view of the higher public penetration of broadcasting and the higher authority which radio and TV appear to enjoy, according to statistical analysis, in the public mind.

24.02 The rules restricting publicity contained in the Contempt of Court Act 1981 apply to broadcasts as well as printed publications, but their effect may be different in practice. Live broadcasts can and occasionally do catch the commission of crime during transmission of a news programme. Although strictly speaking the act of arrest makes proceedings "live" under the 1981 Act, there has not yet been a case where a broadcaster has been accused of contempt in these circumstances. Logically, the law cannot strike out what has been shown on TV up to the point of arrest. But after arrest the commission of the crime cannot be shown again. So the footage of the incident already broadcast cannot be repeated. Nor can newspapers cover the incident as the Contempt of Court Act will apply at their publication time.

24.03 As there have been so few cases concerning broadcasters in a Scottish court it is difficult to analyse the approach of the Scottish judiciary to broadcasting. It is clear, however, that the transitory nature of a broadcast (unlike the written newspaper report which can be read and re-read) can be cited by the broadcasters' lawyers in court both as a defence and also as a mitigating factor in the event of a finding of guilt. Support for this approach can be found in England in the case *Attorney-General v. ITN and Others* in May 1994. There the English Divisional Court accepted that a television broadcast was transitory and therefore less likely to cause a risk of prejudice than a newspaper article. The competing qualities of high penetration and the authority enjoyed by broadcasting on the one hand and the counterbalancing factor of its transitory nature have not been fully discussed in a Scottish case. It must suffice at present to warn broadcasters that the courts will undoubtedly attach weight to the argument that TV and radio broadcasts reach large audiences and enjoy high authority. It follows that defamation or a contempt by a broadcaster could be regarded as more serious than that by a print journalist. If there is no sufficient counterbalancing argument available then it may be thought that the broadcasters expect a heavier penalty for contempt or suffer a higher award of damages for defamation.

CONTRAST BETWEEN BROADCASTS AND NEWSPAPERS IN CONTEMPT CASES AND DEFAMATION CASES

24.04 On the question of contempt some small degree of guidance might be obtained from the experience of newspapers and radio broadcasting in 1979 in the case of *Stuurman*. In that case the English police unfortunately put out a press release indicating that a Mr Stuurman, his wife and two other individuals arrested in Scotland and charged with crimes under the Misuse of Drugs Act were members of an international drugs running gang who had been sought by Interpol for many years. Some sections of the Scottish press carried this material and found themselves before the Scottish High Court of Justiciary for contempt (See 10.112 onwards for fuller details of the *Sturman* case).

24.05 The *Herald* was fined £20,000 for carrying the material, whereas Radio Forth was fined £10,000 for carrying basically the same material. It may be difficult to extract principles from one case but it is reasonable to suppose that the High Court took the view that the printed words in the Herald were more likely to reach and be remembered by the public. The newspaper article, therefore, might have a greater effect on potential jurors than the brief broadcast on Radio Forth.

24.06 Two recent cases which came before the Scottish courts show a surprising disparity of approach in the Scottish courts to allegedly defamatory material which is broadcast rather than printed. In 1992, the case of Anthony Gecas against Scottish Television was finally decided. In that case Mr Gecas, a Lithuanian national living in Edinburgh, had sued STV in respect of their programme "Crimes of War" which alleged he was involved in the death squad extermination of many Lithuanian Jews. Gecas claimed £600,000.

Lord Milligan's judgement was in favour of STV and accordingly, no award was made. Lord Milligan did however state that had he found in Mr Gecas's favour he would have awarded only £20,000— above £30,000 at today's prices. One has to remember that the programme alleged that Mr Gecas was a mass murderer.

24.07 In contrast, in 1999, Temporary Judge Gordon Coutts, Q.C. awarded £186,000 to Mr Raymond Baigent and his wife Margaret and their three adult children, the operatives of Orchard House Nursing Home in Lanarkshire. The award was made against the BBC in respect of a programme in the "Frontline" series, which had alleged that the nursing home was poorly run and that residents were badly treated. These damages included an element for aggravated damages, due to the basis of truth (*veritas*). But there is no exemplary damages in these sums.

24.08 Such wildly different approaches to defamation damages by two Scottish judges are very difficult to reconcile.

24.09 It would be difficult to draw any conclusions from these two recent defamation cases. All that may be said is that the Scottish courts do not appear yet to have come to any view as to whether defamation on television is more or less serious than defamation in newspaper.

INTERDICTS

24.10 In a few cases attempts have been made to obtain interim interdicts against radio or TV broadcasts on the basis that the material to be broadcast was defamatory. The first of cases was an application to the Court of Session by George Galloway, M.P., in respect of a BBC Scotland programme which made reference to his activities while secretary of the charity, War on Want. The court refused interim interdict. So far as it is possible to elicit a principle from a case when no written judgment has been issued, it seems that the court's basis for refusing the application was that, if the material was defamatory, Mr Galloway had a remedy by suing BBC Scotland for damages. The application had been made when the broadcast was imminent. So too was an application by Touche Ross, chartered accountants, in connection with a BBC Scotland "Focal Point" programme on Glasgow's Year as European City of Culture in 1990. Touche Ross were accountants to the company formed in connection with Glasgow's Exhibition, which was part of the 1990 Year, and claimed that the programme defamed them by alleging that they had not carried out their work properly and professionally. BBC Scotland maintained that no such innuendo could be taken from the words used in the programme. In that case, with only minutes to go before transmission time, the Court of Session decided Touche Ross had not made out a prima facie case and interim interdict was refused. The case illustrated the fundamental legal rule that to obtain an interim order the pursuer must at least demonstrate a prima facie case of defamation. In 1991 Sheriff Ewen Stewart was successful in obtaining an interim interdict against a "Focal Point" programme which basically alleged that he was unfit for office. Lord Penrose granted the interim interdict but this was later withdrawn by agreement a few days later at a review hearing. (Sheriff Stewart was later removed from the shrieval bench on the motion of both Houses of Parliament on the basis of his unfitness for office.)

In contrast to the Scottish courts' approach, the English courts **24.11** very rarely grant "prior restraint orders". The authority of *Bonnard v. Perriman*, 1893 is to the effect that, if the media defender claims that the defamatory allegations are true, an English judge will allow the broadcast to take place. This approach seems to accord with Article 10 of the European Convention on Human Rights. When incorporating the Convention into United Kingdom law, Parliament specifically dealt with the question of balancing the Article 10 right to freedom of expression with other Convention rights, such as the Article 8 right to privacy. Accordingly, section 12 of the Human Rights Act 1998 makes it clear that the courts must afford great weight to freedom of expression when considering an application for an injunction/interdict against the media. It may therefore reasonably be expected that the approach taken by the Scottish courts in future to pre-publication interdicts will be similar to that taken for the past 100 years by the courts in England and Wales.

There is no authoritative Inner House decision laying down **24.12** guidelines as to when interim interdict is appropriate against an allegedly defamatory broadcast. There have not been a sufficient number of cases to work out the principles on which our courts approach such situations. It is clear, however, that broadcasters would be foolish not to lodge *caveats* in the Court of Session to ensure that they have the chance of appearing to make representations against the granting of an interim interdict order. It is arguable that section 12 of the Human Rights Act 1998 makes the lodging of *caveats* unnecessary, but for safety's sake it is still wise to take this precaution. So, too, broadcasters should be prepared to defend controversial programmes in court (even, at the last minute). They must also be mindful of the fact that it seems likely that if an application for interim interdict were made and failed and later the programme was proved to be defamatory, the court would probably award higher damages against the broadcaster. Although the Scottish courts do not award exemplary damages, it seems reasonable to suppose that a judge would be sympathetic to a party who had in effect warned the broadcaster by applying for an interim interdict of the defamatory nature of material to be broadcast. If the broadcaster went ahead despite that warning it can be anticipated that the broadcaster would suffer more severe treatment from the court by way of damages. As stated above, the whole question of our courts' approach to this matter will inevitably be affected by the incorporation of the European Convention on Human Rights and in particular the guarantees of freedom of expression contained in Article 10 of the Convention. Section 12 of the Human Rights Act 1998 suggests that the courts should give considerable force to the freedom of expression article in such cases.

SPECIAL PROBLEMS OF TELEVISION

24.13 The medium of television is an unusual form of communication in that it simultaneously conveys to the viewer words and visual images. This gives rise to particular legal problems. The juxtaposition of the pictures and commentary/script can frequently give rise to the broadcast becoming defamatory. Often this is accidental and completely unintentional. An example will illustrate the point.

24.14 In 1994 a BBC Television news broadcast on the Public Account's Committee's investigation into the activities of certain statutory bodies in Wales made reference to the PAC's findings of wasteful, fraudulent and corrupt behaviour on the part of the Welsh statutory bodies, particularly the Welsh Development Agency. During the course of these news reports the BBC used a Welsh Development Agency video which included pictures of a factory in North Wales run by a company called Sharp Electronics UK Limited. The company name and logo could be clearly seen. Sharp Electronics sued in the English courts for defamation claiming that there was an implication that their company was involved in the sort of activities the PAC was criticising. They succeeded in obtaining an apology, damages and payment of their costs.

24.15 In the same year, court proceedings were raised at Glasgow Sheriff Court by a Glasgow solicitor, John Carroll, who argued that an item on "Reporting Scotland" had been "cut" in such a way as to make it appear that some remarks by Duncan Campbell applied to him. A full text of Duncan Campbell's remarks made it clear that he was talking not about the solicitor but about the solicitor's client, David Donaldson, the so-called "Fettesgate Raider". The sheriff principal dismissed Mr Carroll's action and Mr Carroll later abandoned an appeal to the Court of Session. Nevertheless, the case illustrates the necessity for journalists to take care when editing television tape to make sure insofar as possible that the juxtaposition between words and pictures does not lead to even the possibility of confusion in the mind of the public.

The lesson to be learned for journalists working in television is **24.16** that extreme care must be taken to prevent critical words in news reports which are aimed at one particular target from hitting another by accident. Even in situations where an interviewee is intending to criticise one individual it is perfectly possible that as a matter of law his words are held to be defamatory of another individual. That will arise due to the television journalist "cutting" the story in such a way that the interviewee's comments would be construed by the viewer in that (quite unintended) way. It is good practice for a television journalist to have a colleague who has not been working on the story in question to view the television tape before transmission if there is doubt as to how the viewer would construe critical references in the report.

LIVE PROGRAMMES

Up until 1996 there was no protection given to live programmes, **24.17** despite the fact that the broadcaster on occasions had very little control over the content of the programme, for example, a vigorous studio debate on a controversial issue. Under the old law, in 1986 BBC Scotland were sued for £500,000 pounds by the late Robert Maxwell over a remark made by Arnold Kemp, editor of *The Herald* in the live discussion programme on Radio Scotland "Taking Issue with Colin Bell". Mr Kemp too was sued by Maxwell for £500,000. The unfairness of the law was recognised when section 1 of the Defamation Act 1996 came into effect. In short, that section allows the broadcaster of live programmes protection if one of the participants in the live programme utters defamatory remarks in circumstances where the broadcaster has no control over this. There have as yet been no cases determining when the broadcaster will be able to use this new "live programme defence" effectively. However, it would appear to be common sense to say that, if the presenter of the programme is encouraging participants to debate particular points and, in response to the presenter's questions, a participant utters defamatory remarks, the broadcaster will probably be held responsible by the courts. In contrast, if a participant departs sufficiently from the areas the presenter is encouraging him or her to speak about, the broadcaster may well have a defence. Although there are no Scottish court cases concerning live broadcast at present, the Section has already proved a discouragement to some would-be libel pursuers. In the case brought by MORI against the BBC in 1999 the "live broadcast defence" was allowed to go to the jury. The BBC had broadcast remarks of Sir Gus Goldsmith on the accuracy of MORI's opinion polls on his Referendum Party's popularity during the 1997 General Election.

24.18 Live programmes, however, enjoy no special position regarding contempt of court. If an "active" court case is to be debated in the course of a live programme, it is necessary to take the utmost care that participants say nothing which would cause the risk of prejudice to the forthcoming trial. It will be necessary for producers and presenters to brief lay participants prior to the programme beginning on the restrictions which apply to any discussion of an outstanding criminal trial.

WHO MAY BE SUED/ACCUSED IN RESPECT OF A BROADCAST

24.19 Again this has never been judicially determined. On the analogy of newspaper cases, it appears that the reporter, the editor, the producer and the broadcasting organisation itself could all find themselves involved in court proceedings. In one contempt case in 1987 involving Radio Clyde, however, the fine of £20,000 imposed on the radio station's news editor, Colin Adams, by Lord Allanbridge at Paisley was reduced to nil on appeal by the High Court. (This case concerned a broadcast during a murder trial to the effect that the accused had offered to plead guilty to culpable homicide—an offer which the broadcast claimed had been rejected by the Crown.)

24.20 This case should not be viewed by news editors as particularly comforting. Mr Adams' pleas that he relied on the expertise of the reporter had more force than normal in that the reporter in question was a freelance and had many years experience in the particular area of work (contemporaneous court reporting). If he had been a staff reporter under the control of Mr Adams the High Court's attitude would probably have been different. Lord Allanbridge refrained from fining the broadcasting limited company, Radio Clyde. It seems likely that such a fine would have received more support from the High Court than one of £20,000 imposed on an individual who the Judge was told earned £22,000 per annum and whose employers were by no means certain to back him financially in respect of the fine. (See also Chapter 10.) It is interesting to note that the freelance reporter did not appeal the fine of £5,000 imposed on him by Lord Allanbridge, although the reporter's earnings at the relevant time were stated to be £7,000 per annum.

INDEPENDENT PRODUCERS AND CONTEMPT/DEFAMATION

The foregoing paragraph has particular force nowadays when so **24.21** much material broadcast comes from independent producers. It seems clear that Scots law allows the pursuer in a defamation action to sue the independent production company as well as the organisation which broadcast the material. It would be possible therefore to have several defenders when, for example, the programme broadcast was produced by an independent production company who employed a freelance reporter. It is suggested that the pursuer could sue all or any of the following:

(a) the broadcaster;
(b) the independent production company as producers;
(c) the reporter(s);
(d) possibly the editor of the programme;
(e) the contributor,

if the alleged defamatory remarks were made by him. There would be no need for the pursuer to sue the broadcasting organisation itself. He could choose to sue the independent producer alone or the reporter alone. In fact, normally a pursuer sues all concerned jointly and severally for the same amount of money. Technically this is incorrect as Lord Fraser's judgment in *Turnbull v. Frome* (1966) makes clear. Liability in defamation cases is individual, not joint and several. It is suggested that it would be wise for independent producers and reporters involved in such programmes to come to some sort of agreement before the broadcast as to who will be responsible in part for the payment of damages in a defamation situation. It must be emphasised, however, on the question of contempt, this is a quasi-criminal matter over which the court alone has jurisdiction. An agreement to pay each other's fines may be informally entered into but nobody can serve your jail sentence for you! Independent producers and their reporters should be mindful of this fact.

CONTEMPT OF COURT: PARTICULAR PROBLEMS FOR BROADCASTERS

24.22 The ability of broadcasters to transmit up-to-the-minute reports of developing news stories is one of the principal strengths of TV and radio. But this very strength creates considerable dangers for broadcasters in the area of contempt of court. If for example there were a dramatic bank raid in the morning, the first newspaper report of the event would not appear until the evening or perhaps in some cities until the next day. But TV and radio could broadcast stories of the raid within minutes of the event. The danger, however, of committing the serious offence of contempt of court in this situation is extremely high. Reference is made to Chapter 9. The various trigger mechanisms which cause the rules of the Contempt of Court Act 1981 to commence operation should be in the forefront of the minds of broadcasters. The principal events which would trigger the operation of the 1981 Act rules in such a situation as envisaged here are (1) arrest or (2) the granting of a warrant to arrest. A broadcaster reporting a bank raid would have to check constantly with the police to see if either event had taken place. If he received no information or received wrong information to the effect that there had been no arrest and no warrant granted, the broadcaster could try to rely upon the defence of innocent publication which is set out in section 3 of the Act. It is emphasised that the law requires that the broadcaster must be able to show that he has "taken all reasonable care".

24.23 It is therefore suggested that broadcasters should operate a working rule of keeping a record of all enquiries to the police and the times they are made regarding the question of arrest and the granting of arrest warrants in this sort of situation. Broadcasters may, however, find that the police reaction to requests from journalists for immediate information on arrests and warrants can be less than helpful—at least in some forces. Some police information services have been known to answer journalists' enquiries as to whether or not an arrest has been made by saying that the journalist and his legal advisers should be able to work that out for themselves. It is submitted that this unhelpful attitude would imperil the Crown's position in any petition for contempt against the broadcasting organisation. The broadcaster could transmit in these circumstances with a reasonable prospect of adopting the innocent publication defence.

24.24 A very good example of developing a news story of dramatic proportions arose late in 1991 when a large number of armed police raided the home of the so-called gangland Godfather Arthur

Thomson in Provanmill, Glasgow in connection with an inquiry into the deaths of two Glasgow gangland figures. Streets in the area were closed off as police surrounded the house and told the occupants via a loud hailer "to come out with their hands up". This they duly did. Later all were released. The police later put out the incredible statement that there had been no arrests and all concerned had attended voluntarily. The situation demonstrates the dangers for broadcast journalists. Had any of these "volunteers" become accused persons the court would undoubtedly have taken the view that they were arrested at Thomson's house and accordingly the terms of the Act operated from that point onwards. That would have had a considerable effect on the way TV could cover the story. Pictures of those taken from the house could not have been used. Identity is almost always an issue in a Scottish criminal case. Once the restrictions of the 1981 Act operate (from arrest, the granting of a warrant, etc.), pictures of the accused cannot normally be used unless there is specific permission from the Lord Advocate—and even then there could be dangers from the defence.

There are some rare exceptions to this general rule. For **24.25** example, television pictures of the Govan M.P. Mohammed Sarwar were used when he gave a press conference after being released on bail, having appeared on petition at Glasgow Sheriff Court in 1998 on a series of charges alleging wrong-doing in relation to his election campaign in the 1997 General Election. Generally speaking, the view of media lawyers appeared to be that Mr Sarwar had indicated by his actions, *i.e.* happily giving full-face interviews to television and newspaper journalists, that he felt his identity was not an issue in the trial and was content for his picture to be used. Similarly, in 1996, the face of the actor, Eric Cullen, who was appearing on charges of indecency and possession of pornographic videos, was used by newspapers and television. Similarly, pictures of the two Libyans accused of the Lockerbie bombing have been used by the media without any complaint being made. It is emphasised, however, that these cases are the exception and that television journalists, like newspaper journalists, must exercise extreme caution before using the picture of an accused person who has not yet been tried.

GOVERNMENT INTERFERENCE IN BROADCASTING

The Secretary of State's powers in relation to broadcasting are **24.26** contained in section 10 of the Broadcasting Act 1990. That states that the Secretary of State can direct the Independent Television

Commission to require the licence holders to publish specific announcements. He may also require the ITC to direct their licence holders to refrain from including any material specified in a Notice served by the Secretary of State or other Minister of the Crown. Such power, which existed since before the 1990 Act, has been used by the Crown in relation to broadcasts containing material from Sinn Fein. For approximately six years it was possible to broadcast the content of a Sinn Fein's official speech/ interview/press release but not to show him speaking the words. In the case of the BBC, the Crown used the terms of the Corporation's Charter to have the Corporation follow a similar practice. The Minister's Notice was challenged in the courts by journalists. The House of Lords refused to set the Notice aside, although they thought it might well be in breach of international law *viz*. Article 10 of the European Convention on Human Rights (*R v. Home Secretary, ex p. Brind* 1991).

24.27 Section 10 therefore has considerable potential for Government interference in broadcasting and it is unclear if the section and the provisions in the BBC's Charter comply with the terms of Article 10 of European Convention on Human Rights for the protection of freedom of expression.

24.28 Part 1 of Article 10 of the Convention states:

> "Everyone has the right to freedom of expression. This right shall include freedom to hold opinions and to receive and impart information and ideas without interference by public authority and regardless of frontiers. This Article shall not prevent States from requiring the licensing of broadcasting, television or cinema enterprises."

24.29 It would appear that the Convention, whilst accepting the principle of licensing broadcasting, does not make any exception in the case of broadcasting from the broad general principle of the right to freedom of expression. It therefore appears reasonable to anticipate that at some point a broadcasting organisation could challenge any use of section 10 of the Broadcasting Act by the Crown in the European Court. Although the *Brind* precedent mentioned above went against the media, it seems reasonable to refer that incorporation of the European Convention on Human Rights by the Human Rights Act 1998 will mean that the courts are more sympathetic to such freedom of expression arguments.

24.30 It should be noted that Part 2 of Article 10 of the Convention contains a proviso to the general right to freedom of expression, stating that:

> "The exercise of these freedoms, since it carries with it duties and responsibilities, may be subject to such formalities, conditions, restrictions or penalties as are prescribed by law and are

necessary in a democratic society, in the interests of national security, territorial integrity or public safety, for the prevention of disorder or crime, for the protection of health or morals, for the protection of the reputation or rights of others, for preventing the disclosure of information received in confidence, or for maintaining the authority and impartiality of the judiciary."

In any hearing before the Court of Human Rights the Crown could have been expected to claim that this proviso was applicable to ministerial control over broadcasting matter emanating from an organisation such as Sinn Fein.

POLICE POWERS

In terms of the Broadcasting Act 1990, section 167, a justice of the **24.31** peace may authorise a police constable to require a broadcaster to produce a visual or sound recording of any matter contained in a programme where there is reasonable ground for suspecting that a "relevant offence" has been committed, namely an offence under section 51 of the Civic Government (Scotland) Act 1982 or under section 22 of the Public Order Act 1986. Accordingly, if there were reasonable ground for suspicion that obscene or racially inflammatory material had been broadcast such authority could be given to a constable requiring compliance with any order made by a justice of the peace.

It would appear that the inclusion of this section in the Act **24.32** indicates that, rather than finding themselves embarrassed by the controversy surrounding the Zircon raid on the Queen Margaret Drive premises of BBC Scotland in 1987, the Government has persuaded Parliament to grant powers to the police to obtain copies of material from broadcasters as a statutory right.

Section 167 appears only to cover the situation where the **24.33** material has already been broadcast. If the Crown wished to stop a broadcast being made on the basis that the suspected material might be obscene, racially inflammatory or might offend against some other statute or Scots common law, then it would require to proceed by way of interim interdict.

It is specifically stated in section 167(6)b that the reference to a **24.34** justice of the peace shall include a reference to the sheriff. No default provision was inserted as a direct result of the considerable controversy at the time of the Zircon raid that the warrant had been signed by a sheriff rather than a justice of the peace which appeared to offend against the terms of the Official Secrets Act 1911.

24.35 Finally, broadcasters should note that in terms of section 145(5) they have a duty to keep recordings of their programmes for the purposes of assisting the police under this section.

BROADCASTING STANDARDS COMMISSION

24.36 The 1996 Broadcasting Act amalgamated the old Broadcasting Complaints Commission and Broadcasting Standards Council. The new amalgamated body has the title the Broadcasting Standards Commission. The Commission's duty is to draw up a code of giving guidance for particular areas of broadcasting, as follows:

  (a) practices to be followed in connection with the portrayal of violence in programmes to which this part of the Act applies;
  (b) practices to be followed in connection with the portrayal of sexual conduct in such programmes;
  (c) standards of taste and decency for such programmes generally.

24.37 The relevant part of the Act applies to:

  (a) a television or sound programme broadcast by the BBC;
  (b) any television programme by the Welsh Authority;
  (c) any television or sound programme included in a licensed service,

in effect to all United Kingdom television and radio broadcasters. It is in addition the Commission's duty to monitor the programmes broadcast in relation to:

  (1) unjust or unfair treatment;
  (2) unwarranted infringements of privacy;
  (3) the portrayal of violence and sexual conduct; and
  (4) on the standards of taste and decency maintained.

24.38 The Commission, whose functions and powers are laid down by sections 106 to 130 of the 1996 Act, has the duty to consider complaints made to it. It must make findings regarding such complaints. The complainer must put his case in writing and the Commission will not entertain a complaint which is made more than two months after a television programme or three weeks after a sound programme unless it appears to it that in the particular circumstances it is appropriate to do so. It is suggested that "particular circumstances" might arise for example if the complainer was the person mentioned in the programme and was absent from the country for a while. The Commission has the power if appropriate to have a hearing on a complaint. Normally such a hearing will be in private, although the Commission does have power to direct that it be in public. A copy of the complaint must be sent to "the relevant person" and, if the programme was included in a licensed service, to the appropriate regulatory body. "The relevant person" is defined as (a) in a case where the relevant programme was broadcast by a broadcasting body, that body; and (b) in a case where the relevant programme was included in a licensed service, the licence holder providing that service. A broadcasting body is defined in the Act as meaning the BBC or the Welsh Authorities. Once the Commission has considered and made findings in respect of the complaint it will direct that a summary of the complaint and its findings and any observations on it are broadcast. The broadcaster must comply with any such direction.

The Commission has a duty to produce an annual report which **24.39** is laid before Parliament by the relevant Secretary of State.

JUDICIAL REVIEW OF DECISIONS OF BROADCASTING STANDARDS COMMISSION

The Broadcasting Standards Commission's decisions can be chal- **24.40** lenged in the court. The BBC have taken judicial review proceedings on two occasions. On the first occasion the BBC took proceedings in respect of a decision by the former Broadcasting Complaints Commission on the Panorama programme "Babies on Benefit". The BCC had found that the programme had been unfair to single parents. The court found that the group which had complained to the BCC, namely "The Council for One-Parent Families" had no locus to make a complaint as they had not been mentioned in the programme. Accordingly, the BCC's decision was set aside by the court.

In July 1999 the BBC successfully judicially reviewed the deci- **24.41** sion of the Broadcasting Standards Commission upholding a complaint by the electrical retailers, Dixons, against the "Watchdog" programme. In this case, the BSC had upheld a complaint by Dixons that their privacy had been infringed when the programme-makers had surreptitiously filmed some of the retailing procedures in Dixons' stores. The Divisional Court upheld the BBC's contention that the BSC decision was unjustified as these activities took place in public. In addition, the court took the view that a company such as Dixons did not have a right to privacy. That right was enjoyed by individuals rather than companies. However, the Court of Appeal upheld the BSC's approach to the case, including the idea that a corporate body has a right of privacy. At the time of writing this case is likely to go to the House of Lords.

RACIAL HATRED: PUBLIC ORDER ACT 1986

24.42 Section 164 of the 1990 Act extends the law in the Public Order Act 1986 relating to incitement to racial hatred to apply to broadcasting. So if a programme involves threatening, or abusive or insulting visual images then each of a group of persons will be guilty of an offence if—(a) he intends to stir up racial hatred, or (b) having regard to all the circumstances racial hatred is likely to be stirred up. Those who may be guilty of an offence are:

(a) the person providing the broadcast;
(b) any person by whom the programme was produced or directed, and
(c) any person by whom offending words or behaviour are used.

It is a defence for the person providing the service, or a person by whom the programme was produced or directed, to prove that (a) he did not know and had no reason to suspect that the programme would involve the offending material, and (b) having regard to the circumstances in which the programme was broadcast it was not reasonably practicable for him to secure the removal of the material. While this defence might well apply to the broadcasting organisation providing the service, it is difficult to see that either a producer or director is likely to be able to use it, by the nature of their job it would be difficult to claim ignorance. The decision of the European Court of Human Rights in *Jersild v. Denmark* (September 23, 1994) indicates that this statutory provision could offend against Article 10 of the European Convention on Human Rights. During the General Election in May 1997, the National Front party election broadcast was believed by some viewers to offend against this statutory provision. Complaints were made to the prosecuting authorities but proceedings were not brought in respect of the broadcast.

OBSCENITY

24.43 Section 163 of the 1990 Act modifies the terms of the Civic Government (Scotland) Act 1982 so as to allow prosecution of anyone responsible for the inclusion of any obscene material in a programme. The section appears wide enough to include the reporter, an independent production company (if there is one) and the broadcasting organisation itself, and possibly also the editor and producer of such a programme.

The Obscene Publications Act of 1959 (covering the broadcast- **24.44** ing of obscene material in England) does not apply in Scotland.

Although Scottish journalists are in the same legal position as **24.45** their English colleagues it may well be that the attitude of the Crown in Scotland to prosecution of obscenity was affected by the failure of the prosecution in the so-called "Glasgow Obscenity Trial" which took place in the early 1980s. This involved three men accused of running a "sex shop" selling allegedly obscene material. The trial lasted for many weeks in Glasgow Sheriff Court and the jury unanimously found the accused not guilty of all the charges.

BROADCASTING AT ELECTION TIME: THE OBLIGATION OF IMPARTIALITY AND THE REPRESENTATION OF THE PEOPLE ACT

At election time print journalists are entitled to be (and frequently **24.46** are) extremely selective and biased in their reporting of events. Such an approach in the world of tabloid newspapers is the norm rather than the exception. In contrast broadcasters have to be particularly aware of the obligations imposed upon them to be impartial. As has previously been noted in the case of the BBC this arises in terms of the BBC's Charter. In the case of the independent broadcasting companies it arises in terms of the licence which they hold from the ITC and under the Broadcasting Acts

In the latter years of the Major administration, broadcasters **24.47** began to find themselves beset by political "spin doctors", who accused radio and television journalists of bias against their particular party. Matters became increasingly heated in the run-up to the May 1997 election, during which political parties took to timing the interviews of politicians, the number of questions asked, the degree of hostility in the questions, and other matters. All of these points were then put forward as examples of a failure to be impartial. Court proceedings were raised in the course of the 1997 election, accusing broadcasters of a lack of impartiality. The Referendum Party sued the BBC, ITV and ITC in the High Court in London on the basis that they were allocated what they claimed were insufficient party political broadcasts. Their action failed. An action on the same legal basis by Sinn Fein in the Northern Irish courts against the BBC failed. An action in the Court of Session in

Scotland by the Scottish National Party against Scottish Television, ITV and the ITC, based on the claim that Alex Salmond might not be allowed to participate in the so-called "great debate" between the leaders of the main political parties, likewise failed. Despite the success of broadcasters in these proceedings, it is obvious that the obligation of impartiality must be in the forefront of the mind of every broadcast journalist when covering political matters, particularly in the run-up to General Elections.

Representation of the People Act

24.48 Although they are much less likely to cause difficulties than the obligation of impartiality, broadcasters must remember that certain duties are imposed by the Representation of the People Act 1983 on broadcasters, both in relation to parliamentary and local government elections. In the case of parliamentary elections, in a General Election the obligation arises from the date of dissolution of Parliament or from the announcement of the Queen's intention to dissolve Parliament. In the case of a parliamentary by-election the date of the issuing of the writ for the election imposes the obligation. In the case of a local government election the obligation arises five weeks before the date of the election.

24.49   The legal duty is that broadcasters must not transmit any item about the constituency or electoral area if any of the candidates at the election takes part in the item, unless that individual gives his consent, s. 93 of the 1983 Act. Further, it is an offence to broadcast from outside the United Kingdom with intent to influence voters. Broadcasts from outside the United Kingdom would, however, be permissible if they were for the purpose of supplying material to the BBC or if it were in the pursuance of an arrangement made with the ITC.

Decided cases

24.50 Journalists working in the field of broadcasting at election time should be aware of two court decisions which are instructive as to how to approach election broadcasts. The first case is English— *Marshall v. BBC* [1979]. In this case Mr Marshall (a Labour candidate in an English constituency) wished to prevent a broadcast which included reference to one of his rival candidates who was standing for the National Front. He indicated to the BBC he was unhappy about being involved in any broadcast which included reference to the National Front candidate. The BBC proposed a broadcast showing Mr Marshall taking part in electioneering— stopping people in the streets, calling at doors, etc. Initially he obtained an injunction against the BBC broadcast on the basis that he was refusing to give his consent to the transmission. On appeal, however, the Court of Appeal held that the 1983 Act, which gave a candidate a right of veto in respect of a programme in which he took part, did not entitle Mr Marshall to an injunction in this case, because the phrase "takes part in" in the context which it appeared in the Act meant an active part. Accordingly, TV pictures showing the candidate campaigning did not fall within the definition of "taking part in", and the injunction was lifted so that the programme could go ahead.

It is interesting to note that the Court of Appeal felt that if they **24.51** had come to the opposite decision they would have been allowing Mr Marshall to compel the BBC to become partial in their reporting. He would have been able to veto any broadcast which referred to the National Front candidate and therefore would force the BBC to be partisan in their broadcasting on this particular parliamentary election. That, the Court of Appeal felt, was precisely what Parliament had intended to avoid. Parliament's intention was that broadcasters should be impartial and objective during the "run-up" to an election.

The second case is from the Northern Irish Courts—*McAliskey v.* **24.52** *BBC,* 1980. It was brought by Bernadette McAliskey (formerly Bernadette Devlin) in connection with a European election. She claimed that the treatment she was to receive in a BBC programme indicated that she and various others who were standing for election to the European Parliament were more minor candidates than some of the other candidates. She made this claim on the basis that the BBC broadcast proposed to divide the candidates into two groups. In the case of one group (of which she was a member) less time would be allocated in the broadcast to their views and accordingly, she claimed, the impression would be given that they were less serious candidates.

She therefore refused her consent to the proposed broadcast and **24.53** applied to the Court for an injunction. She claimed that the BBC had a duty under its Royal Charter and licence to act fairly and impartially at election time. She also alleged that the proposed broadcast would constitute a breach of section 9(1) of the Representation of the People Act 1969.

In reply the BBC argued that the proposed broadcast did not **24.54** breach the Act and so was not an unlawful broadcast. It also alleged that it had no obligation laid upon it in terms of its charter and licence to secure a fair balance.

Mr Justice Murray in the Irish High Court delivered a full and **24.55** interesting judgment on this complex area of law. For present purposes suffice it to say that his conclusion was that the BBC had to get the consent of all 13 candidates before the item could be broadcast. If consent were not obtained from all candidates then the broadcast would become an illegal broadcast in terms of section 9 of the Act.

24.56   The new law which is contained in section 93 of the Representation of the People Act 1983 is in the same terms as section 9 of the 1969 Act so the position remains as it was when the case of McAliskey was decided by Mr Justice Murray.

24.57   Interestingly, the Representation of the People Act did not apply to the elections to the Scottish Parliament which took place in May 1999. This was undoubtedly due to the difficulty of applying the Act, which was intended for a "first past the post" system to the list system of proportional representation used for the Scottish elections. In terms of the Scotland Act, the Secretary of State for Scotland could have made an order applying the Representation of the People Act in whole or in part to the Scottish elections. In the event, he did not do so. The Representation of the People Act is criticised by broadcasters as being an obsolete piece of legislation which takes no account of the fact that General Elections are fought on a nation-wide basis, rather than being a series of 632 individual electoral contests within separate constituencies. The Government has expressed a willingness to consider the appropriateness of the Representation of the People Act continuing in its present form.

THE STRUCTURE OF BROADCASTING: BROADCASTING ORGANISATIONS

The British Broadcasting Corporation

24.58   The BBC is a Corporation incorporated by Royal Charter. The current Royal Charter was granted in 1996 and is due to run for ten years. As in previous Charters, the BBC's principal objective is to provide broadcasting services for general reception at home and abroad. In addition to the Royal Charter, the BBC has a subsidiary constitutional document which is the agreement between the BBC and the Secretary of State for Culture, Media and Sport.

24.59   The powers, responsibilities and obligations laid upon the Corporation are vested in the Board of Governors who exercise them through a permanent staff headed by the Director General as the BBC's Chief Executive Officer, and the Board of Management. The 12 Governors—who include the Chairman, Vice-chairman and three who are respectively national Governors for Scotland, Wales and Northern Ireland are appointed by the Queen in Council (on the nomination of the Government of the day). The appointment is normally for five years. Sir Robert Smith, Chief Executive of Morgan Grenfell Asset Management, is currently the National Governor for Scotland. BBC Scotland has its own Management Board, which is headed by the Chief Executive, who is entitled Controller, Scotland. The current Controller, Scotland is John McCormick.

The Government's Powers in relation to the BBC: In terms of **24.60** clause 13 (4) of the licence the Home Secretary "may from time to time by notice in writing require the Corporation to refrain at any specified time or at all times from sending any matter or matters of any class specified in such notice". Formally this clause confers on the Government absolute power to determine what the BBC may or may not broadcast. The clause has never been used to ban any specific programmes. As noted above, in October 1988 the clause was used to restrict broadcast coverage of statements supporting terrorism in Northern Ireland. This was the first exercise of the Government's power under Clause 13 (4). The Home Secretary's decision has been vigorously challenged by journalists in the courts. The House of Lords, however, has refused to interfere with the notice. The notice was revoked in 1994.

The BBC's Obligations: In terms of section 13 of the licence and **24.61** Agreement the BBC is required to "broadcast an impartial account day by day prepared by professional reporters of the proceedings of both Houses of Parliament". This obligation does not cover the Scottish Parliament in its present form but, as a matter of practice, BBC Scotland will broadcast daily coverage of the Scottish Parliament and its Committees. The BBC is also required to broadcast official announcements whenever asked to do so by one of Her Majesty's Ministers. In reality this is achieved without ministerial intervention. Normally major Government announcements are reported naturally as a matter of news interest in BBC broadcasts.

The BBC is forbidden in terms of its licence to transmit **24.62** television images of very brief duration which "might convey a message to influence the minds of an audience without their being aware, or fully aware, of what has been done". This is a safeguard against subliminal advertising or indoctrination. In terms of its Licence the BBC is required to refrain from expressing its own opinion on current affairs or on matters of public policy other than broadcasting. This requirement underlines one of the major differences between the press and the broadcasting media in Britain.

Newspapers are at liberty to express their own editorial views on any subject they choose. Broadcasting authorities are specifically prohibited from doing so.

24.63 *Finance*: The BBC relies on two principal sources of income:

(1) The licence fees paid by the public;
(2) A grant from the Treasury in respect of World Services provided for overseas listeners.

24.64 *Broadcasting Councils*: These are set up in terms of article 10 of the BBC's Charter. There is also a Broadcasting Council for Scotland which was established in 1952. There are similar Councils for both Wales and Northern Ireland. The Councils' main functions are to control the policy and content of radio and television services of the BBC which are provided primarily for reception in the countries they represent. In this they are required to have full regard to the distinctive culture, language, interests and taste of the peoples of the respective country. They may also advise the Corporation on any other broadcasting matters which may affect the peoples in these countries. Constitutionally, the Councils' link with the Corporation is through their chairmen who are Governors of the BBC and are entitled National Governors. In the Broadcasting Council for Scotland the National Governor is assisted by 11 members of the Council, who are part-time appointees to reflect a reasonable cross-section of Scottish interests, and are appointed by the Corporation on the recommendation of a special panel.

24.65 The BBC is a legal entity and can sue and be sued in the courts. It does not enjoy any special rights or privileges, under the laws of defamation or contempt of court.

Independent broadcasters

24.66 In contrast, independent broadcasters, such as Granada and STV, are limited companies who enjoy the right to broadcast in terms of a licence held for a fixed period. The holders of licences in Scotland are Scottish Television and Grampian (Border TV, based in Carlisle, broadcasts in the Lake District and the Scottish Border area). Their licences were awarded in 1991 and last for a 10-year period from January 1, 1993. Since the award of these licences Scottish Television and Grampian have come under the common ownership of Scottish Media Group plc.

The Independent Television Commission

24.67 The Broadcasting Act of 1990 set up a new organisation—the Independent Television Commission, with headquarters at 70 Brompton Road, London SW3 1EY and a Scottish office at 123

Blythswood Street, Glasgow G2 4AN. The ITC has replaced the old IBA and Cable Authority. The ITC is not a broadcasting organisation but a licensing body with supervisory and regulatory powers. It issues licences for (a) terrestrial television, (b) satellite television and (c) cable television. There are eight to 10 members of the ITC, one of whom has to be Scottish. Members of the Commission are appointed for up to five years at a time.

The Commission, an independent body which is intended to be **24.68** financially self-supporting, is accountable to the Secretary of State, to whom it must submit annual reports to be laid before Parliament.

The Commission's function is to regulate in accordance with the **24.69** Act the provision of:

(a) television programme services from places in the United Kingdom by persons other than the BBC and the Welsh Authority;
(b) additional services from places in the United Kingdom —in effect, Teletext services and sub-titling for the deaf;
(c) multiplex services;
(d) digital additional services (in the case of digital, these are likely to be "super" teletext services, such as financial and business information).

The Commission's duty is to discharge its functions in respect of **24.70** the licensed services so as to ensure that a wide range of such services is available throughout the United Kingdom and to ensure fair and effective competition in the provision of such services. It is also its job in respect of licensing to ensure the provision of such services are of high quality and offer a wide range of programmes. Principally therefore the Commission is an organisation which grants licences to television and radio broadcasters other than the BBC and Welsh Authority. The Commission has a discretion as to whom to award the licence and regarding the terms of a licence.

REQUIREMENTS AS TO LICENSED SERVICES

The ITC is required to do all that it can to ensure that every **24.71** licensed service complies with certain requirements. These are listed in the Broadcasting Act 1990:

(a) That nothing is included in the programmes which offends against good taste or decency or is likely to encourage incitement to crime or lead to disorder or to be offensive to public feelings;

(b) That any news given (in whatever form) in its programmes is presented with due accuracy and impartiality;

(c) That due impartiality is preserved by the person providing the service on matters of political or industrial controversy or relating to current public policy;

(d) That due responsibility is exercised with respect to the content of any of its religious programmes; and

(e) That subliminal broadcasting does not take place.

24.72 For Independent Television broadcasters the ITC's regulatory function is extremely important. Journalists working in this sector should familiarise themselves with the ITC Programme Code. In most cases Independent Television broadcasters will have in-house Compliance Officers who should be able to liase and advise the working journalist in the field on aspects of the ITC Code. The current Code was promulgated in January 1993.

24.73 Perhaps the most important areas of the Code for journalists are that it covers filming and recording members of the public, the use of hidden microphones and cameras, interviewing of children and recognises the citizen's right to a degree of privacy. For the broadcaster the Code has something to say on the use of foul language, sex and nudity, bad taste in humour, the portrayal of violence, hypnotism, the portrayal of people with disabilities and a great deal to say on the scheduling of particular programmes. It contains rules on Party Political and Parliamentary broadcasting. It covers the reporting of terrorism, crime and anti-social behaviour. If its Code is breached the ITC has the power to impose financial penalties on its licence holders. Currently, that penalty is 3 per cent of "qualifying revenue" (defined in the Broadcasting Act 1990, s. 19) for the first breach. For subsequent breaches the ITC can fine up to 5 per cent of qualifying revenue.

24.74 The ITC can also require the licence holder to broadcast a correction or an apology. Finally, the licence holder can be required by the ITC not to repeat the offending programme.

24.75 The existence of the ITC as a regulatory body means that programme makers working in the independent sector are in the unenviable position of facing criticism and possible penalties from not one but two regulatory bodies, namely, the ITC and the BSC. It is, of course, perfectly possible for one of these bodies to reject a complaint while the other upholds it.

Radio Authority

24.76 The Broadcasting Act 1990 established an entirely new regulatory body for independent radio. The Radio Authority established by section 83 of the 1990 Act consists of a Chairman, Deputy Chairman and between four and ten other members. Appointments are made by the Secretary of State. No Governor or employee of the BBC, member or employee of Channel 4, member of the Welsh Authority, member of the BCC or the BSC can be a member of the Radio Authority. Appointments are made for a maximum period of five years. The Authority's function is to grant licences for and regulate the provision of independent radio services. Independent Radio has only been a phenomenon in this country since 1973, having been illegal (or pirate) before that time. The explosion in the market has meant that the Radio Authority, although a very new arrival on the broadcasting scene is an enormously important body.

The Radio Authority grants independent radio services licenses. **24.77** It must be satisfied that a person applying for the licence is a fit and proper person to hold it. Licences can be transferred but the Radio Authority has to approve such transfers. The 1990 Act, s. 87 lays down general conditions which apply to all licences granted by the Radio Authority. In terms of section 90 the Radio Authority is placed under an obligation to do all it can to secure that every licensed service complies with the requirements that;

(a) nothing is included in its programmes which offends against good taste or decency, is likely to encourage or incite crime, to lead to disorder or to be offensive to public feeling;

(b) any news given (in whatever form) in its programmes is presented with due accuracy and impartiality;

(c) its programmes do not include any technique which exploits the possibility of conveying a message to, or otherwise influencing the minds of, persons listening to the programmes, without their being aware of, or fully aware of, what has occurred (*i.e.* subliminal messages).

These, of course, are similar provisions to those found in the ITC's Code for Television.

If the Radio Authority is satisfied that the holder of a sound **24.78** broadcasting licence has failed to comply with any licence condition, or with any direction, given by the Authority, then it may serve on him a notice. The independent radio broadcaster has a period within which to comply with the notice. If he fails to do so, the licence can be withdrawn.

For journalists it is important to note that in terms of section **24.79** 109(3) the Radio Authority has the power in the event of an independent radio broadcaster failing to comply with one of the terms of its licence to enforce the broadcasting of a correction or an apology. Further, by section 110, the Radio Authority has the power to impose financial penalties or to suspend or shorten licence periods should the licence holder fail to comply with the conditions of the licence. A fine can be up to £50,000. The Secretary of State has power to increase this sum.

Broadcasting and the Scottish Parliament

24.80 Broadcasting is not a devolved function. It follows that the Scottish Parliament has no legal role to play in this area. However Scottish broadcasters have agreed to appear before the Culture Committee of the Parliament—the first appearance was in March 2000.

KEY POINTS

24.81 The law of defamation and contempt of court apply equally to journalists working in the field of radio or TV broadcasting. In addition to the courts, journalists working in broadcasting have to concern themselves with regulatory bodies. The Broadcasting Standards Commission will look at (1) unfairness; (2) unwarranted infringement of privacy; (3) taste and decency; and (4) portrayal of sex and violence.

24.82 In the private or independent sector, radio broadcasters must observe the Code promulgated by the Radio Authority. Similarly, in the independent television sector the ITC's Code must be obeyed. Both the Radio Authority and the ITC have the power to instruct the broadcasting of apologies and/or corrections. They have the power to modify or revoke licences. They have the power to fine.

CHAPTER 25

HUMAN RIGHTS ACT 1998 AND PRIVACY

From a journalistic point of view, the European Convention on **25.01**
Human Rights contains two important rights: Article 8, the right to
privacy; and Article 10, the right to freedom of expression.

Despite being an early signatory to it, the United Kingdom did **25.02**
not incorporate the Convention into domestic law. Therefore,
when a United Kingdom citizen felt that these rights had been
breached, his or her only redress was to go to the European Court
of Human Rights in Strasbourg. (Neither the Court nor the
Convention has any connection with the European Union.)

The United Kingdom has fallen foul of Strasbourg's rulings on a **25.03**
very large number of occasions, and notably in relation to freedom
of expression. In most cases, Westminster has legislated with a view
to getting into line with Strasbourg's rulings. As a result, thus far
the United Kingdom has had to alter its laws on legal health,
prisoners' rights, corporal punishment, telephone tapping,
homosexual discrimination, interrogation procedures and access to
children. Nevertheless, going to the European Court of Human
Rights has always been slightly unwieldy.

With the coming into force of the 1998 Human Rights Act, **25.04**
United Kingdom citizens can rely upon their Convention rights in
"domestic courts, tribunals and 'disputes with public authorities'".

Public authorities

There is some dispute as to who "public authorities" are. They are **25.05**
defined somewhat vaguely in the Act as "any person certain of
whose functions are functions of a public nature", unless the
"nature of the [unlawful] act is private". If, for example, the BBC is
a public authority for the purposes of allotting party election
broadcasts, does it follow that it remains a public authority in
relation to employment disputes?

It is anticipated that the Press Complaints Commission and the **25.06**
Broadcasting Standards Commission will be public authorities,
certainly in relation to their decisions. So will the Scottish courts
and tribunals.

25.07 Many lawyers feel that the "public authorities" argument does not matter, since the most important decision makers, *i.e.* the courts, have to take account of European Convention rights in deciding disputes, even between individuals. The courts and tribunals will also require to take account of existing Strasbourg case decisions. But they will not be "bound" by individual Strasbourg decisions. It is recognised, first, that individual States have what Strasbourg calls a "margin of appreciation"—a degree of cultural discretion as to how they implement law within their own courts. Secondly, the Convention is to be a "living instrument", growing and changing to meet particular social circumstances. Thirdly, membership of the Court has changed often and newer democracies are joining in, so the approach of Strasbourg will not be static or even predictable.

Acts of Parliament

25.08 The Human Rights Act does not permit the courts to strike down Westminster legislation because it does not comply with the Convention. Instead, if they cannot, by any stretch of interpretation, reconcile the domestic legislation with the Convention right, they are to issue a "Declaration of Incompatibility". It is expected that remedial legislation with then be put in place quickly.

25.09 In relation to the Scottish Parliament, the position is somewhat different. Since the Scotland Act 1998 does not permit the Scottish Parliament to legislate in contravention of international treaty obligations (including the European Convention on Human Rights), any Scottish Acts which the Scottish judiciary considers do not comply with the Convention may be treated as void. This is why temporary sheriffs are no longer used in Scottish courts. It is expected, however, that every attempt will be made, both north and south of the border, to interpret legislation so as to make it fit with the Convention and avoid such political embarrassments. The legislation is also to be looked at carefully before it is passed, to check for compliance.

Privacy

25.10 Article 8 of the Convention states:

> "1. Everyone has the right to respect for his private and family life, his home and his correspondence.
> 2. There shall be no interference by a public authority with the exercise of this right except such as is in accordance with the law and is necessary in a democratic society in the interests of national security, public safety or the economic well-being of

the country, for the prevention of disorder or crime, for the protection of health or morals, or for the protection of the rights and freedoms of others."

Freedom of expression

Article 10 states: **25.11**

"1. Everyone has the right to freedom of expression. This right shall include freedom to hold opinions and to receive and impart information and ideas without interference by public authority and regardless of frontiers. This Article shall not prevent States from requiring the licensing of broadcasting, television or cinema enterprises.

2. The exercise of these freedoms, since it carries with it duties and responsibilities, may be subject to such formalities, conditions, restrictions or penalties as are prescribed by law and are necessary in a democratic society, in the interests of national security, territorial integrity or public safety, for the prevention of disorder or crime, for the protection of health morals, for the protection of the reputation or rights of others, for preventing the disclosure of information received in confidence, or for maintaining the authority and impartiality of the judiciary."

Conflicts between privacy and freedom of expression

Other Articles of the Convention may also be of significance to the   **25.12**
journalist. The Article 6 right to a fair trial may be expected to have a place in arguments about contempt of court and disclosure of sources. The Article 11 right of freedom of assembly and association may be of assistance in relation to the investigative and reporting process. However, it is the interplay between the Article 8 right of privacy and the Article 10 right of freedom of expression which is likely to be of most interest to the journalist in the years to come. Here there are grounds for optimism, since the European Court has consistently defended freedom of expression as having a very high place within the hierarchy of human rights.

What is privacy?

There has never been a coherent attempt of the Strasbourg Court   **25.13**
to draw the line between public and private life. Most of the cases relate either to children or to sexuality, although some deal with noise and other environmental pollution. Significance has been attached to whether the person concerned had "a legitimate

expectation of privacy" in the circumstances, *e.g.* in using the telephone in her own office. Few deal with the issue of when media coverage of a celebrity becomes unacceptably intrusive.

25.14 Earl Spencer and his former wife were unsuccessful in arguing that the United Kingdom had failed to protect their rights in relation to photographs and coverage of Countess Spencer's treatment in a clinic for eating disorders and alcoholism. This was on the basis that they had not "exhausted their domestic remedies", *i.e.* tried everything before the English courts. The Spencers' argument was that English law did not include an action for breach of privacy on the basis of which they could claim damages. It was held that they could have pursued an action for breach of confidence as well as getting non-financial remedies from the Press Complaints Commission. The Court in Strasbourg does not itself tend to make large financial awards.

Home and family

25.15 There have been cases where search of a home for civil or criminal proceedings in the United Kingdom has been held to amount to violation, even if the premises are partly used for business purposes. In particular circumstances, however, this may be justified as being for protection of the rights of others.

25.16 Family life includes the extended family, grandparents and grandchildren. What is necessary is evidence of a genuine and close family tie—fostering, step-parenting, cohabitation and adoption have all been included. Something may fall within "private life" category even if it does not fall within the "family" as such—homosexual relationships have so far been dealt with in this way.

Prisoners

25.17 The position of prisoners has generated a lot of Article 8 case law. In particular, the European Court has allowed substantial freedom to a prisoner to correspond with his lawyer and to seek media intervention to investigate an alleged miscarriage of justice.

Telephone tapping

25.18 Telephone tapping is accepted in principle by the United Kingdom, but has to be "prescribed by law" and kept within bounds. The United Kingdom lost a case brought by senior policewoman Alison Halford because the safeguards then in place were inadequate.

Conflicting interests of privacy and confidence

25.19 In *Gaskin v. U.K.*, a man who had spent almost all his life in jail was refused access to his Social Security records, which he said he needed to establish his identity. Some of the information had been given in confidence. The Strasbourg Court said that the United Kingdom had violated Article 8 not so much by refusing to disclose the records, which might have been justified, but because there was no independent adjudication system to decide on the appropriate balancing of conflicting interests in such a situation.

Freedom of expression: the case law

The European Court has consistently held that freedom of expres- **25.20** sion, including unpopular expression, is an essential foundation of democracy and an important line of defence for human rights. Therefore, any limit on freedom of expression must be "proportionate" to the aim pursued. There are certain limits on freedom of expression. The European Court has upheld in the past the imprisonment of a soldier for publishing an article critical of army officers, the denial of state teaching posts to persons sympathetic to communism, the prosecution of artists for painting explicit pictures in public and the prosecution of a journalist for asserting that two judges were not independent.

The public's right to be informed

However, the European Court did find against the United King- **25.21** dom and for the *Sunday Times* on the Thalidomide issue. There was an injunction against the appearance of an article on the Thalidomide tragedy whilst there was an ongoing litigation on the amount of compensation due. The Court said: "The Thalidomide disaster was a matter of undisputed public concern . . . Article 10 guarantees not only the freedom of the press to inform the public but also the right of the public to be properly informed." The Court is also looking increasingly closely at large defamation awards. In the recent case of *Bergens Tidende v. Norway*, a defamation award against newspaper articles critical of a cosmetic surgeon was held to be a breach of Article 10. Regardless of the facts of the case, the mere size of the damages, in an extreme case, may breach Article 10.

National security and prior restraints

The Strasbourg jurisprudence is especially wary of "prior **25.22** restraint", *i.e.* gagging orders. In relation to the famous *Spycatcher* excerpts to be published by the *Observer, Sunday Times* and *Guardian*, the Court held that the original injunctions were valid because the State was given great leeway in the name of national security. However, after the book had been published in the USA, national security no longer amounted to an adequate reason for restriction.

Licensing

25.23 Article 10 allows States to licence broadcasting. Article 10 does not constitute a right of access to broadcasting facilities, but it does include the right not to have properly-licensed broadcasts jammed or disrupted. The Court is willing to scrutinise and sometimes overturn licence refusals.

Commercial speech

25.24 Advertising and commercial activities are protected as exercises of free speech, although the level of protection is less than that accorded to the expression of political ideas. Strasbourg has stepped in to protect the rights of members of professional bodies who have been reprimanded by these bodies for certain types of free speech.

Political speech

25.25 The Court also found in favour of an Austrian journalist who was taken to court for calling a politician's ideas "Nazi". They upheld that a journalist was entitled to be provocative in order to draw the public's attention to the ideas and attitudes of political leaders. A high level of protection is given to political speech. This was recognised by the House of Lords in *Derbyshire County Council v. Times Newspapers*. This English case held that a local authority had no right to sue for libel in respect of its administrative reputation, when no financial loss was alleged. The principal reason for this finding was that it would otherwise interfere with Article 10 freedom of expression.

25.26 In an Icelandic case in 1992, the applicant was prosecuted for defamation, having published an article containing reports of police brutality. The Court held that interference was unjustified having regard to the importance of the subject, the fact that the language used was not excessive and that the purpose of the article was to prompt debate about the need for a reformed police complaints system. In another 1992 Austrian case, the court held that there had been a violation when a journalist was prosecuted for referring to a politician's spent conviction for a traffic offence 20 years earlier.

The public domain

25.27 In 1990, an environmental campaigner was fined for having disclosed, at a press conference, steps taken by an investigating judge in pending proceedings. The Court considered that at the time of disclosure most of the relevant information was already in the public domain and therefore no restriction on the applicant's right to freedom of expression was justified.

Section 12 of the Human Rights Act 1998

Section 12 of the Human Rights Act 1998 was introduced as a **25.28** result of strong representations from the media. However, section 12 can be employed by anyone, not just "the media". It applies if a court is considering whether to grant any relief which, if granted, might affect the exercise of the Convention right to freedom of expression. This section reflects the pre-eminence given to the Article 10 right to freedom of expression by the European Court jurisprudence and its distaste for prior restraints. Section 12 is intended to stop gagging orders from being obtained behind the journalist's (or other defender's) back. The defender has to be notified of the hearing unless "there are compelling reasons" why not. There is to be no restraint on publication unless the Court is satisfied that the applicant is "likely to establish that publication should not be allowed" in a full hearing at the end of the day.

Section 12 does not cover merely obvious areas such as defam- **25.29** ation cases, but any order which, in effect, would operate as a gag. Thus, breach of confidence and breach of copyright actions may also come under this heading. So might orders preventing the identification of people involved in civil actions.

The Court must have particular regard to the importance of the **25.30** Convention right to freedom of expression. Where the proceedings relate to material which the respondent claims, or which appears to the Court, to be journalistic, literary or artistic material (or to conduct connected to such material), the Court must give weight to:

- (a) the extent to which:
    - (i) material has, or is about to become, available to the public; or
    - (ii) it is, or would be, in the public interest for the material to be published.
- (b) any relevant privacy code.

"Courts" includes a tribunal and "relief" includes "any remedy **25.31** or order (other than in criminal proceedings)".

Contempt of Court and Article 6

Contempt of court rulings which affect freedom of expression may **25.32** bear—at any rate as regards pre-trial publicity—on the right to a fair trial. This right is guaranteed by Article 6 of the Convention and is also regarded as extremely important by Europe. This Article 6 right does not relate simply to criminal trials, but applies to the determination of "civil rights and obligations". This could be pled against the media when they are refusing to reveal sources who may be in breach of, for example, their contracts of employment or duties of confidentiality.

The Future

25.33 The effects of the Human Rights Act are expected to be striking initially. The impact of the privacy right, in particular, will be novel. Privacy has been protected to some extent within the United Kingdom by actions for breach of confidence, copyright and (more in England than in Scotland) trespass. Breach of the peace may be an issue also, where Scottish journalists have been felt to be intrusive. Early attempts to challenge the wide-ranging breach of the peace offence in Scotland as being too vague to pass muster in ECHR terms have failed.

25.34 The Human Rights Act attaches significance to codes such as the PCC and BSC produce, as well as any internal guidelines which the media organisation may have. In some cases, these guidelines (such as the BBC's Producers Guidelines) may be a deal more restrictive than the law would require, and failure to follow them will be a factor weighing against the journalist before the Court. It should also be remembered that the Human Rights Act 1998 does not exist in isolation from other important contemporary legislation on access to personal information—notably the Data Protection Act 1998 and the pending Freedom of Information legislation from Westminster and Holyrood.

25.35 The real concern about the privacy law which is, in effect, being introduced by the Human Rights Act is that it will choke off investigation and evidence-gathering for journalistic purposes, *e.g.* undercover filming. The right to publish or broadcast is, however, strengthened because of the emphasis in the Strasbourg jurisprudence on freedom of expression.

KEY POINTS

25.36 The Human Rights Act 1998 requires public authorities—including courts—to respect the fundamental rights set out in the European Convention of Human Rights, and to have regard to the decisions of the Strasbourg Court. Two of these fundamental rights are the Article 10 right to freedom of expression and the Article 8 right to privacy. Freedom of expression covers political, commercial and other speech and writing in all media. Privacy covers the home, family life, correspondence and associated areas. Balancing these rights when they conflict may not be easy or obvious, but a high value is given to freedom of expression. Section 12 of the Act should operate to prevent prior restraints on freedom of expression in most cases. Although reporting restrictions on trials, contempt findings, etc, will require to be justified as necessary, the right to a fair trial is also enshrined in the Convention and Act, so there needs to be a balance there also. The Act gives added emphasis to voluntary codes like the PCC.

CHAPTER 26

THE REHABILITATION OF OFFENDERS ACT 1974

Purpose of Act

26.01 The purpose of this Act is to enable people with criminal convictions to wipe certain old offences off their records and continue their lives free from the constant threat of disclosure. The Act achieves its purpose by prohibiting the telling of the truth and legalising lying. It uses two key concepts, the "rehabilitated person" and the "spent" conviction.

Restriction of information about spent convictions

26.02 From the journalist's point of view one of the main effects of the Act is that it restricts the availability of information about the spent convictions of a rehabilitated person. A rehabilitated person is, in general, to be treated for all purposes in law as if he had not committed the offence in question or been charged, prosecuted, convicted or sentenced as a result. Evidence of spent convictions is not normally admissible in any judicial proceedings in Great Britain and a person is not, in such proceedings, liable to be asked or bound to answer any question relating to his past which cannot be answered without acknowledging or referring to a spent conviction.

26.03   However, there are important exceptions to these rules. The Act does not affect the admission of evidence as to a person's previous convictions (a) in any criminal proceedings before a court in Great Britain, (b) in service disciplinary proceedings, (c) in most proceedings (such as children's hearings, or adoption, guardianship or custody proceedings) relating to children under 18. A party or witness in any proceedings can also waive the protection of the Act and consent to the admission of evidence about his spent convictions or the determination of an issue involving such evidence.

26.04   In most non-judicial contexts too, such as applying for a job or filling in a proposal form for an insurance policy, a person is not bound to disclose spent convictions in answer to any question about his past and is not to be subjected to any legal liability or prejudice for his non-disclosure. The Secretary of State has power to make orders excluding or modifying the application of these provisions in particular circumstances.

It is also an offence for a person, such as a court official, police **26.05** officer or civil servant, who in the course of his duty has access to official records, to disclose, "otherwise than in the course of those duties", information about spent convictions. There is a defence which covers disclosure to, or at the express request of, the rehabilitated person.

The phrase "otherwise than in the course of those duties" **26.06** probably relates to disclosure by one official to another, and is probably not intended to cover, for example, disclosure by a press officer to the press. If such disclosure to the press were regarded as covered by the phrase, the further question would arise whether the journalist receiving the information was a "person who, in the course of his official duties . . . had custody of or access to any official record of the information contained there". It would be difficult to argue that he was. He would receive the information in the course of his job but he would not have custody of or access to it in the course of his official duties.

On a proper reading of the Act the obligation would seem to be **26.07** on court officials, police officers and other officials to hold back the relevant information and not on the press. This view is supported by section 9(4), which makes it an offence to obtain information about spent convictions from any official record by means of any fraud, dishonesty or bribe. The purpose of section 9 of the Act, in short, is to keep information on spent convictions within the confines of official records, and the effect of sections 4 and 9 is to restrict the information available to the press and public.

Effects on law of defamation

The other main effect of the Act from the point of view of the **26.08** media is that it limits the availability of certain defences to an action of defamation. First, a defender in such an action cannot rely on the defence of *veritas* in relation to a spent conviction if the publication is proved to have been made with malice.

It is not clear exactly what is meant by "malice" in this context. **26.09** It cannot include, as it does in some other areas, the lack of any honest belief in the truth of the statement made. On the other hand it probably includes an intention to injure wholly or mainly for the gratification of personal spite or ill will. A newspaper which published details of a rehabilitated person's spent convictions because it was annoyed by his unco-operative attitude over some other matter would, if its malice could be proved, be unable to rely on the defence of *veritas*.

26.10   Secondly, a defender in an action for defamation cannot rely on the privilege attaching to a fair and accurate report of judicial proceedings if it is proved that the report contained a reference to evidence which was ruled to be inadmissible in the proceedings because it related to a spent conviction. This provision does not apply to bona fide law reports and reports or accounts of judicial proceedings "published for bona fide educational, scientific or professional purposes, or given in the course of any lecture, class or discussion given or held for any of these purposes".

26.11   These are the only two areas in which the law of defamation is altered by the Act, which expressly provides that spent convictions can be referred to in other respects to enable a defender to rely on any defence of *veritas* or fair comment or of absolute or qualified privilege which is available to him. Moreover, the law of defamation is not in any way altered by the Act if the publication complained of took place before the conviction was spent.

Sentences subject to rehabilitation

26.12 Some sentences are excluded from rehabilitation under the Act. The convictions to which these sentences relate accordingly never become spent convictions and the person on whom they are imposed never becomes a rehabilitated person in relation to them. These sentences excluded from rehabilitation are as follows:

(a) a sentence of imprisonment for life;
(b) a sentence of imprisonment or corrective training for a term exceeding 30 months;
(c) a sentence of preventive detention; and
(d) a sentence of detention during Her Majesty's pleasure or for life, or for a term exceeding 30 months, passed under section 53 of the Children and Young Persons Act 1933 or under section 57 of the Children and Young Persons (Scotland) Act 1937 (section 5).

All other sentences are subject to rehabilitation.

Effect of subsequent conviction

26.13 A subsequent conviction after the rehabilitation period does not revive the earlier conviction: it remains spent.

26.14   The effect of a subsequent conviction during the rehabilitation period depends on its nature. If it is a conviction for a minor offence (in Scotland, an offence within the jurisdiction of the district courts) it has no effect on rehabilitation. If it is a more serious offence but does not involve a sentence excluded from rehabilitation (i.e. heavier than 30 months' imprisonment or detention) it delays the expiry of the rehabilitated period until the end of the rehabilitation period applicable to the new offence or the old offence whichever ends later. If the subsequent conviction involves a sentence excluded from rehabilitation then it precludes rehabilitation altogether and the old offence never becomes spent.

Rehabilitation periods

The Act provides for different rehabilitation periods depending on **26.15** the gravity of the sentence and the age of the offender. In the case of adult offenders the scale is as in Table A.

In the case of persons under 17 these periods are reduced by half **26.16** and there is a special scale for certain sentences confined to young offenders (Table B).

The rehabilitation period applicable to an order discharging a **26.17** person absolutely for an offence is six months from the date of the conviction and the same period applies to a discharge by a children's hearing. If a person is put on probation the rehabilitation period ends one year after the date of the conviction or when the probation order ceases to have effect, whichever is the later. The same rule applies if a person is conditionally discharged, or bound over to keep the peace or be of good behaviour.

A similar rule—one year or the duration of a period of care, **26.18** residential training or supervision, whichever is the longer—applies in relation to various orders dealing with children and young persons, including a supervision requirement. If a convicted person is made the subject of a hospital order under the Mental Health Act 1959 or the Mental Health (Scotland) Act 1983 or the Mental Health (Scotland) Act 1984 (with or without an order restricting discharge) the rehabilitation period ends five years after the date of the conviction or two years after the hospital order ceases to have effect, whichever is later.

Finally, if a convicted person has any disqualification imposed on **26.19** him (such as a disqualification from driving) the rehabilitation period ends when the disqualification ceases to have effect. The same rule applies to a "disability, prohibition or other penalty".

These are the main rules on rehabilitation periods but the Act **26.20** contains other provisions and also empowers the Secretary of State to make orders varying the periods. The result is a complex piece of legislation. It will often be difficult to know whether a conviction is spent. Fortunately, as we have seen, the main sanction of the Act lies in the law of defamation and, so long as there is no malice, and no reference in a report of judicial proceedings to evidence actually ruled to be inadmissible under the Act, the journalist has the protection of the usual defences and privileges and has nothing to fear from the Act.

"Rehabilitated person" and "spent conviction"

26.21 On the expiry of the relevant length of time, the person concerned becomes a rehabilitated person and the conviction becomes a spent conviction. This is subject to the rules on subsequent conviction considered above, since rehabilitation under the Act is designed for those who do not commit other serious offences during the rehabilitation period. It is also subject to the sentence being served, at least in the case of imprisonment and other custodial sentences. Non-payment of a fine does not prevent rehabilitation; nor does failure to comply with any requirement of a probation order, suspended sentence or supervision order). The escaped convict does not become a rehabilitated person.

Application to service disciplinary proceedings

26.22 Findings of guilt by army, navy or air force courts-martial or other competent authorities are treated as convictions for purposes of the Act but only if (a) the offence is also a civil offence or comes within a specified list of service offences or (b) the punishment is imprisonment; cashiering, discharge with ignominy or dismissal with disgrace from Her Majesty's service; dismissal from Her Majesty's service; or detention for a term of three months or more. The rehabilitation period for cashiering, discharge with ignominy or dismissal with disgrace from Her Majesty's service is 10 years; for dismissal from Her Majesty's service, seven years; and for a sentence of detention, five years: these periods are halved if the person sentenced was under 17 years of age when found guilty.

Application to children's hearings

26.23 Children's hearings do not convict or sentence the children who come before them. Their approach is intended to be therapeutic rather than punitive. Nevertheless it was thought desirable that people brought before them on an offence ground should have the chance of becoming rehabilitated persons under the Act. If that were not the case, a boy sent to a residential school for stealing lead from a roof would be denied the opportunity of living down his offence.

26.24 Accordingly, the Act provides that if a child is referred to a children's hearing on an offence ground and that ground is either accepted by the child (and, where necessary, his parent) or established to the satisfaction of the sheriff on a referral to him, then the acceptance or establishment of the ground shall be treated for the purposes of the Act as a conviction and any disposal of the case by a children's hearing as a sentence.

Application to foreign courts

The Act applies to convictions by or before courts outside Great **26.25** Britain. In calculating rehabilitation periods in relation to such convictions a sentence is treated as if it were the nearest British equivalent. But a conviction by a court outside Great Britain does not delay or preclude rehabilitation in relation to a previous conviction.

KEY POINTS

The aim of the Rehabilitation of Offenders Act is to allow people **26.26** with convictions to live without the constant threat of having their past dredged up. The rehabilitated person is generally to be treated as if he had never committed the offence. After a certain period of time, the conviction is regarded as "spent".

Evidence of previous convictions is, however, admitted in crimi- **26.27** nal proceedings.

In a defamation action involving a spent conviction a journalist **26.28** cannot rely on a defence of *veritas* if the publication is proved to have been made with malice. Sentences of imprisonment or detention of more than 30 months are not subject to rehabilitation.

CHAPTER 27

PRINTER AND PUBLISHER

27.01 There are various Acts of Parliament which apply primarily to the editorial or managerial side of the newspaper business but which journalists should know. These provisions apply to both Scotland and England unless otherwise stated.

Name of printer

27.02 The name and address of the printer must be printed on the first or last page of every newspaper, periodical and most other printed matter in Scotland or England (Newspapers, Printers and Reading Rooms Repeal Act 1869; Printers Imprint Act 1961). If this is not done, printers, publishers and distributors can be fined up to £50 for each offending copy. Prosecutions must be brought in the name of the Lord Advocate in Scotland.

Registration

27.03 Newspapers must register annually with the General Post Office in London to enjoy the benefit of reduced rates of postage.

Keeping copies

27.04 The printer of a paper (if it is printed for hire, reward, gain or profit—which covers most cases) must keep at least one copy, showing on it the name and address of the person for whom it was printed. He must preserve it for six months and show it to any justice of the peace requiring to see it in that time. Failure to comply may result in a fine (Newspapers, Printers and Reading Rooms Repeal Act 1869).

Delivering copies to museums and libraries

27.05 The publisher of every newspaper, periodical or book published in the United Kingdom must within a month of publication deliver a copy to the British Library, at his own expense (Copyright Act 1911).

On written demand within 12 months of publication, he must **27.06** also deliver a copy to the Bodleian Library, Oxford; the University Library, Cambridge; the National Library, Scotland; the Library of Trinity College, Dublin and in certain cases the National Library of Wales. A separate demand need not be made for each copy of a newspaper. One demand can cover all numbers subsequently published.

There is a fine and the value of the paper, book or magazine, for **27.07** failure to comply with these provisions.

Obscene matter

Section 51 of the Civic Government (Scotland) Act 1982 makes it **27.08** an offence to display any obscene material (any book, magazine, bill, paper, print, film, tape, disc or other kind of recording, photograph, drawing or painting) in a public place, which means a place to which the public are allowed access, whether on payment or otherwise. It bans the publication, reproduction, sale, distribution, printing and keeping of obscene material.

The penalty for contravention is, on summary conviction, a fine **27.09** not exceeding £2,000 or imprisonment for up to three months, or, on indictment, a fine of no stated limit or imprisonment for up to two years, or both in each case. There is a defence where it can be proved all due diligence was used to avoid an offence.

The section was extended to television and sound broadcasts by **27.10** the Broadcasting Act 1990.

CHAPTER 28

ADVERTISEMENTS

28.01 The publication of certain advertisements is illegal and can result in a fairly heavy fine or imprisonment or both.

Medical advertisements

28.02 It is an offence to take part in the publication of an advertisement containing an offer to treat any person for cancer, or to prescribe a remedy or give advice on the treatment of that disease (Cancer Act 1939, section 4).

28.03 The Medicines Act 1968 introduced a set of offences concerning medical advertisements generally. Under the Act it is an offence to issue, at the request or with the consent of "a commercially interested party" (a term which includes most manufacturers and suppliers of medicines), a false or misleading advertisement relating to medicinal products.

28.04 An advertisement is false or misleading for this purpose if it falsely describes the medicinal products or if it is likely to mislead as to their nature, quality, uses or effects.

28.05 In the case of certain medicinal products which are subject to a licence it is also an offence to issue an advertisement containing recommendations other than those authorised by the licence. In both cases, however, it is a defence for an accused person to prove that he did not know, and could not with reasonable diligence have discovered, that the advertisement was false or misleading or contained unauthorised recommendations.

28.06 Where a product licence is in force for medicinal products of a particular description only the holder of the licence can authorise advertisements relating to such products. Accordingly, it is an offence under section 94 of the Medicines Act 1968 to issue any such advertisement at the request or with the consent of any other commercially interested party. It is, however, a defence for an accused person to prove (a) that he exercised all due diligence to secure that the section would not be contravened, and (b) that the contravention was due to the act or default of another person.

28.07 The Medicines Act 1968 also empowers the appropriate Ministers to make regulations prohibiting, or regulating, particular types of advertisements for medicinal products. The regulations may, for example, prohibit the advertising of treatments for particular diseases, or prohibit advertisements containing particular misleading words or phrases, or require medical advertisements to take a certain form and contain specified particulars. The defence mentioned in paragraph 28.06 above is available where a contravention of these regulations is alleged.

Food advertisements

It is an offence to be a party to the publication of an advertisement **28.08** giving a false or misleading description of any food or drug (Food and Drugs (Scotland) Act 1956). There are special provisions for margarine advertisements designed, it seems, to prevent all possibility of confusion with butter (Labelling of Food (Amendment) Regulations 1955). However, it is a defence to prove that the advertisement was published in the ordinary course of business by a person whose business it is to publish or arrange for the publication of advertisements. This will normally protect newspapers.

Experiments on animals

It is an offence to publish an advertisement of a public exhibition **28.09** of an experimental or scientific procedure on an animal which may have the effect of causing the animal pain, suffering, distress or lasting harm (Animals (Scientific Procedures) Act 1986).

Fraudulent advertisements

It is a serious offence to distribute circulars which to one's **28.10** knowledge fraudulently induce or attempt to induce people to invest money. This will not involve a newspaper proprietor, publisher or distributor in liability unless he knows of or is a party to the fraud (Prevention of Fraud Investments Act 1958).

Consumer credit advertisements

The Consumer Credit Act 1974 contains provisions on consumer **28.11** credit advertisements, such as most advertisements of hire-purchase facilities and most moneylenders' advertisements. Regulations will provide for the form and content of such advertisements to ensure, among other things, that they give a fair indication of the credit or hire facilities offered and of their true cost. The Act itself makes it an offence to publish a consumer credit advertisement which conveys information which is misleading in a material respect. It also prohibits certain advertisements of credit facilities for goods or services which are not available for cash. There are similar restrictions on advertisements by credit brokers, debt adjusters and debt counsellors.

28.12 All these provisions apply expressly to the publisher of an advertisement as well as to the advertiser, but newspapers and others are protected by a provision that it is a defence for a person charged to prove (a) that the advertisement was published in the course of a business carried on by him, and (b) that he received the advertisement in the course of that business, and did not know and had no reason to suspect that its publication would be an offence.

Adoption and care of children

28.13 It is an offence to publish knowingly an advertisement indicating that a parent or guardian wants a child adopted, or that a person wants to adopt a child or that any person other than a registered adoption society or local authority is willing to make arrangements for the adoption of a child (Adoption (Scotland) Act 1978).

28.14 The Children Act 1958 makes it an offence to publish knowingly an advertisement that a person will undertake or will arrange for the care and maintenance of a child, unless the advertisement truly states the person's name and address.

Licensed betting office advertisements

28.15 It was formerly an offence to publish or permit to be published an advertisement of a particular licensed betting office or of licensed betting offices in general. However, the Deregulation (Betting and Gaming) Order, which came into effect in April 1997 allowed the advertisement of betting shops in the print media, although not the broadcast media. It also removed all restrictions on bingo advertising including advertising on radio and television.

Lotteries

28.16 A lottery is a scheme for distributing prizes by lot or chance. With certain exceptions, all lotteries are unlawful. It is an offence to print or advertise lottery tickets; to print, publish or distribute any advertisement of a lottery, or any list of lottery winners, or anything concerning a lottery calculated to induce people to participate in it or in other lotteries (Lotteries and Amusements Act 1976). It is, however, a defence to prove that the lottery in question was one of the few types of lawful lotteries mentioned below and that the person charged believed, and had reasonable ground for believing, that none of the statutory conditions applying to the lottery had been broken.

The types of lawful lottery mentioned above are as follows: **28.17**

(1) The National Lottery.
(2) Small lotteries incidental to certain entertainments such as bazaars, sales of work, fetes, dinners, dances and sporting or athletic events. There must be no money prizes and tickets must be sold and the result declared only at and during the entertainment in question. The lottery must not be the only, or the only substantial, inducement to people to attend the entertainment. The whole proceeds of the entertainment (including the proceeds of the lottery), less expenses and a small sum for the purchase of prizes, must be devoted to purposes other than private gain. This exception would cover, for example, an announcement in an advertisement of a football match that a bottle of whisky would be raffled.
(3) Private lotteries. These are lotteries held by and for people belonging to the same society, working on the same premises or living on the same premises. The main conditions applying to this kind of lottery are that the sale of tickets must be restricted to the people mentioned, the net proceeds must be devoted only to the provision of prizes or the purposes of the society holding the lottery and there must be no outside advertisement. The tickets must contain certain information and must all be the same price. This exception would cover, for example, an announcement in a newspaper that Mr X had won the local golf club's Derby sweepstake.
(4) Lotteries promoted by societies established and conducted wholly or mainly for charitable, sporting, cultural or other purposes not for private gain or any commercial undertaking. A society must register with the appropriate district or islands council if it wishes to promote lawful lotteries, and it must keep within certain financial and other limits.
(5) Local lotteries promoted by local authorities in accordance with an approved scheme.
(6) Art union lotteries. Art unions are societies which purchase works of art or raise money for their purchase and distribute works of art or money among their members by lot or otherwise.

Amusements with prizes

None of the restrictions relating to lotteries apply to amusements **28.18** with prizes provided as an incident to entertainments such as a bazaar, sale of work, fete, dinner, dance or sporting or athletic event. The proceeds must be devoted to purposes other than private gain and the opportunity to win prizes must not be the only substantial inducement to attend the entertainment. The restrictions on lotteries do not apply to amusements with prizes provided on premises authorised by the local authorities or at funfairs held by travelling showmen.

28.19   A newspaper will generally be quite safe in advertising fetes, bazaars, funfairs, etc., even if the advertisement states that certain amusements with prizes will be provided.

Prize competitions

28.20 It is an offence to conduct in or through any newspaper, magazine or other periodical (a) any competition in which prizes are offered for forecasts of the result of a future event or of a past event the result of which is not yet ascertained or not yet generally known, or (b) any other competition, in which success does not depend to a substantial degree on the exercise of skill.

28.21   In 1973 the House of Lords decided that the *News of the World's* "Spot-the-ball" competition did not infringe this provision. The paper published a photograph of an actual incident in a football game but with the ball eliminated. Competitors were asked to mark with a cross the position where the ball was most likely to be. The winning entry was that which corresponded most closely with the opinion of a panel of experts as to the logical position of the ball in the circumstances (which might not be the same as the true position of the ball in the original photograph). The court took the view that competitors were being asked to use their skill and judgment and not just to forecast a future event (the decision of the panel of experts).

Advertisements of foreign betting

28.22 It is an offence, subject to certain limited exceptions, to advertise foreign pool betting or coupon betting or betting with a bookmaker outside Great Britain (Betting and Gaming Duties Act).

Gaming advertisements

28.23 The Gaming Act 1968 defines gaming as "the playing of a game of chance for winnings in money or money's worth, whether any person playing the game is at risk of losing any money or money's worth or not". The term is wide enough to include shove-halfpenny and bingo as well as the more sophisticated games normally played in casinos.

28.24   The Act makes it an offence to publish any advertisement informing the public that any premises in Great Britain are premises on which gaming takes place or inviting the public to take part in such gaming. It is also an offence to publish advertisements inviting the public (a) to apply for information about taking part in any gaming in Great Britain, or (b) to subscribe money or money's worth to be used in gaming anywhere, or (c) to apply for information about facilities for such subscriptions.

There are, however, exceptions for advertisements of certain **28.25** kinds of gaming. The first relates to gaming as an incident of a bazaar, sale of work, fete, dinner, dance, sporting or athletic event or other entertainment of a similar character. The second relates to games played at an entertainment promoted otherwise than for purposes of private gain and complying with certain stringent conditions. This exception could cover, for example, advertisements of a bingo session held to raise funds for a football supporters' club. The third exception relates to gaming at amusement arcades or similar premises which are used wholly or mainly to provide amusements by means of gaming machines and which have a permit from the local authority to do so. The fourth exception covers gaming at any travelling showmen's pleasure fair.

The Gaming Act 1968 provides for the licensing of certain **28.26** gaming premises including bingo clubs. The mere fact that premises are licensed to carry on gaming does not mean that they can be advertised (other than by a sign or notice displayed on the premises themselves). However, there is a specific provision allowing the publication in any newspaper of a notice stating that a licence under the Gaming Act has been granted. The notice must be published not later than 14 days from the date when the licence was granted or from such later date as the licensing board may specify and provided it is in a form approved by the licensing board. The Act also requires applications for licences to be advertised in a newspaper, so there can clearly be no objection to publishing these.

The provisions restricting gaming advertisements do not apply to **28.27** the publication of an advertisement in a newspaper which circulates wholly or mainly outside Great Britain.

Finally, it is a defence to a prosecution under these provisions **28.28** for the accused to prove that he is a person whose business it is to publish or arrange for the publication of advertisements and that he received the offending advertisement for publication in the ordinary course of business and did not know and had no reason to suspect that its publication would amount to an offence.

False trade descriptions

Trade Descriptions Act 1968 prohibits false trade descriptions (as **28.29** defined in the Act) and various other mis-statements, such as false indications that goods are being offered at a cut price. The Act also gives the Department of Trade power to require certain advertisements to include certain particulars if they think this is necessary or expedient in the interests of consumers. Although the Act is aimed primarily at misstatements by those supplying goods and services, certain of its provisions apply to publishers of advertisements. If a newspaper knew that an advertisement contained a false trade description (*e.g.* that goods advertised as new were in fact second-hand or reconditioned) it would be guilty of an offence under the Act if it published it. Obviously, however, newspapers cannot be expected to investigate the accuracy of every statement made in their advertising columns. The Act therefore provides that it shall be a defence for the publisher of an advertisement to prove that he is a person whose business it is to publish or arrange for the publication of advertisements and that he received the advertisement for publication in the ordinary course of business and did not know and had no reason to suspect that its publication would amount to an offence under the Act.

Pirate radio stations

28.30 Under the Marine etc. Broadcasting (Offences) Act 1967 it is an offence to publish the times or other details of broadcasts to be made from pirate radio stations or to publish advertisements calculated to promote their interests.

Cars

28.31 An advertisement for new cars which contains any statement about fuel consumption must include information about results of relevant official tests.

Surrogacy arrangements

28.32 The Surrogacy Arrangements Act 1985 makes it an offence to publish any advertisement containing an indication (a) that any person is or may be willing to enter into a surrogacy arrangement or to negotiate or facilitate the making of a surrogacy arrangement or (b) that any person is looking for a woman willing to become a surrogate mother or is looking for persons wanting to carry a child as surrogate mother.

Obscene publications

28.33 Obscenity is an offence at common law in Scotland. The broad test is whether the publication complained of is calculated to deprave and corrupt those who are likely to read it. The Indecent Advertisements Act 1889 deals mainly with placing indecent advertisements on walls and similar places and the distribution or exhibition of indecent matter in the streets. The Civic Government (Scotland) Act 1982 makes it an offence to publish any advertisement to the effect that the advertiser distributes or intends to distribute an indecent photograph of a child under 16.

Harmful publications

It is an offence to print, publish, sell or hire "horror comics" **28.34** (Children and Young Persons (Harmful Publications) Act 1955). This will not affect the average newspaper as the statute applies only to works which consist wholly or mainly of picture stories portraying the commission of crimes or acts of violence or cruelty or incidents of a repulsive or horrible nature in such a way that the work as a whole would tend to corrupt a child or young person into whose hands it might fall. It would apply, *e.g.* to "video nasties". A child is defined as someone under 14 and a young person as someone under the age of 17.

Election matter

It is an offence to incur expense without the written authority of **28.35** the election agent in issuing advertisements, circulars or publications with a view to promoting or procuring the election of a candidate at an election (Representation of the People Act 1983). This does not prevent newspapers commenting on an election with complete freedom and presenting a candidate or his views or disparaging another candidate. It has been held that there was an offence when a publication advised electors to vote against a candidate but did not advise them to vote for his opponent. It nevertheless tended to promote the opponent's election.

But to offend, the publication must tend to promote or procure **28.36** the election of a particular candidate and not merely a political party as a whole. This was decided in a case in 1952 (*R. v. Tronoh Mines Ltd*) in which the proprietors of *The Times* and others were prosecuted over an advertisement condemning the financial policy of the Labour Party and saying that an election would give an opportunity of saving the country from being reduced to bankruptcy through the policies of a socialist government. The judge observed that no reasonable jury could find that this advertisement presented to the electors of any particular constituency any particular candidate.

It is also an offence to print, publish, post or distribute any bill, **28.37** placard or poster referring to an election unless the name and address of the printer and publisher appear on its face (Representation of the People Act 1983). This provision might apply, for example, to newspaper posters proclaiming "Vote for Blogg".

Accommodation agencies

28.38 It is an offence under the Accommodation Agencies Act 1953, to issue any advertisement describing any house as being to let without the authority of the owner of the house or his agent. It is also an offence under the Act to demand or accept certain illegal commissions for registering people seeking tenancies or for supplying particulars of houses to let. However, the Act expressly provides that:

> "[A] person shall not be guilty of an offence under this section by reason of his demanding or accepting any payment in consideration of . . . the publication in a newspaper, of any advertisement or notice, or by reason of the . . . publication . . . of an advertisement or notice received for the purpose in the ordinary course of business".

Sex Discrimination Act 1975

28.39 Under section 38 of this Act it is unlawful to publish or cause to be published an advertisement which indicates, or might reasonably be understood as indicating, an intention by a person to do any act which is or might be unlawful discrimination on grounds of sex in the employment field or in other fields. This provision does not apply to an advertisement if the intended act would not in fact be unlawful. For example, the 1975 Act does not apply to employment for the purposes of a private household or where the number of persons employed by the employer does not exceed five. A private householder or, say, a solicitor employing only three people could therefore lawfully advertise for a male gardener or a female secretary respectively even though such advertisements are in general unlawful.

28.40   The section provides that for its purposes the use of a job description with a sexual connotation (such as "waiter", "salesgirl", "postman" or "stewardess") shall be taken to indicate an intention to discriminate, unless the advertisement contains an indication to the contrary. It would obviously be impossible for newspapers and others in a similar position to check the lawfulness of each advertisement submitted to them. They could not be expected, for example, to carry out independent inquiries into the number of people employed by a particular advertiser. The section therefore provides a defence for the publisher of an advertisement if he proves (a) that the advertisement was published in reliance on a statement made to him by the person who caused it to be published to the effect that the intended act would not in fact be unlawful and (b) that it was reasonable for him to rely on the statement.

Equal opportunities

In 1981 the Equal Opportunities Commission issued guidance **28.41** notes on the advertising provisions of the Act which included points for the guidance of advertisers. These included the following: "Watch out for words like salesman, storeman/woman. If these are used, make sure the ad clearly offers the job to both sexes. Make sure that advertisements for jobs which have in the past been done mainly by men or women only (e.g. mechanic, typist) could not be understood to indicate a preference for one sex. If the ad contains words like he, she, or him, make sure that they are used as alternatives, e.g. he or she, or him/her, and are consistent throughout the advertisement. In one way or another the ad must make it clear that the vacancy is open to both men and women. Pictures can give a biased impression too. If they are used, ensure that men and women are shown fairly, in both numbers and prominence. Otherwise a bold disclaimer should be placed as close to the illustration as possible".

Advertising standards

Publishers should be familiar with the British Code of Advertising **28.42** Practice, administered by the Advertising Standards Authority. Although the code is not statutory, the Authority has power, where an advertisement is found to have contravened the code, to order the advertiser to amend or withdraw it from publication. The aim of the code is to protect consumers from unacceptable or misleading advertising, its philosophy, in brief, being that "if an advertiser can't prove it, he can't say it"; and the Authority summarises its message thus: "All advertisements should be legal, decent, honest and truthful".

The code, which is under constant review, makes special pro- **28.43** vision for political and religious advertising, to avoid undue suppression of freedom of speech. Publishers of newspapers and periodicals are entitled to withdraw any advertisement they think is contrary to the code. There are separate codes dealing with television, radio, cable and satellite broadcasting.

In December 1990, the Advertising Standards Authority ruled **28.44** that a leading research charity, the Imperial Cancer Research Fund, had exaggerated its role in pioneering a new breast cancer therapy and had made misleading claims about the therapy.

In the same month a former boxing champion Tony Sibson **28.45** threatened to take legal action after an advertisement for Audi cars used a picture of his bruised and battered face accompanied by the words: "In our eyes, it's better to avoid a hit than take one". Mr

Sibson said that the advertisement, which had been published without his permission and without warning, had caused distress to his whole family and carried the implication that his only talent had been to endure punishment.

28.46 The Advertising Standards Authority said that its code of practice did not require advertisers to seek the permission of people in the public eye although they were advised to do so. It pointed out however, that it had recently endorsed a complaint by Mr Arthur Scargill, President of the National Union of Mineworkers, over an advertisement for an anti-perspirant which used his picture with the caption: "For when you're really sweating". The authority described this as "highly distasteful" at a time when Mr Scargill was involved in an inquiry over missing union funds.

28.47 The British Code of Advertising Practice says advertisements should contain nothing which might cause children physical, mental or moral harm, or which exploits their credulity, lack of experience or sense of loyalty and should not encourage them to be a nuisance to their parents or anyone else with the aim of persuading them to buy an advertised product.

KEY POINTS

28.48 A fine and/or imprisonment can be imposed for the publication of certain types of illegal advertisement. For example, it is an offence to publish false or misleading advertisements about medicines or medical treatment, food and drugs.

28.49 There are also strict rules governing advertisements on consumer credit, betting and lotteries.

28.50 Advertisements are supposed to be "legal, decent, honest and truthful" and the Advertising Standards Authority has power to order an advertiser to amend or withdraw an advertisement which fails to meet these criteria.

CHAPTER 29

RACE RELATIONS

It is an offence under section 19 of the Public Order Act 1986 to **29.01** display, publish or distribute written material which is threatening, abusive or insulting if the intention is to stir up racial hatred or, taking all the circumstances into account, racial hatred is likely to be stirred up. The penalties for a breach of the Act are up to six months' imprisonment or a fine or both for summary conviction and up to two years' imprisonment or a fine or both on indictment. The Broadcasting Act 1990 extended these provisions to radio and television broadcasts (see also Chapter 24).

The important point to note is that an offence can be committed **29.02** under the Act without any intention of stirring up racial hatred. An editor could be prosecuted for publishing a racist speech, just as an extremist politician could be for making it. The editor would have to decide whether in all the circumstances racial hatred was likely to be stirred up. He might have to consider toning down the language of the original by taking the controversial parts out of direct speech so that they were no longer threatening, abusive or insulting in terms of the Act.

Under section 22 of the 1986 Act journalists involved in televi- **29.03** sion or radio broadcasts may be guilty of an offence if the programme involves the use of threatening, abusive or insulting visual images or sounds in circumstances in which racial hatred is likely to be stirred up. The offence covers each of the people providing the programme service; any person by whom the programme is produced or directed and any person by whom the offending words or behaviour are used. (See para. 22.30).

The Act defines racial hatred as hatred against a group of people **29.04** in Great Britain by reference to colour, race, nationality (including citizenship) or ethnic or national origins. This can include a particular racial group such as Jews, Sikhs or Romanies. In October 1991 the Dowager Lady Birdwood was conditionally discharged and ordered to pay £500 towards prosecution costs after being convicted of distributing anti-Jewish leaflets intended to stir up racial hatred.

29.05　　In a test case in 1983, the House of Lords, overruling the English Court of Appeal, decided that Sikhs qualify for protection under the Race Relations Act 1976 as a racial group. The Court of Appeal had held that they were a religious community and did not enjoy such protection. The Lords ruled that a Birmingham headmaster unlawfully discriminated against a Sikh pupil in refusing to allow him to wear a turban in the school. Lord Fraser of Tullybelton (a Scottish Lord of Appeal), said the Sikhs were a group defined by reference to ethnic origins for the purposes of the Act. The court laid down a test of whether a group regarded itself and was seen by others as a distinct community because of certain characteristics such as a long shared history, a cultural tradition of its own, a common ancestry, common language and literature, a common religion and being a minority.

29.06　　In a case in April 1991 an employment appeal tribunal decided that Rastafarians were a religious sect but not a racial group defined by ethnic origin within the meaning of the Race Relations Act. In allowing an appeal from an employer from a finding of racial discrimination by an industrial tribunal, the employment appeal tribunal stated that Rastafarians were not sufficiently distinguishable from the rest of the Afro-Caribbean community. It also took the view that as a movement which went back only 60 years, the Rastafarians did not possess a long shared history, one of the tests for establishing a racial group.

29.07　　It is a defence for someone who is not shown to have intended to stir up racial hatred to prove that he was not aware of the content of the material or did not suspect, and had no reason to suspect that it was threatening, abusive or insulting. The defence must be proved on a balance of probabilities.

29.08　　The Act does not apply to fair, accurate and contemporaneous reports of public hearings before any court or tribunal exercising judicial authority, or to reports of proceedings in Parliament.

29.09　　During 1986 the Press Council dealt with a series of complaints about the practice of some newspapers of specifying the skin colour or race of the offender or defendant in reports of cases of violence or serious crime—dubbed by some writers "adjectival racism". Its decisions had no legal force, but they at least gave editors a basis for considering how to proceed in this sensitive area. One of the grounds of complaint was that while reports sometimes described offenders as black, no mention was made of the fact, in other similar kinds of case, that the offenders were white.

29.10　　The council upheld a complaint against the *Daily Telegraph* over its description of a rape gang as black, and held that this was an irrelevant, prejudicial description which tended to exacerbate hostility against minority groups. The then editor, William Deedes, maintained that there would always be differences on what was or was not relevant in a particular case.

The council ruled that reference to race or colour was objection- **29.11** able where it was both irrelevant to the report and in a prejudicial context. There might be cases where it would be relevant to refer to race or colour without substantial risk of prejudice. Where, however, the reference was to a person convicted or accused of violent crime as black, this was both irrelevant and prejudicial. It tended to exacerbate hostility against minority groups, who were at risk of serious prejudice within the community. Accepting that there were different views on the matter, the council believed that its view served the interest of better community race relations and should be respected.

In another case the council heard a complaint that the same **29.12** paper reported that a 16-year-old white girl told the Old Bailey she was raped "about 30 times" by a gang of black youths. The council held that no evidence was reported that the crimes had been racially motivated and the paper should not have introduced the defendants' colour or race into the story. But it was held not improper that the paper failed to identify the colour or race of defendants or victims in other reports cited.

The council rejected a complaint against the *Daily Telegraph* that **29.13** in reporting the Tottenham riots it specified that alleged offenders later brought before the court in connection with the disturbances were black. The editor, Max Hastings, said he was determined to preserve editorial discretion as to whether or not it was appropriate to mention the colour of a person named in news items. The council took the view that the colour of those involved in the Tottenham riots was relevant to the reports of the court cases covered by the paper. The *Daily Telegraph*, it may be noted, in other reports of violent crimes during the year, specified the colour of assailants where this was not black.

In another case, the council found it was not improper or **29.14** irrelevant for the *Daily Telegraph* to refer to the colour of two armed burglars in a report of their trial. It said counsel's descrip- tion of one of the accused as black was relevant to the trial. It was the way in which a principal witness distinguished between the two in her evidence of what they did and said. The complaint in this case also was rejected.

In February 1989 the Press Council decided that a newspaper's **29.15** reference to a man's dreadlocked hairstyle and his white girlfriend clearly implied his race or colour, which was irrelevant to the report. The council upheld a complaint that by describing a rapist as "dreadlocked" the *Daily Mail* had improperly identified his race and religion. The complaint stated that the use of the word "dreadlocked" was a description of the man as a black Rastafarian, although it might be that he was neither.

29.16 In April 1990 the Press Council upheld a complaint against the *Sun*, *Star* and *Daily Mail* that their coverage of a trial had unnecessarily identified the defendant as a black ballet dancer. The man denied the charge and was acquitted. The Press Council ruled that the newspapers should have avoided revealing the man's colour "in the interests of avoiding unjustified discrimination in the minds of the readers".

29.17 The following month the Press Council upheld a complaint that the *Sun* had improperly identified the colour of the white victim of a rush-hour knife attack. The complaint against the newspaper was that although it was acceptable to describe the attacker as black, since this could help in his capture, reference to the colour of the white victim suggested a racial motive and was likely to exacerbate racism. The managing editor of the newspaper had argued that it was a fact that a black man had stabbed a white man and that the colour of the victim was relevant to the story.

29.18 The subject of discrimination was dealt with in a Code of Practice drawn up by the newly-established Press Complaints Commission. The Code, which came into effect on January 1, 1991, stated:

> (1) The Press should avoid prejudicial or pejorative reference to a person's race, colour, religion, sex or sexual orientation or to any physical or mental illness or handicap.
> (2) It should avoid publishing details of a person's race, colour, religion, sex or sexual orientation, unless these are directly relevant to the story.

KEY POINTS

29.19 It is an offence to publish threatening, abusive or insulting material with the intention of stirring up racial hatred, or if racial hatred is likely to be stirred up (Public Order Act 1986). Racial hatred is defined as hatred against a group of people by reference to colour, race, nationality or ethnic or national origins.

29.20 Guidelines for dealing with issues of race and colour are contained in the Code of Practice drawn up by the Press Complaints Commission.

CHAPTER 30

OFFICIAL SECRETS

The Official Secrets Acts

In the pursuit of news the journalist may come up against the **30.01**
Official Secrets Acts which make it an offence to be in or around a
prohibited place for any purpose prejudicial to the safety or
interests of the State (Official Secrets Act 1911, s. 1). Prohibited
places include Her Majesty's arsenals, naval or air force establishments, factories, stations, dockyards, camps, ships and aircraft.
They also include places where the Crown has munitions or models
or papers relating to munitions. Various other places may be
specifically declared to be prohibited. A journalist can be convicted
if his conduct or the circumstances of the case indicate that his
purpose was prejudicial to the interests of the State. This purpose
need not be expressly proved by the prosecution.

It is also an offence under the Act to make sketches, photo- **30.02**
graphs or notes which might be useful to an enemy. The same
applies to obtaining, communicating or publishing documents or
information which might be useful to an enemy. In these cases a
purpose prejudicial to the safety or interests of the State is usually
presumed unless the contrary is proved (Official Secrets Act 1911,
s. 1).

Under the all-embracing provisions of section 2 of the 1911 Act **30.03**
it was an offence for anyone with access to official secrets to
communicate them to unauthorised persons. Of more importance
to journalists was the provision that a person who knowingly and
willingly received a communication of this kind was also guilty of
an offence (s. 2). Under a strict interpretation of section 2 it was an
offence to disclose how many cups of tea were drunk each week in
the Ministry of Defence or how much toilet paper was used.

However, in a number of English cases in the 1960s and 1970s **30.04**
juries could not be persuaded to convict people charged under
section 2, and the Official Secrets Act 1989 was introduced to
replace the "catch-all" approach of section 2 with a series of
measures to deal with specific types of official information.

The information protected by the Act falls into one of the **30.05**
following categories: security and intelligence; defence (including

the size, organisation, deployment and training of the armed forces and defence policy and strategy); international relations; crime (information which, if disclosed, does or is likely to result in the commission of a crime, assist an escape from custody or impede the prevention or detection of offences); information entrusted in confidence to other States or international organisations; special investigation powers (information on State telephone-tapping, interception of letters or other communications). The offence of deliberate disclosure carries a maximum penalty of two years' imprisonment.

30.06 The Act is primarily aimed at unauthorised disclosures of protected information by members of the security and intelligence services, Crown servants and government contractors, but also applies to disclosures by anyone, including journalists. However, if a journalist disclosed information connected with security, intelligence, defence or international relations, the prosecution would have to prove that the disclosure was "damaging", and that the journalist knew or had reasonable cause to believe it to be damaging.

30.07 Where a journalist disclosed information relating to crime and special investigation powers, the Crown would not have to prove damage (damage is assumed) or that the journalist knew or had reasonable cause to believe the disclosure to be damaging. A disclosure would be regarded as damaging if, for example, it harmed the capability of the armed forces or endangered the interests of the United Kingdom abroad.

30.08 It is not a defence under the 1989 Act that the disclosure was made in the public interest, for example that it revealed the existence of criminal conduct. Nor is there a prior publication defence—that the information is no longer secret because it has already been published—although, as the *Spycatcher* case illustrates, this plea would be likely to succeed in the European Court of Human Rights. In the case of the journalist, however, the fact that information was already in the public domain could provide the basis for an argument that further publication could no longer cause any damage.

30.09 In certain cases a police officer above the rank of inspector can require a person to give information relating to an offence or suspected offence under the Official Secrets Acts. It is an offence to fail to comply with such a requirement or knowingly to give false information. But the officer must have the authority of the chief officer of police and, except in emergencies, a Secretary of State must have given his express permission (Official Secrets Act 1939, s. 1).

The *Zircon* case

As was illustrated by the *Zircon* case in 1987, section 9 of the 1911 **30.10**
Act remains of considerable significance to journalists, as it gives
the police wide powers to carry out searches. If satisfied that an
offence under the Act has been or is about to be committed, a
magistrate may grant a warrant authorising police to enter premises named in the warrant, to search the premises or anyone found
on them and to seize material which is evidence of an offence
under the Act. Armed with the warrant, detectives searched and
removed from the BBC's offices in Glasgow, material connected
with a programme on the Zircon intelligence-gathering satellite. It
was to be one of a six-part series, "The Secret Society", produced
by BBC Scotland and presented by the journalist Duncan Campbell. The programme claimed that the Government had deceived
Parliament by concealing the fact that it was spending £500 million
on the Zircon project.

One of the many controversial aspects of the *Zircon* case was that **30.11**
the warrant was in fact granted by a sheriff rather than a
magistrate. The Broadcasting Act 1990 made it clear that a sheriff
as well as a magistrate can grant a warrant authorising the seizure
of film and other material from a broadcasting organisation.

The DA-notice system

The system of "DA-notices", formerly known as "D-notices", is **30.12**
important in the field of official secrets, although it is a matter of
practice, not law. The system is administered by the Defence, Press
and Broadcasting Advisory Committee which has both media and
civil service representatives. The service departments bring cases
before the committee and make known their wishes as to whether
the information should be published. The committee considers the
case and then sends DA or Defence Advisory notices to the
participating sections of the media. The notices indicate what
information should not be published. Doubts about the interpretation or application of notices are generally resolved by consulting
the secretary of the committee. The whole system is a voluntary
one.

The system has operated for more than 80 years and is generally **30.13**
thought to have worked well, apart from one or two isolated
incidents. The most notable of these was the "D-notice affair" of
1967 which arose out of the disclosure by the *Daily Express* that
cables sent out of Britain were regularly made available to the
security authorities for scrutiny. The Government said this was a
breach of D-notices: the *Express* maintained it was not. A committee of inquiry found for the *Express*, but the Government
purported to "reject" this finding.

30.14 The system was subjected to careful examination but survived. It was revised in 1982 after a lengthy examination, and four subjects were dropped—advice on Royal Navy warship construction and equipment; aircraft and aero-engines; prisoners of war and evaders; and the whereabouts of the former K.G.B. chief in Canberra, Vladimir Petrov, and his spy wife, who defected to Australia in 1954.

30.15 Terrorism figured in the revised list. The introduction to the up-dated set of notices, presented in simpler and more general terms than before, stated: "Dissemination of sensitive information . . . can also be of value to terrorist groups who lack the resources to obtain it through their own efforts". The system then covered:

(1) Defence plans, operational capability, state of readiness and training;

(2) Defence equipment;

(3) Nuclear weapons (this item bears the warning that publication of design information could assist nuclear weapon states to improve their nuclear capability and non-nuclear states to acquire one or sub-national groups to produce explosive nuclear devices);

(4) Radio and radar transmissions;

(5) Cyphers and communications (with the request that extreme discretion should be used in reporting ostensible disclosures of information published at home or overseas about British codes and cyphers and that such information should not be elaborated upon without reference to the secretary of the committee);

(6) British security and intelligence services (the names "security service" (MI5) and "secret service" (MI6) were dropped);

(7) War precautions and civil defence;

(8) Photographs of defence establishments, installations, dock-yards and factories.

30.16 In 1988 press representatives on the Defence, Press and Broadcasting Committee expressed their concern over a number of incidents in which the Government had pursued legal action against the press although the information in question had been referred to the secretary of the D-Notice Committee and no further action had been taken. The chairman replied to these concerns by reaffirming the Government's commitment to the D-notice system and by pointing out that questions of breaches of the duty of confidentiality owed to the Crown by members and former members of the security and intelligence services were outwith the remit of the D-Notice Committee.

The first D-notice for six years was issued in December 1990 **30.17** shortly before the bombing of Iraq. It requested the media not to publish any details about the theft from an RAF officer's car of a lap-top computer and classified documents containing information about the Gulf. The machine was returned to the Ministry of Defence in January, apparently by the thief, after a nationwide search. In October 1992 the Defence, Press and Broadcasting Committee announced a thorough review of the system. This was said to be as a result of Prime Minister John Major's insistence on more government openness and the end of the Cold War.

In July 1993 an update of the system was announced reducing **30.18** the number of DA-notices to six. They now cover "operations, plans and capabilities", "non-nuclear weapons and operational equipment," "nuclear weapons and equipment", "cyphers and secure communications", "identification of specific installations" and "United Kingdom security and intelligence services." D-Notices were renamed DA-Notices or Defence Advisory Notices, and the D-Notice Committee, the Defence Press and Broadcasting Advisory Committee.

Scots law and *Spycatcher*

Ban a book and make it a best-seller: that was the bitter lesson **30.19** facing the British Government as it pursued its relentless efforts through the English civil courts, and elsewhere, including New South Wales and Hong Kong, in 1987 to stop publication of extracts from the book *Spycatcher* written in retirement in Australia by Peter Wright, a former MI5 officer. A more pointed lesson for Scottish journalists was the impotence of the English interim injunctions north of the Border. While the English proceedings were going through all stages to the House of Lords the book was published in the USA and copies entered Britain and were put on sale unhindered.

The understandable object of the Government, through the **30.20** Attorney-General, was to stop Wright's breach of a lifelong obligation of confidence which he owed it. The legal mechanisms available to it proved, however, unequal to the task outside the jurisdiction of the English courts. Scottish editors were alive to the fact that orders made by English courts did not rule in Scotland. Some of them, having taken legal advice, published extracts from the book and reports of the court proceedings in Sydney, all prohibited to English editors by interim injunctions.

The House of Lords decision was intended to preserve the ban **30.21** in the interests of national security, pending a full hearing of the case, and to prevent future repetition of Wright's breach of duty by other members of the British secret service. Although the Lord Advocate issued a warning that he would take proceedings in the Court of Session against any Scottish publication which breached the House of Lords ban, no action was in fact taken in the Scottish courts—tacit confirmation that the legal advice on which Scottish editors decided to publish was well founded, and a tribute to the special care taken to ensure that nothing they printed or broadcast reached across the Border.

30.22   Nothing could have better illustrated the special place of Scottish editors under their separate and independent legal system. The alleged revelations made by Wright about the internal workings of MI5, and the issues raised by the efforts to have him silenced, were of undoubted public interest—having been already published in the USA and also circulating in other countries. Had he been living in the United Kingdom he could have been prosecuted under the Official Secrets Acts.

30.23   The final decision of the House of Lords on a full hearing of the case was in fact that due to extensive prior publication of the information in the book in other jurisdictions, further publication in England would not pose a threat to national security. All the injunctions were lifted and the court ruled that anyone could now publish the information.

30.24   In November 1991 the 24 judges of the European Court of Human Rights ruled unanimously that the Government had been in breach of the European Human Rights Convention by banning the media from publishing material from *Spycatcher* between July 1987 (when the book was published in the USA) and October 1988 (when the House of Lord lifted the injunctions). The Court upheld claims by the *Sunday Times*, *Observer* and *Guardian* that the Government had infringed Article 10 of the Convention governing freedom of expression. In assessing whether a ban had been "necessary in a democratic society" the European Court said confidentiality in *Spycatcher* had been destroyed by publication abroad. However, the European Court also decided, by a narrow majority, that the Government had not violated Article 10 when it obtained the original injunctions against publication in 1986, because at that time no information had been published in the United States.

Inside Intelligence

30.25 The case of *Lord Advocate v. The Scotsman Publications Ltd.* (The *Inside Intelligence* case) is the closest Scottish equivalent to *Spycatcher*. It involved a petition by the Lord Advocate for interdict against *The Scotsman* and "any other person having notice" of the interdict, to ban publication of any of the information contained in the book *Inside Intelligence*, written by former MI6 member Anthony Cavendish. The Scottish case followed the granting of an injunction in England banning further publication after extracts from the book appeared in the *Sunday Times*.

As in *Spycatcher*, the final decision of the House of Lords in **30.26** *Inside Intelligence* was in favour of publication, although on different grounds. In this case, the Law Lords' decision hinged more on the fact that the Lord Advocate had failed to establish that further publication would do any significant damage to the public interest.

This may seem to be another victory for freedom of speech and **30.27** the press, but in fact the judgments of the Lords laid down a number of categories in which the Crown could succeed in an action to restrain publication of information, provided they could fit the case into one of these categories. These include the situation where the specific information concerned is shown to pose a direct threat to national security (provided there has not been extensive prior publication) and of course the court pointed out that the chances of an interdict being granted were greater if there had been no prior publication at all.

As we have seen earlier in this chapter, the Official Secrets Act **30.28** 1989 has now gone further in setting out the specific categories of information in which disclosure is prohibited.

Another important issue for the media, which was discussed in **30.29** the course of *Inside Intelligence* although not decided by the House of Lords, was the scope of the interdict sought by the Crown. The Lord Advocate's attempt to gain an interdict effective against the world in general (not just The *Scotsman* but any person having notice of the interdict) was rejected by the Court of Session as contrary to Scots law. However, there was no decision on whether an action of contempt of court (rather than breach of interdict) would be available in Scotland in the case of a third party disclosing information subject to a court order banning publication. Such an order was granted by the Court of Appeal in England and approved by the House of Lords in the *Spycatcher* case and might prove persuasive in Scotland (see also Chapter 10).

The ineffectiveness of an English injunction in Scotland was also **30.30** underlined when the *Herald* published the contents of a confidential despatch from H.M. Ambassador to Saudi Arabia in 1986. An injunction had been granted by the English courts to prohibit publication of the despatch by the *New Statesman*, but the editor of the *Herald* took the view that the order had no application north of the Border. Similarly, The *Scotsman* published a story concerning an extra-marital affair by Liberal Democrat leader Mr Paddy Ashdown in 1992 when an injunction existed in England banning publication of the information. Indeed, the English injunction banned mention of the fact that the injunction existed!

30.31 In the Saudi Arabian letter case the Government did seek an interim interdict in the Court of Session against the *Herald*. However, by the time an interdict was granted by Lord Davidson at his home in the early hours of the morning, the paper was already on the streets with the despatch reproduced in full.

KEY POINTS

30.32 The Official Secrets Act 1911 makes it an offence to be in and around certain areas such as dockyards, naval or air force establishments for purposes prejudicial to the interests of the State. It is also an offence to take pictures or make sketches or notes which might be useful to an enemy.

30.33 The "catch-all" section 2 of the 1911 Act, under which a journalist risked prosecution for receiving secret information however trivial, was repealed in the 1989 Official Secrets Act. In most cases, the journalist will now be guilty of an offence only where the disclosure of specific types of classified information is damaging.

30.34 The Defence Press and Broadcasting Advisory Committee provides guidance to the media on publication of national security matters through the "DA-Notice" system. The system is voluntary and has no legal authority.

30.35 An injunction granted by the English courts is not effective in Scotland. In the *Inside Intelligence* case, the Court of Session refused to grant an interdict aimed at all sections of the media, not just the newspaper named in the court action.

30.36 However, the question of whether an action for contempt of court (rather than breach of interdict) might be brought in Scotland against a third party who disclosed information subject to a court order was not decided.

CHAPTER 31

REPORTS OF ENGLISH COMMITTAL
PROCEEDINGS

Scots lawyers have often been critical of the English system of **31.01** holding a preliminary public inquiry before examining magistrates to decide whether or not there is stateable case for sending someone for trial by jury on an indictable offence. It has been pointed out that this could result in publicity which might prejudice potential jurors against the accused. The system has been contrasted with the Scottish system of preliminary proceedings held almost entirely in private.

Before the law was changed prosecution evidence in "old-style" **31.02** committal proceedings in which witnesses gave evidence was often widely reported in sensational cases, making it difficult to find an unbiased jury for a later trial at the Crown Court. A notorious example was the case of Dr John Bodkin Adams in 1957. The doctor stood trial for one murder but at the committal proceedings mention was made of the deaths of other patients although these did not form part of the eventual trial at which the doctor was acquitted despite the previous adverse publicity.

The purpose of committal proceedings is to decide whether **31.03** there is an arguable case against an accused and the object of reporting restrictions contained in the Magistrates Courts Act 1980 is to ensure that potential jurors at a future Crown Court trial are not swayed by what they see or hear in media reports. The reporting restrictions apply to both "either-way" offences—triable at Crown Court or magistrates court-and indictable offences such as murder or rape triable only at the Crown Court.

In practice old-style committals have been abolished and **31.04** replaced by "paper" committals allowing magistrates to send an accused for trial on the basis of written statements. Witnesses are no longer called to give evidence.

The details which may be included in a report even though it is **31.05** published before the trial, are restricted to the following 10 points:

(a) the identity of the court and the names of the examining justices;

331

(b) the names, addresses and occupations of the parties and witnesses and the ages of the accused and witnesses;

(c) the offence or offences, or a summary of them, with which the accused is or are charged;

(d) the names of counsel and solicitors involved in the proceedings;

(e) any decision of the court to commit the accused or any of the accused for trial, and any decision of the court on the disposal of the case of any of the accused not committed;

(f) where the court commits the accused for trial, the charge or charges, or a summary of them, on which he is committed and the court to which he is committed;

(g) where the committal proceedings are adjourned, the date and place to which they are adjourned;

(h) any arrangements as to bail on committal or adjournment;

(i) whether legal aid was granted to the defendant or any of the defendants;

(j) any decision of the court to lift or not to lift reporting restrictions.

31.06 In 1996 the former editor and the owners of The Citizen newspaper in Gloucester were each fined £4,500 over a story of the first appearance before magistrates of the mass murderer Fred West. Although the report was accurate it included a statement that West had admitted killing his daughter.

30-07 The restrictions no longer apply if the magistrates decide not to commit any of the accused for trial, the court decides to try one of the accused summarily, when they have all finally been tried at Crown Court or one of the accused asks for restrictions to be lifted. If there is more than one accused all are allowed to make submissions before a decision is taken on whether restrictions should be lifted. If one accused objects reporting restrictions will be lifted only if it is decided to be in the interests of justice to do so. This is designed to avoid the situation that arose in the Jeremy Thorpe case in 1979 in which the committal proceedings were widely reported although only one of the accused had asked the court to dispense with reporting restrictions. The kind of consideration the court might have to have in mind in deciding whether to lift restrictions is whether one accused wants publicity in the hope of encouraging an important witness for his defence to come forward.

Indictable-only offences

31.08 A new method of committing for trial at the Crown Court for indictable offences involving accused over the age of 18 was introduced on a trial basis in some parts of England and Wales by the Crime and Disorder Act 1998. The plan was to extend the procedure to the rest of the country in the year 2000. The prosecution supplies the defence with a copy of the evidence on which the case against the accused is based and the magistrates court must send him for trial. A copy of the case is also provided to the Crown Court and at that stage the accused can apply to the Crown Court for any charge to be dismissed because of a lack of evidence.

An application for dismissal of an indictable-only offence at the **31.09** Crown Court stage is also subject to reporting restrictions under the 1998 Act. The only details that can be reported at that stage are the identity of the judge and the court, the names, ages, addresses and occupations of the accused and witnesses, the offences involved, the identity of counsel and solicitors, bail arrangements and whether legal aid was granted.

The restrictions no longer apply if the application to have the **31.10** case dismissed is successful. The judge can lift reporting restrictions but where there is more than one accused and he objects, it must be in the interests of justice to lift restrictions.

Either-way offences

When someone over 18 appears before magistrates charged with **31.11** an either-way offence he is asked how he intends to plead in what is referred to a plea-before-venue procedure. If he indicates that he wishes to plead guilty the magistrate will deal with the case and pass sentence after hearing the prosecution case and a plea in mitigation. The case does not go to the Crown Court for trial. However it can be sent there for sentence if the magistrates take the view that their sentencing powers are inadequate. The thinking behind this procedure (introduced by the Criminal Procedure and Investigations Act 1996) is to give the accused the chance to plead guilty as soon as possible and keep in the magistrates court cases that can properly be dealt with at that level. If the accused charged with an either-way offences indicates that he is pleading guilty, reporting restrictions no longer apply.

If the accused indicates that he wishes to plead not guilty to an **31.12** either-way offence the magistrates court must decide whether it can try the case summarily or whether it must go to the Crown Court. The accused must be asked whether he is agreeable to a summary trial and can elect for jury trial at the Crown Court in which case reporting restrictions will remain in force. If the accused agrees to a summary trial of an either-way offence the restrictions no longer apply.

The coverage of committal proceedings can also be affected by **31.13** section 4(2) of the Contempt of Court Act 1981, which gives courts

power to postpone publication of reports of proceedings to avoid
prejudicing other proceedings which are pending or imminent. In
an appeal against an order made by Horsham magistrates under
the section in 1981 the English High Court ruled that magistrates
must not make an order that is wider than necessary to prevent
prejudice to the administration of justice. In deciding that the
magistrates' order was too wide, the court said it should have been
limited to sensitive matters disclosed during the committal hearing.

CHAPTER 32

BREACH OF CONFIDENCE

Journalists should be aware of the existence of the law of confi- **32.01** dence. The legal complexities will almost inevitably require that legal advice is taken in a case where there is a question of breach of confidence.

The law of confidence is not fully developed in Scots law, but **32.02** recent events have made it clear that the law is sufficiently advanced for courts to grant remedies against journalists, when they attempt to use information which the court decides should be protected by the law of confidence. The *Spycatcher* litigation in England and the *Cavendish* litigation in Scotland both involved the law of confidence. It is commonly supposed by journalists that these cases are of limited relevance because they involved the use by journalists of material obtained by Peter Wright and Anthony Cavendish when both were working for the security services as spies.

The law of confidence is not restricted to matters involving State **32.03** secrets. Nor is it restricted to cases, such as *Spycatcher* and *Cavendish*, in which the duty of confidence is owed to the Government.

In fact, the legal principles involved in these cases have a much **32.04** wider application. Basically, the law protects information which is itself confidential and which is given in confidence by one person (the confider) to another (the confidant). Examples would be communication between husband and wife, employer and employee, from business to business on contractual matters and between the Government and civil servants. The obligation of confidentiality may not be confined to the two parties to the confidential communication. It can extend to third parties who come into possession of confidential information. As the *Cavendish* litigation made clear, the obligation will extend even to situations where the third party comes into possession of the confidential information without any positive steps on his part. The law of confidence will apply just as much to the journalist who receives the confidential information anonymously in a brown paper parcel as to the journalist who, in the course of an investigative piece of work, uncovers the confidential information by his own efforts. The law, of course, requires that there is knowledge that the material is of a confidential nature. However, it seems clear that the courts will take the view that certain material, by its very nature, must put the recipient on his guard that it is confidential. The approach the courts will take is basically a common sense one. If, applying common sense, it is obvious that the material is of a confidential nature, then the journalist should be alert and takes a risk if he publishes without making further inquiries.

32.05   In England it was the law of confidence that enabled the late Princess of Wales to obtain an injunction against the *Daily Mirror* newspaper from further publication of photographs of her working out in a health club gym in London in November 1993. It might also have been possible for her to obtain damages against the *Mirror* newspaper for profits they obtained from the use of these pictures which were obtained and published in breach of the obligation of confidence which existed between the Princess and the owners and operators of the health club. The right to claim damages was affirmed in the *Spycatcher* litigation by the House of Lords where it awarded damages to the Attorney-General against *The Times* newspaper for the profits that newspaper obtained by increased circulation when it published part of Peter Wright's book.

32.06   Similarly, in Scotland, the parents of the children removed by the Social Work Department from Orkney were successful in November 1992 in obtaining an interim interdict in the Court of Session against the BBC "Panorama" programme from using tapes of the disclosure sessions between the children and officials of the Royal Scottish Society for the Prevention of Cruelty to Children. The interim interdict was granted by Lord Cameron, despite the fact that the BBC had given an undertaking that the children could not be seen in the interview and their voices would be disguised.

32.07   Scottish actions for breach of confidence in recent years have centred around employment contracts and trade information, rather than freedom of speech interests. However, the two can interact. Recently, the owner of a funeral parlour which had been the subject of undercover filming sought an injunction in the English courts against Channel 4 on the basis that their undercover journalist was an employee of the funeral parlour and owed it a duty of confidentiality. The court refused an injunction. (*Service Corporation International plc & Associated Funeral Directors Limited v. Channel Four Television* (1998) Ent. L.R. Vol. 9, Issue 6, pp 211–215.)

Information does not automatically become confidential simply **32.08** because it is gleaned from being on what one might think of as private premises. Thus the English courts refused injunctions both in the funeral parlour case, and in a 1998 case where the BBC had shown a film taken in the home of a woman convicted of neglecting animals (*Clutterbuck v. BBC,* 13 November 1998). It held that the film was simply a means of conveying information which was not in itself confidential, although a person's proper expectation of confidentiality might well be greater in his own home.

A recent Scottish case on breach of confidence is *Osborne v.* **32.09** *BBC.* Dr Osborne was the former Head of Social Work at Orkney Islands Council. She obtained an interim interdict against the BBC and the *Orcadian,* to prevent them disclosing information about her sexuality, reason for leaving the Council, or the Council's employment practices. She based this on an alleged confidentiality clause in the termination agreement. The BBC reclaimed, *i.e.* appealed, successfully. The court held that two parties could not simply contract together to decide retrospectively that certain information was confidential, and prevent third parties from discussing it.

The law of confidence is presently a developing area, particularly **32.10** in view of the courts' current interest in protecting the privacy of private citizens and the advent of the Human Rights Act 1998. On the other hand, it is clearly part of the journalists' trade to make some material public despite the fact that it was communicated in confidence. For example, journalists would hardly be doing their work properly if they failed to expose wrongdoings simply because the communication between the wrongdoers was confidential.

Generally speaking, the law of confidence allows the parties to **32.11** the confidential communication to ask the court to grant an interim interdict against publications of the confidential information. If there are counterbalancing interests such as the public interest in being informed on certain matters then journalists can, quite properly, have their legal representatives make these points in court.

The general rule is that "there is no confidence in iniquity", *i.e.* **32.12** you cannot tell someone of your wrongdoing and then insist upon their keeping it quiet. That cannot always be relied upon, however. In a recent English case, *Bunn v. BBC,* it was heard that an apparent admission of guilt in relation to the Maxwell frauds, made in a statement to the police, was confidential. This was so notwithstanding that the BBC wanted to use it in a programme, "Fraudbusters", about the workings of the SFO, and the court accepted this was a legitimate focus of public interest in the

Maxwell case. The judge's point was that the police had the information already, and, whilst it was reasonable for the BBC to want to pass it on to the public, there was a greater public interest in allowing confidential statements to be made to the police. An injunction (*i.e.* English interdict) was refused, however, because the information had already been made public.

32.13 Journalists should be mindful of the fact that although public interest may well provide a defence to an action of breach of confidence, the courts define "public interest" in a way quite different from that of journalists. Judges have repeatedly told the press that public interest in law does not mean that in which the public has an interest. For example, there might be a wide (prurient) interest amongst the public at large in seeing the pictures of Princess Diana in the gym. But in law, that sort of interest is not deemed to be the public interest. In law, the public interest in this context is confined to the likes of exposure of fraudulent activity, discovery of a crime or revelation of political hypocrisy.

32.14 It is suggested that, particularly where sensitive commercial information comes into the hands of journalists, they would be wise to seek legal advice as to the remedies which might be sought by confider/confidant as the publication of such information could open the door to claims for substantial damages.

32.15 An action for breach of confidence is also sometimes made as an alternative to breach of copyright. For example, if an unsolicited script treatment or manuscript is sent to a publisher or broadcaster which rejects it, and a book or programme of considerable similarity later appears from that stable, the writer may argue that it was a breach of confidence to "steal" the idea. The writer would require to prove that the script was confidential; that the idea was developed to an extent that showed it was not common knowledge or unoriginal; and that unauthorised use was made of it. Because copyright does not protect ideas, but only their expression, a breach of confidence action might succeed where a copyright action would fail.

32.16 Up until October 2000, the courts applied the balance of convenience test in cases involving the law of confidence. The pursuer needed only to show that he had a prima facie case against the defender and that the balance of convenience favoured an interim interdict being granted.

32.17 In the law of libel, courts were more likely to permit publication on the premise that damages could correct most defamatory publications. In cases involving confidential information, however, it was of the essence that damage would be done if the information ₛs made public. The mere fact of publication mean that the information loses its confidential quality. On the other hand, it might be felt that it is more invidious to ban publication of something that is admittedly true than something which is said to be false.

Actions seeking interdict for anticipated breach of confidence **32.18** will now fall under section 12 of the Human Rights Act 1998, which makes getting "bans" on publication more difficult.

Breach of confidence is criticised by many as a very sprawling, **32.19** unpredictable and rapidly-sprouting barrier to free speech. However, in principle the European Commission on Human Rights has implied that it is a valid action. It refused to hear an application by the Countess Spencer in relation to a breach of privacy when photographs of her outside an eating disorders clinic were published on the basis that she had a domestic right of action for breach of confidence and should have used that.

Journalists are only too aware of the fact that although an **32.20** interim interdict can be overturned once the court has heard all the evidence, that this will usually be of no comfort as the newsworthiness of the material will not endure until the court hears the evidence (this can be a year or two later). So victory at the interim stage is vital for the media. For this reason journalists should be mindful of the fact that the standard the courts will apply when considering an application for interim interdict in confidence cases has hitherto been, in practice, lower than in defamation cases. However, section 12 of the Human Rights Act 1998 should address this.

KEY POINTS

Material passing between individuals (including corporate individ- **32.21** uals) who owe a duty of confidence to each other will still have the quality of confidence if it comes into the hands of the journalist as third party. Such a duty cannot, however, be transferred just by the two individuals concerned making a contract to that effect. To use such information is a breach of confidence and can give rise to an application to the court by one of the original parties to the confidential communication for interdict preventing publication. An action for damages to recover any profits received from a publication made in breach of confidence could follow. Legitimate public interest in the information is a defence in some cases. The Human Rights Act may have an impact here.

CHAPTER 33

THE INTERNET

33.01 The Internet has been described as a "network of networks" of computers. Internet communication is based on the copying of digital email, divided into packets and reassembled after transmission, through various routes, in networks around the world.

33.02 The growth of the Internet will have an impact upon every area of the law. Already there have been international cases involving harassment by email, obscenity, commercial disputes, data protection and privacy. In the Canadian case of *Phillips*, an Internet Service Provider was ordered to disclose the identities of its users, whereas in an American case, *ACLU v. Reno*, an attempt to control Internet content through the Communications Decency Act was challenged as an unconstitutional infringement of free speech. In other words, the culture of the country (privacy-centred, freedom of speech-centred, public order-centred, etc.) will strongly colour its attitude towards regulation of the Internet.

33.03 The difficulty with this, obviously, is that the Internet is global. For those who wish to control content on the Internet, the fact that the "wrong-doers" may be in another jurisdiction thousands of miles away makes the task acutely complicated. For the Internet user to know, and abide by, the laws of all the countries to which one transmits materials, is equally impossible on the face of it.

33.04 Apart from its global reach, the Internet has various features as a means of communication which make it particularly risky in legal terms. It is rapid, so there can be no adequate time for second thoughts. It is easy to publish, for example, a defamatory statement by mistake—sending it to the wrong person, or even to the wrong list of people, at the press of a button. Because it is easy to forward emails, objectionable material can be further distributed very quickly. It is easier to tell, face-to-face, if someone will find material objectionable. As well, the culture of the Internet is informal and uninhibited. It appears informal and anonymous, but actually e-communication leaves a long "paper trail".

33.05 Part of the explanation of the distinctive and informal culture lies in its origins. The Internet is about 30 years old. It developed from the U.S. military-sponsored ArpaNet. This was deliberately designed to create a means of communication which operated so randomly that it would not be possible to prevent messages getting through altogether, even if individual elements of the system were attacked or sabotaged. Later, university researchers and Government agencies began to use it. So its whole background is one of unstoppable, international, interactive discussion—making it highly difficult to control at this stage.

Although all areas of law will have an impact on the Internet **33.06** (and vice versa), three areas in particular are of concern to the journalist: intellectual property rights; defamation; and contempt of court.

Intellectual property rights

Intellectual property rights—copyright, moral rights, trademarks, **33.07** and so on—are increasingly valuable. Furthermore (unlike contempt of court or defamation), considerable international efforts have already been made to secure a baseline for them to be protected, by treaty.

Nonetheless, novel questions have been raised by the Internet. **33.08** In a recent Scottish case, the electronic publisher "Shetland News" created unauthorised hypertext linking from its own website to the *Shetland Times* site. *Shetland Times* sued for copyright infringement. (The problem from the *Shetland Times'* perspective is that the hypertext links enabled the reader to go straight to the *Shetland Times* piece, bypassing the advertising on the front pages.) Lord Hamilton granted interim interdict to stop Shetland News from doing this. He took the view that the *Shetland Times* website was a cable programme and rights in it were infringed by the links to it, which were themselves items in a cable programme. This case is quite unusual on its facts—for example, it was conceded by both sides that the headlines which formed part of the links were copyright. Some commentators think that the case might have gone against the *Shetland Times* at the end of the day. In the event, it settled out of court.

Analogies with existing means of communication, like print, are **33.09** not very exact. In the *Shetland Times* case, for example, it was not the Shetland News as such which was making use of the *Shetland Times'* copyright material, rather, it was showing other users where they could read it. Also, the new technology is much more concerned with using the material, rather than the old-fashioned act of "copying". Some people argue that every act of access entails breach of copyright.

However, straightforward commercial piracy of intellectual prop- **33** erty rights over the Internet is unlikely to appeal to judges in the

United Kingdom. "Cyber-squatting", *i.e.* unrelated parties register-ing famous names like "Scottish Widows" and then trying to sell the websites to those companies, has been attacked successfully, as "passing off", on both sides of the Border.

Defamation

33.11 When a statement has gone over the world, whose laws should govern content? And where, in which "jurisdiction", can one sue? In many cases, there will be an embarrassment of choices of courts in different countries, leading Lars Davies, Research Fellow in Internet Law at University College London to remark:

> "The Internet is the most regulated entity in existence . . . it is impossible to avoid infringing regulations."

33.12 In practice, this may mean that those making claims in defam-ation go "forum shopping" and choose the courts that award higher damages. London is already a popular choice in "forum shopping" for defamation actions against the international press. Whether the court of a particular country will regard itself as having jurisdiction is a matter for that country. Thus, in 1998, a Virginian district court claimed personal jurisdiction in a libel case over Texan residents, because they posted a news-group message via an AOL account with headquarters in Virginia, even though the Internet service provider was based in California. It should also be borne in mind that defamation can be a criminal offence in some countries, including England. In reality, there is no way to comply in each and every jurisdiction. The journalist has to make a risk assessment, having regard to where he and his assets are.

33.13 Nonetheless, some effort is being made at least in the European countries to set common standards. There is already a European Commission Electronic Commerce Directive. This aims, amongst other things, to protect Internet Service Providers when they host material which they did not, and could not, know was unlawful.

33.14 This is probably already the case in the United Kingdom under section 1(1) of the 1996 Defamation Act, to judge from the recent case of *Godfrey v. Demon Internet*. There, the defamatory material was posted to a Demon Internet news-group, purporting to come from one of its subscribers, an academic named Laurence Godfrey. ʻe asked for it to be removed as it was a forgery, but Demon ᵈd to do so. They were held liable for defamation, not so much ᵗting the material as for failing to remove it when asked.

ᵘation is an area where the swift and wide transmissibility ᵗt communication can prove expensive. In July 1997, ᵗion Healthcare paid out £450,000 to Western Provid-ᶜ settlement of a libel action in relation to rumours spread on Norwich Union's internal email system about Western's financial standing. The sports broadcaster Jimmy Hill has also sued the sponsors of a website known as "The Tartan Army" for defamatory comments.

Contempt of court

The Scots and English courts have traditionally interpreted the **33.16** same Contempt of Court Act in different ways—sometimes to the disadvantage of Scots journalists. In part, this arises from fundamental differences in the legal systems of the two countries. In a Scottish criminal trial, identification of the accused is almost always a vital issue, so the use of photographs of him is always risky. However, cultural differences between countries can make it very difficult for them to agree upon issues such as the pre-trial publicity and the identification of under-age offenders.

Even disregarding the Internet, this can cause problems. When **33.17** the Home Secretary's son, William Straw, was involved in a cannabis-supply incident, there was a High Court injunction against naming the 17-year-old boy. The Scottish newspapers decided to identify father and son on the basis that the High Court injunction did not apply to Scotland. The upshot of this was that the injunction became clearly pointless and was swiftly lifted.

The Internet obviously goes far beyond the boundaries of the **33.18** United Kingdom. It would not have been possible to extend such an injunction to, for example, the United States. This is a matter of considerable topical importance because of the pending trial of the Libyans accused in relation to the 1988 Lockerbie bombing. That trial is presently proceeding without a jury in the Netherlands and in front of a panel of senior Judges. The Scottish court—wherever it was sitting—would be in no position to prevent an influx of apparently prejudicial American comment through the Internet and, to a lesser extent, through the conventional media.

Canada found this out, to its cost, when it imposed a highly **33.19** controversial publication ban on the 1993/1994 trials of Karla Homolka and Paul Bernardo in connection with grotesque double murders. The police, the prosecution and the victims' families supported the ban. The ban was felt to be necessary because Bernardo's wife, Karla Homolka, had been sentenced to 12 years for manslaughter in relation to the deaths, as part of her plea-bargain in which she gave critical evidence against her husband when he was tried for murder. Internet users criticised, ignored and ultimately substantially undermined the ban.

Even where newspapers originate in one country, they may be **33.20** concerned as to the position in relation to a ban in a neighbouring jurisdiction. The William Straw case suggests that at least some Scottish papers were given pause. The BBC in Scotland could not carry the story either, because BBC Scotland's signal extends into Cumbria and North Yorkshire. Thus, whatever the proper position in law, the effect of a ban on the conventional media can be to create a *cordon-sanitaire* in relation to the immediate geographical surroundings of the trial. There is no such insulation on the Internet, where the sender of the information can be a very long way from the scene of any enforcement action.

33.21   This is not a matter which is likely to be resolved by international agreement. Canada believes strongly that the accused has a right to be protected from the potentially damaging effects of adverse pre-trial publicity; America believes strongly that freedom of expression is a primary social good. In relation to trials of international interest, a state can only attempt physically to exclude foreign journalists. This is plainly easy to circumvent in a variety of ways. Few democracies, whatever their attitude to the purity of the trial process, are willing to ban journalists altogether. Nor, obviously, would that operate to prevent the leakage, through the Internet, of information from other sources.

33.22   Most trials are not of international interest. In relation to those that are, however, countries with a Scottish/Canadian approach are going to be unable to enforce their usual standards in relation to control of pre-trial publicity. Solutions may have to be practical. The Lockerbie trial arrangements were plainly elaborate, but they set a precedent for trial by a high-calibre judicial panel, rather than by a jury. Alternatively, we could use American-style tactics, such as examination of the jury before its selection, sequestration of it, or, simply, careful instructions to jurors to disregard extraneous information. The last route is obviously the simplest—the others are not in use in Scotland—but the idea that pre-trial publicity can be entirely cured by telling the jurors to ignore it, has never won much confidence from the Scottish judiciary. Research into ways in which juries actually reach their decisions might provide empirical evidence to undermine this scepticism but is itself limited at present by the Contempt of Court Act 1981.

33.23   Conversely, although Internet sites are accessible throughout the world, it does not follow that substantial numbers of people actually will access them, or even be able to find them, still less that they will implicitly believe in their contents if they do. The fact that the Internet is a free-for-all might be felt to diminish its credibility as a purveyor of information, at least in relation to the details of a trial, where the jury are being provided with high-quality evidence designed to convince. Ready correction is also possible. The Court of Session recently agreed to issue an Opinion reflecting that the Law Society had withdrawn allegations of dishonesty against two disbarred solicitors, because the earlier Opinion suggesting the contrary had been published online. This is one of the ways in which analogies with conventional print media may be false.

The Federal District Court in Philadelphia said in the *ACLU v.* **33.24** *Reno* case that four characteristics of the Internet were "of transcendent importance":

> "First, the Internet presents very low barriers to entry. Second, these barriers to entry are identical for users and listeners. Third, as a result of these low barriers, astoundingly diverse content is available on the Internet. Fourth, the Internet provides significant access to all who wish to speak . . . and even creates a relative parity . . . The Internet is a far more speech-enhancing medium than print, the village green, or the mails . . ."

Later, the U.S. District Court agreed that: "Just as the strength **33.25** of the Internet is chaos, so the strength of our liberty depends upon the chaos and cacophony of the unfettered speech the First Amendment protects."

Emphasis on "soft law", such as ethical codes, is suggested as a **33.26** solution in some American quarters. This amounts to a recognition of the fact that "hard law" may make itself look ridiculous. However, codes have recently been given emphasis in the United Kingdom by section 12 of the Human Rights Act. Certain forms of self-restraint, *e.g.* the media not naming rape victims (although in Scotland this is not statutory), indicates that self-control is possible.

KEY POINTS

The Internet is a fast-growing and ineffectively controlled medium **33.27** of mass communication. There is at present no international consensus as to whether and how content should be regulated.Particular challenges lie ahead in terms of the enforcement of copyright and other intellectual property rights, in dealing with defamation risk and in reassessing contempt law in internationally-reported trials. Although States vary enormously in their views on appropriate controls, they nonetheless can and do attempt to enforce their existing laws on intellectual property, defamation and contempt in the context of the Internet; individuals and companies have fallen foul of such attempts already. Pragmatically, avoiding this is an issue of risk assessment and likely to remain so for some time.

CONTEMPT OF COURT ACT 1981

(1981 c.49)

NOTE
Shown as applied to Scotland: see s.21(4).

An Act to amend the law relating to contempt of court and related matters.

[27th July 1981]

Strict liability

The strict liability rule

1.—In this Act; the strict liability rule; means the rule of law whereby conduct may be treated as a contempt of court as tending to interfere with the course of justice in particular legal proceedings regardless of intent to do so.

Limitations of scope of strict liability

2.—¹(1) The strict liability rule applies only in relation to publications, and for this purpose; publication; includes any speech, writing, programme included in a programme service or other communication in whatever form, which is addressed to the public at large or any section of the public.

(2) The strict liability rule applies only to a publication which creates a substantial risk that the course of justice in the proceedings in question will be seriously impeded or prejudiced.

(3) The strict liability rule applies to a publication only if the proceedings in question are active within the meaning of this section at the time of the publication.

(4) Schedule 1 applies for determining the times at which proceedings are to be treated as active within the meaning of this section.

²(5) In this section; programme service; has the same meaning as in the Broadcasting Act 1990.

NOTES
[1] As amended by the Cable and Broadcasting Act 1984 (c. 46), Sched. 5, para. 39(1), and the Broadcasting Act 1990 (c. 42), Sched.20, para.31(1).
[2] Inserted by the Broadcasting Act 1990 (c. 42), Sched.20, para.31(1), with effect from January 1, 1991.

Defence of innocent publication or distribution

3.—(1) A person is not guilty of contempt of court under the strict liability rule as the publisher of any matter to which that rule applies if at the time of publication (having taken all reasonable care) he does not know and has no reason to suspect that relevant proceedings are active.

(2) A person is not guilty of contempt of court under the strict liability rule as the distributor of a publication containing any such matter if at the time of distribution (having taken all reasonable care) he does not know that it contains such matter and has no reason to suspect that it is likely to do so.

(3) The burden of proof of any fact tending to establish a defence afforded by this section to any person lies upon that person.

(4) Section 11 of the Administration of Justice Act 1960 is repealed.

Contemporary reports of proceedings

4.—(1) Subject to this section a person is not guilty of contempt of court under the strict liability rule in respect of a fair and accurate report of legal proceedings held in public, published contemporaneously and in good faith.

(2) In any such proceedings the court may, where it appears to be necessary for avoiding a substantial risk of prejudice to the administration of justice in those proceedings, or in any other proceedings pending or imminent, order that the publication of any report of the proceedings, or any part of the proceedings, be postponed for such period as the court thinks necessary for that purpose.

[1][(2A) Where in proceedings for any offence which is an administration of justice offence for the purposes of section 54 of the Criminal Procedure and Investigations Act 1996 (acquittal tainted by an administration of justice offence) it appears to the court that there is a possibility that (by virtue of that section) proceedings may be taken against a person for an offence of which he has been acquitted, subsection (2) of this section shall apply as if those proceedings were pending or imminent.]

(3) For the purposes of subsection (1) of this section a report of proceedings shall be treated as published contemporaneously

(a) in the case of a report of which publication is postponed pursuant to an order under subsection (2) of this section, if published as soon as practicable after that order expires;

²(b) in the case of a report of committal proceedings of which publication is permitted by virtue only of subsection (3) of section 8 of the Magistrates' Courts Act 1980, if published as soon as practicable after publication is so permitted.

(4). . .

NOTES
¹ Prospectively inserted by the Criminal Procedure and Investigations Act 1996 (c. 25) s.57.
² Prospectively amended (England and Wales) by the Criminal Justice and Public Order Act 1994 (c. 33), Sched. 4, para. 50.

Discussion of public affairs

5.—A publication made as or as part of a discussion in good faith of public affairs or other matters of general public interest is not to be treated as a contempt of court under the strict liability rule if the risk of impediment or prejudice to particular legal proceedings is merely incidental to the discussion.

Savings

6.—Nothing in the foregoing provisions of this Act

(a) prejudices any defence available at common law to a charge of contempt of court under the strict liability rule;

(b) implies that any publication is punishable as contempt of court under that rule which would not be so punishable apart from those provisions;

(c) restricts liability for contempt of court in respect of conduct intended to impede or prejudice the administration of justice.

. . .

Other aspects of law and procedure

Confidentiality of jury's deliberations

8.—(1) Subject to subsection (2) below, it is a contempt of court to obtain, disclose or solicit any particulars of statements made, opinions expressed, arguments advanced or votes cast by members of a jury in the course of their deliberations in any legal proceedings.

(2) This section does not apply to any disclosure of any particulars—

(a) in the proceedings in question for the purpose of enabling the jury to arrive at their verdict, or in connection with the delivery of that verdict, or;

(b) in evidence in any subsequent proceedings for an offence alleged to have been committed in relation to the jury in the first mentioned proceedings,

or to the publication of any particulars so disclosed.

(3) . . .

Use of tape recorders

9.—(1) Subject to subsection (4) below, it is a contempt of court—

(a) to use in court, or bring into court for use, any tape recorder or other instrument for recording sound, except with the leave of the court;

(b) to publish a recording of legal proceedings made by means of any such instrument, or any recording derived directly or indirectly from it, by playing it in the hearing of the public or any section of the public, or to dispose of it or any recording so derived, with a view to such publication;

(c) to use any such recording in contravention of any conditions of leave granted under paragraph (a).

(2) Leave under paragraph (a) of subsection (1) may be granted or refused at the discretion of the court, and if granted may be granted subject to such conditions as the court thinks proper with respect to the use of any recording made pursuant to the leave; and where leave has been granted the court may at the like discretion withdraw or amend it either generally or in relation to any particular part of the proceedings.

(3) Without prejudice to any other power to deal with an act of contempt under paragraph (a) of subsection (1), the court may order the instrument, or any recording made with it, or both, to be forfeited; and any object so forfeited shall (unless the court otherwise determines on application by a person appearing to be the owner) be sold or otherwise disposed of in such manner as the court may direct.

(4) This section does not apply to the making or use of sound recordings for purposes of official transcripts of proceedings.

Sources of information

10.—No court may require a person to disclose, nor is any person guilty of contempt of court for refusing to disclose, the source of information contained in a publication for which he is responsible, unless it be established to the satisfaction of the court that disclosure is necessary in the interests of justice or national security or for the prevention of disorder or crime.

Publication of matters exempted from disclosure in court

11.—In any case where a court (having power to do so) allows a name or other matter to be withheld from the public in proceedings before the court, the court may give such directions prohibiting the publication of that name or matter in connection with the proceedings as appear to the court to be necessary for the purpose for which it was so withheld.

. . .

Legal aid

13.—(1)—(3) [*Repealed by the Legal Aid Act 1988, Sched.6.*]

(4) [*Repealed by the Legal Aid (Scotland) Act 1986, Sched.5.*]

(5) This section is without prejudice to any other enactment by virtue of which legal aid may be granted in or for purposes of civil or criminal proceedings.

. . .

Penalties for contempt of court in Scottish proceedings

15.—(1) In Scottish proceedings, when a person is committed to prison for contempt of court the committal shall (without prejudice to the power of the court to order his earlier discharge) be for a fixed term.

[1](2) The maximum penalty which may be imposed by way of imprisonment or fine for contempt of court in Scottish proceedings shall be two years' imprisonment or a fine or both, except that—

    (a) where the contempt is dealt with by the sheriff in the course of or in connection with proceedings other than criminal proceedings on indictment, such penalty shall not exceed three months' imprisonment or a fine of level 4 on the standard scale or both; and

    (b) where the contempt is dealt with by the district court, such penalty shall not exceed 60 days' imprisonment or a fine of level 4 on the standard scale or both.

[2](3) The following provisions of the Criminal Procedure (Scotland) Act 1995 shall apply in relation to persons found guilty

of contempt of court in Scottish proceedings as they apply in relation to persons convicted of offences—

- (a) in every case, section 207 (restrictions on detention of young offenders);
- (b) in any case to which paragraph (b) of subsection (2) above does not apply, sections 58, 59 and 61 (persons suffering from mental disorder);

and in any case to which the said paragraph (b) does apply, subsection (5) below shall have effect.

(4)...

[3](5) Where a person is found guilty by a district court of contempt of court and it appears to the court that he may be suffering from mental disorder, it shall remit him to the sheriff in the manner provided by section 7(9) and (10) of the Criminal Procedure (Scotland) Act 1995 and the sheriff shall, on such remit being made, have the like power to make an order under section 58(1) of the said Act in respect of him as if he had been convicted by the sheriff of an offence, or in dealing with him may exercise the like powers as the court making the remit.

(6) [*Added by the Criminal Justice (Scotland) Act 1987, Sched. 1, para. 19, but repealed by the Prisoners and Criminal Proceedings (Scotland) Act 1993, Sched. 7 (effective 1st October 1993: S.I. 1993 No. 2050).*]

NOTES

[1] As amended by the Criminal Justice Act 1982 (c. 48), Sched. 7, and the Criminal Procedure (Consequential Provisions) (Scotland) Act 1995 (c.40), Sched. 4, para. 36.

[2] Substituted for subss. (3) and (4) by the Criminal Procedure (Consequential Provisions) (Scotland) Act 1995 (c. 40), Sched. 4, para. 36 (effective April 1, 1996: s.7(2)).

[3] As amended by the Criminal Procedure (Consequential Provisions) (Scotland) Act 1995 (c.40), Sched. 4, para. 36 (effective April 1, 1996).

. . .

Supplemental

Interpretation

[1]**19.**—In this Act—

"court" includes any tribunal or body exercising the judicial power of the State, and "legal proceedings" shall be construed accordingly;

"publication" has the meaning assigned by subsection (1) of section 2, and "publish" (except in section 9) shall be construed accordingly;

"Scottish proceedings" means proceedings before any court, including the Courts-Martial Appeal Court, the Restrictive Practices Court and the Employment Appeal Tribunal, sitting in Scotland, and includes proceedings before the House of Lords in the exercise of any appellate jurisdiction over proceedings in such a court;

"the strict liability rule" has the meaning assigned by section 1;

"superior court" means the Court of Appeal, the High Court, the Crown Court, the Courts-Martial Appeal Court, the Restrictive Practices Court, the Employment Appeal Tribunal and any other court exercising in relation to its proceedings powers equivalent to those of the High Court, and includes the House of Lords in the exercise of its appellate jurisdiction.

NOTE

[1] As amended by the Cable and Broadcasting Act 1984, Sched.5, para.39(2), and the Broadcasting Act 1990, Sched.20, para.31(2) and Sched.21.

Tribunals of Inquiry

20.—(1) In relation to any tribunal to which the Tribunals of Inquiry (Evidence) Act 1921 applies, and the proceedings of such a tribunal, the provisions of this Act (except subsection (3) of section 9) apply as they apply in relation to courts and legal proceedings; and references to the course of justice or the administration of justice in legal proceedings shall be construed accordingly.

(2) The proceedings of a tribunal established under the said Act shall be treated as active within the meaning of section 2 from the time when the tribunal is appointed until its report is presented to Parliament.

Short title, commencement and extent

21.—(1) This Act may be cited as the Contempt of Court Act 1981.

(2) The provisions of this Act relating to legal aid in England and Wales shall come into force on such day as the Lord Chancellor may appoint by order made by statutory instrument; and the provisions of this Act relating to legal aid in Scotland and Northern Ireland shall come into force on such day or days as the Secretary of State may so appoint.

Different days may be appointed under this subsection in relation to different courts.

(3) Subject to subsection (2), this Act shall come into force at the expiration of the period of one month beginning with the day on which it is passed.

(4) Sections 7, 8(3), 12, 13(1) to (3), 14, 16, 17 and 18, Parts I and III of Schedule 2 and Schedules 3 and 4 of this Act do not extend to Scotland.

SCHEDULES

Schedule 1

Times when Proceedings are Active for Purposes of Section 2

Preliminary

1. In this Schedule "criminal proceedings" means proceedings against a person in respect of an offence, not being appellate proceedings or proceedings commenced by motion for committal or attachment in England and Wales or Northern Ireland; and "appellate proceedings" means proceedings on appeal from or for the review of the decision of a court in any proceedings.

2. Criminal, appellate and other proceedings are active within the meaning of section 2 at the times respectively prescribed by the following paragraphs of this Schedule; and in relation to proceedings in which more than one of the steps described in any of those paragraphs is taken, the reference in that paragraph is a reference to the first of those steps.

Criminal proceedings

3. Subject to the following provisions of this Schedule, criminal proceedings are active from the relevant initial step specified in paragraph 4 or 4A until concluded as described in paragraph 5.

4. The initial steps of criminal proceedings are:—

    (a)   arrest without warrant;

    (b)   the issue, or in Scotland the grant, of a warrant for arrest;

    (c)   the issue of a summons to appear, or in Scotland the grant of a warrant to cite;

    (d)   the service of an indictment or other document specifying the charge;

    (e)   except in Scotland, oral charge.

[1][4A. Where as a result of an order under section 54 of the Criminal Procedure and Investigations Act 1996 (acquittal tainted by an administration of justice offence) proceedings are brought against a person for an offence of which he has previously been acquitted the initial step of the proceedings is a certification under subsection (2) of that section; and paragraph 4 has effect subject to this].

5. Criminal proceedings are concluded—

    (a)   by acquittal or, as the case may be, by sentence;

    (b)   by any other verdict, finding, order or decision which puts an end to the proceedings;

    (c)   by discontinuance or by operation of law.

6. The reference in paragraph 5(a) to sentence includes any order or decision consequent on conviction or finding of guilt which disposes of the case, either absolutely or subject to future events, and a deferment of sentence under section 1 of the Powers of Criminal Courts Act 1973, section 219 or 432 of the Criminal Procedure (Scotland) Act 1975 or Article 14 of the Treatment of Offenders (Northern Ireland) Order 1976.

7. Proceedings are discontinued within the meaning of paragraph 5(c)—

    (a)   in England and Wales or Northern Ireland, if the charge or summons is withdrawn or a *nolle prosequi* entered;

(b)　　in Scotland, if the proceedings are expressly abandoned by the prosecutor or are deserted *simpliciter;*

(c)　　in the case of proceedings in England and Wales or Northern Ireland commenced by arrest without warrant, if the person arrested is released, otherwise than on bail, without having been charged.

8. Criminal proceedings before a court-martial or standing civilian court are not concluded until the completion of any review of finding or sentence.

9. Criminal proceedings in England and Wales or Northern Ireland cease to be active if an order is made for the charge to lie on the file, but become active again if leave is later given for the proceedings to continue.

[2]10.Without prejudice to paragraph 5(b) above, criminal proceedings against a person cease to be active—

(a)　　if the accused is found to be under a disability such as to render him unfit to be tried or unfit to plead or, in Scotland, is found to be insane in bar of trial; or

(b)　　if a hospital order is made in his case under section 51(5) of the Mental Health Act 1983 or paragraph (b) of subsection (2) of section 62 of the Mental Health Act (Northern Ireland) 1961 or, in Scotland, where a transfer order ceases to have effect by virtue of section 73(1) of the Mental Health (Scotland) Act 1984,

but become active again if they are later resumed.

NOTES

[1] Prospectively inserted by the Criminal Procedure and Investigations Act 1996 (c. 25) s.57.

[2] As amended by the Mental Health Act 1983, Sched. 4, para. 57(c), and the Mental Health (Scotland) Act 1984, Sched. 3, para. 48.

---

11. Criminal proceedings against a person which become active on the issue or the grant of a warrant for his arrest cease to be active at the end of the period of twelve months beginning with the date of the warrant unless he has been arrested within that period, but become active again if he is subsequently arrested.

Other proceedings at first instance

12. Proceedings other than criminal proceedings and appellate proceedings are active from the time when arrangements for the hearing are made or, if no such arrangements are previously made, from the time the hearing begins, until the proceedings are disposed of or discontinued or withdrawn; and for the purpose of this paragraph any motion or application made in or for the purposes of any proceedings, and any pre-trial review in the county court, is to be treated as a distinct proceeding.

13. In England and Wales or Northern Ireland arrangements for the hearing of proceedings to which paragraph 12 applies are made within the meaning of that paragraph—

(a)　　in the case of proceedings in the High Court for which provision is made by rules of court for setting down for trial, when the case is set down;

(b) in the case of any proceedings, when a date for the trial or hearing is fixed.

14. In Scotland arrangements for the hearing of proceedings to which paragraph 12 applies are made within the meaning of that paragraph—

(a) in the case of an ordinary action in the Court of Session or in the sheriff court, when the Record is closed;
(b) in the case of a motion or application, when it is enrolled or made;
(c) in any other case, when the date for a hearing is fixed or a hearing is allowed.

Appellate proceedings

15. Appellate proceedings are active from the time when they are commenced—

(a) by application for leave to appeal or apply for review, or by notice of such an application;
(b) by notice of appeal or of application for review;
(c) by other originating process,

until disposed of or abandoned, discontinued or withdrawn.

16. Where, in appellate proceedings relating to criminal proceedings, the court—

(a) remits the case to the court below; or
(b) orders a new trial or a *venire de novo*, or in Scotland grants authority to bring a new prosecution,

any further or new proceedings which result shall be treated as active from the conclusion of the appellate proceedings.

SCHEDULE 2

Sections 13, 14

Amendments

Part I

[Repealed by the Legal Aid Act 1988, Sched.6.]

Part II

[Repealed by the Legal Aid (Scotland) Act 1986, Sched.5.]

BROADCASTING STANDARDS COMMISSION

CODES OF GUIDANCE

JUNE 1998

Section 107 of the Broadcasting Act 1996

(1) It shall be the duty of the Broadcasting Standards Commission to draw up, and from time to time review, a code giving guidance as to principles to be observed, and practices to be followed, in connection with the avoidance of—

- (a) unjust or unfair treatment in programmes to which this section applies, or
- (b) unwarranted infringement of privacy in, or in connection with the obtaining of material included in, such programmes.

(2) It shall be the duty of each broadcasting or regulatory body, when drawing up or revising any code relating to principles and practice in connection with programmes, or in connection with the obtaining of material to be included in programmes, to reflect the general effect of so much of the code referred to in subsection (1) (as for the time being in force) as is relevant to the programmes in question.

Section 108 of the Broadcasting Act 1996

(1) It shall be the duty of the Broadcasting Standards Commission to draw up, and from time to time review, a code giving guidance as to—

- (a) practices to be followed in connection with the portrayal of violence in programmes to which this section applies,
- (b) practices to be followed in connection with the portrayal of sexual conduct in such programmes, and,

(c) standards of taste and decency for such programmes generally.

(2) It shall be the duty of each broadcasting or regulatory body, when drawing up or revising any code relating to standards and practice for programmes, to reflect the general effect of so much of the code referred to in subsection (1) (as for the time being in force) as is relevant to the programmes in question.

These codes are provided in fulfilment of that statutory obligation.

CODES OF GUIDANCE

Introduction

The Broadcasting Standards Commission produces its Fairness and Standards Codes in fulfilment of its statutory duty under the 1996 Broadcasting Act. The Act requires the general effect of these codes to be reflected in the detail of the codes and guidelines of all UK broadcasters and broadcasting regulators.

The Code on Fairness and Privacy was first published in November 1997, effective from 1 January 1998 and the same version is produced here. The Code on Standards is based on the Code of the former Broadcasting Standards Council and has been updated, following consultation with the broadcasters and a range of interested parties. Revisions have also been made in light of research, trends identified, the consideration of complaints and the Commission's Roadshows.

Through its codes, the Commission seeks to inform and sustain the debate about issues of fairness and standards in broadcasting. Within the areas of the Commission's particular responsibilities, these codes express the considerations which the Commission believes should be kept in the mind of everyone concerned with standards in broadcasting, whether as providers, citizens or consumers. They will be kept under review in light of the Commission's experience and research as well as further changes in the broadcasting landscape.

June 1998

CODE ON FAIRNESS AND PRIVACY

PREAMBLE

1. In any democratic society, there are balances to be struck between the citizen's right to receive information and ideas, and the responsibilities of broadcasters and journalists to behave reasonably and fairly and not to cause an unwarranted infringement of a citizen's basic right to privacy.

The guidance in this Code cannot resolve that dilemma. But it sets out what the Broadcasting Standards Commission considers are the principles to be observed and practices to be followed by all broadcasters (including the providers of teletext services) to avoid unjust or unfair treatment in radio and television programmes, and to avoid the unwarranted infringement of privacy in the making and broadcasting of such programmes. Broadcasters and broadcasting regulatory bodies should reflect this guidance in their own codes and guidelines.

The Commission will, as required by the Act, take the provisions of this Code into account as it considers complaints and the Code will be revised, as necessary, in light of its experience. But the guidance in a code can never be exhaustive. Whether the needs of fairness and privacy have been met can only be judged by considering each particular case in light of the information the broadcaster had available after diligent research at the time the programme was made or broadcast.

FAIRNESS

General

2. Broadcasters have a responsibility to avoid unfairness to individuals or organisations featured in programmes in particular through the use of inaccurate information or distortion, for example, by the unfair selection or juxtaposition of material taken out of context, whether specially recorded for a programme, or taken from library or other sources. Broadcasters should avoid creating doubts on the audience's part as to what they are being shown if it could mislead the audience in a way which would be unfair to those featured in the programme.

Dealing Fairly with Contributors

3. From the outset, broadcasters should ensure that all programme-makers, whether in-house or independent, understand the need to be straightforward and fair in their dealings with potential participants in factual programmes, in particular by making clear, wherever practicable, the nature of the programme and its purpose and, whenever appropriate, the nature of their contractual rights. Many potential contributors will be unfamiliar with broadcasting and therefore may not share assumptions about programme-making which broadcasters regard as obvious.

4. Contributors should be dealt with fairly. Where they are invited to make a significant contribution to a factual programme, they should:

    (i) be told what the programme is about;

    (ii) be given a clear explanation of why they were contacted by the programme;

    (iii) be told what kind of contribution they are expected to make—for example by way of interview or as part of a discussion;

    (iv) be informed about the areas of questioning, and, wherever possible, the nature of other likely contributions;

    (v) be told whether their contribution is to be live or recorded; and, if recorded, whether it is likely to be edited;

    (vi) not be coached or pushed or improperly induced into saying anything which they know not to be true or do not believe to be true;

    (vii) whenever appropriate, be made aware of any significant changes to the programme as it develops which might reasonably affect their original consent to participate, and cause material unfairness; and

    (viii) if offered an opportunity to preview the programme, be given clear information about whether they will be able to effect any change in the programme.

The requirements of fairness in news reports pose particular challenges. The speed of newsgathering means that it is not always possible to provide contributors to news reports with all the information mentioned above. However, that does not absolve journalists from treating contributors fairly or ensuring that the reports compiled meet the needs of fairness and accuracy.

5. Broadcasters should take special care that the use of material originally recorded for one purpose and then used in a later or different programme does not create material unfairness or unwarrantably infringe privacy. The inclusion of such material, should be carefully considered, especially where this involves instances of personal tragedy or reference to criminal matters. This applies as much to material obtained from others as to material shot by the broadcaster itself.

6. All reasonable steps should be taken to ensure that guarantees given to contributors, whether as to content, confidentiality or anonymity, are honoured.

Accuracy

7. Broadcasters should take special care when their programmes are capable of adversely affecting the reputation of individuals, companies or other organisations. Broadcasters should take all reasonable care to satisfy themselves that all material facts have been considered before transmission and so far as possible are fairly presented.

8. Broadcasters should also be alert to the danger of unsubstantiated allegations being made by participants to live 'phone-ins and discussion programmes and ensure that presenters are briefed accordingly.

9. Contemporary drama which is based on the lives and experience of real people or organisations should seek to convey them fairly. It should be made clear in advance to the audience whether the drama is loosely based on the events it describes or rather purports to be an accurate account of what happened. In neither case should drama distort the verifiable facts in a way which is unfair to anyone with a direct interest in the programme. Care should also be taken not to convey through characterisation, or casting, or on-air promotion an unfair impression of the characters on whom the drama is based.

Correction and Apology

10. Whenever the broadcaster recognises that a broadcast has been unfair, if the person affected so wishes, it should be corrected promptly with due prominence unless there are compelling legal reasons not to do so. An apology should also be broadcast whenever appropriate.

Opportunity to Contribute

11. Where a programme alleges wrongdoing or incompetence, or contains a damaging critique of an individual or organisation, those criticised should normally be given an appropriate and timely opportunity to respond to or comment on the arguments and evidence contained within that programme.

Non-Participation

12. Anyone has the right to refuse to participate in a programme, but the refusal of an individual or organisation to take part should not normally prevent the programme from going ahead. However where an individual or organisation is mentioned or discussed in their absence, care should be taken to ensure that their views are not misrepresented. (See also paragraph 25.)

Deception

13. Factual programme-makers should not normally obtain or seek information or pictures through misrepresentation or deception, except where the disclosure is reasonably believed to serve an overriding public interest (see also paragraphs 14, 16, 18, 23, 26, 27, 28, 31, 32, 33) and the material cannot reasonably be obtained by any other means. Where the use of deception is judged permissible, it should always be proportionate to the alleged wrongdoing and should wherever possible avoid the encouragement of conduct which might not have occurred at all but for the intervention of the programme-maker. Prior editorial approval at the most senior editorial levels within the broadcasting organisation should be obtained for such methods. The programme should also make clear to the audience the means used to obtain access to the information, unless this places sources at risk.

PRIVACY

General

14. The line to be drawn between the public's right to information and the citizen's right to privacy can sometimes be a fine one. In considering complaints about the unwarranted infringement of privacy, the Commission will therefore address itself to two distinct questions: First, has there been an infringement of privacy? Second, if so, was it warranted?

An infringement of privacy has to be justified by an overriding public interest in disclosure of the information. This would include revealing or detecting crime or disreputable behaviour, protecting public health or safety, exposing misleading claims made by individuals or organisations, or disclosing significant incompetence in public office. Moreover, the means of obtaining the information must be proportionate to the matter under investigation.

15. Privacy can be infringed during the obtaining of material for a programme, even if none of it is broadcast, as well as in the way in which material is used within the programme.

16. For much of the time, the private lives of most people are of no legitimate public interest. It is important that when, for a short time, people are caught up, however involuntarily, in events which have a place in the news, their situation is not abused or exploited either at the time or in later programmes which revisit those events. When broadcasters are covering events in public places, they should ensure that the words spoken or images shown are sufficiently in the public domain to justify their broadcast without the consent of the individuals concerned. When filming or recording in institutions, organisations or agencies where permission has been given by the relevant authority or management, broadcasters are under no obligation to seek the individual consent of employees or others whose appearance is incidental or where they are essentially anonymous members of the general public. However, in clearly sensitive situations in places such as hospitals or prisons or police stations, individual consent should normally be obtained unless their identity has been concealed. Broadcasters should take similar care with material recorded by CCTV cameras to ensure identifiable individuals are treated fairly. Any exceptions to the requirement of individual consent would have to be justified by an overriding public interest.

17. People in the public eye, either through the position they hold or the publicity they attract, are in a special position. However, not all matters which interest the public are in the public interest. Even when personal matters become the proper subject of enquiry, people in the public eye or their immediate family or friends do not forfeit the right to privacy, though there may be occasions where private behaviour raises broader public issues either through the nature of the behaviour itself or by the consequences of its becoming widely known. But any information broadcast should be significant as well as true. The location of a person's home or family should not normally be revealed unless strictly relevant to the behaviour under investigation.

The Use of Hidden Microphones and Cameras

18. The use of secret recording should only be considered where it is necessary to the credibility and authenticity of the story, as the use of hidden recording techniques can be unfair to those recorded as well as infringe their privacy. In seeking to determine whether an infringement of privacy is warranted, the Commission will consider the following guiding principles:

   (i) Normally, broadcasters on location should operate only in public where they can be seen. Where recording does take place secretly in places, the words or images recorded should serve an overriding public interest to justify:

- the decision to gather the material;
- the actual recording;
- the broadcast.

(ii) An unattended recording device should not be left on private property without the full and informed consent of the occupiers or their agent unless seeking permission might frustrate the investigation by the programme-makers of matters of an overriding public interest.

(iii) The open and apparent use of cameras or recording devices on both public and private property, when the subject is on private property, must be appropriate to the importance or nature of the story. The broadcaster should not intrude unnecessarily on private behaviour.

19. When broadcasting material obtained secretly, whether in public or on private property, broadcasters should take care not to infringe the privacy of bystanders who may be caught inadvertently in the recording. Wherever it is clear that unfairness might otherwise be caused, the identity of innocent parties should be obscured.

20. Broadcasters should apply the same rules to material shot secretly by others as they do to their own recordings in taking the decision whether to broadcast the material.

21. When secret recording is undertaken as part of an entertainment programme, care should also be taken to prevent the unwarranted infringement of privacy. Those who are the subjects of a recorded deception should be asked to give their consent before the material is broadcast. If they become aware of the recording and ask for it to stop, their wishes should be respected. In a live broadcast, especial care should be taken to avoid offence to the individuals concerned.

Telephone Calls

22. Broadcasters should normally identify themselves to telephone interviewees from the outset, or seek agreement from the other party, if they wish to broadcast a recording of a telephone call between the broadcaster and the other party.

23. If factual programme-makers take someone by surprise by recording a call for broadcast purposes without any prior warning, it is the equivalent of doorstepping (see paragraphs 25, 26, 27) and similar rules apply. Such approaches should only take place where there is reason to believe that there is an overriding public interest and the subject has refused to respond to reasonable requests for interview, or has a history of such failure or refusal, or there is good reason to believe that the investigation will be frustrated if the subject is approached openly.

24. Other recordings of telephone conversations for broadcast purposes made with the agreement of one of the parties but without the knowledge of the other party are to be assessed by the criteria which apply to secret recording on private property. (See paragraph 18.)

Doorstepping

25. People who are currently in the news cannot reasonably object to being questioned and recorded by the media when in public places. The questions should be fair even if they are unwelcome. If the approach is made by telephone, the broadcaster should make clear who is calling and for what purpose. Nevertheless, even those who are in the news have the right to make no comment or to refuse to appear in a broadcast. Any relevant broadcast should make clear that a person has chosen not to appear and mention such person's explanation, if not to do so could be materially unfair. (See also paragraph 12.)

26. Outside the daily news context, different considerations apply. But surprise can be a legitimate device to elicit the truth especially when dealing with matters where there is an overriding public interest in investigation and disclosure. Doorstepping in these circumstances may be legitimate where there has been repeated refusal to grant an interview (or a history of such refusals) or the risk exists that a protagonist might disappear.

27. Repeated attempts to take pictures or to obtain an interview when consent has been refused can, however, constitute an unwarranted infringement of privacy and can also constitute unfairness. Care must also be taken not to make it easy to locate or identify the refuser's address unless it is strictly relevant to the behaviour under investigation and there is an overriding public interest.

Suffering and Distress

28. Broadcasters should not add to the distress of people caught up in emergencies or suffering a personal tragedy. People in a state of distress must not be put under any pressure to provide interviews. The mere fact that grieving people have been named or suggested for interview by the police or other authorities does not justify the use of material which infringes their privacy or is distressing. Such use is justified only if an overriding public interest is served. Broadcasters should take care not to reveal the identity of a person who has died, or victims of accidents or violent crimes unless and until it is clear that the next of kin have been informed.

29. Programme-makers should also be sensitive to the possibility of causing additional anxiety or distress when filming or recording people who are already extremely upset or under stress, for example at funerals or in hospitals. Normally, prior consent should be obtained from the family or their agents.

- At funerals, programme-makers should respect their requests to withdraw.
- No attempt should be made to enter wards or other places of treatment in hospitals without clear and informed authorisation from the medical staff and the individuals concerned or those acting on their behalf.

Broadcasters should also respect any reasonable arrangements made by the emergency services to supervise media access to victims of crime or accident or disaster, or their relatives, in the immediate aftermath of a tragedy.

30. Broadcasters should ask themselves whether the repeated use of traumatic library material is justified if it features identifiable people who are still alive or who have died recently.

Revisiting Past Events

31. Programmes intended to examine past events involving trauma to individuals, including crime, should try to minimise the potential distress to surviving victims or surviving relatives in retelling the story. So far as is reasonably practicable, surviving victims or the immediate families of those whose experience is to feature in the programme, should be informed of the programme's plans and its intended transmission. Failure to do this might be deemed an unwarranted infringement of privacy, even if the events or material to be broadcast have been in the public domain in the past.

Children

32. Children's vulnerability must be a prime concern for broadcasters. They do not lose their rights to privacy because of the fame or notoriety of their parents or because of events in their schools. Care should be taken that a child's gullibility or trust is not abused. They should not be questioned about private family matters or asked for views on matters likely to be beyond their capacity to answer properly. Consent from parents or those in loco parentis should normally be obtained before interviewing children under 16 on matters of significance.

Where consent has not been obtained or actually refused, any decision to go ahead can only be justified if the item is of overriding public interest and the child's appearance is absolutely necessary.

Similarly, children under 16 involved in police enquiries or court proceedings relating to sexual offences should not be identified or identifiable in news or other programmes.

Agency Operations

33. Broadcasters should be clear about the terms and conditions upon which they are granted access to police operations and those of other law enforcement agencies, emergency services or bodies working directly with vulnerable people. When accompanying such operations, crews should identify as soon as practicable for whom they are working and what they are doing. If asked to stop filming on private premises by the property owner or occupier, or to leave, they should do so unless there is an overriding public interest. Bystanders caught on camera should have their identities obscured, where unfairness might arise.

CODE ON STANDARDS

Preamble

1. Broadcasting is a creative medium. It is a living, cultural force in which broadcasters interact with their many audiences in a relationship of respect. That is what gives them the right to experiment and to challenge conventions by presenting controversial work. At the same time, broadcasters must also be wary of causing unjustified offence. It is part of the broadcasters' duty to find ways of striking a balance between their creative freedom and their responsibility to their diverse audiences.

A distinction has to be made between attitudes which are subject to rapid changes of fashion, such as style of dress or modes of address, and those which reflect more enduring views of right and wrong. Matters of taste are ephemeral, while matters of decency, such as the dignity to be accorded to the dead and bereaved, reflect ideals that acknowledge our shared values.

The purpose of this Code is to provide guidance on how to strike that balance: guidance that has been established after extensive research by the Broadcasting Standards Commission into audience views and expectations. It applies to radio and all forms of television, including satellite and cable channels, and also includes broadcast advertisements, unless otherwise stated.

The Code aims to give broadcasters, their regulators and the public an understanding of the thinking and the approach of the Broadcasting Standards Commission ('the Commission'). It sets out the factors which should be taken into account when making editorial judgments. Editorial responsibility lies with the broadcasters themselves, though on occasion the Code draws attention to specific issues, and offers clear advice. Broadcasters and their regulators must reflect the general effect of this Code in their own codes or guidelines.

Stating principles will always provoke questions about their interpretation in individual circumstances. It is the responsibility of the programme-makers and broadcasters to explain their policies clearly and for the audience and the Commission to add its voice to the debate.

The Commission's role is to offer advice and guidance through the Code. It takes into account public's views about matters of taste and decency, as reflected in the Commission's own research, and the way in which they shift over time. Judgments will depend on the editorial context and audience expectations surrounding a particular programme, channel or radio station, the timing of the broadcast, or the clarity with which the intentions of the programme are signalled in advance. The Commission will take this Code into account when considering complaints.

The Code begins with general issues of scheduling, taste and decency which should apply to all programming. Then, in line with the Broadcasting Act 1996, it focuses specifically on the portrayal of violence and sexual conduct.

Scheduling

2. There is an implied contract between the viewer, the listener and the broadcaster about the terms of admission to the home. The most frequent reason for viewers or listeners finding a particular item offensive is that it flouts their expectation of that contract— expectations about what sort of material should be broadcast at a certain time of day, on a particular channel and within a certain type of programme, or indeed whether it should be broadcast at all.
3. The composition of audiences to open access channels changes throughout the day and the content of broadcasts reflects this. For example, at certain times, parents will want to be confident that their children can watch or listen to programmes without the risk of being exposed to disturbing material. At other times there will be more challenging material. The majority of parents accept that they are expected to take greater control over the choice of their children's viewing after the Watershed.
4. Broadcasters have a clear duty to give enough information about the nature and content of programmes so as to allow parents to make an informed judgment on a programme's suitability for their children to see or hear.
5. Special consideration is given to the child audience in other sections of the Code.

The Watershed

6. The television Watershed, which starts at 9.00 pm and lasts until 5.30 am, is well established as a scheduling marker to distinguish clearly between programmes intended mainly for family viewing and those intended for adults. Some 90% of adults are aware of the Watershed and its significance. The Watershed should not be an abrupt change from family viewing to adult programming. It is not a waterfall, but a signal to parents that they need to exercise increasing control over their children's viewing after this time. Parents should also be aware that even programming leading up to the Watershed might not be suitable for all children. The child audience covers a wide age range from very young children to adolescents, and even some 'children's' programmes or news programmes may be unsuitable for younger child audiences. Broadcasters should provide sufficient information to assist parents and others to take the degree of responsibility they feel appropriate for the children in their care.

7. Broadcasters should further bear in mind that children tend to stay up later than usual on Friday and Saturday nights and during school holidays and that programmes which start before 9.00 pm and run through the Watershed may continue to be viewed by a family audience. Care should also be taken in the scheduling of daytime programmes in and out of term-time.

8. Cable and licensed satellite services operate with the standard 9.00 pm Watershed for all channels, except for specially encrypted services with restricted availability to children, which have two Watersheds: one at 8.00 pm (equivalent to the 9.00 pm change on other channels) and the second at 10.00 pm when material of a more adult nature can be shown. Other cable and licensed satellite services are expected to follow similar standards to the terrestrial channels. The programmes and the versions of the films they broadcast should be suitable for the time of day.

9. Pay Per View services give subscribers greater choice over what is available to view in the home. Given their stricter security systems, the Watershed does not apply in the same way. However, the expectation is that the films or programmes shown will conform to the same basic principles set out in this Code.

10. Although there is no Watershed for radio, caution should be exercised at the times children tend to listen, especially during breakfast programmes.

Programme Repeats, Trails and Advertisements

11. Broadcasters need to assess the suitability of material for its time slot. When repeats are rescheduled from evening to daytime their suitability for that particular slot should be considered with care, particularly when the original scheduling decision was based on the programme's level of violence, sexual explicitness or language. Care should also be applied to material repeated during the school holidays.

12. Broadcasters should be aware that trails come upon audiences without warning so they cannot make informed choices about whether or not to be exposed to them. Special care needs to be taken to ensure that trails which are in themselves unsuitable for children are not broadcast before the Watershed.

13. Advertisements also appear without warning and have the power to surprise and shock an audience which cannot selectively screen them out. Broadcasters should be sensitive to commercials which are out of step with their surrounding programmes and might cause offence—especially programmes which appeal to children. They should ensure that the content and style of an advertisement is suitable for the time of its transmission and likely audience.

Labelling and Warnings

14. Breaches of taste and decency in broadcasting can cause particular offence when they are encountered with little or no warning. Broadcasters have to fulfil the conflicting objectives of attracting audiences whilst simultaneously warning other viewers or listeners that they may find a programme offensive. Providing as much advance information as possible about the nature of programmes can often fulfil both objectives. Research also suggests that clearly worded warnings are appreciated so that people can make informed choices about what to watch and what to allow their children to view. Respondents are able to differentiate between the sorts of warnings appropriate to different programme genres.

Taste and decency

15. Challenging or deliberately flouting the boundaries of taste in drama and comedy is a time-honoured tradition going back to Shakespeare, Chaucer and beyond. The tradition has a rightful place in broadcasting. Comedy has a special freedom but this does not give unlimited licence to be crude or cruel, or to humiliate individuals or groups gratuitously.

16. Matters of taste shift quite quickly and vary from one age or social group to another. They often relate to subjects which can cause embarrassment or upset. Matters of decency, however, are based on deeper, more fundamental values and emotions: the respect owed to the bereaved at funerals is one example. Offence to decency has the potential to cause more significant difficulty, and should thus be given the highest priority when considering the suitability of items for broadcast.

Respect and Dignity

17. Broadcasting touches the lives of its audiences in many ways, and from time to time involves them in an aspect of programme making. Whatever the relationship, it has a responsibility to preserve, as far as possible, the dignity of the individual. Individuals should not be exploited needlessly or caused unnecessary distress, nor should the audience be made to feel mere voyeurs of others' distress.

18. The line between the public's right to information and the citizen's right to privacy can be fine, and difficult to draw. This issue is dealt with in the Code on Fairness and Privacy.

Occasions of Grief and Bereavement

19. Modern communications can confront the programme-maker, the reporter and the audience with the reality of the grief and bereavement of strangers more starkly than even a few years ago. The details can be available to every household within minutes.

20. Not every community, nor every family, nor indeed every individual, deals with disasters in the same way—for example, the very public displays of grief practised in some cultures or the wish of some bereaved parents to talk about their immediate sense of loss while others take refuge in silence. But viewers and listeners are offended if they consider that a broadcaster has failed to observe basic decencies. Care must be taken not to take advantage of people in deep shock, or persuade them into an expression of their emotions or views, for example, which they may later regret. Such approaches must be made with discretion and sensitivity.

21. If the consent of the bereaved is obtained, the significance of funerals as a turning-point in the story of an individual tragedy or a major disaster can justify the presence of reporters and their equipment. There should, however, be an accompanying readiness not to exploit the drama of such events by too close a concentration on the bereaved, whether they are public figures or not. Memorial services generally have a different role, deliberately bringing a more public element into the situation of private grief. But the stress which can be caused to the family by such events should never be discounted. In planning coverage of any kind, in circumstances of this sort, it is important to seek as much local advice as possible.

Scheduling

22. Some tragic events, such as the death of Diana, Princess of Wales or the Dunblane shootings, have such a strong impact on the public imagination that broadcasters have to alter their schedules to adjust to the public mood. Careful consideration should be given to the broadcast and scheduling of programmes where the subject matter is very close to that of such a tragic event or on its anniversary.

Swearing

23. The use of language of all kinds is never static; words acquire new meanings and interpretations and levels of offence undergo constant change. The impact of particular words can differ between generations and between different parts of the country, as well as between different tones of voice. There is a range of words, such as 'bugger', 'sod' and 'bastard', which can be terms of near-affection in some places when spoken with particular emphasis. In other circumstances or places, they remain terms of strong abuse. Language may be offensive because of political, religious or social sensitivities; though language can occasionally have a shock value, expressing moments of extreme stress or even outrage. There is also a concern that, in constant use, expletives can represent an impoverishment of language and a barrier to communication.

24. A significant number of complaints arise from the impact on a group of people from watching together—different generations of a family or a mixed group of men and women. Each generation has its own language for use among its peers, often including words which if used between generations or strangers would give the deepest offence.

25. The protests which are often provoked by bad language in programmes, especially those intended for children, are often protests at breaches of these assumptions. Research has indicated that audiences consider the use of bad language to be unacceptable in certain circumstances and its repetitive use was disliked by 86% of respondents. Significantly, the level of protest is reduced when the audience accepts the relevance of the language used to the situation portrayed. In recent research, 65% of those questioned favoured the use of a later transmission time rather than editing, particularly for films containing bad language.

26. The paramount concern of most adults is for children, especially children under 10. In research conducted by the Commission, most respondents (89%) said that all programmes shown before the Watershed should contain language suitable for a family audience. Respondents were also concerned about the use of bad language by those whom children take as role models, for example footballers or pop stars.

27. The Commission does not lay down rigid rules or a list of banned words. Common sense and a study of the relevant research should indicate where the areas of difficulty lie. However, words and phrases which have sexual origins or applications cause particular offence. For example, the Commission would expect the abusive use of any of the synonyms for the female genitalia to have been referred to the most senior levels of management.

28. The Commission considers there is hardly ever any justification for the use on television of offensive language before the Watershed. This rule should be broken very rarely and never without discussion at the most senior levels within the broadcasting organisations.

29. While no Radio Watershed exists, the use of words which give particular offence should also be carefully overseen at senior levels within the broadcasting organisations.

30. The Broadcasting Standards Council's research in 1991, repeated in 1998, showed how racist terms and terms implying disability and mental illness have come to be regarded as deeply offensive, outpacing some traditional terms of abuse. Broadcasters should be sensitive to the offence caused by these words to the majority, as well as the minorities directly affected.

Offences against Religious Sensibilities

31. The casual use of names, words or symbols regarded as sacred by different sets of believers can cause hurt as well as offence. People of all faiths are distressed by affronts to their sacred words. This should not be underestimated. For example, while many may not themselves be offended, a majority would not wish to cause offence to others by the casual use of the Christian holy names as expletives. There is particular offence taken by the linking of the names with sexual swear words. Often, the offence is not intended, but arises from an unawareness of the weight attached to words or symbols which have religious connotations for some of the audience.

Lyrics

32. The lyrics of contemporary music can also cause problems. Care should be taken over material which glamorises crime and drug-taking, incites aggression, or debases human relationships.
33. Music videos should observe the limits applied to drama, bearing in mind the different times at which they are likely to be transmitted. The precise time of scheduling all music videos should be chosen with care.

Drugs

34. Drugs provide a legitimate subject matter for both factual and fictional programmes, but nothing should be done to promote their irresponsible or illegal use.

Alcohol and Smoking

35. Given the health and other risks, neither smoking nor the abuse of alcohol should be glamorised, especially in programmes directed mainly towards the young.

People with Disabilities or Mental Health Problems

36. Over six million people in the UK have some form of physical disability or mental health problem. Programmes should seek to avoid anything which might encourage prejudice.

37. Within most groups of people with disabilities, there are those who consider themselves in danger of being patronised for displaying a courage they would not claim. Other stereotypes persist, for example the bitter and twisted disabled person, or the disabled person incapable of a loving relationship. Programmes should seek to avoid stereotypes by consulting disabled people, when appropriate, through the production process.

38. People with mental health difficulties are also sometimes treated in similar ways, while words like 'loony', 'nutter' and 'schizo' may cause great offence. Care should be taken neither to propagate myths nor to stigmatise. Programme-makers should also take care not to add to a stereotype, for example to suggest that people with a schizophrenic illness are invariably black or dangerous. Programmes should seek to avoid stereotypes by consulting with people with mental health difficulties through the production process whenever appropriate.

39. Some forms of human behaviour seem incomprehensible, but that is not a reason to assume that the people concerned are mentally ill. It is important in portraying acts of criminal violence not to associate them uncritically with questions about the mental health of their perpetrators.

Race

40. Apart from the strict requirements of the law governing race relations in Britain, there needs to be sensitivity towards the differences which exist between people from different ethnic backgrounds. There are times when racial or national stereotypes, whether physical or behavioural, may be used without offence in programmes, but their use and likely effect should always be considered carefully in advance.

41. Almost invariably, the use of derogatory terms in speaking of men and women from particular ethnic backgrounds and nations gives offence and should be avoided unless the context warrants it. Great distinctions exist between many people within single countries, let alone whole continents, and a broad community of interest or a common identity cannot always be assumed. The presentation of minority groups as an undifferentiated mass, rather than a collection of individuals with limited interests in common, should be discouraged.

42. Research points to the desire for positive British minority ethnic role models. Respondents suggest that too many of the racial role models provided for the young, particularly young black men, are derived from programming produced outside the UK, especially films and programmes originating in the US. For many, this is a problem, not least because of the stereotype it suggests to others.

Stereotypes

43. Much humour depends on stereotypes and there are many occasions when their use can be justified for the purposes of a particular programme. Care, however, is needed to avoid the unthinking or lazy adoption of stereotypes: for example, in the portrayal of male and female behaviour; the creation of an impression of older people as a single, vulnerable group; or the representation of people with mental health problems as violent. The same is true of a number of groups which may be singled out on grounds of race, religion, or sexuality.

Archive Material

44. When using archive material, it should be borne in mind that attitudes towards past events change at different rates. For instance, the spectacle of First World War troops going over the top of the trenches to their deaths is still profoundly moving after 80 years, even though relatively few people now remain with a personal involvement as either a participant or a relative. Judgment is called for rather than a blanket ruling. Events such as the Hillsborough Stadium deaths, the Marchioness drownings, the Piper Alpha disaster or the tragedy at Dunblane are still raw events for the relatives and friends of those who perished or survived. More recent archive material should be used with even greater care. Programme-makers should also bear in mind the distress that can be caused to survivors or the relatives of victims when coverage of previous disasters or serious incidents is used to illustrate current news stories. Images and sounds which retain a deep hold on the imagination of many should be used in circumstances appropriate to the weight of the message they convey.

Crime

45. Programmes should neither glamorise nor condone criminals or their actions as crime is rarely without victims.

46. The retelling by criminals or their relatives of their stories of criminal or antisocial behaviour should not result in personal gain unless there is an overriding public interest both in the telling of the story and in the making of payments. It is also important for the media not to the lives of offenders or their families.

47. Documentaries on prison life can expose its realities. It has also become possible to arrange interviews with named criminals—

sometimes with the legitimate aim of drawing attention to injustice or with the declared intention of helping the audience to understand the criminal mind. Both are proper ambitions for broadcasters with a purpose of serving the public interest, but each is capable of being exploited for sensational ends. Programme-makers should be clear about the purpose of such an interview and ensure that its presentation is consistent with that goal. Broadcasting authorities should, where practical, take into account the need to inform victims who may have been involved in the crime, or their families.

Portrayal of violence

48. Violence takes many forms. War. The outrages committed by terrorists. Human conflict in daily life and popular fiction. The antics of cartoon characters. Body contact sports. The ravages of natural disaster. They are facts of life. So long as it exists in society, television and radio programmes will reflect it, portray it and report it. Broadcasters have a duty to show real life in a violent world where natural disasters and human actions wreak havoc. To seek to prevent broadcasters from telling and retelling hard truths about the world would be a substantial disservice both to democracy and to our understanding of the human condition. The portrayal of violence has played a major part in popular storytelling throughout human history, and continues to have a place in the civilising process of which broadcasting is a part.

49. There are some significant concerns about the portrayal of violence which broadcasters need to take into consideration. These include the fear that repeated exposure to violence desensitises audiences, making them apathetic towards increases in actual violence or indifferent to the plight of victims or the copycat effect—outbreaks of violence similar to those shown on the screen—which could be a consequence of showing it in detail. Viewers might identify screen violence with the reality of their own lives and become unreasonably fearful, for instance, being scared to go out at night alone. It could also encourage the view that violence is acceptable as the means of resolving disputes.

50. In scheduling a programme containing violence, especially where it is violence with which viewers may identify closely, broadcasters should consider the programmes placed each side of it, as well as the time of transmission. A sequence of programmes containing violence can rarely be justified.

Violence in News, Current Affairs and Documentary Programmes

51. News and factual programmes play an important part in informing citizens about their own society and the state of the world. By its nature, news will often be about violent events such as war, crime, accidents and natural disaster. The immediacy and speed with which images and reports can be relayed into people's homes means that decisions about the suitability of items for different time slots sometimes have to be made swiftly with little time for consultation. Complete items packaged at distant locations can be fed directly into bulletins as they are transmitted. News channels or services relying on a rotating sequence of items, some repeated many times in succeeding cycles, need to consider issues of suitability as they pass through various phases of the television day.

52. The increasing availability of amateur and CCTV videos provides another source of material where careful editorial decisions are called for, balancing the immediacy of the material with its suitability for transmission at one time of the day or another. Broadcasters will have to make difficult decisions on occasions about how much detail of shocking material is necessary or acceptable, and to what degree material must be edited before it can be shown at all—even where the piece is designed to evoke outrage at the violence shown.

53. News bulletins are now part of the day-long output of many broadcast services. At some times of the day large numbers of children are viewing or listening, so broadcasters must continue to practise discretion over what is transmitted at different times and provide appropriate warnings.

54. Images shown on television can have an overwhelming impact. While broadcasters should not shy away from showing the consequences of violence, they must also take care in the choice of accompanying words to ensure that they put the scenes into the right perspective and ensure that those exercising editorial judgments are aware of the impact such material may have on the audience.

55. Reports of attacks on children or on older people, which might engender the fear of crime, should be handled with particular sensitivity.

Explicitness

56. A balance needs to be struck between the demands of truth and the danger of desensitising people. Where scenes of violence are included in television news bulletins, the fact that violence has bloody consequences should not be glossed over. There is also a danger of sanitising violence. However:

- the dead should be treated with respect and not shown in close-up unless there are compelling reasons for doing so;

- close-ups of the injuries suffered by victims should generally be avoided;
- care should be taken not to linger unduly on the physical consequences of violence.

57. Decency requires that people should be allowed to die in private. Only in the rarest circumstances should broadcasters show the intimate moments of death itself.

58. Neither explicit hangings nor other judicial executions should be shown before the Watershed, except in the rarest of circumstances. Careful editorial consideration ought to be given at the most senior levels of management before such material is broadcast. Subsequent broadcasts should happen only after their relevance in a new context has been carefully assessed.

Radio News

59. Radio can also respond rapidly to news events, but it too faces the difficulty of maintaining a perspective on the violence it reports. The choice of language is crucial. Where casualties occur, accurate reporting of the details will be equally important. In reporting certain kinds of crime, such as sexual assaults or incidents involving children, the time of transmission must be taken into account and the degree of explicit detail matched to the probable presence of children in the audience. A balance needs to be struck between accurate and full news reporting and engendering unjustified fear.

60. Natural sounds, whether on radio or television, can be as distressing as pictures and should be treated with care.

Suicides

61. There should normally be no detailed demonstration nor description of the means of suicide before the Watershed. It is particularly important to avoid detailed portrayal of a suicide when there is some novel aspect which may be copied. Care also needs to be taken over the use of words to describe the event.

62. There is evidence that both imitative suicide attempts and the presence of curious spectators can be discouraged by leaving details as to method or location imprecise. It should be borne in mind that late evening and early morning are periods when loneliness and isolation are at their most intense for vulnerable people.

63. Broadcasters are reminded that The Samaritans are available to offer help and advice in this area.

Reconstruction of Violent Crimes

64. Reconstructing a crime, sometimes with fresh details of which the victims and their families are unaware, can disturb not only those directly affected, but also others in similar situations. The people involved should be informed, wherever appropriate. Where co-operation is withheld, especially in drama-documentary programmes, justification for the programme should have some overriding public interest, such as the illumination of public policy or the disclosure of significant new facts, and be considered at the most senior levels within the broadcasting organisation. (See also the Code on Fairness and Privacy, Paragraph 9).

65. It is important not to over-emphasise the dramatic aspects of reconstructed crime by the insensitive use, for instance, of slow motion, music or other special dramatic effects. The weapons used should not be discussed in unnecessary detail.

Violence in Drama

66. Violence is a legitimate ingredient of drama, but should seldom be an end in itself. The context of the violence, and the audience's ability to appreciate the conventions within which the drama is being played out, will be key. Research indicates that respondents are most shocked when violence occurs in locations that seem familiar to them, and with which they can identify, particularly if that violence 'erupts' and cannot be foreseen. Violence in situations which are more distant, and which are further from their own reality, are less likely to impact; whereas the apparently gratuitous intrusion of violence into locations regarded as places of safety can be deeply shocking.

67. The impression of violence goes beyond the number of punches thrown or guns fired and is connected with the audience's expectations. Research suggests that people are more concerned when the act of violence is personal and shown explicitly and realistically. Action films and thriller or adventure series create a perception of violence because of the subject matter, and the noise of running feet, shouting and squealing tyres and the firing of weapons, but these are considered to be less realistic and therefore less disturbing. It is the combination of pain, cruelty and viciousness in a recognisable situation which causes anxiety as fictional violence is seen by some as more real than the actual violence of war in a far off place.

68. But the serious consequences of violence should not be glossed over—in real life a blow to the head which fells a man is unlikely to be cured by a ritual head-shaking as the victim swiftly gets to his feet.

Genre Movies

69. Some film genres, such as the Western, sci-fi, action adventures, Japanese cartoons or action thrillers present violence as cartoon. In depicting violence which in other contexts would be unacceptable, it is important to schedule programmes appropriately and ensure that they are trailed so that audiences can exercise informed judgment on whether to watch. It is also important to have pre-transmission announcements where appropriate. (See Scheduling paragraphs 2 *et seq.*)

70. Broadcasters should also consider whether a cartoon breaches unacceptable limits of violence.

Children and Drama

71. Some pre-Watershed drama, especially soaps, will deal with adult issues. But broadcasters should be aware that some children can be disturbed by violence in familiar surroundings. Contemporary domestic violence is potentially distressing, while violence set in a distant land or in another era may be less disturbing for children. The general principles covering violence in drama will need to be observed with even greater care.

72. In drama produced for children, the themes and content will cover a narrower range than drama for adult audiences. The levels of violence permissible in some adult plays would be unacceptable for broadcasts aimed at children or when children are likely to be viewing.

Care should be taken to avoid:

    (i) suggesting that violence does not injure people or have consequences for the perpetrator as well as the victim;

    (ii) implying that violence does not cause long-term damage or psychological harm;

    (iii) showing dangerous conduct which might be copied by children;

    (iv) suggesting that characters, especially those likely to be children's heroes, resort easily to violence as the means of resolving differences capable of resolution by other means.

73. Traditional children's cartoons do not normally raise concerns, but the character of some modern day cartoons means that parents should not assume that all cartoons will be suitable for younger audiences. Broadcasters should also alert parents by both scheduling and providing adequate information about a cartoon's content.

Imitation

74. On television the use of weapons, particularly knives or other objects readily available in the home, should be considered carefully. Care should also be taken not to give detailed instructions on how to make explosives.

Animals

75. Violence which involves animals is especially upsetting to many members of the audience, particularly children—even when no harm comes to the animals during production. If it needs to be included in a programme, it should not be dwelt on. It may also be helpful to indicate that no harm was caused to the animals in an appropriate transmission announcement.

Suicide

76. The presentation of suicide in drama requires care. In particular, programmes should avoid giving too much detail of the means of suicide or suggesting that there is a simple explanation, as suicide is rarely caused by a single factor. This would also include suggesting that suicide brings together people who are estranged or that the person committing suicide is loved more in death than in life. Particular care needs to be taken over suicides involving attractive role models, especially in soaps. It is also important to depict the realities and the consequences of their actions.

77. Explicit hanging scenes should never be shown before or close to the Watershed; storylines involving the detailed depiction of suicide should be considered at senior levels within the broadcasting organisation.

78. Broadcasters are reminded that The Samaritans are available to offer help and advice in this area.

Portrayal of sexual conduct

79. Research shows that audiences in Britain have generally become more liberal and relaxed about the portrayal of sex, but broadcasters cannot assume a universal climate of tolerance towards sexually explicit material. Offence may be given by making public and explicit what many people regard as private and exclusive.

80. Radio and television have to meet the expectations of wide audiences which will encompass a spectrum of tolerance towards the portrayal of sexual relationships. However, even those unlikely to be offended themselves may be concerned about viewing some programmes in the company of others, and are likely to be mindful of the effects on children. Broadcasters have a duty to act responsibly and reflect the fact that relations within and between the sexes normally reflect moral choices. Audiences should not be reduced to voyeurs, nor the participants to objects. The youth and physical attractiveness of the participants are no justification for explicitness.

81. Sensitive scheduling, especially within the hour around the Watershed, is particularly important for items involving sexual matters. Broadcasters should provide straightforward labelling in clear language and sufficient warnings about programmes containing explicit material.

82. Encrypted subscription and Pay Per View services offering explicit sexual content cater to self-selected adult audiences. But the depiction of sex is bound by the law relating to hard-core pornography and obscenity.

Factual Programmes

83. Where a news story involves a sexual aspect, it should be presented without undue exploitation. The relative explicitness of such reports must, in any case, be measured by the broadcaster against the time of day at which they are transmitted and the likely presence of children in the audience. Other factual programmes deal with a variety of sexual themes. But producers should ask themselves whether an explicit representation is justified.

Discussion and 'Phone-in Programmes

84. There is a wide difference of attitudes, particularly between the generations, towards the open debate of sexual topics. Programmes need to be scheduled with care and labelled to give warning of their likely content.

Fiction

85. Broadcasters must ensure that actual sexual intercourse is not transmitted.

The broadcast of sexually explicit scenes before the Watershed should always be a matter for judgment at the most senior levels within the broadcasting organisations. On radio, broadcasters must take into account the likely composition of the audience before scheduling more explicit portrayals of sexual activity.

86. When a scene involves rape or indecent assault, careful consideration must always be given to achieving the dramatic purpose while minimising the depiction of the details. Rape should not be presented in a way which might suggest it was anything other than a tragedy for its victim.

Children

87. A sexual relationship between an adult and a child or between under-age young people can be a legitimate theme for programmes: it is the treatment which may make it improper, or even unlawful. The treatment should not suggest that such behaviour is legal or is to be encouraged.

Explicit sexual acts between adults and children should not be transmitted.

88. The Protection of Children Act, 1978, makes it an offence to take an indecent photograph, film or video-recording of a child under the age of 16, or involve a child below 16 in a photograph or recording which is itself indecent—even if the child's role in it is not. Even when legal advice judges material to be on the right side of the law, it should be subjected to careful scrutiny at the highest level over the need to include the sequence in the programme. This applies even when the child is played by an older actor or actress.

Incest and Child Abuse

89. The inclusion of these subjects in well-established serials or single programmes may be justified as public information, even in programmes directed at older children. These programmes may also play a legitimate role in warning children of the dangers of abuse, and advising them of the help available.

90. Where a play or film takes incest as its theme, there should be particular awareness of the relative ease with which some people, including children, may identify characters or actions with their own circumstances, and may also take them as role models.

91. In television, material of this kind should be accompanied by clear labelling of the programme's content, while sensitive scheduling and labelling are also called for in radio.

Animals

92. Explicit sexual conduct between humans and animals should never be shown and should be referred to in programmes only after consultations at a senior level.

Nudity

93. There is now a greater relaxation about the human body. The appearance of the nude human body can have a justifiable and powerful dramatic effect and be a legitimate element in a programme, provided it does not exploit the nude person. But it can also be disturbing and cause offence, especially where it appears that there is no clear editorial rationale. The justification must come from the intention and the merit of the individual programme itself.

Innuendo

94. Sexual humour and innuendo may cause offence especially if broadcast when there are children and young people in the audience. It may pass over the heads of the young, but may nevertheless cause embarrassment to older people watching or listening with them. Care is needed therefore in the scheduling of risqué programmes and programmes which would not normally be expected to contain material of this kind.

PRESS COMPLAINTS COMMISSION

CODE OF PRACTICE

DECEMBER 1, 1999

All members of the press have a duty to maintain the highest professional and ethical standards. This code sets the benchmarks for those standards. It both protects the rights of the individual and upholds the public's right to know.

The code is the cornerstone of the system of self-regulation to which the industry has made a binding commitment. Editors and publishers must ensure that the code is observed rigorously not only by their staff but also by anyone who contributes to their publications.

It is essential to the workings of an agreed code that it be honoured not only to the letter but in the full spirit. The code should not be interpreted so narrowly as to compromise its commitment to respect the rights of the individual, nor so broadly that it prevents publication in the public interest.

It is the responsibility of editors to co-operate with the PCC as swiftly as possible in the resolution of complaints.

Any publication which is criticised by the PCC under one of the following clauses must print the adjudication which follows in full and with due prominence.

The public interest

There may be exceptions to the clauses marked * where they can be demonstrated to be in the public interest.

1. The public interest includes:

    (i) Detecting or exposing crime or a serious misdemeanour.
    (ii) Protecting public health and safety.
    (iii) Preventing the public from being misled by some statement or action of an individual or organisation.

2. In any case where the public interest is invoked, the Press Complaints Commission will require a full explanation by the editor demonstrating how the public interest was served.

3. There is a public interest in freedom of expression itself. The Commission will therefore have regard to the extent to which material has, or is about to, become available to the public.

4. In cases involving children editors must demonstrate an exceptional public interest to over-ride the normally paramount interest of the child

1. Accuracy

(i) Newspapers and periodicals should take care not to publish inaccurate, misleading or distorted material including pictures.

(ii) Whenever it is recognised that a significant inaccuracy, misleading statement or distorted report has been published, it should be corrected promptly and with due prominence.

(iii) An apology must be published whenever appropriate.

(iv) Newspapers, whilst free to be partisan, must distinguish clearly between comment, conjecture and fact

(v) A newspaper or periodical must report fairly and accurately the outcome of an action for defamation to which it has been a party.

2. Opportunity to reply

A fair opportunity for reply to inaccuracies must be given to individuals or organisations when reasonably called for.

*3. Privacy

(i) Everyone is entitled to respect for his or her private and family life, home, health and correspondence. A publication will be expected to justify intrusions into any individual's private life without consent.

(ii) The use of long lens photography to take pictures of people in private places without their consent is unacceptable.

Note—Private places are public or private property where there is a reasonable expectation of privacy.

*4. Harassment

(i) Journalists and photographers must neither obtain nor seek to obtain information or pictures through intimidation, harassment or persistent pursuit.

(ii) They must not photograph individuals in private places (as defined by the note to clause 3) without their consent; must not persist in telephoning, questioning, pursuing or photographing individuals after having been asked to desist; must not remain on their property after having been asked to leave and must not follow them.

(iii) Editors must ensure that those working for them comply with these requirements and must not publish material from other sources which does not meet these requirements.

*5. Intrusion into grief or shock

In cases involving personal grief or shock, enquiries should be carried out and approaches made with sympathy and discretion. Publication must be handled sensitively at such times but this should not be interpreted as restricting the right to report judicial proceedings.

*6. Children

(i) Young people should be free to complete their time at school without unnecessary intrusion.

(ii) Journalists must not interview or photograph a child under the age of 16 on subjects involving the welfare of the child or any other child in the absence of or without the consent of a parent or other adult who is responsible for the children.

(iii) Pupils must not be approached or photographed while at school without the permission of the school authorities.

(iv) There must be no payment to minors for material involving the welfare of children nor payments to parents or guardians for material about their children or wards unless it is demonstrably in the child's interest.

(v) Where material about the private life of a child is published, there must be justification for publication other than the fame, notoriety or position of his or her parents or guardian.

*7. Children in sex cases

1. The press must not, even where the law does not prohibit it, identify children under the age of 16 who are involved in cases concerning sexual offences, whether as victims or as witnesses.

2. In any press report of a case involving a sexual offence against a child:

(i) The child must not be identified.
(ii) The adult may be identified.
(iii) The word "incest" must not be used where a child victim might be identified.
(iv) Care must be taken that nothing in the report implies the relationship between the accused and the child.

*8. Listening Devices

Journalists must not obtain or publish material obtained by using clandestine listening devices or by intercepting private telephone conversations.

*9. Hospitals

(i) Journalists or photographers making enquiries at hospitals or similar institutions should identify themselves to a responsible executive and obtain permission before entering non-public areas.
(ii) The restrictions on intruding into privacy are particularly relevant to enquiries about individuals in hospitals or similar institutions.

*10. Reporting of crime.

(i) The press must avoid identifying relatives or friends of persons convicted or accused of crime without their consent.
(ii) Particular regard should be paid to the potentially vulnerable position of children who are witnesses to, or victims of, crime. This should not be interpreted as restricting the right to report judicial proceedings.

*11. Misrepresentation

(i) Journalists must not generally obtain or seek to obtain information or pictures through misrepresentation or subterfuge.
(ii) Documents or photographs should be removed only with the consent of the owner.
iii) Subterfuge can be justified only in the public interest and only when material cannot be obtained by any other means.

12. Victims of sexual assault

The press must not identify victims of sexual assault or publish material likely to contribute to such identification unless there is adequate justification and, by law, they are free to do so.

13. Discrimination

    (i) The press must avoid prejudicial or pejorative reference to a person's race, colour, religion, sex or sexual orientation or to any physical or mental illness or disability.

    (ii) It must avoid publishing details of a person's race, colour, religion, sexual orientation, physical or mental illness or disability unless these are directly relevant to the story.

14. Financial journalism

    (i) Even where the law does not prohibit it, journalists must not use for their own profit financial information they receive in advance of its general publication, nor should they pass such information to others.

    (ii) They must not write about shares or securities in whose performance they know that they or their close families have a significant financial interest without disclosing the interest to the editor or financial editor.

    (iii) They must not buy or sell, either directly or through nominees or agents, shares or securities about which they have written recently or about which they intend to write in the near future.

15. Confidential sources

Journalists have a moral obligation to protect confidential sources of information.

*16. Payment for articles

    (i) Payment or offers of payment for stories or information must not be made directly or through agents to witnesses or potential witnesses in current criminal proceedings except where the material concerned ought to be published in the public interest and there is an overriding need to make or promise to make a payment for this to be done. Journalists must take every possible step to ensure that no financial dealings have influence on the evidence that those witnesses may give.

(An editor authorising such a payment must be prepared to demonstrate that there is a legitimate public interest at stake involving matters that the public has a right to know. The payment or, where accepted, the offer of payment to any witness who is actually cited to give evidence should be disclosed to the prosecution and the defence and the witness should be advised of this.)

(ii) Payment or offers of payment for stories, pictures or information, must not be made directly or through agents to convicted or confessed criminals or to their associates—who may include family, friends and colleagues—except where the material concerned ought to be published in the public interest and payment is necessary for this to be done.

DEFAMATION ACT 1996

SCHEDULE 1

QUALIFIED PRIVILEGE

PART I

Statements having qualified privilege without explanation or contradiction

1. A fair and accurate report of proceedings in public of a legislature anywhere in the world.
2. A fair and accurate report of proceedings in public before a court anywhere in the world.
3. A fair and accurate report of proceedings in public of a person appointed to hold a public inquiry by a government or legislature anywhere in the world.
4. A fair and accurate report of proceedings in public anywhere in the world of an international organisation or an international conference.
5. A fair and accurate copy of or extract from any register or other document required by law to be open to public inspection.
6. A notice or advertisement published by or on the authority of a court, or of a judge or officer of a court, anywhere in the world.
7. A fair and accurate copy of or extract from matter published by or on the authority of a government or legislature anywhere in the world.
8. A fair and accurate copy of or extract from matter published anywhere in the world by an international organisation or an international conference.

PART II

Statements privileged subject to explanation or contradiction

9.—(1) A fair and accurate copy of or extract from a notice or other matter issued for the information of the public by or on behalf of—

(a) a legislature in any member State or the European Parliament;
(b) the government of any member State, or any authority performing governmental functions in any member State or part of a member State, or the European Commission;

(c)   an international organisation or international conference.

(2) In this paragraph "governmental functions" includes police functions.

10. A fair and accurate copy of or extract from a document made available by a court in any member State or the European Court of Justice (or any court attached to that court), or by a judge or officer of any such court.

11. —(1) A fair and accurate report of proceedings at any public meeting or sitting in the United Kingdom of—

(a)   a local authority or local authority committee;

(b)   a justice or justices of the peace acting otherwise than as a court exercising judicial authority;

¹(c)   a commission, tribunal, committee or person appointed for the purposes of any inquiry by any statutory provision, by Her Majesty or by a Minister of the Crown, a member of the Scottish Executive or a Northern Ireland Department;

(d)   a person appointed by a local authority to hold a local inquiry in pursuance of any statutory provision;

(e)   any other tribunal, board, committee or body constituted by or under, and exercising functions under, any statutory provision.

(2) In sub-paragraph (1)(a)—

"local authority" means—

(a) in relation to England and Wales, a principal council within the meaning of the 1972 c. 70 .Local Government Act 1972, any body falling within any paragraph of section 100J(1) of that Act or an authority or body to which the 1960 c. 67 .Public Bodies (Admission to Meetings) Act 1960 applies,

(b) in relation to Scotland, a council constituted under section 2 of the Local Government etc. (Scotland) Act 1994 or an authority or body to which the Public Bodies (Admission to Meetings) Act 1960 applies,

(c) in relation to Northern Ireland, any authority or body to which sections 23 to 27 of the Local Government Act (Northern Ireland) 1972 apply; and

"local authority committee" means any committee of a local authority or of local authorities, and includes—

(a) any committee or sub-committee in relation to which sections 100A to 100D of the Local Government Act 1972 apply by virtue of section 100E of that Act (whether or not also by virtue of section 100J of that Act), and

(b) any committee or sub-committee in relation to which sections 50A to 50D of the Local Government (Scotland) Act 1973 apply by virtue of section 50E of that Act.

(3) A fair and accurate report of any corresponding proceedings in any of the Channel Islands or the Isle of Man or in another member State.

12.—(1) A fair and accurate report of proceedings at any public meeting held in a member State.

(2) In this paragraph a "public meeting" means a meeting bona fide and lawfully held for a lawful purpose and for the furtherance or discussion of a matter of public concern, whether admission to the meeting is general or restricted.

13.—(1) A fair and accurate report of proceedings at a general meeting of a UK public company.

(2) A fair and accurate copy of or extract from any document circulated to members of a UK public company—

(a)   by or with the authority of the board of directors of the company,
(b)   by the auditors of the company, or
(c)   by any member of the company in pursuance of a right conferred by any statutory provision.

(3) A fair and accurate copy of or extract from any document circulated to members of a UK public company which relates to the appointment, resignation, retirement or dismissal of directors of the company.

(4) In this paragraph "UK public company" means—

(a)   a public company within the meaning of section 1(3) of theCompanies Act 1985 or Article 12(3) of the S.I. 1986/1032 (N.I. 6).Companies (Northern Ireland) Order 1986, or
(b)   a body corporate incorporated by or registered under any other statutory provision, or by Royal Charter, or formed in pursuance of letters patent.

(5) A fair and accurate report of proceedings at any corresponding meeting of, or copy of or extract from any corresponding document circulated to members of, a public company formed under the law of any of the Channel Islands or the Isle of Man or of another member State.

14. A fair and accurate report of any finding or decision of any of the following descriptions of association, formed in the United Kingdom or another member State, or of any committee or governing body of such an association—

(a)   an association formed for the purpose of promoting or encouraging the exercise of or interest in any art, science, religion or learning, and empowered by its constitution to exercise control over or adjudicate on matters of interest or concern to the association, or the actions or conduct of any person subject to such control or adjudication;
(b)   an association formed for the purpose of promoting or safeguarding the interests of any trade, business, industry or profession, or of the persons carrying on or engaged in any trade, business, industry or profession, and empowered by its constitution to exercise control over or adjudicate upon matters connected with that trade, business, industry or profession, or the actions or conduct of those persons;
(c)   an association formed for the purpose of promoting or safeguarding the interests of a game, sport or pastime to the playing or exercise of which members of the public are invited or admitted, and empowered by its constitution to exercise control over or adjudicate upon persons connected with or taking part in the game, sport or pastime;
(d)   an association formed for the purpose of promoting charitable objects or other objects beneficial to the community and empowered by its constitution to exercise control over or to adjudicate on matters of interest or concern to the association, or the actions or conduct of any person subject to such control or adjudication.

15.—(1) A fair and accurate report of, or copy of or extract from, any adjudication, report, statement or notice issued by a body, officer or other person designated for the purposes of this paragraph—

(a)   for England and Wales or Northern Ireland, by order of the Lord Chancellor, and
(b)   for Scotland, by order of the Secretary of State.

(2) An order under this paragraph shall be made by statutory instrument which shall be subject to annulment in pursuance of a resolution of either House of Parliament.

NOTE
[1] As amended by the Scotland Act 1998 (c.46), Sched. 8, para.33(3) (effective May 6, 1999: S.I. 1998 No. 3178).

———

Part III

Supplementary provisions

16.—(1) In this Schedule—

"court" includes any tribunal or body exercising the judicial power of the State;

"international conference" means a conference attended by representatives of two or more governments;

"international organisation" means an organisation of which two or more governments are members, and includes any committee or other subordinate body of such an organisation; and

"legislature" includes a local legislature.

(2) References in this Schedule to a member State include any European dependent territory of a member State.

(3) In paragraphs 2 and 6 "court" includes—

(a) the European Court of Justice (or any court attached to that court) and the Court of Auditors of the European Communities,

(b) the European Court of Human Rights,

(c) any international criminal tribunal established by the Security Council of the United Nations or by an international agreement to which the United Kingdom is a party, and

(d) the International Court of Justice and any other judicial or arbitral tribunal deciding matters in dispute between States.

(4) In paragraphs 1, 3 and 7 "legislature" includes the European Parliament.

17.—(1) Provision may be made by order identifying—

(a) for the purposes of paragraph 11, the corresponding proceedings referred to in sub-paragraph (3);

(b) for the purposes of paragraph 13, the corresponding meetings and documents referred to in sub-paragraph (5).

(2) An order under this paragraph may be made—

(a) for England and Wales or Northern Ireland, by the Lord Chancellor, and

(b) for Scotland, by the Secretary of State.

(3) An order under this paragraph shall be made by statutory instrument which shall be subject to annulment in pursuance of a resolution of either House of Parliament.

GLOSSARY

Ab ante	before, previously
ab initio	from the beginning
absolvitor	decree absolving defender
actus Dei	act of God
ad factum praestandurn	obligation to perform an act other than payment of money
adhere	(court) affirm; (spouse) live with
ad hoc	for this purpose
ad interim	in the interval; meantime
Adjournal, Acts of	procedural rules made by High Court
ad litem	as regards the action
adminicle	piece of supporting evidence
ad valorem	according to value
advise	give judgment
advocation	form of criminal appeal usually by prosecution at preliminary stage
a fortiori	all the more
agnate	related through father
alibi	elsewhere (special defence plea)
aliment	maintenance enforceable by law
aliquot	integral factor
aliunde	from a different source
a mensa et thoro	from bed and table (separation)
ante omnia	first of all
apparent insolvency	insolvency which has become public
a posteriors	reasoning from effect to cause
appoint	to order, direct
a priori	reasoning from cause to effect
arbiter	one chosen by parties to settle difference (in England-arbitrator)
as accords (of law)	in conformity with the law
assize	jury
assoilzie (z silent)	absolve
aver	to state in written pleadings
a verbis legis non est recedendum	the words of a statute must be strictly adhered to
avizandum	to be considered (reserved judgment)
Back letter	document qualifying another which purports to give an absolute right
bairns' part of gear	(see legitim)
barratry	acceptance of bribes by a judge
before answer (allowance of proof)	before the law of the case is determined

397

bill of suspension	form of a peal to Justiciary Appeal Court
bona fide	in good faith
brevi manu	short cut; summarily
brutum fulmen	harmless thunderbolt; vain attack
Calling	first step in civil action
calumny, oath of	formerly oath (in divorce cases) that facts pleaded are believed to be true
Candlemas	February 2, quarter-day
casual homicide	blameless killing
caution (pronounced "cay-shun")	security
caveat	"let him take care"; legal document lodged by part to ensure no order passes against him in his absence
certiorate	give formal notice of a fact
champerty	offence of assisting a party in a suit without having an interest except to share in any pecuniary outcome
circumvention	dishonest taking advantage of a facile person for gain
cite	to summon to court
cognate	related through mother
commit	consign to prison to await further procedure
compear	to appear and participate in an action
compos mentis	of sound mind
conclusion	relief sought in an action
condescendence	statement of averred facts or contentions
conditio si testator sine liberis decesserit	principle by which a will not dealing with children is revoked by birth of a child
consanguinean	relationship between brothers or sisters who have the same father but different mothers
consistorial	relating to questions of status, such as matrimonial proceedings
continue	adjourn (case) to later date
contra bonos mores	in breach of moral law
contumacy	failure to obey court order
courtesy	widower's liferent of his wife's heritage (now obsolete)
crave	formally ask court (as in petition)
curator ad litem	officer appointed by court to assume responsibility for interests of litigant
curator bonis	officer appointed by court to manage a person's estate
cy-pres	as near as possible (applied to necessary variation of terms of trust, will, etc.)
Damnum	harm, loss
damnum fatale	loss due to act of God
data	statements acknowledged as true
decern	give formal, final decree
deciarator	binding statement of rights of a party issued by court
declinature	refusal of judge to take jurisdiction because of his interest or relationship
de die in diem	from day to day
de facto	in point of fact; actual
deforcement	offence of resisting officer of law to prevent him carrying out his duties

de futuro	in the future
de jure	in point of law; legal (as opposed to actual)
delectus personae	choice of person who is thereby excluded from delegating his duty
delict	a wrong
de minimis (non curat lex)	the law ignores trifles
de novo	of new; afresh
de plano	summarily; simply; without further procedure
de presenti	now
desert	to abandon (diet)
design	to set forth person's occupation and address
dies non	a non-legal day
diet	date fixed for a hearing of a case
diligence	execution against a debtor; procedure for recovery of document
disentail	release from entail (*q.v.*)
dispone	to convey (land)
DA-notice	Defence Advisory (see Chapter 29)
dominus litis	person controlling lawsuit who is not actually a party to it
Edictal citation	method of citing persons who are furth of Scotland or sheriffdom
effeir	to correspond, appertain
embracery	attempt to corrupt a jury, or acceptance of bribe by juror
entail	restriction of heritage to prescribed line of heirs (incompetent since 1914)
eo ipso	by the thing itself
ergo	therefore
error calculi	error in calculation
escheat	forfeiture of a person's estate
esto	assuming; let it be assumed
ex adverso	opposite to; adjacent
ex animo	willingly; intentionally
excambion	contract for exchange of one piece of land for another
ex concesso	from what has been admitted
executor-dative	executor appointed by court
executor-nominate	executor appointed by testator
ex facie	on the face of it
ex hypothesi	by the hypothesis
ex justa causa	for just cause or sufficient reason
ex offido	by virtue of office
ex parte	in absence of a party; one-sided; partisan
expenses	payment for legal services (in England—costs)
expose	put up for sale
ex post facto	after the event; retrospectively
ex proprio motu	on (the court's) own initiative
ex re	arising in the circumstances
ex tempore	without premeditation
extract	authenticated copy of decree, etc.
Facsimile	exact copy
fee	full right of property (as opposed to liferent, *q.v.*)
fiar	owner of a fee

fiars (prices)	average prices of grain fixed annually to determine ministers' stipends
filiation	determination by court of paternity
force and fear	duress vitiating a contract
force majeure	something beyond the control of man; that cannot be prevented
forisfamiliation	departure of child from family on becoming independent
forum (or fora)	platform; court; tribunal
fugitation	outlawry
fulmen brutum	vain threat
fund in medio	amount under dispute in action of multiplepoinding (*q.v.*)
furtum grave	theft which formerly merited death penalty
furth	outside (*e.g.* the country)
Garnishment	order not to pay creditor(s) before first settling debt to third party holding judgment against his creditors
gift	bequest
glebe	land in parish to which minister has right apart from stipend
grassum	single payment made in addition to periodic one, such as rent
Habeas corpus	writ releasing person from prison (English law)
Habile	apt
habit and repute	reputation of being married without formal ceremony, entitling parties to declarator of marriage
hamesucken	assault upon man in his own home
haver	person holding documents he is required to produce in court
heritage	land and buildings passing to an heir on owner's death
holograph	wholly handwritten and signed by the author
homologate	approve and thereby validate
horning	ancient procedure for public denunciation of a debtor
hypothec	security for debt, such as right of landlord over tenant's goods in premises let to him
Impeachment	special defence accusing another of the crime charged (known also as incrimination)
impetrate	procure, to another's prejudice
in camera	behind closed doors
in causa	in the case (of)
incompetent	in conflict with the law applicable
indictment	accusation of a crime made in name of Lord Advocate
induciae	time limit
in extenso	in full
in faciendo	in doing
in favorem	in favour
infeft	having a feudal title to heritage
in forma pauperis	in the character of a pauper
in foro	in court
in futuro	in the future
in gremio	in the body (of a deed etc.)
in hoc statu	at this stage; in the present state of affairs
in initio litis	at the outset of the action

in jure	in right
in limine	at the outset (threshold)
in litem	in the case
in loco parentis	in the place of a parent (*e.g.* guardian)
in mala fides	in bad faith
Inner House	appellate department of Court of Session comprising First and Second Divisions
in re	in the case of
in rem suam	in one's own affairs
in rem versum	to one's own account
in retentis	kept for the record
in solidum	for the whole sum
instruct	to vouch or support
inter alia	among other things
inter alios	among other persons
interdict	judicial prohibition (in England-injunction)
interlocutor	formal minute of court decision
interpone	authority to give court's approval to
joint minute	agreement between parties
interrogatories	written questions put to witness excused from attending court
in toto	totally
inter vivos	between living persons (with reference to deeds)
intromit	to handle, deal with, funds, property, etc.
ipse dixit	bare assertion
ipso fact	by the fact itself
ipso jure	by the force of law alone
irritancy	forfeiture of a right due to neglect or contravention (*e.g.* lease)
irrelevant	even if proved, would not justify remedy sought
ish	termination, usually of lease
Judicial factor	person appointed by court to manage affairs of another
jus mariti	right of husband to part of wife's moveable property (now abolished)
jus quaesitum tertio	contractual right of a person arising out of a contract between two others to which he is not a party
jus relictae	widow's right to share of husband's moveable property
jus relicti	widower's right to share of wife's moveable property
jus tertii	right of a third party
Justidar	ancient term for Lord Justice-General
justifiable homicide	killing in exercise of public duty
justo tempore	in due time
Lammas	August 1, quarter-day
lawburrows	ancient process for security against apprehended molestation
legitim	children's right to share of parent's moveable property at death
legitimation per subsequens matrimonium	rendering child legitimate by subsequent marriage of parents
lenocinium	procuring by husband of his wife's adultery
lesion	detriment, loss, injury
lex loci contractus	law of the place where contract was made

lex patriae	law of one's own country
lien	right to retain property of a debtor until he pays
liferent	right entitling a person for life to use of another's property
light	property owner's obligation not to obstruct neighbour's light
liquid (sum)	of ascertained amount
List D	category of school which replaced "special" school
loco parentis, in	in the place of a parent (*e.g.* guardian)
locus	place
locus standi	right to be heard in court
Mala fides	bad faith
mala in se	bad in itself
Martinmas	November 11 or 28, quarter-day
medio tempore	in the meantime
medium concludendi	ground of action
medium filum	centre line of river
minute	document by which party defines his position to the court
misfeasance	doing of an act in an unlawful manner
missives	writings exchanged by parties negotiating for a contract
modus	mode, manner
Moorov doctrine	the principle that, where an accused is charged with a series of similar offences closely linked in time and circumstances, the evidence of one witness as to each offence will be taken as mutually corroborative
mora	delay in making claim
mortis causa	to take effect after death
muirbum	seasonal burning of heather
multiplepoinding	action raised nominally by one party but in which a number of conflicting claims are made to a fund in medio
murmur (a judge)	to slander him
Necessitas juris	by necessity of law
nemo	no one
next-of-kin	relatives entitled to succeed to moveable property under common law
nihil novit	he knows nothing
nobile offidum	equitable jurisdiction of High Court of Justiciary or Inner House of Court of Session by which strictness of common law may be mitigated, or a remedy given where not otherwise available
nolle prosequi	decision by prosecutor to stop proceedings
nomine damni	in name of damages
nominal raiser	holder of fund in a multiplepoinding when another initiates proceedings
non compos mentis	not of sound mind
non constat	it is not evident, not agreed
nonfeasance	omission to do a legal duty
notour bankruptcy	insolvency which has become public, a prerequisite in most cases of sequestration now, apparent insolvency

Obiter dictum	judge's expression of an opinion not forming part of court's decision
obtemper	obey (court order)
onerous	granted for value
onus	burden (*e.g.* of proving case)
oppression	use of office or process of law to commit injustice
Outer House	department of Court of Session exercising jurisdiction of first instance
outputter	one who passes counterfeit coins
Pactum illicitum	unlawful contract
panel, pannel	prisoner at bar
paraphernalia	woman's clothes and adornments which remained her own on marriage (obsolete)
pari passu	share and share alike; side by side
parole (evidence)	oral (term borrowed from England)
particeps criminis	accomplice
patrimonial	pertaining to property; pecuniary
party-minuter	party entering proceedings by lodging a minute
penal action	one in which not only damages are sought, but also a sum as penalty
per capita	divided equally among persons
per incuriam	by mistake
per se	of itself; by himself
per stirpes	division among children of the shares that would have been their parents' (as opposed to per capita)
plagium	child-stealing
poind (pronounced "pind")	to take debtor's moveable property by way of execution
praepositura	wife's implied agency to purchase household supplies on husband's credit (obsolete)
precognition	statement from witness of evidence he is prepared to give
prescription	restriction of a right owing to passage of a specific period of time
prima facie	at first sight
primo loco	in the first place
probable cause	case satisfactory on the face of it
probative document	one which by its nature appears to afford proof of its contents
process	documentary course of an action from first step to final judgment
pro confesso	as if conceded
pro forma	as a mere formality
pro hac vice	for this occasion
pro indiviso	undivided
pro loco et tempore	for the place and time
proof	hearing of evidence by a judge
pro rata	proportionately
prorogate	extend time allowed; or submit to court's jurisdiction
pro tanto	to that extent
pro tempore	for the time being
protestation	procedure whereby defender compels pursuer to proceed with his case or end it
prout de jure	by all the means known to the law

pro veritate	as if true
punctum temporis	point of time
Quantum lucratus	as much as he has profited
quantum meruit	as much as he has earned; what is due
quantum valeat	for what it is worth
Queen's and Lord Treasurer's Remembrancer	administrator of Crown revenues in Scotland
quid pro quo	exchange of equivalents
quoad ultra	otherwise; with regard to other matters
Rank	to admit a claimant to his rightful place (*e.g.* in multiplepoinding)
ratio decidendi	line of reasoning; basis of judgment
real raiser	party who, holding fund in medio, initiates action of multiplepoinding
reclaim	to appeal to Inner House of Court of Session against Outer House judgment
record	statement by parties to an actionof their claims and answers; document containing these
reduce	annul; rescind; set aside (by action of reduction)
regalia majora	Crown rights, *e.g.* to hold seashore in trust for public (inalienable)
regalia minora	Crown rights, such as salmon fishing, which may be subject of grant
rei interventus	rule barring a party, who knowingly permits another to depart from form, to challenge the resulting contract
relevant	applied to case where, if facts stated are proved, pursuer would be entitled to remedy he seeks
relocation	re-letting
repel	reject (a plea or objection)
repone	to restore a party as a litigant
res gestae	things done
res judicata	matter already judicially decided
res noviter	information newly discovered
res publicae	things owned by the state
resting-owing	unpaid (debt)
respondentia	money lent on ship's cargo subject to certain conditions
review	revision by appeal court
rider	addition b jury to its verdict; claim lodged in multiplepoinding
rolls	list of cases to be heard in court
roup	auction
rubric	head-note; summary given at head of law report
Saevitia	legal cruelty (obsolete)
Sanctuary	protection against claims once enjoyed by debtor (*e.g.* by taking refuge in Holyrood Abbey)
Sasine	a putting into possession of land
Scienter	knowledge of animal's dangerous tendency
Sederunt, Acts of	procedural rules made by Court of Session
separatim	separately
sequestrate	render bankrupt (strictly it is the estate which is sequestrated)
seriatim	singly, in regular order

serve	to deliver (a court document)
servitude	burden or obligation on a piece of land
simpliciter	simply, absolutely, without qualification
sine die	without a date being fixed
sine qua non	indispensable condition
Single Bill	motion in the Inner House of the Court of Session
singular successor	person obtaining property otherwise than as heir
sist	to stay or stop a process; to summon or call a party
sleep	a civil action may fall asleep after a year without any step of procedure being taken; it may be revived by a minute of wakening
socius criminis	accomplice in a crime
solatium	damages for injured feelings, grief, pain
solum	ground, foundation, bed of river
special case	method of obtaining legal opinion of Inner House of Court of Session where facts are agreed
spei emptio	purchase of a chance (*e.g,* succession)
spes successionis	hope of succession (as heir apparent)
status	standing, rank
status quo	existing situation
subjects	property, usually heritable
subpoena	under penalty
sui generis	of its own kind
summons	court writ bearing royal mandate; document served on defender by which pursuer initiates civil action
superior	grantor of a feu
supersede	postpone
superinduction	unwarranted alteration of a deed
supra	above
suspension	stay of diligence
Tacit relocation	implied re-letting
taciturnity	keeping silent about a debt leading to inference of payment
tailzie (z silent)	entail (*q.v.*)
teind	tithe, tenth part of annual produce of land
tender	offer in settlement made by defender to pursuer
tenor, proving the	establishing the effect of a document (*e.g.* will) the principal copy of which has been lost
terce	widow's liferent of one-third of husband's heritage (abolished)
thole an assize	undergo trial, after which no further trial on same charge may take place
tinsel of feu	forfeiture for non-payment of feu duty
title to sue	legal right to bring an action
tocher	dowry
trepass	temporary intrusion on land without owner's consent or permission
trial	hearing of a case before a jury
Truck Acts	legislation limiting payment of wages in kind (now repealed)
tutor	guardian of child
Ultimus haeres	last heir (the Crown), to whom estate falls when all other claims fail
ultra valorem	beyond the value

ultra vires	beyond (one's legal) powers
unum quid	one thing; single unit
upset price	price at which property is exposed for sale by auction
uterine	born of same mother but different father
utter	to put false writing or currency into circulation
Veritas	truth (deference to action of slander)
vice versa	conversely
vis et metus	force and fear (*q.v.*)
viva voce	orally
volenti non fit injuria	no injustice is done to a party by an act to which he consents (defence to action for damages)
Wakening	step taken to revive action which has gone to sleep (*q.v.*)
warrandice	guarantee of a right contained in a deed, usually disponing heritage
white-bonnet	one who bids at auction to enhance price
Whitsunday	May 15 or 28, quarter day
writ	a writing possessing legal significance
writer	old name for solicitor

INDEX

absolvitor, 4.22
access rights, 23.01–29
  court proceedings, 23.04
  local authorities, 23.13–23
  Parliament, 23.06–12
  public bodies, 23.21–23
  public meetings, 23.24–25
  quasi-judicial proceedings, 23.05
  tribunals, 23.05
Act of Union, 1.04
acts of adjournal, 1.16
acts of sederunt, 1.16
adjustment rolls, 8.27–29
adoption
  advertising, 28.13
  proceedings, 7.21, 13.37–39
advertising, 28.01–50
  adoption, 28.13
  amusements with prizes, 28.18–19
  betting offices, 28.15
  British Code of Advertising Practice,
    28.42 43, 28.47
  cars, 28.31
  consumer credit, 28.11–12
  defamation, 19.02, 19.10–14
  discrimination, 28.39–41
  election matters, 28.35–37
  experiments on animals, 28.09
  food, 28.08
  foreign betting, 28.22
  fraudulent investments, 28.10
  gaming, 28.23–28
  lettings, 28.38
  lotteries, 28.16–17
  medical advertisements, 28.02–07
  obscenity, 28.33
  pirate radio, 28.30
  prize competitions, 28.20–21
  standards, 28.42–47
  surrogacy arrangements, 28.32
  trade descriptions, 28.29
Advertising Standards Authority,
  28.44, 28.46

Advocate General, 1.42
advocates
  and barristers, 2.12
  chambers, 2.13
  clerks, 2.13
  discipline, 6.54
  forms of address, 15.04, 15.07
  monopoly, 2.02
  QCs, 2, 10
  role, 2.08
  training, 2.09
advocates-depute, 3.30, 3.41, 15.04
AIDS, defamation, 16.27
aliment, 15.09
animal experiments, 28.09
appeals
  children's hearings, 3.17, 13.24
  civil jury trials, 4.44
  contempt of court, 10.72–78
  convictions for contempt, 10.106–110
  courts-martial, 5.29–30
  district courts, 3.07
  divorce actions, reporting
    restrictions, 12.23
  from children's hearings, 3.17
  hospital orders, 3.61
  kirk sessions, 5.17
  licensing, 5.15
  Lyon Court, 5.14
  National Health Service tribunals,
    6.15
  professional disciplinary bodies, 6.45
  Restrictive Practices Court, 5.08
  summary appeals, 3.74–77
Architects Registration Council, 6.47
armed services
  courts, 5.20–33
  rehabilitation of offenders, 26.22
arrest, 3.51
  warrants, 3.51
  without warrant, 3.51
assault
  by photography, 11.42–45

assault—*cont.*
journalists, 7.52
trespass, 23.29
assessors, summary appeals, 3.59
avizandum, 8.72

bail, 3.87–95
appeals, 3.95
publicity, 3.95, 7.20
applications, 3.60
bonds, 3.88
breaches, 3.92
conditions, 3.85, 3.87
considerations, 3.92
human rights, 3.60, 3.93
non-bailable crimes, 3.93
pending appeals, 3.94
police bail, 3.90
submissions, 8.78
banning orders, 7.10–13
barristers, 2.11
and advocates, 2.12
monopoly, 2.14
specialisations, 2.13
BBC, 24.58–65
Board of Governors, 24.59
broadcasting councils, 24.64
finance, 24.63
government powers, 24.60
legal entity, 24.65
obligations, 24.61
impartiality, 24.62
Royal Charter, 24.58
subliminal broadcasting, 24.62
betting, advertisements
amusement with prizes, 28.18–19
betting offices, 28.15
foreign betting, 28.22
gaming, 28.23–28
lotteries, 28.16–17
bills of advocation, 3.84
bills of suspension, 3.74, 3.76
breach of confidence, 9.03, 32.01–20
cases, 32.05–09
criticism, 32.19
developing area, 32.10
employment, 32.07
interim interdicts, 32.11
anticipated breaches, 32.18
balance of convenience, 32.16
standard of proof, 32.20
or breach of copyright, 32.15
public interest, 32.13

breach of confidence—*cont.*
right to privacy, 32.19
scope of the law, 32.03–04
Scots law, 32.02
wrongdoings, 32.12
breach of the peace
and human rights, 25.33
journalists, 7.52
photographers, 11.44–45
bribery, elections, 5.10
broadcasting *see also* **television**
1996 Act, application, 24.37
BBC, 24.58–65
contempt of court, 24.01 03,
24.22–25
active proceedings, 24.22
contrasts with newspapers, 24.04–09
defamation, 24.01–03
elections
case law, 24.50–57
duty of impartiality, 24.46–57
Representation of the People Act,
24.48–49
government interference, 24.26–30
and freedom of expression, 24.28,
25.23
ministerial notices, 24.26
Sinn Fein, 24.26
incitement to racial hatred, 24.42,
29.03
independent broadcasters, 24.66
Independent Television Commission,
24.67–70
interdicts, 24.10–12
liable persons, 24.19–20
independent producers, 24.21
obscenity, 24.43 45, 27.10
pirate radio, 28.30
police powers, 24.31–35
Radio Authority, 24.67–79
reserved matter, 24.80
standards, App 2
Broadcasting Standards Commission,
9.02, 24.36–39
codes, 24.36, App 2
duties, 24.38
judicial review, 24.40
bye-laws, 1.16

calling lists, 8.04–08
cameras
hidden cameras, 9.05
in court, 11.15–16

Campaign for Freedom of Information, 8.109
cancer treatment, 28.02
captions, photographs, 11.13
cars, advertisements, 28.31
Carstairs, 3.66
case law, 1.17–18
caveats, 8.61, 8.62, 18.13, 18.14
Chancery, 4.64
charge sheets, 8.75
children
  abuse, 3.13
  adoption proceedings, 7.21, 13.37–39
  advertisements
    adoption, 28.13
    childcare, 28.14
  compulsory supervision, 3.10
  identification ban in legal actions, 3.14, 13.01–16
    children's hearings, 13.25
    custody hearings, 13.32–36
    dead children, 13.05
    fatal accident inquiries, 13.40–43
    in other proceedings, 13.12
    incest, 13.17–19
    intention, 13.16
    legislation, 13.02–03
    lifting of ban, 13.04
    penalties, 13.07
    photographs, 11.47–48
    public interest, 13.06, 13.14
    small communities, 13.31
    stage of proceedings, 13.09
  meaning, 3.09, 13.27
  offences, 3.11
    rehabilitation of offenders, 26.18
  photographs, 11.46–48
    indecency, 11.50
  presence in court, 3.45
  proceedings, rehabilitation of offenders, 26.03
  publications for, 28.34
  referral hearings, 3.12
  reporting, 13.26
  witnesses, 13.30
children's hearings, 1.08, 3.09–18, 13.20–28
  appeals, 3.17, 13.24
  children's panels, 3.14, 13.21
  constitution, 13.23
  contempt of court, 10.183–185
  curators *ad litem,* 3.16, 13.28
  grounds of referral, 3.11

children's hearings—*cont.*
  jurisdiction, 13.20
  Orkney case, 3.18
  privacy, 13.25
  rehabilitation of offenders, 26.23–24
  reporters, 3.14, 13.22
  reporting, privilege, 17.19
  role of media, 3.18
  safeguarders, 3.17, 13.28
church courts, 5.16–19
civil courts, 4.01 12 *see also* individual courts
  in England, 4.64
civil jury trials, 4.02, 4.19, 4.36–51, 14.01–16
  appeals, 4.44, 4.47–49
  defamation, 4.41
  justification, 4.50
  numbers, 4.45, 4.51
  procedure, 4.42 43
  proof, 14.14–16
  special causes, 4.38 39
civil law, meanings, 1.23–24
civil procedure, 4.13–54
  standard of proof, 4.29
closed proceedings, 7.19 25, 7.27–30
closed records, 4.18, 4.24
  changes, 8.46
  choice of material, 8.47
  publication, 8.35–46
Clyde inquiry, 3.18
Commercial Court, 4.27–31
  judicial review, 4.30
  petitions, 4.28
committal proceedings, 31.01–13
  either-way officers, 31.11–13
  indictable only officers, 31.08–10
committees of inquiry, 6.23
common law, meaning, 1.22
companies
  defamation, 16.39
  right to privacy, 9.02, 20.12
compensation orders, 3.72
complaints, 3.02, 8.75
  access to, 8.80
compulsory purchase, 6.19
computer programmes, copyright, 22.37
confidence *see* **breach of confidence**
confidential information
  breach of confidence, 9.03, 32.04
  journalists' sources, 10.37
  jury rooms, 10.91–93

confirmation of executors, 4.03
conflict of laws, Internet, 33.12
consumer credit, advertisements,
  28.11–12
contempt of court, 1.12, 3.49,
  10.01–199, App 1
  abortion of trials, 10.118–121
    Joseph Trainer case, 10.125–128
    Tom King case, 10.120–121
  active proceedings, 10.18–29, 10.165
  and freedom of expression, 10.02,
    10.04, 10.74
    Daily Record case, 10.143
    shift in favour of freedom, 10.150
  appeals, 10.106–110
  application, 5.01
  behaviour in court, 10.187
    interruptions, 11.23
  broadcasting *see* **broadcasting**
  calling lists, 8.05
  children's hearings, 10.183–185
  civil proceedings, 10.158–174
  common law, 10.94–99
    photographs, 11.02
    Sunday Times case, 10.100–105
  complaints, judicial attitudes,
    10.114–121
  coroner's inquests, 10.187
  criminal proceedings, 3.40
    appeals, 10.72–78
    background information,
      10.111–113
    Daily Record case, 10.137–150
    detention period, 10.30
    end of risk, 10.65–71
    Evening Times case, 10.152–156
    Julian Danskin case, 10.157
    legal debate in jury's absence,
      10.51–56
    Lockerbie case, 10.79–91
    mistakes in reports, 10.129–136
    postponement, 10.57–60
    public confidence in legal system,
      10.78, 10.81
    reports, 10.47–50
    restrictions, 10.57–61
    retrials, 3.65
  criticism of courts, 10.188–190
  defences
    innocent publication, 10.31
    public interest, 10.32–34
    reasonable care, 10.31

contempt of court—*cont.*
  dignity of courts, 10.187–188
  escaped prisoners, 10.192–195
  fatal accident inquiries, 10.176–183
  inquiries, 10.171–174
  Internet, 33.16–26
    difference in national attitudes,
      33.21
  journalists' sources, 10.37–46
  jurisdiction, 5.04
  jury proceedings, 10.91–93
  legislation, 10.06
  open records, 8.31
  Parliamentary proceedings, 1.32
  penalties, 10.157
  persons liable, 10.127
  photography *see* **photographs**
  pre-trial publicity, 10.02
  risk of prejudice, 10.01–03, 10.20,
    10.23, 10.28, 10.68
    appeals, 10.70
  Scottish cases, 10.07–17
  statutory basis, 10.06
  strict liability, 10.18, 10.89–90
  tribunal proceedings, 6.05,
    10.167–174
Convention rights *see* **human rights**
convicium, 20.02–03, 20.12
copyright
  artistic works, 22.10
  assignation, 22.18
  duration, 22.36–41
  fair dealing, 22.23–25
  infringement, 22.16
    breach of confidence, 32.15
    damages, 22.39, 22.40
    defences, 22.39
  Internet, 33.07–10
  legislation, 22.02
  length of works, 22.11
  letters to editor, 22.40
  licences, 22.18
  literary works, 22.08
  meaning, 22.03, 22.15
  moral rights, 22.31–33
  music, 22.09
  nom de plumes, 22.14
  original works, 22.05–07
  ownership, 22.17
    rights, 22.16
  performance rights, 22.34–35
  photographs, 11.40, 22.17, 22.19–22

copyright—*cont.*
protection of persons, 22.04
purpose, 22.01
spoken word, 22.26–30
titles, 22.12
coroner's inquests, contempt of court,
10.184
Coulsfield Report, 4.27
Counsel, 2.08
court documents
access to information, 8.01 117
adjustment rolls, 8.27–29
calling lists, 8.04–08
court rolls, 8.03, 8.67–71
interlocutors, 8.73
opinions, 8.73
petitions, 8.54–56
privilege, 17.18
records, 8.28–46
summons, 8.09–26
types, 8.02
Court of Appeal, 4.64
Court of Session, 4.07–11
Extra Division, 4.08
holiday sittings, 7.25
Inner House, 4.08, 4.10
divisions, 4.09
judges, 15.01–02
judicial titles, 15.01–02
optional procedure, 4.26
Outer House, 4.08, 4.09
procedure, 4.13–23
supervisory jurisdiction, 4.11
court reporting
accuracy, 7.06, 7.50, 10.128, 17.14
balance, 7.15 18, 7.45–46
banning orders, 7.10–13
civil proceedings, 10.159–167
closed proceedings, 7.19 25, 7.27–30
contempt of court, 10.47–50
appeals, 10.72–78
background information,
10.111–113
Daily Record case, 10.137–151
end of risk, 10.65–71
Evening Times case, 10.152–156
Julian Danskin case, 10.157
legal debate in jury's absence,
10.51–56
mistakes in reports, 10.129–136
public confidence in legal system,
10.78, 10.81

court reporting—*cont.*
fairness, 7.07, 10.50, 17.14
importance, 7.03–05
incitement to racial hatred, 29.08
interpretation, 7.48–54
mentally disabled, 7.17
mitigation pleas, 7.08
non disclosure of names, 7.31
notebooks, retention, 7.35–36
open court hearings, 8 49 53
out of court statements, 7.09
party litigants, 7.43–47
postponement, 10.57–61
privilege, 7.32 47, 17.14–24
rape, 7.30
restrictions, 10.57–61
statements, attribution, 7.37–42
tape recorders, 10.93, 17.14
courts
access rights, 23.04
access to documents *see* **court
documents**
civil courts, 4.01–12, 4.64
criminal courts, 3.01–45
precincts, meaning, 11.24–26
courts martial, 5.20–32
appeals, 5.29–30
right to fair trial, 5.31, 5.32
criminal appeals, 3.31, 3.42–45
additional evidence, 3.84
leave, 3.42, 3.77
solemn appeals, 3.78–85
summary appeals, 3.73–77
criminal courts, 3.01–45 *see also*
individual courts
criminal procedure, 3.46–96
1995 Act, 3.55–59
access to information, 8.75–81
England
committal proceedings, 31.09–09
investigation, 3.49
solemn proceedings *see* **solemn
procedure**
standard of proof, 4.29
summary proceedings *see* **summary
procedure**
criminal trials
absence of accused, 3.64
adverse publicity, 3.48
insanity, 3.66
jury directions, 3.66
no case to answer, 3.65, 3.80

criminal trials—*cont.*
　opening speeches, 3.65
　summary trials, 3.54
　time limits, 3.63
cross-examination, 3.54
Cullen Inquiry, 6.22, 10.171
curators *ad litem,* 3.16, 13.28
custom, 1.21

DA notices, 30.12–18
damages
　actions, 4.23
　by offenders, 3.81
　defamation, 18.01–11
　　aggravation, 18.06–08
　　England, 18.05
　　exemplary damages, 24.12
　　injury to feelings, 18.02
　　mitigation, 18.09–11
　　trends, 18.03
data protection
　1998 Act, 8.82–84
　criminal offences, 8.91–92
　exemptions, 8.98 100
　Information Commissioner, 8.97,
　　9.06, 9.07
　manual files, 8.85
　news gathering, 9.06–07
　non-sensitve data, 8.87
　notification, 8.97
　personal rights, 8.88–90
　publication in public interest, 8.101
　security, 8.93–96
　sensitive data, 8.86
death, declarators, 12.24–25
deception, 9.04
decrees
　absolvitor, 4.22
　in absence, 4.17
　superseding extract, 8.74
defamation, 16.01–40 *see also* **verbal**
　injury
　Act, App 4
　advertisements, 19.02, 19.10–14
　after death, 16.37–38
　and rehabilitation of offenders,
　　16.14, 26.08–09
　broadcasting, 24.01–03
　　contrasts with newspapers,
　　　24.04–09
　burden of proof, 16.11, 17.01
　civil jury trials, 4.41

defamation—*cont.*
　civil wrong, 16.09–10
　closed records, 8 37
　communication, 16.10
　contributions by third parties,
　　19.01–14
　　letters to editor, 19.03–09
　defamatory statements, 16.16–27
　　AIDS, 16.27
　　competence, 16.26
　　criminality, 16.17
　　dishonesty, 16.22
　　drunkenness, 16.22
　　insanity, 16.27
　　insolvency, 16.25
　　sexual immorality, 16.19–21
　defences, 17.01–38
　　English law, 21.05–08
　　fair comment, 11.41, 17.07–11,
　　　19.06
　　fair retort, 17.10
　　innocent dissemination, 16.06,
　　　16.07
　　intentions, 16.32, 17.24–28
　　offers of amends, 17.29–32
　　privilege *see* **privilege**
　　public figures, 16.04, 17.35, 17.36
　　recent developments, 17.35–36
　　veritas, 16.11, 16.15
　　words *in rixa,* 17.06
　English law, 21.01–10
　　criminal libel, 21.04
　　defences, 21.05–08
　　frequency of actions, 21.10
　　libel and slander, 21.02–03
　falsity, 16.11–15
　　proof, 16.11–13
　freedom of speech, 16.04
　headlines, 19.01
　innuendoes, 16.28–33
　Internet, 33.11–15
　legal developments, 16.04
　liable persons, 16.05
　　disseminators, 16.06
　limitation of actions, 16.340, 17.34
　　repetitions, 17.02
　malice, 16.14
　minimisation of damages, 17.33
　Parliamentary proceedings, 1.32
　pursuers
　　corporate bodies, 16.39
　　local authorities, 17.04

defamation—*cont.*
  pursuers—*cont.*
    nationalised utilities, 17.04
    political parties, 17.04
  remedies, 18.01–14
    damages *see* **damages**
    interdicts, 18.12–14
  reporting from summons, 8.11–26
  statements or otherwise, 16.34
    about a person, 16.35–36
  television *see* **television**
defenders, 15.10
desertion of actions, 10.66, 10.67
detention
  intimation, 3.57
  mental health, 3.66
  safeguards, 3.57
  suspects, 3.56
devils, 2.09
devolution, 1.26–42
  issues, 1.31, 4.54
disability discrimination, 6.13
discrimination, advertisements,
    28.39–41
dismissal of cases, 4.22, 14.15
district courts, 3.04–08
  appeals, 3.07
  clerks, 3.06
  jurisdiction, 3.05
  prosecutors, 3.06
  territorial jurisdiction, 3.01
divorce actions, 12.01–40
  closed proceedings, 7.29
  decrees
    absolute, 12.21
    delay, 12.22
    nisi, 12.21
  procedure
    commencement, 15.10
    reform, 12.08
  reporting restrictions
    1926 Act, 12.01–07
      continuing applicability, 12.02,
        12.26–40
      purpose, 12.37, 12.40
    appeals, 12.23
    categories of material, 12.03
    defended cases, 12.10–20
      points of law, 12.15
      preliminary matters, 12.18–19
    information allowed, 12.06
    jurisdiction, 12.34–39
    penalties, 12.07

divorce actions—*cont.*
  reporting restrictions—*cont.*
    time and place, 12.35–39
    undefended cases
      details, 12.10
      list, 12.09

election courts, 5.09–11
elections
  additional member system, 1.29
  broadcasting
    case law, 24.50–57
    duty of impartiality, 24.46–57
    Representation of the People Act,
      24.48–49
  defamatory statements, 16.09
  expenses, 28.35–37
employment
  gagging clauses, 9.03
  references, 20.10
Employment Appeal Tribunal, 6.07
employment tribunals, 6.06–13
  disability discrimination, 6.13
  hearings, 6.08
  restricted reporting orders, 6.09–13
  sexual misconduct, 6.09–12
English law
  committal proceedings, 3.84,
    31.01–13
  defamation, 18.05, 21.01–10
  offences
    either way, 31.11–13
    indictable only, 31.08–10
  photographs in court, 11.18–23
  removal of judges, 6.62
Equal Opportunities Commission,
    28.41
EU law
  compatible legislation, 1.30
  electronic commerce directive, 33.13
  supremacy, 1.09–11
**European Commission of Human
    Rights,** 10.43
**European Convention on Human
    Rights**
  incorporation into British law, 4.60
    effect, 16.01
    privacy, 20.11
  UK infringements, 25.03
European Court of Human Rights,
    1.12, 4.58–59
  defamation, burden of proof, 17.01
  Spycatcher case, 10.105

European Court of Justice, 4.55–57
evidence
  additional evidence, criminal
    appeals, 3.93
  on commission, transcripts, 8 53
  transcripts, 8.70
expenses, 15.09
extracts, superseding extract, 8.74

Faculty Services, 2.13
Family Division, 4.64
family life, 25.16
Faslane, nuclear weapons, 3.44
fatal accident inquiries, 6.28–30
  contempt of court, 10.176–186
  identification of children, 13.40–43
  photographs, 11.49–50
First Minister, 1.33
food, advertisements, 28.08
fraud, 9.04
  advertisements, 28.10
freedom of expression, 1.12, 9.15,
    25.01, 25.11
  advertising, 28.43
  and contempt of court, 10.02, 10.04,
    10.77
    Daily Record case, 10.143
    shift in favour of freedom, 10.89,
      10.150
  and disclosure of journalists' sources,
    10.43
  and government interference in
    broadcasting, 24.28–30
  and law of defamation, 16.04
  and right to fair trial, 10.156, 25.32
  commercial expression, 25.24
  conflict with privacy, 25.12
  data in public domain, 25.27
  gagging orders, 25.22
  incitement to racial hatred, 24.42
  licensing of broadcasting, 25.22
  limits, 25.20
  national security, 25.22
  official secrets, 30.24, 30.27
  political expression, 25.25–26
  prohibition on limitations, 25.28–31
    anticipated breach of confidence,
      32.18
  right to be informed, 25.21
freedom of information
  Bill, 8.102 109, 9.08–10
    exemptions, 8.104–106, 9.09

freedom of information—*cont.*
  Bill—*cont.*
    Information Commissioner, 9.10
    prejudice to conduct of public
      affairs, 8.105, 8.106
    watering down, 8.103
  in Scotland, 8.107–110, 9.11–14
    exemptions, 9.14
    harm test, 9.12
    police, 8.109
    presumption of openness, 8.107

gagging clauses, 9.03
General Dental Council, 6.46
General Medical Council, 6.46
General Optical Council, 6.46
Glasgow rape case, 3.46
guilty pleas, 3.68

harassment, 7.52
headlines
  court reporting, 17.16
  defamation, 19.01
hearsay evidence, 6.03
High Court, 3.28–31
  at Kamp van Zeist, 3.28
  criminal appeals, 3.31, 3.42–45
  full court hearings, 3.45
  in England, 4.64
  judges, 15.01
    appointment, 3.28
    temporary judges, 3.28
  prosecutions, 3.30
  solemn proceedings, 3.03
  territorial jurisdiction, 3.01
homelessness, 4.30
  judicial review, 14.17
hospital orders, 3.66
  appeals, 3.66
House of Lords, 4.12, 4.64
human rights *see also* **freedom of
    expression; privacy; right to fair
    trial**
  1998 Act, 9.15
    applicability, 9.16
    impact, 25.33–35
  bail, 3.60, 3.93
  compatibility with, 1.13
    legislation, 1.30, 4.61
  courts martial, 5.31
  interdicts against defamation, 18.13
  introduction, 4.62

human rights—*cont.*
  scope
    Acts of Parliament, 25.07–08
    public authorities, 25.05–06

ice-cream wars, 3.93
identification parades, 3.58
incest, 13.17–19
incitement to racial hatred *see* **race relations**
Independent Television Commission, 24.67–70
  regulatory functions, 24.71–75
    code for journalists, 24.73
indictments, 3.03, 8.75
  access to, 8.80
  publication, 8.76
induciae, 4.14, 4.24
Information Commissioner, 8.97, 9.06, 9.07, 9.10
initial writs, 4.24
injurious falsehoods, 21.09
innocence, presumption, 3.48, 3.96
inquiries, 6.20–41
  committees of inquiry, 6.23
  contempt, 10.171–174
  fatal accident inquiries, 6.28–30
  local inquiries, 6.26–27
  royal commissions, 6.24–25
  shipping and railway inquiries, 6.31–36
  tribunals of inquiries, 6.21–22
insanity
  criminal trials, 3.66
  defamation, 16.27
institutional writers, 1.20, 1.21
intellectual property, 22.01–43
  copyright *see* **copyright**
  Internet, 33.07–10
  patents, 22.43
  registered designs, 22.43
  trademarks, 22.42
    registration, 22.43
interdicts, 15.09 *see also* **interim interdicts**
  broadcasting, 24.10–12
  defamation, 18.12–14
    and human rights, 18.13
interests of justice, 10.37, 10.43
interim interdicts, 8.57–66
  balance of convenience, 8.64
  defamation, 18.12

interim interdicts—*cont.*
  breach of confidence, 32.11
    balance of convenience, 32.16
    standard of proof, 32.20
  broadcasting, 24.10
    defamation, 24.12
interlocutors, 8.73
international law, nuclear weapons, 3.44
Internet, 33.01–26
  contempt of court, 33.16–26
  defamation, 33.11–15
    e-mail, 33.15
    liable persons, 33.11, 33.14
  EU law, 33.13
  forum shopping, 33.12
  global reach, 33.03–04
  intellectual property rights, 33.07–10
  origins, 33.05
  regulation, 33.24–26
  Shetland Times, 33.08–09
investigatory powers
  regulation
    England, 08.111–114
    Scotland, 08.115

judges
  appointment, 1.36, 6.57
  removal, 6.58–59
    England, 6.62
  temporary judges, 03.19, 03.28, 4.07
Judicial Committee of Privy Council, 4.52–54
  devolution issues, 4.54
  references, 1.31
judicial examinations, 3.62
judicial review, 14.01–12
  Broadcasting Standards Commission, 14.07
  grounds for review, 14.10
  Press Complaints Commission, 14.07
  procedure, 14.03
  remedies, 14.06
  Scotland Act 1998, 14.11
  use, 14.41
juries, 3.03, 3.55
  civil juries *see* **civil jury trials**
  directions, 3.66
  objections, 3.65
  proceedings, confidentiality, 10.91–93
jurisdiction
  meaning, 3.01
  territorial jurisdiction, 3.01

justices of the peace, 3.04
  appointment, 3.04
  supplemental list, 3.08

kirk sessions, 5.17

Labour Government, 1.26, 4.60
Land Court, 5.13
Lands Tribunal, 6.19
Lands Valuation Appeal Court, 5.05
Lands Valuation Court, 5.03
law officers, 1.37–42, 15.05–11
law reporting, 8.01
legal aid
  defamation, 20.08
  verbal injury, 20.08
legal profession, 2.01–17
Legal Services Ombudsman, 6.51–53
legal terms, 7.49–50, 15.10
legislation, 1.15
  compatibility with Convention rights,
    1.30, 25.07–08
  compatibility with EU law, 1.30
  Scottish Parliament, 1.30
    legislative competence, 1.31
letters to editor
  copyright, 22.40
  defamation, 19.03–09
letting agencies, 28.38
libels *see* **defamation**
licensing boards, 5.15
limitation of actions, defamation,
  16.34, 17.34
  repetitions, 17.02
local authorities
  access rights, 23.13–23
  documents, 23.19–20
  exclusions, 23.14–18
  defamation, 17.04
local inquiries, 6.26–27
local ombudsmen, 6.37–41
Lockerbie trial, 1.40
  contempt of court, 10.77–90
  Internet, 33.18, 33.22
  pressure on judiciary, 3.28, 4.07
  proceedings without jury, 3.03
locus standi, private prosecution, 3.46
Lord Advocate, 1.13, 1.33, 1.37–41
  appointment, 3.47, 15.07
  functions, 15.05–06
  independence, 1.39, 1.40, 1.41
  place in court, 15.05–06
  prosecutor, 3.24

Lord Advocate—*cont.*
  references to High Court, 3.44
  responsibility for prosecutions, 3.47
  separation of powers, 1.41
  right to fair trial, 25.09
Lord Chancellor, separation of powers,
  1.41
Lord Justice-Clerk, 3.28, 4.07, 4.09,
  15.01
Lord Justice-General, 3.28, 15.01
Lord President, 4.07, 4.09, 15.01
loss of society, 4.23
lotteries, 28.16–17
Lyon Court, 5.14

malice
  defamation, 16.14, 17.10
  employment references, 17.23, 20.10
  letters to editor, 19.05
  malicious falsehood, 20.04–05
  meaning, 26.09
matrimonial proceedings *see* **divorce**
  actions
medical advertisements, 28.02–07
mental health detention, 3.66
mentally disabled, court reporting, 7.17
microphones, hidden microphones,
  9.05
Minister of Justice, 1.35–36
miscarriages of justice, appeals
  by prosecutors, 3.78
  solemn procedure, 3.78, 3.82
mistakes, court reporting, 10.129–136
mitigation, 3.54
moral rights, 22.31–33
murder, sentencing, 3.69

National Health Service ombudsman,
  6.37
National Health Service tribunals,
  6.14–15
  appeals, 6.15
national security
  disclosure of journalists' sources,
    10.37, 10.40
  freedom of expression, 25.22
  official secrets, 30.21
negligent statements, 20.09–10
  employment references, 20.10
Newspaper Society, 8.109
newspapers
  registration, 27.03
  retention of copies, 27.04

nobile officium, 4.10, 14.28
  appeals against contempt of court
    convictions, 10.108, 10.110
not-proven verdict, 1.05, 3.54
notaries public, 2.07
nullity of marriage, 7.22, 7.29

obiter dicta, 1.19
obscenity, 27.08–10
  advertising, 28.33
  broadcasting, 24.43 45, 27.10
official secrets, 30.01–31
  communication, 30.03
  convictions, 30.04
  DA notices, 30.12–18
  freedom of expression, 30.24, 30.27
  information on offences, 30.09
  Inside Intelligence, 30.25–31
  legislation, 30.01–09
  photographs, 11.51, 30.02
  prohibited places, 30.01
  protected categories, 30.05
  public interest, 30.08
  Scots law, 30.25–31
    Spycatcher, 30.22
  Spycatcher, 10.105, 30.19–24
  terrorism, 30.15
  unauthorised disclosures, 30.06
  Zircon case, 30.10–11
ombudsmen, 6.37–41
  privileged communications, 17.13
open records, 8.28, 8.30–34
  publication, 8.30–33
opinions, 8.73
optional procedure, 4.26
options hearings, 4.25
Orders in Council, 1.15
ordinary causes, 4.06
Orkney case, 3.18
  breach of confidence, 32.06
  photographs, 13.25

Parliament
  access rights, 23.06–12
  breach of privilege, 23.07–12
    complaints, 23.12
  ombudsman, 6.37
  proceedings
    contempt of court, 1.32
    incitement to racial hatred, 29.08
    privilege, 1.32, 17.12
  sovereignty, 1.10

party litigants, court reporting, 7.43–47
passing-off, 22.14
  Internet domain names, 33.10
performance rights, 22.34–35
petitions, 8.54–56
  answers, 8.56
  in chambers, criminal proceedings,
    14.26
  interim interdicts, 8.57–66
    publication, 8.63–66
Pharmaceutical Society, 6.47
photographs, 11.01 52 *see also*
  television
  and privacy, 11.38, 11.41
  assault by photography, 11.42–45
  breach of the peace, 11.44, 11.45
  captions, 11.13
  children, 11.46–48
    children's hearings, 13.25
    indecency, 11.50
  civil cases, 11.14
  contempt of court, 11.01
    common law, 11.02
    Scotland and England, 11.03–12
  copyright, 11.40, 22.17, 22.19–22
  defamation, 16.34
  English legislation, 11.18–23
  fatal accident inquiries, 11.49–50
  inside courts, 11.15–17
  official secrets, 11.51, 30.02
  outside courts, 11.35–41
  precincts of courts, 11.24–26
  witnesses, 11.12
pirate radio, 28.30
planning, local inquiries, 6.26
pleadings
  reporting, 8.40
    privilege, 17.16
  summary procedure, 3.52
police
  freedom of information, 8.109
  powers, broadcasting, 24.31–35
political parties
  advertising, 28.43
  defamation, 17.04
Portsmouth defence, 7.08
precedents, 1.17–18
Press Complaints Commission, App 3
prevention of crime, disclosure of
  journalists' sources, 10.37, 10.41,
    10.42
printers, identification, 27.02
prior restraint orders, 24.11

prisoners
  escaped prisoners, contempt of
      court, 10.192–195
  privacy, 25.16
privacy, 9.02, 25.01, 25.10
  and photographs, 11.38, 11.41
  and searches, 25.15
  breach of confidence, 9.03, 32.19
  breaches, 20.11–12
  code, Broadcasting Standards
      Commission, App 2
  confidence, 25.19
  conflict with freedom of expression,
      25.12
  Human Rights Act, 9.16
  inhibition of investigations, 25.35
  meaning, 25.13–14
  prisoners, 25.16
  right, 20.11
  telephone tapping, 25.18
  trespass, 23.29
private law, 1.25
privilege *see also* **defamation**
  common law, 17.23
    discharge of duties, 17.23
  communications with ombudsmen,
      17.13
  court reporting, 7.32–47, 17.13–22
    attribution of statements, 7.37–42
    calling lists, 8.06
    children's hearings, 17.18
    closed records, 8 36, 8 52
    documents, 17.16
    foreign courts, 17.21
    headlines, 17.15
    party litigants, 7.43–47
    summons, 8.11–26
    tribunals, 6.03–05, 17.20
  defence against defamation, 17.11–23
    rehabilitation of offenders, 26.10
  parliamentary proceedings, 1.32,
      17.13
  public communications, 16.01
  report privilege, 16.02, 16.03
  scope, 8.23
prize competitions, 28.20–21
processes, 4.15
procurators fiscal, 3.21, 3.47
  prosecutions
    discretion, 3.47
    in district courts, 3.06
professions, disciplinary bodies,
      6.42–56

proof, 4.19, 4.20, 4.21
  civil jury trials, 14.14–16
prosecutions
  district courts, 3.06
  High Court, 3.24
  private prosecutions, 3.30
  summary appeals, 3.60
  time limits, 1.05
public authorities, meaning, 25.05–06
public interest
  and breach of confidence, 32.13
  and contempt of court, 10.32–34
  and data protection, 8.101
  and law of defamation, 16.04
  breach of privacy, 9.02
  damage, information from Lord
      Advocate, 1.39
  deception, 9.04
  identification of children, 13.06,
      13.14
  official secrets, 30.08
  publication of data without consent,
      8.87
  restricted reporting orders, 6.12
  television in courts, 11.27
public law, 1.25
public policy
  access to complaints, 8.80
  access to documents of criminal
      cases, 8.81
publishing
  deposit copies, 27.05–07
  election matters, 28.35–37
  identification of printers, 27.02
  newspapers
    registration, 27.03
    retention of copies, 27.04
  obscenity, 27.08–10
  place and time, 12.34–39
  protection of children, 28.34
pursuers, 15.08

Queen's Bench, 4.64
Queen's Counsels, 2.10

race relations, 29.01–18
  Code of Practice, 29.18
  incitement to racial hatred, 29.01
    adjectival racism, 29.09
    broadcasting, 24.42, 29.03
    cases, 29.10–17
    court proceedings, 29.08
    defences, 29.07

race relations—*cont.*
 incitement to racial hatred—*cont.*
  intentions, 29.02
  parliamentary proceedings, 29.08
  racial hatred, meaning, 29.04
  Rastafarians, 29.06
  Sikhs, 29.05
Radio Authority, 24.76–79
 licences, 24.81
  withdrawal, 24.82
  penalties, 24.83
railways, inquiries, 6.35–36
rape, 7.30, 03.32–03.41
 closed proceedings, 03.32, 03.33
 England, 03.35–03.38
 restrictions
  application, 03.39
  identification of victims, 03.32,
   03.38
  lifting, 03.40, 03.41
Rastafarians, 29.06
records, 8.28
 closed records, 8.28, 8.29, 8.35–46
 open records, 8.28, 8.30–34
Registration Appeal Court, 5.12
rehabilitation of offenders, 26.01–25
 and defamation, 16.14, 26.08–09
  privilege, 26.10
 application of legislation
  armed services, 26.22
  children's hearings, 26.23–24
  foreign courts, 26.25
 exceptions, 26.03
 excluded sentences, 26.12
 purpose of Act, 26.01
 rehabilitated persons, 26.21
 rehabilitation periods, 26.15–20
 spent convictions, 26.21
  restriction of information,
   26.02–07
 subsequent convictions, 26.13–14
remedies *see* damages; interdicts
reserved matters, 1.27
respondents, 15.08
restricted reporting orders, 6.09–13
Restrictive Practices Court, 5.06–08
right to fair trial, 1.12, 1.13
 and freedom of expression, 10.156,
  25.32
 and temporary sheriffs, 3.19
 courts martial, 5.31, 5.32
 position of Lord Advocate, 25.09
right to life, 1.12

road haulage, 6.18
rolls of court, 8.03, 8.67–71
 incidental motions, 8.69
Royal College of Veterinary Surgeons,
 6.46
royal commissions, 6.24–25
Royal Faculty of Procurators, 2.06
Runciman Inquiry, 6.24

safeguarders, 3.15, 13.28
Salmon Committee, 10.173–174, 10.181
schools, List D schools, 13.28
Scotland Act, 1.13
Scots law, 1.01–13
 distinctiveness, 1.05
 pioneering areas, 1.08
 publishing, 1.07
Scottish Administration, 1.33–42
 law officers, 1.37–41
Scottish Criminal Cases Review
  Commission, 3.43, 3.86
Scottish Executive, 1.33
Scottish Law Commission, 1.06
Scottish Parliament, 1.01–03, 1.26
 broadcasting powers, 24.84
 election system, 1.29
 legislation, 1.30
  competence, 1.31
 Presiding Officer, 1.31
 report of proceedings, 1.32
 terms, 1.29
Scottish Solicitors' Discipline
  Tribunal, 6.48–50
searches, and privacy, 25.15
Secretary of State for Scotland, 1.34
sentencing, 3.67
 appeals, 3.82
  by Crown, 3.83
 compensation to victims, 3.72
 life sentences, 3.69
 rehabilitation of offenders, 26.12
 s 76 hearings, 3.68
separation of powers, position of Lord
  Advocate, 1.41
 right to fair trial, 25.09
service courts, 5.20–33
 application of Rehabilitation of
  Offenders Act, 26.22
 courts martial, 5.20–32
 standing civilian courts, 5.33
sex discrimination, 28.39–41
sexual misconduct, employment
  tribunals, 6.09–12

sheriff clerks, 3.21
sheriff courts
  civil jurisdiction, 4.01–06
    confirmation of executors, 4.03
    ordinary causes, 4.06
    small claims, 4.05
    summary causes, 4.04
  civil procedure, 4.24
    options hearings, 4.25
    rules, 4.25
  criminal jurisdiction, 3.19–21
    prosecutors, 3.21
    solemn proceedings, 3.03, 3.22
    summary proceedings, 3.02, 3.22
    territorial jurisdiction, 3.01, 3.20
  law reporting, 8.01
sheriffdoms, 3.19, 4.01
sheriffs
  appointment, 3.19
  forms of address, 15.03
  removal, 6.60–61
  temporary sheriffs, 1.13, 3.19
  titles, 15.03
sheriffs principal, 3.19, 4.01
shipping, inquiries, 6.31–34
Sikhs, 29.05
slander *see* **defamation**
slander of goods, 20.06
small claims, 4.05
Society of Advocates, 2.06
Society of Editors, 8.109
Society of Solicitor-Advocates, 2.03
solatium, 4.23
solemn appeals, 3.78–85
  retrials, 3.78
    prejudice, 3.65
solemn procedure, 3.03, 3.33, 3.44-57
  see also **criminal trials**
  and summary procedure, 3.57
  committal diets, 3.44
  first appearance, 3.44
    publication, 3.44
  judicial examination, 3.46
  preliminary diets, 3.45
solicitor-advocates, 2.02–04
  prosecuting in High Court, 2.04
Solicitor-General, 1.33, 1.38
  appointment, 3.47, 15.07
  place in court, 15.05
  prosecutor, 3.30, 15.05
  responsibility for prosecutions, 3.47
solicitors
  becoming judges, 2.16

solicitors—*cont.*
  rights of audience
    in England, 2.15, 2.16
    in Scotland, 2.02
  role, 2.01
  societies, 2.06
  training, 2.05
Solicitors in the Supreme Court, 2.06
solvent abuse, 3.13
sources, contempt of court, 10.37–46
sources of law, 1.14–21
spent convictions, defamation, 16.14
Spycatcher case, 10.100–105, 30.19–24
standard of proof, 4.29, 14.20–21
stated cases
  children's hearings, 3.17
  summary appeals, 3.74
    adjustments, 3.75
statutory instruments, 1.16
stipendiary magistrates, 3.04
  appointment, 3.04
subordinate legislation, 1.15–16
summary appeals, 3.83–86
  assessors, 3.84
  by prosecutors, 3.85
summary causes, 4.04
summary procedure
  and solemn procedure, 3.73
  criminal cases, 3.02, 3.49, 3.52–54
  intermediate diets, 3.53
  pleading, 3.52
summary trials, 3.54
  Court of Session, 7.26–31
  time limits, 3.59
summons, 4.04, 4.14, 8.09–26
  reporting from, 8.11–26
    contempt of court, 10.162
surrogacy arrangements, 28.32

tape recorders, in court, 10.93, 17.14
telephone tapping, 25.18
television *see also* **BBC; broadcasting;**
  Independent Television
  Commission
  channels, 24 76 79
  court proceedings, 11.17, 11.27–34
  defamation, 24.13–16
    live programmes, 24.17–18
  independent broadcasters, 24.66
terrorism, 30.15
time limits, criminal prosecutions, 1.05
  solemn procedure, 3.83
  summary trials, 3.59

trade descriptions, 28.29
Traffic Commissioner, 6.16–17
Transport Tribunal, 6.17–18
trespass, 23.26–29
  assault, 23.29
  right to privacy, 23.29
trials *see* civil jury trials; criminal
  trials
tribunals, 6.01–19
  access rights, 23.05
  Council on Tribunals, 6.02
  decisions, reasons, 6.02
  employment tribunals, 6.06–13
  meaning, 5.02
  mental health tribunals, 6.05
  National Health Service tribunals,
    6.14–15
  of inquiries, 6.21–22
  proceedings
    contempt of court, 10.168–175
    qualified privilege, 6.03, 6.03 05,
      17.20
trusts, variation, 4.32–35

UN Convention on the Rights of the
  Child, 3.15

utilities, defamation, 17.04

valuation courts, 6.05
verbal injury, 20.01–12
  breach of privacy, 20.11–12
  convicium, 20.02–03, 20.12
  legal aid, 20.08
  malicious falsehood, 20.04–05
  negligent statements, 20.09–10
  onus of proof, 20.07
  slander of goods, 20.06
verdicts, 3.50
  majority verdicts, 3.66
  not-proven verdicts, 1.05, 3.54

warrants, arrest, 3.51
water authorities, access rights, 23.23
witnesses
  children, 13.30
  pictures, 11.12
Writers to the Signet (WS), 2.06

young offenders
  murder, 3.69
  sentencing, 3.70